Racial Fever

Racial Fever

Freud and the Jewish Question

Eliza Slavet

FORDHAM UNIVERSITY PRESS
NEW YORK 2009

Fordham University Press has no responsibility for the persistence or accuracy of URLs for external or third-party Internet websites referred to in this publication and does not guarantee that any content on such websites is, or will remain, accurate or appropriate.

Library of Congress Cataloging-in-Publication Data

Slavet, Eliza.
   Racial fever : Freud and the Jewish question / Eliza Slavet.
      p.   cm.
   Includes bibliographical references and index.
   ISBN 978-0-8232-3141-6 (cloth : alk. paper)
   ISBN 978-0-8232-3142-3 (pbk. : alk. paper)
      1. Psychoanalysis and religion.   2. Jews—Psychology.
3. Jews—Identity.   4. Race—Religious aspects—Judaism.
I. Title.
BF175.4.R44S53   2009
155.8'4924—dc22

                                                    2009008226

Printed in the United States of America
11 10 09   5 4 3 2 1
First edition

Traduttore—Traditore!

—Freud, *Jokes and Their Relation to the Unconscious*

CONTENTS

ACKNOWLEDGMENTS

When I first read Yosef Hayim Yerushalmi's book *Freud's Moses: Judaism Terminable and Interminable* in April 2001, I had no idea that the author and I were connected by a series of fateful coincidences. Forty-three years before I read this book, Yerushalmi was the rabbi at the synagogue that my mother's family attended in the suburbs of New York City. There, he became friends with my grandparents Ruben and Elsa Farro, and he charmed a thirteen-year-old girl named Susan Farro who would later name her child, Eliza, after her recently deceased mother. She did not know that Yerushalmi and I were born on the same day (May 20), albeit separated by 42 years. On April 29, 2001, I called my mother from Berlin to tell her that I had just been reading a book by Yerushalmi that I thought she might find interesting. It was then that she told me that he had been her rabbi forty-odd years before. A week later (on May 6, the 145th anniversary of Freud's birth), my mother had a massive stroke that severely damaged her brain and paralyzed the left side of her body for the rest of her life. While she retains most of her long-term memories, she sometimes misremembers or adds new materials to stories that could never have happened the way she now recalls them. I would like to thank my mother for sharing her memories both before and after her brain was transformed by what now goes by the names of biology, chemistry, and circuitry. More important, I would like to thank both my parents, Susan Farro Slavet and Jerry Slavet, for their constant encouragement and unfailing support while I wrote and revised this book over the last seven years.

In April 2006, I finally met Yosef Hayim Yerushalmi in person. Since this book began as a long letter to him, I would like to thank him for his warm hospitality and for his moving scholarship, which drew me into this work.

Racial Fever is largely based on my doctoral dissertation, "Freud's *Moses*: Memory Material and Immaterial" (2007). During my time as a graduate student at the University of California, San Diego (UCSD) and since then, I have been blessed to have three wonderful mentors who have also become dear friends. Marcel Hénaff chaired my doctoral committee and has been gracious and supportive throughout the past eight years. Hillel Schwartz not only read numerous drafts and responded to countless emails in which I posed my most difficult and embarrassing questions about writing in general and about my project in particular; he has also been a collaborator and a model of independent scholarship. Geoffrey Bowker generously answered my calls and emails and encouraged me to pursue even the most meandering paths of scholarship and inspiration.

A number of friends encouraged, prodded, advised, and assisted me along the way. I am continually grateful for the friendship and sage advice of Ruth Mack. In the early stages of writing, I enjoyed exchanging ideas with Shahrokh Yadegari, whose own independent approach to writing his doctoral dissertation was inspiring. Ronald Robboy sent me *Jewish Wit* at a crucial moment and more generally reminded me of the meaningful meandering paths of scholarship and performance. Ruth Liberman generously shared her mother tongue and helped me translate particularly thorny German passages. Yvonne Shafir tirelessly read drafts, shared comments, and posed difficult questions. My short-lived but enlightening dissertation writing group was an education in itself: I learned a lot from reading the work and comments of Tamar Barzel, Holly Dugan, Libby Garland, Nick Syrett, Margie Weinstein; special thanks to Tamar for major help with editing in the post-dissertation phase. Brigid Hains's extensive editorial commentary and pointed questions got me back on track a number of times; her loyal missives traveled the farthest (from both Melbourne, Australia and London, England), but they consistently managed to reach me at the perfect moments. Finally, Steve Ausbury provided me not only with artistic and poetic inspiration, he also created an artwork for the cover of this book.

In the all-important administrative, funding, and library category, I would like to thank the UCSD Center for the Humanities and the UCSD Literature Department for grants that allowed me to take time off from teaching and focus exclusively on writing. A grant from the Deutsche Akademische Austausch Dienst in 2000 allowed me to go to Berlin, where the seeds of this work were first planted. The Interlibrary Loan staff at UCSD's

Geisel Library and New York University's Bobst Library were indispensable and much appreciated. I am grateful to Matthew von Umwerth, librarian for the Brill Library at the New York Psychoanalytic Institute, for both early and last-minute bibliographic assistance as well as intellectual stimulation. Michael Molnar and J. Keith Davies of the Freud Museum in London quickly and thoroughly answered a number of queries.

When I moved from San Diego to New York City, I joined a number of independent researchers who spend their days at the New York Public Library. I was particularly grateful to be granted access to the Wertheim Study and to discover NYPL's Dorot Jewish Division, both of which made the experience of research at a huge public library a little more intimate and user friendly. Many thanks to Michael Terry for locating hard-to-find materials. Special thanks to Michael for making my fantasy of an event to celebrate the 150th anniversary of Freud's *bris* a reality. The lecture I presented as part of "Freud's Foreskin: A Sesquicentennial Celebration of the Most Suggestive Circumcision in History" on May 10, 2006, led me to further develop my ideas about circumcision, which appear in the third chapter.

I am grateful to Gabriel Goldstein and the staff at the Yeshiva University Museum for hiring me to be the greeter at the exhibit "Vienna: Jews and the City of Music, 1870–1938." Not only was I encouraged to read and write in the hours between tours, I also had the good fortune to sit among a number of inspiring historical objects, including Ludwig Wittgenstein's clarinet, a number of photos of Gustav Mahler, and a copy of Arnold Schoenberg's document of (re)conversion (back to Judaism) signed by Marc Chagall. While each of these figures were unquestioningly incorporated into the exhibit, each of them posed difficult questions about the very definition of Jewishness, questions that somehow—perhaps mysteriously—shaped my work.

Writing this book has given me the chance to become acquainted with a number of scholars whom I would not have met otherwise. Many of these individuals generously answered queries, shared unpublished manuscripts, and read portions of my manuscript before we had ever met in person. These include (in alphabetical order) Nadia Abu El-Haj, Aleida Assmann, Alan Bass, Sander Gilman, Sander Gliboff, Ilse Grubrich-Simitis, Robin Judd, Veronika Lipphardt, Eric Santner, Peter Schäfer, Eric Kline Silverman, and Paul Weindling. I am particularly grateful to David Biale, Warren Breckman, Steven Cassedy, Jay Geller, Bruce Rosenstock, and Eric Santner for reading earlier drafts of the fifth chapter. The third chapter benefited from editorial suggestions made by Paul Farber and by the anonymous reviewers for the *Journal of the History of Biology*, which published the chapter separately in 2008. I feel lucky to have met Jan Assmann the very first time I presented material from this book at a conference in 2003. Since then, I have learned much from his published works and also from lectures and correspondence that he has graciously shared with me.

It is common for scholars to completely revise their doctoral dissertations before they are published as books. While I made a series of minor revisions to the manuscript, I am grateful to have had the advice of Geof Bowker to simply send the thing off. I was perhaps even luckier to meet Helen Tartar (thanks to Diana Fuss for introducing us on a subway platform!) who encouraged me to send her my manuscript without too much ado. Helen quickly shepherded the manuscript through the review process. Most of all, I am grateful that she was warm and open even before reading the manuscript, and that she was willing to take a chance on an unknown such as myself. Many thanks to Eric Newman for guiding me through the final rounds of editing, and to all the hard-working people at Fordham University Press.

There is one person who has lived through the ups and downs of this book as much as (or perhaps more than) I: Anthony Burr brilliantly and unflaggingly played the roles of editor, tech support, cheerleader, provocateur, coach, cook, dog walker, lover, husband, and much, much more. There is no way to thank him enough for his support throughout this process, but as a beginning, I dedicate this book to him.

Unless otherwise indicated, quotations from Freud's works are from *The Standard Edition of the Complete Psychological Works of Sigmund Freud*, translated and edited by James Strachey and Anna Freud, 24 vols. (London: Hogarth Press and the Institute of Psycho-Analysis, 1953–1974), abbreviated as *S.E.* In the case of certain problematic or repeated terms, the German is periodically included; unless otherwise indicated, these German quotations are from Sigmund Freud, *Gesammelte Werke, chronologisch geordnet*, ed. Anna Freud, 17 vols. (London: Imago Publishing Company, 1940–1952).

Racial Fever

Introduction

Autobiographical Preface

On most Friday afternoons, a Chassidic man stands on a street corner in Manhattan, searching the crowd for people who look as if they might be Jewish. As soon as he spots a potential Jew, he approaches and says, "Excuse me, are you Jewish?" If he gets a "yes," he tells the person that the Sabbath is about to begin. Does the person know how to light the candles? How to say the blessings? If there is any hesitancy, he tries to help by offering a pair of Sabbath candles and a brochure with the blessings printed in Hebrew and English. By seeking out non-observant Jews and helping them "return" to a life of Jewish ritual and practice, the Chassidic man believes that he is doing a *mitzvah*, a good deed. By doing such *mitzvot*, he believes that he will hasten the coming of the Messiah. Thus, he searches. . . . He sees a man who he *knows* must be Jewish: curly black hair, dressed in a suit, he's even wearing a Star of David around his neck. The Chassid confidently approaches. "Excuse me, sir, are you Jewish?" The man pauses, and looks at the Chassid with a grin. "No," he says. "Why? Are you?"

There is something unsettling about being stopped and asked about one's Jewishness on a street corner. Move the scene to a different time and place, and the consequences of this question are a matter of life and death. Since the Holocaust, it has often been difficult to employ a racial definition of Jewishness without sounding obscene or anti-semitic. And yet, within Jewish communities and families—both observant and secular, both conservative and liberal—there is often an almost obsessive desire to know whether a person is Jewish. The definition of Jewishness in these cases is almost always purely genealogical in that the question is not whether a person feels, thinks, acts, or looks Jewish but whether such suggestive signs are evidence of the "real thing"—the fact that the person has a Jewish parent (or even a grandparent), the fact that the person "really" is Jewish. Indeed, it is not uncommon to hear (both Jewish and non-Jewish) people say that someone is "half-Jewish"[1] or a "quarter Jewish" or even a "mixed breed," even as they are fully aware of the racial (and possibly racist) logic of such descriptions. For better and often for worse, the concept of race is a historical reality whose influence reaches far beyond the color line.[2] This book is an attempt to explore race as a concept beyond the realm of physical variation and to consider racial thinking without reducing it to racism.

Before beginning to write this book, I was dimly aware that such racial definitions of Jewishness were part of a persistent phenomenon. I became conscious of this while I was living in Berlin, Germany, in 2000–2001.[3] Prior to becoming deeply involved with this project, I had no long-standing (scholarly, artistic, conscious) interest in psychoanalysis or Jewish identity. My interest in these subjects emerged from my work developing a sound-art installation for which I record the sounds of individuals' breathing. "Breathing Traces" is designed as a sort of anti-archive that stores only the sounds of a person's life: the inhales, exhales, sighs, grunts, and sniffs. Unlike the numerous archives that many institutions developed with increasing speed and enormity in the late nineteenth century, my archive exhibits none of the distinct attributes often used to define an individual—not gender, height, weight, or age, and not sexual orientation, ethnicity, religion, or nationality.[4] None of these characteristics is perceivable—at least not immediately or dependably so—by listening to the recordings of my collected "specimens," each one exhibited (heard) through a separate loudspeaker. The project began with a sort of universal aesthetic beyond the questions of identity; the sounds of breathing seemed to elicit uncanny feelings of absent presence and distant intimacy. Nonetheless, listening to the sounds of breathing evoked fantasies, memories, and lurking questions about the histories of the individuals whose lives were being technologically replayed.

In 2001, I proposed this project to the Jewish Museum in Berlin, suggesting that I would record and exhibit the sounds of Jews presently living (and breathing) in that city. Whereas many of the museum's other exhibited materials had obvious Jewish content—kitschy Judaica, rescued dusty items from European ghettos, or various art that somehow alludes to Jewish images (an abstract menorah or a Star of David, for example)—the only thing I would exhibit would be the sounds of Jewish people living and breathing in Berlin. On the surface, the project would exhibit the continuity of Jewish *life*; the breathing would undulate, mixing the old with the young, the past with the future. The only qualifications for including individuals in the exhibit were their Jewishness and their capacity to breathe. While the latter (aliveness) is generally easily determined, the former (Jewishness) quickly emerged as a deeply problematic matter. Indeed, the questions of how individuals determine and demonstrate their Jewishness became the heart of the proposed project. If a person wants to be counted as Jewish in Germany today (to get various state benefits or to join a synagogue), she or he must appeal to the rabbi in whichever city she or he lives. Each rabbi in each city has a slightly different method for deciding whether a person is Jewish: Can the person read Hebrew? Is he circumcised? Can she chant the *Sh'mah*? Does she have evidence of a Jewish mother? What sort of evidence? What about the mother's mother? Some rabbis are more strict than others, whether because of their particular interpretations of the Jewish legal tradition or because of their experience dealing with border cases such as post-Soviet individuals whose Jewishness is apparently more questionable (having been suppressed during Communism).[5] In addition to the exhibition of the Jewish breathers, I proposed an accompanying chart that would document the Jewishness of each breather: the column on the left would list the breathing individuals' names, and the top row would contain various historical and contemporary judges (rabbis, government officials in Israel and Germany, "regular" individuals, and so on). For each breather, there would be at least one judge who would count the person as Jewish, and one who would count the person as non-Jewish.[6]

It was in the course of developing the proposal for "Breathing Traces Berlin" that I came across Jacques Derrida's book *Archive Fever: A Freudian*

Impression (1996). In an anticipation of the return of the repressed, my breathing project and *Archive Fever* held all the traces of the book you are now reading. Derrida explores the nature of "archive fever": the "compulsive, repetitive, and nostalgic desire for the archive, an irrepressible desire to return to the origin, a homesickness, a nostalgia for the return to the most archaic place of absolute commencement."[7] Such returns are ultimately impossible: They make people sick or crazy in their desire to resuscitate a past that is gone forever but continues to haunt the present. And yet, the desire rages, the compulsion to repeat repeats. "The archivist produces more archive, and that is why the archive is never closed. It opens out of the future."[8] While *Archive Fever* retraces many classic Derridean themes (such as the questions of trace, presence and absence, and the [im]possibilities of interpretation), it is an explicit response to Yosef Hayim Yerushalmi's book *Freud's Moses: Judaism Terminable and Interminable* (1991), which is itself a response to Freud's *Moses and Monotheism* (1939). Derrida reads Yerushalmi's book with an ear for his rhetorical flourishes and inconsistencies, traces that ultimately suggest cracks in the very project of being both an "objective" historian and a historian who deeply cares about his object of study. In my own work, Derrida's *Archive Fever* has been the source of an "anxiety of influence."[9] His very rhythms have sometimes threatened to crowd out the rationality expected of someone attempting to establish her scholarly credentials and the independence needed to forge one's own style. *Archive Fever* has "tormented me like an unlaid ghost."[10] Throughout this book, there are traces of *Archive Fever*, but there are very few explicit references to it.

This is not the case for Yerushalmi's book. While Derrida's meditations haunted me, Yerushalmi's compelled me to begin writing. Whereas other scholars had found ample evidence that Freud felt ambivalent about or distant from the Jewish tradition, in *Freud's Moses* Yerushalmi meticulously and feverishly combs Freud's archives and finds traces of his positively Jewish affection. While Yerushalmi insists that he has no need to "claim" Freud for "an already crowded Jewish pantheon,"[11] he spends much of the book demonstrating that Freud was not simply a "Psychological Jew," but something more: more substantive than "pure subjectivity," more "content" than merely "character."[12] Yerushalmi begins with the fact that, unlike many of his contemporaries, Freud never disavowed his Jewish identity; to the contrary, he insisted "on a Jewishness that resisted definition."[13] Despite his insistence that he is interested only in Freud's "conscious intentional-ity,"[14] and that he has no interest in psychoanalyzing the original psychoan-alyst, Yerushalmi shows that in private, Freud demonstrated a deep connection to Judaism, regardless of his public protestations to the contrary. As Yerushalmi notes (using a particularly Freudian logic of negation),

> the very violence of Freud's recoil against Jewish religious belief and ritual must arouse our deepest suspicion. It displays an aggressive intensity that normally accompanies a rebellion against an equally intense former attachment, more typi-cal of a former Yeshiva student in revolt against Judaism than of one who had received a minimal Jewish education.[15]

Ultimately, he demonstrates that it is not only Freud's Jewish genealogical origins that matter, but his Jewish life—his transmission of a new kind of Judaism to the future. The question, which Yerushalmi asks in a monologue addressed to Freud's ghost in the last section of *Freud's Moses*, is whether Freud finally saw psychoanalysis as a sort of godless Judaism, a "Jewish sci-ence" for the future.

Yerushalmi's historiography is inextricably linked to his position as a son and a father, someone who has received a legacy and someone who hopes to leave a legacy, a Jewish legacy, to the future.[16] It is also, I think, subtly linked to the fact that before becoming one of the foremost historians of the Jewish people and Jewish tradition, Yerushalmi briefly worked as a rabbi.[17] As an authority on Jewish liturgy and history, he can convincingly reveal the Jewishness of an anecdote or a slip of the tongue, illuminating not only the slip but also its resonance with classical Jewish texts. In addition to the more general archive fever at the heart of Yerushalmi's historiogra-phy, then, there is a particularly Jewish fever: a desire to discover not simply the past, but the *Jewish* past, as if discovering traces of such a past could ensure its future. Nonetheless, he explicitly acknowledges that "the future, in spite of the appearances, always remains open. . . . The historian's task, luckily, is to try to understand the past."[18] A historian's task may be to understand the past, but the ultimate hope is that he will leave something for the future, indeed that he can even help produce a better future.

Yerushalmi's archive fever is alluring yet troubling. He seems to com-mand his audience to bow before his rabbinic and scholarly authority. (Who could be a better judge of whether something or someone is "authentically" Jewish?[19]) And yet, there is a violence at the heart of a project (not only

Yerushalmi's) whose archive fever is fuelled by a desire to root out the Jewish traces—to show *how* Jewish a person *really* is. This fever derives at least in part from the ideas that there are some people who are more Jewish than others, and that there are certain individuals (other than God or oneself) who can determine who is truly Jewish.[20] I was able to diagnose this fever only upon reading the book that elicited Yerushalmi's book: Freud's *Moses and Monotheism*.[21] Here I discovered that Freud had developed a complex theory of Jewishness that addresses why many individuals feel overcome with the burdens of their ancestral past, even as this past is unverifiable and ultimately unknowable. In Freud's *Moses*, Jewishness emerges as both a matter of genealogical bodily inheritance and as a matter of immaterial memory and its material representations. In the case of the Jewish people, Freud suggests that regardless of any attempts to repress, suppress, or repudiate Jewishness, it will survive, for better and for worse.

These are symptoms of racial fever: the irrepressible desire of individuals and communities to define themselves and others through genealogy, to discover (and sometimes invent) ancestral memories that can somehow explain the tensions and compulsions of the present, and to reconstruct and return to these narratives as if they were indisputable history and palpable facts. Racial fever is felt in and on the body, even as it is invisible, indefinable, and ultimately indecipherable. Sometimes it seems to take the form of a sickness; at other times it is a fervor, an intense craving, or a zealous enthusiasm. Now and then it seems to lie dormant, biding its time.

The idea of racial fever emerges directly out of psychoanalysis. Throughout his life, Freud explored the ways in which individuals' lives seem ruled by their pasts, tracing patients' physical symptoms to psychical traumas and identifying their compulsions to repeat as the result of memories of a distant past. In his earliest work, Freud rejected his teachers' over-emphasis on heredity by proposing that his patients suffered not from familial degeneracy but from "reminiscences." As such, he initially resisted the idea that an individual's memories reached further back than childhood. Along the way, however, he realized that there were certain conflicts and patterns that were inexorable; individuals seemed to be burdened with memories not only of their earliest lives but of the effects "produced on the endlessly *long chain of our ancestors*."[22] Yet it was not until his final book that Freud specified what he meant by "our" ancestors and explicitly explored the Jewish Question.

Written during the last five years of his life, Freud's *Moses and Monotheism* has long been regarded as an autobiographical curiosity that, while shedding light on his feelings about his own Jewishness, potentially compromises some of the more convincing aspects of psychoanalysis. At first glance, the book is a bizarre reconstruction of the "real" story behind Moses, monotheism, and the Jewish people. It incorporates what seem to be tortured twists of logic, drawing from dubious and apparently outmoded theories of race and heredity, as well as (what were then) recent discoveries in archaeology and ethnology. However, *Moses and Monotheism* is a serious work in which Freud proposes a theory of Jewishness—what it is, how it is transmitted, and how it continues to survive. Rather than an aberration, Freud's last book is the culmination of a lifetime spent investigating the relationships between memory and its rivals: heredity, history, and fiction. By proposing that certain events in the distant past were so traumatic that their memories were inherited by successive generations, Freud eventually integrated the two realms—the biological, permanent, and racial on the one hand, and the psychic, experiential, and cultural on the other. In *Moses and Monotheism* he theorized that Jewishness is constituted by the inheritance of a specific archaic memory that Jewish people are inexorably compelled to transmit to future generations, whether consciously or unconsciously. It is for this reason that I consider Freud's theory of Jewishness to be a racial theory of memory.

The Plot

But first, a joke: A precocious boy comes home from school and announces that he has learned all about Moses. His mother asks him, "So who was Moses?" The boy answers, "Moses was the son of an Egyptian princess." The mother, obviously concerned, replies, "No, Moses was the son of a *Jewish* woman. The princess only took him out of the water." To which the boy answers, "Says *she!*"[23]

The explicit narrative of *Moses and Monotheism* is in some ways a retelling of this joke. It is also a complicated re-reading of the Biblical account of Moses and the origins of the Jewish people. Freud outlined the plot of the new work in a letter to his friend Lou Andreas-Salomé in January 1935. In its most simple formulation, he writes, his new work "started out from the question as to what has really created the particular character of the Jew, and came to the conclusion that the Jew is the creation of the man Moses. Who was this Moses and what did he bring about?"[24] The narrative of the book itself is a detailed account of how Moses formulated Mosaic monotheism, how this became Jewish tradition, and how the Jewish people have survived despite millennia of anti-semitic oppression. While Freud uses the Hebrew Bible as his main source of information, he also draws from the scholarship of contemporary archaeologists, Egyptologists, Biblical scholars, anthropologists, and biologists, as well as his own psychoanalytic theory and methodology.

According to Freud, Moses was not an Israelite but rather an Egyptian. It was Moses (not God) who chose a rowdy band of Semites as his people, upon whom he imposed a harsh and strict monotheism (based on the Egyptian pharaoh Akhenaten's monotheistic sun-god cult). Unlike the earlier Egyptian religions, Mosaic monotheism was devoid of magic and mysticism: It rejected the idea of the afterlife and strictly prohibited any representation of god. Finding the Mosaic tradition too difficult, the band of Semites killed this Moses and apparently forgot all about the episode. Meanwhile, this band joined up with a Midianite tribe who happened to worship a volcano god named Yahweh and whose leader also happened to be named Moses. Over centuries, tradition "fused" the two tribes, the two gods, and the two Moseses such that the Biblical text contains records of just one tribe, one god, and one Moses. The monotheistic and aniconic religion of the first Moses remained a "half-extinguished tradition" for many centuries, but eventually it "triumphed." While some traces of these events are found in the Biblical text, according to Freud the decisive memory-traces of Moses—and the Mosaic tradition itself—were biologically transmitted from one generation to the next.[25]

Freud was well aware that his reconstruction of the "true" origins of the Jewish people was bound to offend—not only scholars of ancient history, religion, ethnology, and biology, but also religious and secular Jews as well as both anti-semitic and philo-semitic non-Jews. As he exclaimed in a letter to Arnold Zweig in 1938, "Can one really believe that my arid treatise would destroy the belief of a single person brought up by heredity and training in the faith, even if it were to come his way?"[26] For many readers, the proposal that Moses was not an Israelite but rather an Egyptian has been the most shocking and disturbing, for (as Freud acknowledges) it seems to "deprive a people of the man whom they take pride in as the greatest of their sons."[27] Yet Freud knew that he was neither the first nor the last person to assert the Egyptian origins of Moses and his monotheism.[28] Long before, authors such as Manetho (in the third century B.C.E.) and Strabo (in the first century C.E.) proposed that Moses was actually an Egyptian, while Enlightenment authors such as John Toland, John Spencer, and Friedrich Schiller proposed that Moses was culturally Egyptian even if he was ethnically Hebrew.[29] As the Egyptologist Jan Assmann explains, though "there are no traces of his earthly existence outside the tradition," elaborate reconstructions of Moses' origins have been a significant element of interpretations of the Exodus story in a wide range of historical, cultural, and religious contexts.[30] Contrary to what most readers have assumed, by insisting on the Egyptianness of Moses Freud did not hope to disavow his own Jewishness or the Jewishness of his institution (that is, psychoanalysis). Instead, he subtly questioned the self-evidence of such definitions. Even in the Biblical narrative, Moses was an Israelite only by virtue of his genealogy; after he was weaned he was brought back to Pharaoh's daughter and "he became her son" (Exodus 2:10). Thus this passage suggests that while Moses' genealogy may have been Israelite, his education and culture were Egyptian.

This genealogical element is the key to Freud's theory of Jewishness and his explanation of how this tradition survived. Though he uses texts, traditions, and rituals as the basis of his reconstruction of the origins of the Jewish people, he ultimately concludes that such forms of direct communication are not enough to explain the deep power and persistence of the Mosaic tradition. Freud explains this conundrum in one paragraph whose elements are cited in every chapter of this book. I quote it here in its entirety:

> On further reflection, I must admit that I have behaved for a long time as though the inheritance of memory-traces of the experience of our ancestors, *independently of direct communication* and of the influence of education by the setting of an example, were established beyond question. When I spoke of the *survival of a tradition* among a people or of the formation of a people's character, I had mostly in mind *an inherited tradition* of this kind and *not one transmitted by communication.* Or at least I made no distinction between the two and was not clearly aware of my audacity in neglecting to do so. My position, no doubt, is made more difficult by the present attitude of biological science, which *refuses to hear of the inheritance of acquired characters by succeeding generations.* I must, however, in all modesty

confess that nevertheless I cannot do without *this factor in biological evolution*. The same thing is not in question, indeed, in the two cases: in the one it is a matter of acquired characters which are hard to grasp, in the other of memory-traces of external events—*something tangible*, as it were. But it may well be that at bottom we cannot imagine one without the other.[31]

According to Freud, Jewishness is constituted by the memory-traces of Moses and his tradition. Once "acquired," these memory-traces were persistently transmitted from generation to generation through textual and oral communication, education by example, gestures, rituals, and other cultural means. However, Freud insists that these media cannot account for the persistence of the Jewish tradition, including the compulsion to *be* Jewish. Ultimately, he cannot do without the idea that the memory of Moses (and hence, Jewishness) was *biologically* transmitted. Thus, while *Moses and Monotheism* can be considered a work of literary fiction, Biblical criticism, and religious history, it is also an explicit response to the debates about biological theories of evolution, heredity, and race that were already being turned to disturbing effect in 1938. So too, my own interpretation of Freud's theory of Jewishness is not only a study in literary and religious hermeneutics but also an exploration of the permeable boundaries between literature and science; between the categories of race, religion, and culture; and between the realms of textual history and lived bodily experience.

What Was Freud Thinking? (The Biographical Context)

Despite widespread doubts about the truth or scientific value of psychoanalysis, Freud's oeuvre contains some of the most literary and rhetorically impressive writing of the twentieth century. This, however, is not the case with *Moses and Monotheism*, a text burdened with hesitations, repetitions, gaps, and oddly misleading rhetoric. Many scholars have speculated about the reasons for the apparent idiosyncrasies of Freud's final book: from ambivalence about his Jewishness to anxieties about the historical foundations of his narrative to the precarious political and personal situation in which he wrote the work.[32] When he began to write it in 1934 at age 78, he was already suffering from the jaw cancer that had been diagnosed eleven years before and that would lead to his death five years later. The first page of the manuscript is dated August 9, 1934, but it would be at least another four years before he completed the work. In addition to suffering from cancer, in 1934–38 Freud witnessed his country fall into the darkness of anti-semitic "barbarism" and watched as it was annexed by Nazi Germany in March 1938. Finally, in June 1938, Freud and most of his family left Vienna for London, where he published the final sections of *Moses and Monotheism* in March 1939, and where he died six months later on September 23, 1939.

Freud originally thought of the book as a historical novel, and in his first draft he gave it the title *The Man Moses: A Historical Novel* [*Der Mann Moses, Ein historischer Roman*]. As a whole, the book is disjointed and consists of three essays, each an attempt to improve, extend, and recast the findings of the previous one.[33] Indeed, when he published the first two parts of the work as separate essays in *Imago* in 1937, there was hardly any indication that there would be more forthcoming material. The third essay—which is more than twice the length of the first two put together—is preceded by two prefatory notes, the first written in Vienna "before March 1938," and the second written in London in June 1938. In the first preface, Freud explains that he has no intention of publishing this third essay. By contrast, in the second preface he evinces a new confidence deriving at least in part from the fact that he was now living in relative safety in London. Finally, half-way through the third essay, he stops again to present a summary that reads like yet another preface, with "extensive explanations and apologies" for the repetitive and "inartistic" nature of the work. He confesses that he "deplores it unreservedly." However, he could not put the work aside: It "tormented" him "like an unlaid ghost."[34]

As in many of his other works from the last decade of his life, in *Moses and Monotheism* Freud takes a long and wide view of the most fundamental questions of psychoanalysis. In his correspondence with Arnold Zweig between 1927 and 1939, he explored many of the subjects that would become central to his final book: the future of German Jewry; the tensions between various versions of realities and their relationship to fantasies, memories, and narratives; the definition and narrative requirements of historical novels; and last, the nature of religious fanaticism.[35] These subjects were also at the forefront of Zweig's mind: Not only had he recently published a book on the problems confronting German Jewry,[36] he was contemplating immigrating to Palestine (from where he wrote Freud many letters) and was planning on writing a historical novel on Nietzsche (which he discussed with

Freud).[37] In September 1934, Freud announced to Zweig that he had begun a new work:

> Faced with the new persecutions, one asks oneself again how the Jews have come to be what they are and why they have attracted this immortal hatred [*unsterbliche haß*]. I soon discovered the formula: Moses created the Jews. So I gave my work the title: *The Man Moses, a historical novel* (with more justification than your Nietzsche novel).[38]

Freud's reconstruction of the Egyptian origins of the Jews' Jewishness is explicitly couched in terms that hover between truth and fiction, history and memory. In this respect, *Moses* is not only a historical novel, but also a belated meditation on the very terms that shaped his earliest psychoanalytic writings.

Freud's final book was neither an exception nor an inevitable conclusion to his life's work. Rather, it was an intensified pursuit of many of the questions that had lingered in the margins of his work throughout his life. In his letters to Zweig, Freud candidly discussed his misgivings about the possibility of Jewish settlement in Palestine and the violence hovering at the edges of racial and religious distinctions between peoples. In response to Zweig's descriptions of Palestine, Freud writes,

> Palestine has never produced anything but religions, sacred frenzies, presumptuous attempts to overcome the outer world of appearance by means of the inner world of wishful thinking. And we hail [*stammen*] from there (though one of us considers himself a German as well; the other does not); our forebears lived there for perhaps half or perhaps a whole millennium (*but this too is just a perhaps*) and it is impossible to say what heritage from this land we have taken over into our blood and nerves (as is mistakenly said).[39]

Though he slips into the language of "blood and nerves," he quickly points out the "perhaps" and the "mistakes" in this narrative. Throughout his life, Freud struggled to make sense of the explanatory power of heredity even as he doubted its exclusive control of the psyche. And though heredity would seem to be a scientific matter, Freud knew that it could easily fall into a category of irrational, non-scientific beliefs and frenzies (to which he alludes in the letter to Zweig). This category could include the possibility of telepathic communication, the existence of invisible gods, and the powers of the past to rule over the present. Despite being fully aware of rational scientific proofs to the contrary, such obscure forces seemed to rule over the lives of individuals and of communities. Indeed, the belief in the continuity with one's forebears and the idea that one's heritage might reside in the body could also fall into the category of irrational belief (even as it has been a subject of scientific inquiry for at least a century).

Before leaving the biographical context of Freud's last work, it seems prudent to include the bare essentials of his Jewish identity. That is, why do we believe that Freud was Jewish? Since many other scholars have already explored the nuances of the Freud family's Jewish life,[40] I include only the basics. Freud's "Autobiographical Study" (1925) begins, "I was born on May 6th, 1856, at Freiberg in Moravia, a small town in what is now Czecho-slovakia. My parents were Jews, and I have remained a Jew myself."[41] His parents, Kallamon Jacob Freud and Amalia Nathanson, named him Sigis-mund Schlomo Freud, and they had him circumcised according to Jewish ritual law on May 13 by Samson Frankel from Mährisch-Ostrau.[42] In nu-merous published works, Freud maintained that he felt neither religiously nor nationally Jewish, but in these very same works he also attempted to define how he *did* feel Jewish. For example, in a letter to the Jewish Press Centre in Zürich in 1925, he asserted that he stood "as far apart from the Jewish religion as from all other religions: that is to say, they are of great significance to me as a subject of scientific interest, but I have no part in them emotionally. . . . On the other hand, I have always had a strong feeling of solidarity with my fellow-people and have always encouraged it in my children as well. We have all remained in the Jewish denomination."[43]

There is no shortage of quotations that demonstrate that, throughout his life, Freud attempted to articulate his relationship to Judaism, Jewishness, and other Jews. Two more statements will suffice. In his 1926 address to the B'nai B'rith Society, a Jewish social group to which Freud presented many of his early lectures, he said,

> That you were Jews could only be agreeable to me; for I was myself a Jew, and it had always seemed to me not only unworthy but positively senseless to deny the fact. What bound me to Jewry was (I am ashamed to admit) neither faith nor national pride, for I have always been an unbeliever and was brought up without any religion though not without a respect for what are called the "ethical" stan-dards of human civilization. Whenever I felt an inclination to national enthusi-asm I strove to suppress it as being harmful and wrong, alarmed by the warning examples of the peoples among whom we Jews live. But plenty of other things

remained over to make the attraction of Jewry and Jews irresistible—many obscure emotional forces, which were *the more powerful the less they could be expressed in words*.[44]

And finally, in the 1930 preface to the Hebrew translation of *Totem and Taboo*, Freud writes,

> No reader of this book [in Hebrew] will find it easy to put himself in the emotional position of an author who is ignorant of the language of holy writ, who is completely estranged from the religion of his fathers—as well as from every other religion—and who cannot take a share in nationalist ideals, but who has yet never repudiated his people, who feels that he is in his essential nature a Jew and who has no desire to alter that nature. If the question were put to him: "Since you have abandoned all these common characteristics of your countrymen, what is there left to you that is Jewish?" he would reply: "A very great deal, and probably its very essence [*Wesentliche*]." He could not now express that essence clearly in words; but some day, no doubt, it will become accessible to the scientific mind.[45]

Freud prepared this preface in 1930, but the Hebrew translation was not published until 1939, the same year he finally published *Moses and Monotheism* in its entirety. *Moses* can be read in part as Freud's attempt to interrogate the origins and survival of a Jewish "essence," to express the "obscure" powers of this tradition in words, and to make such paradoxes of Jewishness "accessible to the scientific mind."

Why Is This Book Different from All Other Studies of Freud's Moses?

Fifty years after the first complete publication of *Moses and Monotheism*, it emerged as the focus of numerous books, articles, and colloquia. It is impossible to determine the reason for this comeback: whether it is due to the publication of Yerushalmi's book in 1989 and Derrida's response in 1995, or a widespread return to addressing the history of the Holocaust (particularly in Germany), or a generally resurgent interest in the questions of national, racial, religious, and ethnic identities, or some combination of all of these.[46]

In addition to the works by Yerushalmi and Derrida, a number of recent studies of Freud's *Moses* have been especially influential in shaping my own

work. Some of these are primarily historiographic; others are more philosophical. Perhaps because Freud's final book reaches far beyond the field of
psychoanalysis into a realm of speculative cultural and religious analysis,
it has often been interpreted as an extended autobiographical statement,
particularly as it reflects his vexed relationship to things Jewish. Since so
many others have made convincing arguments about the nature of Freud's
feelings about being Jewish, I attempt to withhold further commentary
about such questions. Nonetheless, this scholarship laid the groundwork for
much of my own thinking on the subject. Whereas Yerushalmi argues that
Freud ultimately embraced his Jewish identity, Daniel Boyarin's *Unheroic
Conduct: The Rise of Heterosexuality and the Invention of the Jewish Man* (1997)
focuses on the ways in which *Moses* was Freud's attempt to assimilate by
rewriting Judaism as a form of masculine Teutonic Aryanism. As Boyarin
puts it, "Rather than the conversion of the Jews, the total conversion of
Judaism was the solution."[47] Responding to the work of Sander Gilman,
Boyarin shows that in response to the anti-semitic portrayals of the Jewish
man as feminized, homosexual, and overly "carnal," Freud constructed an
image of Judaism that was more masculine and more supremely spiritual
[*geistig*]. Similarly, Jay Geller finds that, in his attempts to mitigate the traumas of anti-semitism, Freud projected the signs of Jewish difference into
his discussions of gender and sexual difference.[48] More generally, Gilman,
Boyarin, and Geller see Freud as a symptom of the complex relationships
between anti-semitism (as well as Jewish self-hatred), misogyny, and homo-
phobia in late-nineteenth- and early-twentieth-century Europe, particularly
as human difference became a matter of secular scientific study. Drawing
from these scholars' work, I argue that Freud's theory of Jewishness is compelling for the ways in which it moves beyond certain binaries that have
long defined discussions of Judaism and Jewishness. Specifically, rather than
trying to determine whether a text positively or negatively represents Jewishness, Freud's work allows us to articulate the compulsions that give rise
to *both* ethnic pride and racial hatred and to see these feelings as part of one
phenomenon. So too, rather than focusing on only the racial, genealogical,
and bodily elements of Jewish identity or on the intellectual and abstract
concepts of Judaism, Freud's work compels us to explore the relationship
between the two.

   In the work of Boyarin, Gilman, and Geller, Freud's *Moses* emerges as a
doomed attempt to alleviate the effects of European anti-semitism, whether

through assimilation or through the creative inversion of stereotypes. By contrast, in the work of Jan Assmann, Freud's final book emerges as a utopian dream: an attempt to heal the wound at the heart of Western civilization. With the institution of monotheism in the ancient polytheistic world, Assmann explains, a new unbridgeable distinction emerged between "Israel in truth" and "Egypt in error." Because this distinction is associated with Moses and his monotheism, Assmann calls this split the "Mosaic distinction."[49] According to Assmann, in the monotheistic tradition, remembering Egypt maintains the distinctions between the past (Egyptian polytheism) and the present (Jewish monotheism), between falsehood (or false gods) and truth (or one true god), as well as between Gentiles and Jews. Remembering Egypt has been central to the process of constructing and maintaining a group identity, for it allows one both to remember and to be liberated from "one's own past which is no longer one's own."[50] Rather than seeing Freud's work as an ambivalent or vexed response to his Jewishness, Assmann shows that Freud's "Egyptomania" was part of an Enlightenment tradition that attempted to move beyond such deep-rooted distinctions. In Assmann's interpretation, the "discovery" that Moses was an Egyptian was seen as an "Egyptian truth" and welcomed as a way of invalidating "the Mosaic distinction and deconstruct[ing] the space separated by this distinction."[51] While Assmann does not focus on Freud's efforts to come to terms with his Jewishness, he admits that his own study of *Moses the Egyptian* is homologous to Freud's work because it was written at least in part as an attempt to make sense of his own historical situation. Whereas Freud tried to come to terms with his position as a "godless Jew" and as the father of psychoanalysis, Assmann tried to come to terms with his position as a German Egyptologist writing two generations after the catastrophe that Freud would never know in its entirety.[52]

Assmann does not explicitly equate the Mosaic distinction with Jewish difference in *Moses the Egyptian* (1997), but he implies that the Egyptian Moses is a fantasy about overcoming such differences, as if doing away with the gap between true and false religion could also do away with religious antagonism and anti-semitism. Indeed, in entitling the final section of his book, "Abolishing the Mosaic Distinction: Religious Antagonism and Its Overcoming," Assmann uses language that comes perilously close to evangelical Christians' claims that the Jewish problem will be abolished when the Jews overcome their resistance to Jesus Christ.[53] Similarly, in the early twentieth century (in Germany and America, for example), Jews and non-Jews both proposed that if Jews simply assimilated and acted less Jewish, they would no longer be so foreign, and there would no longer be a "Jewish problem."[54]

In his more recent work, Assmann retracts his earlier interpretation of Freud's Egyptian *Moses* as an attempt to overcome the Mosaic distinction. Now, he explains, he sees that Freud portrays monotheism as a Jewish "achievement," deriving most particularly from the law against physically or nominally representing G-d. Like Boyarin, Assmann sees Freud's emphasis on the Jewish "advance in intellectuality [*Geistigkeit*]" as an inversion of the historical distinctions between Judaism and Christianity.[55] That is, since Paul, Christian writers have often portrayed the Jewish people as "mired in the flesh" and the "letter of the law," whereas Christianity had supposedly ascended to the heights of universal spirituality. Freud, however, argues that Judaism remained the most supremely "spiritual [*geistig*]," whereas Christianity had regressed to the primitive idolatry that had characterized Egyptian polytheism. Thus Assmann sees Freud's *Moses* (and psychoanalysis more generally) as an affirmation of the Jewish aspiration to free the soul from the captivity of compulsive idolatry of the material world.[56] While Assmann does not explicitly address the consequences of this exit from the physical realm, I extend his thesis to explore how the Jewish Question can illuminate questions of race and belonging beyond the realm of physical materiality.[57]

Like Assmann in his earlier work, Ilse Grubrich-Simitis sees Freud's *Moses* as a utopian "daydream," an attempt to "relativize *one* of the causes of the millennia-old phenomenon of anti-semitism" and "to allay the grinding disquietude he felt about the future of his life-work." Using the example of Moses, Freud "demonstrated to himself how an uncomfortable, demanding doctrine does not perish even when politically persecuted and suppressed, but, on the contrary, returns from repression after a long interval."[58] In other words, the eventual triumph of Moses' monotheism—even after he had been murdered and his ideals had been repressed—suggested to Freud that psychoanalysis might also eventually triumph, even if the current political situation suggested that he might also be murdered and his ideals rejected. In Grubrich-Simitis' interpretation, Freud's most radical move was not that he made Moses an Egyptian, but that he made the Jews' chosenness a matter of human (rather than divine) selection. By blaming Moses (rather than God) for this choice, Freud seems to suggest that humans may also be able to overcome the "paranoid split" between Jews and non-Jews.[59]

Yet Freud's hopeful humanism is tempered by his recognition of man's limitations. What made the Jews Jewish was not only Moses' choice of the rowdy band of Semites as his people, but the Semites' violent murder of their leader. By proposing that the memory-traces were biologically inherited, Freud addresses the ways in which history is experienced as a matter beyond human action; the Jews remained Jewish not because of history, but because of the naturalization and internalization of history in the body. Where Freud's *Moses* has been seen as an attempt to cure the Jewish people (if not also Western civilization) of their collective neurosis,[60] it is far more representative of his skepticism about the potential for such change.

If Freud developed a theory of Jewishness—indeed, if the history of psychoanalysis is inextricably intertwined with the history of the Jewish Question—is it also relevant to other human groups? What is the relationship between questions of Jewish difference and of other human differences? Though Freud often used a language of universalism in his earlier writings, in *Moses and Monotheism* he finally acknowledges the limited applicability of his work. Rather than understanding difference as only a matter of external characteristics or historical vagaries, Freud's emphasis on the inheritance of archaic memory suggests a model of understanding difference as something that is both internal to one's self or one's own community and as something beyond individual predilections and preferences. In attending to the "paranoid split" opened by the "Mosaic distinction," Assmann and Grubrich-Simitis suggest that Freud wishfully dreamed of a time when such differences (between Jews and non-Jews) might be overcome or at least peacefully accepted. By contrast, Eric Santner criticizes the notion of cultural pluralism and instead focuses on the universal difference "opened by the 'Mosaic distinction.'"[61] Rather than emphasizing the particularities that may characterize a person or community as foreign, Santner shifts the focus to those uncanny differences "internal to any and every space we call home."[62] Recalling Hegel's famous phrase that the "enigmas of the ancient Egyptians were also enigmas for the Egyptians themselves," Santner suggests that the strangeness of the "foreign Other" can only be understood when we understand how strange the Other is to himself.[63] Thus we can begin to see utopian visions of "tolerance and multiculturalism" as defenses against the strange and uncanny presence that characterizes human existence "not only in extreme situations but *every day*."[64]

Late in the writing of this book I came across a passage by Grubrich-Simitis that characterizes my own idiosyncratic methodology. She advocates a (non-Lacanian)

> return to Freud's texts—however out of keeping this may be with the times . . . a radical reading anew of his writings, with a view to rediscovering them or indeed to discovering them for the first time . . . a particular reading attitude is recommended, made up of unobtrusiveness, careful alertness and respect even for the most seemingly insignificant detail—an oscillation between proximity and distance that will assure the texts sufficient free space to reveal themselves in all their independence. . . . The reader must approach them [Freud's texts] *not* from a meta-level, *not* as it were looking down from above, and *not* from a vantage point of "superior" knowledge—that is, *not* solely from the plane of present-day psychoanalytic theory and practice. The risk otherwise is of encountering nothing but his own conscious or unconscious expectations or, alternatively, the babel of later interpreters' voices drowning out everything else. . . . The attitude recommended to the reader can perhaps best be likened to that of "evenly suspended attention," which we assume in relation to the analysand's communications in the course of our analytic work.[65]

While I feel an affinity with Grubrich-Simitis' approach, I am not part of the community that she addresses in this statement. First, I had no problem trying to read Freud's writings "anew," since when I began this project I was reading many of his texts for the first time.[66] Second, since I am neither a psychoanalyst nor a psychoanalytic patient, I cannot draw on "our" analytic work. This outsider status puts me both at an advantage and at a disadvantage. Unlike many of the scholars from whose work I extensively draw, I have no need to emancipate myself from Freud's authoritative sway—I do not worship him and I have no need to take him down. Thus my advantage is that I stand outside the "compact majority" of psychoanalytic communities. The disadvantage, of course, is that while I can read about the phenomenon of psychoanalysis, I am presumably not as sensitive to its inner workings and the subtleties of psychoanalytic interaction, a sensitivity that characterizes some of the scholarship I most admire.[67]

In both psychoanalysis and Judaism there is a homologous sense that individuals are either on the inside or the outside. When a text about the Jewish people is published there is often a question that lurks in people's minds: Is the author a Jew or a non-Jew? Do the statements reveal a fetishistic interest—or worse, latent anti-semitism—or do they point to a familiar sense of ironic pride or ambivalence? Discussions of psychoanalysis and of the Jewish people often turn around a central concern about their future existence.[68] For protective insiders, the question is how to protect or salvage psychoanalysis even as it is bombarded and bashed in the popular press and by "serious" scientists (MD's, neurobiologists, and so on). Unlike many other scientific theories that have fallen by the wayside—nearly forgotten except as blips in the forward progress of science—psychoanalysis continues to rankle, to make headlines and to elicit entire books, even if many of these are dedicated to proving it wrong.[69] Similarly, while there is probably no way to measure contemporary anti-semitism, there is a sense that the Jewish people have attained a certain amount of cultural presence and political power in Europe and North America that would have been almost unthinkable only a century ago. Nonetheless, a quick search for "Jews" on the Internet will reveal that anti-semitism is alive and well—that it is, in Freud's words, a form of "immortal hatred."[70] In both the case of psychoanalysis and of Jewishness, opposition, denunciation, and anxiety seem to be some sort of discomforting evidence—proof positive—of their vitality.

Definitions and Disclaimers

The title of Freud's final book makes no reference to Jews, Jewishness, or Judaism; instead, it refers to *monotheism*. Judaism and monotheism are not equivalent: There are many forms of monotheism that are not Jewish, and there are many Jewish texts that invoke the multiplicity of divinity. Since Freud does not clearly distinguish between Mosaic monotheism and Judaism, I do not extensively engage questions regarding their complicated relationship.[71] Throughout the book, I refer to *Jewishness*, a term that is unfortunately awkward and somewhat uncommon. In German, there is the word *Judentum*, which encompasses what, in English, tends to fall under the categories of *Jewry* (the Jewish people), *Judaism* (the Jewish religion), and finally *Jewishness* (the character, customs, and experience of being Jewish). The difficulty of finding the proper word gestures toward the problematic position of *Judentum* itself: if it is not exactly a religion (where believing and practicing defines the community, as in Christianity), and not exactly a race (since Jews come in many different hues, and since individuals can become Jewish through conversion), and not exactly a nationality (since most Jews around the world carry passports from nations other than Israel), what is it? Is it an ethnicity? An ethical position? A set of rituals or texts? An intellectual tradition? A tradition of interpretation or a predisposition to interpretation? Is it an identity one chooses, or one which is imposed? Jay Geller has noted that "how one translates *Judentum* into English betrays one's agenda,"[72] as if one's agenda is something both knowable and stable, even if it is not explicitly addressed. However, I am not so sure. While the translation may betray one's focus (sociological, religious, or cultural), this should not be confused with one's agenda. It is possible to focus on the sociological aspects of the religion, the religious aspects of the culture, or (as in my case) the ways in which the various terms invoke one another.[73] It is also, I hope, possible to explore *Judentum* with multiple (or even conflicting) agendas and with anticipation that one's agenda may change in the process of such explorations.[74]

While Jewishness would seem most similar to the notion of *Jewish identity*, I choose not to use this phrase partially because of its association with the identity politics of the 1980s and '90s, which primarily focused on individuals' personal feelings about their ethnic, cultural, or racial backgrounds. It is probably impossible to avoid engaging with the affective emotions that shape identity (including my own), but throughout this book I attempt to focus on the political, historical, and scientific contexts that shape the very language that individuals use to discuss their identities. Particularly in left-leaning academic circles, identity is often facilely regarded as a question of the individual's choices and beliefs as opposed to the regressive notion of immutable heredity. I have no desire to assert the truth of the latter notion. Rather, this book is an attempt to acknowledge and to explore the ways in which identity (perhaps particularly Jewish identity) is often discussed and experienced—sometimes consciously, sometimes unconsciously—as something that is inherited and that is quite difficult (if not impossible) for individuals to change. Finally, my choice of the term *Jewishness* intentionally provokes the question of whether it is even possible to speak of a quality or character of Jewishness, and, if it is possible, why people feel the need to define such an entity.

In my discussions of Jewishness, I also try to avoid the term *ambivalence*, even though this might be an obvious description of what Freud is talking about. Let me try to explain. According to Freud's terminology, ambivalence is the condition of simultaneously feeling both love and hate toward a person or thing. It is well known that he explored this concept in *Totem and Taboo* and elsewhere. While he speaks of ambivalent feelings for the analyst (particularly through transference), for one's parents, and for "the father," Freud never uses the word "ambivalent" to speak about his feelings of Jewishness. Similarly, I do not use the word "ambivalent" to describe Freud's relationship to things Jewish because the word (in its Anglo-American context) suggests that Jewishness is something that can be measured like sugar and salt or like the charge of a battery: Ambivalence is weak (someone who is ambivalent about his Jewishness is regarded as "less Jewish"), whereas ethnic pride is strong (a proudly Jewish person is regarded as "more Jewish"). In the twentieth century, the term *ambivalence* was often used to refer to the self-conscious wavering between Jewish self-hatred and ethnic pride. Despite the very common usage of this term, I would describe this as a matter of *discomfort*.[75] Regardless of whether a person loves or hates his body, he cannot entirely escape it. Similarly, a person might love or hate Jewishness, but what is most excruciating is the sense of the impossibility of ever escaping it, the feeling that one is trapped within one's own body and the world in which one finds oneself. To suggest that Jewishness can be hated or loved (bought or sold?) is to reduce the enormously overwhelming complexity of the notion—Jewishness, *Judentum*, Judaism—to an alarmingly narrow and fixed object. Indeed, if I can be a little extreme, to reduce Judaism to this level is to suggest that it can be understood and that its existence can be grasped—and perhaps erased—by mere mortals.

In describing his own Jewishness, Freud used the word *race* cautiously. In his published works, in fact, he is far more critical of the term than in his private letters. For example, in his "Autobiographical Study" he writes that when he entered the university he noticed that he "was expected to feel myself inferior and an alien because I was a Jew. I refused absolutely to do the first of these things. I have never been able to see why I should feel ashamed of my descent or, as people were beginning to say, of my 'race.'"[76] The word is in quotation marks, as if to distance himself from the term, to question its self-evidence. Meanwhile, in a letter to Carl Gustav Jung, Freud admitted that Ernest Jones gave him "a feeling of, I was almost going to say racial strangeness [*Rassenfremdheit*]," intensified by Jones' complete denial of the role of heredity.[77] Here, Freud's peculiar use of the word "race" is compounded by the fact that he is writing to Jung, another non-Jew with whom he also felt a certain (though in this case unspoken) "racial strangeness." Indeed, on the very same day that he wrote this letter to Jung, Freud wrote another letter to his friend Karl Abraham. Here he famously declared that with Jung he was always on guard for expressions of anti-semitism, but with Abraham (who was Jewish) he felt a certain "racial kinship [*Rassenverwandtschaft*]."[78] In his correspondence with his colleagues, there is a sense that there are certain things—Jewish things and psychoanalytic things—that could only be discussed "amongst ourselves."[79] Though Freud insisted that there should be no difference between the results in Jewish and Aryan "science," he acknowledged that "the presentation of them may vary."[80] Despite his own protestations to the contrary, Freud knew that language could not present scientific results without also shaping the nature and terms of the science itself.

Though Freud only hesitantly used the word *race* to describe the Jewish people, there are a number of reasons why I describe his theory of Jewishness as a racial theory of memory. That Freud's theory of Jewishness involves questions of memory is less likely to be problematic, even if it is surprising. For Freud and many others, Jewishness derives from a series of events that are recalled in a variety of ways: in the individual's life there are memories of a childhood filled with melodies, scents, objects, and performances; and in the life of the group there are narratives and histories of events that are ritually recalled week after week, year after year. That Freud's theory of Jewishness is a *racial* theory may require more initial explanation. To begin with, there is an extensive scholarship on the racialization of the Jewish people in the late nineteenth and early twentieth centuries in Europe and America. Jews were discussed as being different not only because of their faith or traditions, but because of supposedly *a priori* differences that were thought to have been inherited and that resided somewhere in or on the body: in the blood, on the penis, even in their desires. While this notion of Jewish racial difference emerged in Europe as early as the sixteenth century in the laws regarding *limpieza de sangre* on the Iberian peninsula, in the nineteenth century such difference began to be discussed in terms of the newly developing fields of biology and evolutionary theory.[81]

Much of the groundwork for my own scholarship on Freud and on questions of race and Jewishness has been laid by others—in particular Sander Gilman, whose work on Jewish racial discourses in the eighteenth to the twentieth centuries has become almost (if not oddly) canonical. While Gilman treats racial discourse on Jewishness mostly as an expression of anti-semitism and Jewish self-hatred, recent work by John Efron and Eric Goldstein, for example, has attended to the ways in which European and American Jews used racialized language to defend the Jewish people and to develop positive forms of self-definition in the late nineteenth and early twentieth centuries.[82] What has gone less examined, however, is how these two forms of Jewish definition are not necessarily easily distinguished—the positive from the negative, the internal definitions from the reactionary defenses. Modern historians have made much of the fact that Germans defined their national identity by cordoning it off from the Other: To be German was to be not Jewish. However, the same could be said for Jewish self-identification, with a twist: To be Jewish is to be not not Jewish (Gentile, *goy*, *nochri*).

My use of the term *race* should not be misunderstood as a rejection of the more common-sense definition of this word in various English-speaking contexts, that is, to describe physical differences that mark individuals as belonging to one group or another (white, black, brown, etc.). In America and elsewhere, these differences continue to shape the realities of individuals' lives every day despite the major successes of the Civil Rights movement and the continuing fights against racism. Indeed, some might argue that to refer to Jews as racially marked is to disregard the reality that many European Jews have been able to assimilate as white Americans (and Europeans and Australians) in ways that are not possible for large groups of racially—that is, physically—marked persons whose ancestors originated in Asia, Africa, Latin America, and elsewhere.[83] Nonetheless, there are important homologies between the logic and use of genealogical and physical definitions of race. Most important, the legal definitions of race in America have been co-terminous with genealogy both in the era of the Jim Crow laws and in the era of affirmative action: If an individual has one X (black, Native American, and so on) parent or grandparent, she can be counted as X regardless of her physical appearance or her cultural habits. While physical appearance may be considered as a more obvious method of determining who is X or Y, genealogy is often presented as a counterargument to the misperceptions of physical appearance.[84] More recently, genetics and DNA testing have been introduced as methods for proving and/or determining racial genealogies.[85] My own position on these matters is that neither physical appearance nor genealogy is a perfect or ultimate definition of an individual's identity; indeed, such criteria often reveal their own fallibility as well as their historical and geographical contingency. Yet genealogy and physical appearance are both persistently regarded as natural and definitive markers of difference and identity.[86] Even as there are contexts that require distinct discussions of race and genealogy, throughout this book I subsume the two terms as part of one phenomenon. And, in so doing, I hope to work against the chauvinism and racism inherent in the presumptions that "real" Jews look or act in certain ways and that some Jews are more Jewish than others.[87]

While racial definitions of Jewishness emerged in the nineteenth century as alternatives to religious definitions, they are not entirely separate matters. Indeed, even this common historical narrative is inaccurate. The genealogical definition of Jewishness can be traced back to at least the fifth century, when, partly in response to Paul's assertions of the universal brotherhood of Jesus Christ, the Rabbis established genealogy (as opposed to belief or practice) as the primary definition of Jewishness. As Daniel Boyarin has argued, where "the Church needed 'Judaism' to be a religious 'Other,' and maintained and reified this term as the name of a religion," the Rabbis needed others to maintain a sense of their own community as an emerging *ethnos*.[88] Thus Jews came to be defined as a genealogical community partly in response to the emerging religious cult of Christianity. While this notion was not originally Jewish per se, it became associated with Jewish particularism in contrast to Christian universalism.[89] In the nineteenth century, the notion of genealogical community membership became more generalized in part because of the increasing secularity and economic prosperity of Western Europe;[90] as Jews were no longer immediately identifiable through sight (dress, hair-style) or sound (language, accent), Jewish particularity began to appear less obvious in an everyday kind of way.[91] Yet as I will discuss in more detail, the relationship between the widespread emergence of secularism and of various models of human difference (racial, religious, cultural) is more complicated than a simple replacement of the terms of religion with the terms of race or culture. The new indeterminacy and invisibility of Jewishness compelled people to find new ways to distinguish themselves from Others, the inside from the outside, and the familiar from the alien and strange. Where such distinctions had been adjudicated by the ecclesiastical courts, increasingly people turned to science to understand their place in the world.⁹²

Similarly, while Freud attempted to explain the inexplicable by using scientific methodologies and terminologies, his language was laced with allusions to common descriptions of European Jews. In founding psychoanalysis, Freud showed that humans are never "masters" in their own houses: Within each psyche there are strange and alien elements, "foreign bodies" that can penetrate, unsettle, and overwhelm the psychical organism. Finally, in *Moses and Monotheism*, he attempted to make sense of the origins of this foreignness, the institution of a difference that has guaranteed the survival not only of the "immortal hatred [*unsterbliche haß*]" of the Jews, but also of the immortality [*Unsterblichkeit*] of the Jewish people and of their tradition.

What's Next?

Freud's theory of Jewishness is problematic: It is vexing in its similarities with racial theories that seem to limit the horizon of the individual, and it is potentially illuminating in its affinity with theories of memory that emphasize the creative relationship of the individual to her past. On the surface, it is comparable to any number of theories developed in the nineteenth and early twentieth century that combined the realms of heredity and memory for diverse reasons and with varied effects.⁹³ Freud's notion of inherited memory is made more shocking by the fact that the memories that are supposedly inherited are traces of a bizarre, complicated, and violent series of events. The weight and the challenge of Freud's theory of Jewishness resides in his insistence that (a) these events really occurred (as far as any history really occurs), and (b) that all Jews have literally and biologically inherited the traces of this past. Throughout the book, I explore these two aspects of Freud's theory of Jewishness. What emerges is a narrative that uses Freud's final book as a point of departure to explore questions posed by psychoanalytic theory and history on the one hand, and by Jews, Jewishness, and Judaism on the other hand.

In Chapter 1, "*Moses* and the Foundations of Psychoanalysis," I explore why Freud felt the need to insist on the historical reality of his narrative of Moses the Egyptian. Though he was clearly anxious about publishing *Moses and Monotheism* because of the political and personal situation in which he wrote it, his particular anxiety about establishing its status as history can be traced to two significant episodes in the history of psychoanalysis: first, his initial establishment of psychoanalysis as a theory and practice in the 1890s, and second, his re-assessment of his theory in the wake of his relationship with Carl Gustav Jung between 1907 and 1914. In this final book, as in these earlier episodes, Freud's attempts to establish psychoanalysis as a hybrid science—both medical and historical, both particular and universal—forced him to acknowledge the inexplicable remnants of analysis and the gaps in the foundations of his theory. Throughout this chapter, *Moses* emerges as a case history of both Freud and Moses and of their creations, psychoanalysis and monotheism.

Rather than simply tracing his patients' illnesses to their "degenerate" family lines, in the 1890s Freud turned to their memories of childhood experiences. However, to prove that they suffered from "reminiscences," he had to demonstrate that they were not dishonest degenerates and that their narratives could be trusted as truthful accounts of their childhoods. Though he initially resisted the idea that his patients' memories extended further back than their childhoods, in conversations with Jung in 1907–14 he eventually incorporated the idea that psychical dispositions were the result of real ancestral experiences. In 1914, Freud and Jung parted ways at least in part because Jung would not accept Freud's emphasis on the reality of primal memories and childhood sexuality. Jung's criticisms of Freud are compared to the Pauline criticisms of Judaic preoccupations with literal interpretation and bodily regulations. Jung and Paul both attempted to move beyond these particularities, for they seemed to limit the universalistic reach of their institutions (psychotherapy and Judaism, respectively). But by acknowledging that neither psychoanalysis nor Judaism would ever extend a universal reach, Freud suggests that such particularity may paradoxically be the most critical strength distinguishing them both from their "opposites"—Judaism from Christianity and psychoanalysis from Jungian psychotherapy.

Freud's insistence on the historical truth of his version of the Moses story may seem strange, but his insistence on the idea that the memory-traces of these events were biologically transmitted has been regarded as even more problematic, particularly in light of later developments in the scientific theorization of evolution and heredity. In Chapters 2 and 3, I move from questions of history and epistemology to debates about the relationships between science and society. Since Freud's interest in inherited memory seems similar to the outmoded "Lamarckian" idea that acquired character-istics can be inherited, many scholars have speculated as to why he contin-ued to insist on such pseudoscience in the 1930s when it seemed that he should have known better. Rather than seeing the question of Freud's "La-marckism" in purely scientific terms, in Chapter 2, "Freud's 'Lamarckism' and the Politics of Racial Science," I show that Freud became uneasy about insisting on the inheritance of acquired characters not because it was scien-tifically outmoded but because it was politically charged and suspiciously regarded by the Nazis as Bolshevik and Jewish. I argue that Freud's ideas about race, heredity, and evolution need to be re-examined with an atten-tion to the ways in which scientific debates were inextricably linked with political debates. Where Freud seemed to use the idea of inherited memory as a way of universalizing his theory beyond the individual cultural milieu of his patients, such a notion of universal science itself became politically charged and identified as particularly Jewish. The vexed and speculative in-terpretations of Freud's "Lamarckism" are situated as part of a larger post-War cultural reaction both against Communism (particularly in the 1950s when Lamarckism was associated with the failures of Lysenko) and against any scientific concepts of race in the wake of the Holocaust.

Freud was well aware that there was ample evidence to suggest that ac-quired characteristics were not inherited. Indeed, the most paradigmatic mark of Jewishness—circumcision—would seem to contradict this idea since it must be performed in every generation for its effects to be transmit-ted. In Chapter 3, "Circumcision: The Unconscious Root of the Problem," I show that the topic of circumcision compelled Freud to re-think some of the foundational ideas of psychoanalysis, in particular the question as to whether an individual's archaic memory extended further back than child-hood. Rather than Lamarck, it was the most vociferous anti-Lamarckian, August Weismann, whose theories shaped Freud's explorations of the blurry lines between the physical and psychical realms, between the notions of race and culture, and between the domains of heredity and experience. By applying Weismann's germ-plasm theory to his structure of the psyche and by incorporating the idea that phylogenetic memory is inherited, Freud was able to maintain the tensions between heredity and memory and between race and culture. More broadly, the topic of circumcision forces the terms of religion back into discussions that are otherwise posed solely in terms of race and/or culture.

Though Freud insisted on the biological inheritance of Jewishness (and memory more generally), his understanding of the actual medium of transmission was by no means straightforward. In Chapter 4, "Secret Inclinations Beyond Direct Communication," I show how Freud's explanations of intergenerational transmission [*Übertragung*] were shaped by his earlier discussions of telepathic thought-transference [*Gedankübertragung*] and the psychoanalytic concept of transference [*Übertragung*]. From 1910 to 1933, in published and unpublished essays and especially in his correspondence with Jung and Sandor Ferenczi, Freud expressed anxiety and excitement about these diverse forms of transmissions. Such transmissions seemed dangerous precisely because it was impossible to grasp them or to define them as either material or immaterial. Freud's discussions of intergenerational transmission in *Moses and Monotheism* retrospectively illuminate his earlier meditations on transference and telepathy. Particularly in his discussions of these mysterious transmissions, he flirts with the margins of science and with the irrationality that haunts rationality. In this chapter I explore the question of why the occult language of telepathy, ghosts, and the uncanny is intertwined with the language used to describe the Jewish subject, both by Jews and non-Jews. The question of whether Jewishness is always transmitted to the future is compared to the famous literary debate between Jacques Lacan and Jacques Derrida about whether "the letter always arrives at its destination." Freud suggests that to be Jewish is to be caught up in an interminable process of transference that threatens the borders between past and present and between self and Other. Such phenomena, he suggests, may be more powerful the less they are suspected.⁹⁴

Where Freud explored the mysterious modes of *ghostly* transmission throughout his career, in *Moses and Monotheism* he insists that the defining feature of the Jewish tradition is its *Geistigkeit*, a word that literally refers to ghostliness, but also to intellectuality or spirituality. In Chapter 5, "Immaterial Materiality: The 'Special Case' of Jewish Tradition," I explore the tension between Freud's insistence that Jewish tradition is defined by its supreme *Geistigkeit* and his emphasis on the idea that Jewishness is transmitted through biological genealogy, a medium that seems utterly material. Freud suggests that the intellectual Jewish tradition has survived precisely because it is genealogically transmitted from one generation to the next. To make sense of the apparent contradiction of the supreme *Geistigkeit* and the base materiality of biology, he maintains biology in a realm "beyond sensory perception." Thus he knowingly and ironically inverts the matrilineal principle of Jewish genealogy, making the matter of biological inheritance a purely *geistig* (intellectual-spiritual) issue based not on material evidence (that is, the identity of the mother) but on hypotheses and inferences (about the identity of the father). Like psychoanalysis more generally, Freud's theory of Jewishness emerges as a scientific theory that challenges the scientific standards of proof and evidence and as a cultural theory that questions the definitions and limits of culture.

In defining Jewishness through the inheritance of memory, Freud illuminates and integrates two seemingly contradictory aspects of Jewish definition: In the most material sense, Jewishness is collectively determined by one's ineluctable descent, while in a more non-material sense, Jewishness is individually determined by one's beliefs, choices, and practices. While many Jewish leaders and scholars have understandably rejected racial definitions of Jewishness, laypeople continue to attempt to define their own Jewishness (as well as others') through lineage, genetics, and inherited history. Though this book is primarily a historical analysis of Freud's work, it engages and is informed by contemporary debates regarding the definitions of Jews and other racial, cultural, and religious groups. My reading of Freud addresses the question of why appeals to the language of race and heredity are so persistent even as the scientific establishment roundly rejected biological definitions of race over fifty years ago. A close examination of the relationship between Freud's theory and his historical situation may allow us to reconsider current uses of essentialist racial identifications and genetic studies without simply turning away in horror. Indeed, while the word "race" may be used less often (and more self-consciously) than a century ago, its terms continue to emerge as central points of controversy in disputes over Israeli citizenship, race-based benefits, and definitions of indigenous populations. *Racial Fever* suggests that while there are major dangers in appealing to the language of racial difference, there are even greater pitfalls in ignoring how such appeals continue to shape our lives every day.

Moses and the Foundations of Psychoanalysis

> The historical foundations of the Moses story are not solid enough to serve as a basis for these invaluable conclusions of mine. And so I remain silent. It suffices me that I myself can believe in the solution of the problem. It has pursued me throughout the whole of my life.
>
> F R E U D , letter to Lou Andreas-Salomé, January 6, 1935

> The man Moses, who set the Jewish people free, who gave them their laws and founded their religion, dates from such remote times that we cannot evade a preliminary enquiry as to whether he was a historical personage or a creature of legend.
>
> F R E U D , *Moses and Monotheism*

A Case of Historical Fiction

From the first page of *Moses and Monotheism*, Freud insists that he is writing a work of history. Yet the story he narrates stretches even the most elastic of novelistic imaginations. Using the Biblical text as his evidence, he works like a detective, building a case for his version of the events. Pointing to the Egyptian etymology of Moses' name and the traces of other suppressed narratives, Freud argues that Moses was not an Israelite but rather an Egyptian follower of the Pharaoh Akhenaten's monotheistic cult of the sun god, Aten. After the death of Akhenaten in the fourteenth century B.C.E., the Egyptian people rejected his monotheistic religion. Since Moses continued to "zealously" follow this monotheism, he left his fatherland and found a wandering tribe of Semites upon whom he imposed his monotheistic religion. While Moses "borrowed" the monotheistic idea from Akhenaten, he transformed it into an abstract intellectual tradition by completely eradicating magic and mysticism and by prohibiting any material representation of the deity. Finding the Mosaic tradition too difficult, the Semites killed this Moses, repressed the memory of the murder, and apparently forgot about the episode. Along the way, they joined a Midianite tribe that worshipped a volcano god named Yahweh, and whose leader also happened to be named Moses. Over time, the two became one: one tribe, one Moses, and one god named Jahve. "In reality," notes Freud—as if this were a matter not of mythology or fantasy, but of *reality*!—the events narrated in the Bible never occurred: The original Moses had never even heard of Jahve, the Jews never went through the Red Sea, and they were never at Mount Sinai.[1]

Though Freud originally conceived of his late Moses work as a historical novel, he eventually rejected this genre classification and referred to it as a "purely historical study."[2] If we could sweep aside the bizarre narrative as an imaginative work of fiction, it would be far easier to accept this book as a compelling (if problematic) answer to the Jewish Question. However, Freud's insistence that *Moses* was a work of history is crucial to the critical questions this final book poses for psychoanalysis, for historiography, and for Jewish identity. Freud wrestled with the historical nature of *Moses* not only because of the choice of subject matter or because of the political situation in which he was working—in this final book, he returned to some of the most foundational questions of psychoanalysis: What are the relationships between memory and fantasy, between fact and fiction, and between history and mythology? Which affects a person more: heredity or history, biology or experience? How can psychoanalysis attend to the universality of human experience and the historical particularity of the individual (or the individual group)? While these concerns may seem specific to Freud's *Moses*, they can be traced to two significant episodes in the history of psychoanalysis: first, Freud's initial establishment of psychoanalysis as a theory and practice in the 1890s, and second, his reassessment of his theory in the wake of his relationship with Carl Gustav Jung between 1909 and 1914. In both cases, Freud's attempts to establish psychoanalysis as a hybrid science—both historical and universal, both medical and theoretical—forced him to acknowledge the cracks in the foundations of his theory.

In *Moses*, Freud returned to questions that he had supposedly solved in 1897 when he abandoned the seduction theory—that is, the idea that all hysteria originates in actual sexual events in early childhood. Throughout his life, Freud recalled this shift in his thinking as if it was absolute, yet he continued to question the relationship between his patients' narratives and their actual experiences. Indeed, even as he explored the nuances of fantasies and dreams, he insisted that actual historical events had led to his patients' current conditions. While he rejected the hereditarian theories of his predecessors, he maintained that heredity was at least partially responsible for mental illness. Even so, for many years, he resisted the idea that heredity and history could be combined; that is, he rejected the notion that individuals inherit memory-traces of their ancestors' experiences. Yet from 1912 onward, Freud began to incorporate the idea of phylogenetic memory into the very structure of psychoanalysis. Finally, in *Moses and Monotheism* he acknowledged that "he had behaved for a long time as though the inheritance of memory-traces of the experience of our ancestors were established beyond question."[3] And he went further: "Granted that at the time we have no stronger evidence for the presence of memory-traces in the archaic heritage than the residual phenomena of the work of analysis which call for a phylogenetic derivation, yet this evidence seems to us strong enough to *postulate* that *such is the fact*."[4] Whereas he often remarked on his radical change regarding the reality of his patients' memories, he never commented on his change regarding the inheritance of phylogenetic memory, even though it thoroughly reshaped the foundations of psychoanalysis.

By the time he met Jung in 1908, Freud had high hopes of promoting psychoanalysis beyond Vienna.[5] Inspired by Jung's own mythological studies in *Totem and Taboo* (1912–13), he began to incorporate the idea that individuals were burdened with memories not only of their own childhoods but also of their ancestors. By adding an archaic heritage to the etiological story, Freud could proclaim that psychoanalysis was universally applicable, for he was no longer bound to the particular narratives of his patients. Though he had worried about proving the historical truth of individual patients' earliest memories, he knew that there was no way to establish the veracity of a narrative about the prehistory of human civilization. Yet where Jung seemed to use mythology and phylogenetic memory as a way to avoid questions about the historical authenticity of the primal past, Freud maintained that the reality of this past was the very foundation of psychoanalysis. Indeed, from the earliest years of psychoanalysis, Freud had struggled with the fact that his patients' recollections only erratically corresponded with reality; now, however, he filled the gaps in their narratives by appealing to the storehouse of phylogenetic memory. While he remained in the universal realm of human civilization (in *Totem*), he did not worry so much about questions of evidence or truth. However, as he rewrote the universal narrative as a particular history of the Jewish people in *Moses*, he was once again forced to reexamine the "historical" evidence supporting his theory. Thus throughout *Moses and Monotheism* we find subtle reflections of the seismic shifts affecting the foundations of psychoanalytic theory and its relationship to Freud's theory of Jewishness.

In exploring the origins of the Jewish people, Freud was compelled to reexamine not only the foundations of psychoanalysis but also its scope and its limitations. Throughout his life, Freud attempted to present psychoanalysis as his original creation *ex nihilo*, yet he was often uncomfortably aware of his intellectual debts.[6] In *Moses*, he argues that monotheism was not original to the Jews. Indeed, monotheism was not even Moses' own creation: *he* borrowed the idea from the pharaoh Akhenaten. As Eric Santner notes, at the moment when Freud's "ego was most in danger, most in need of support, he subjects himself as well as his coreligionists to a sort of narcissistic injury."[7] At a time when purity, originality, and universality were heralded as the first and finest distinctions of peoples, philosophies, and artworks, Freud acknowledges the "impurity and secondariness" not only of the Jewish people, but also of psychoanalysis.[8] While Freud notes that Mosaic monotheism is potentially universal, in this final book he struggles to come to terms with the fact that it was never universally embraced. Similarly, though he had envisioned psychoanalysis as a universal science and therapy, he was not oblivious to the particular social milieu in which he worked and the ultimate limitations of its applicability. In composing *Moses*, Freud may have attempted to "fulfill a wish in fantasy:"[9] by re-telling the story of the survival of Mosaic monotheism, he could thereby envision the survival of his own creation.[10] While Freud may have identified with Moses and fantasized that his own "institution" would also eventually triumph, he realized that Moses was not quite as original or as universally triumphant as he had first imagined. Indeed, instead of a daydream, Freud produced a sobering examination of the most unsettling aspects of psychoanalysis, and by extension, Judaism. If psychoanalysis functions as a provocative model of understanding and interpretation, its emphasis on historical narrative averts the possibility of universalization. Finally, Freud's history of the Jewish people suggests a theory of difference that resists universalism.

A Return to the Source of the Nile

From the beginning, Freud based his arguments not upon physical evidence but on rhetoric, narrative, and logic. Indeed, *Moses and Monotheism* is atypical of his oeuvre in that the text is filled with anxious comments, repetitions, and apologetic asides. In the conclusion to the first of the three essays that make up the book, he complains that he needs more firm facts and objective evidence "in order to defend the wealth of emerging possibilities against the criticism of their being a product of the imagination and too remote from reality."[11] And in the opening of the second essay he notes that he feels hesitant about publicly proclaiming his hypotheses, "since they were based only on psychological probabilities and lacked any *objective proof*."[12] He writes that he felt "the need to beware of exposing it without a secure basis to the critical assaults of the world around one—like a bronze statue with feet of clay."[13] Similarly, after composing the first two essays, in December 1934 he complained to his friend Arnold Zweig that his "last creative effort should have come to grief." The work seemed destined to remain uncompleted; the problem was not "any inner uncertainty . . . but the fact that I was obliged to construct so imposing a statue upon feet of clay, so that any fool could topple it."[14]

While a number of scholars interpret these textual idiosyncrasies as signs of Freud's conflicted feelings about his Jewish identity,[15] others such as Yosef Hayim Yerushalmi and Michel de Certeau read them as signs of a dilemma far more intrinsic to *Moses*,[16] a discomfort not with Jewishness but with exploring new territory on the "*foreign* ground in the field of history" and in the lands of Egypt.[17] "For the first time," Yerushalmi explains, Freud "must attempt to corroborate a psychoanalytically derived truth with historical facts quite beyond the purview of psychoanalysis."[18] Yet Freud was confronted with the dilemma of what could count as historical facts forty years earlier when he first attempted to establish such "psychoanalytically derived truths." As Ilse Grubrich-Simitis argues, in this final book Freud explicitly looked back at his career and returned "to his early reflections on the traumatic genesis of psychic illness . . . to weave them into the context of his current research."[19] The dilemmas of "historical truth" are intrinsic not only to the story of Moses and the Jewish people but to the very foundations of psychoanalysis.

In the 1890s, while other scientists were beginning to explore the mysteries of heredity using experiments and microscopes, Freud developed a psychoanalytic method to explore the mysteries of the psyche using individuals' reports of their own memories. Unlike his mentor Jean-Martin Charcot, who generally regarded mental illness as the result of inherited degeneracy, Freud argued that hysteria was a result of sexual traumas experienced in early childhood. However, after only a few years he realized that he could not necessarily be sure that all of his patients had actually experienced such traumatic events. Even as he abandoned the idea that individuals' recollections re-presented what had actually happened, he never gave up on the idea that psychic misery somehow originated in real events in the past. Instead, he struggled to develop an interpretative code that could allow him to make sense of his patients' reports as evidence of a different kind of reality: a psychical reality enigmatically related to external reality and historical truth.

While Freud seems to enter foreign disciplinary territories (of history as well as Egyptology and Biblical criticism) in *Moses*, he actually returns from a long sojourn in the realm of universal theorization to his roots as a medical physician. That is, by presenting the case history of a specific group of people (rather than all of humanity), he uses rhetorical devices and narrative forms that are far more similar to his early work as a medical doctor than with his intervening theoretical works such as *Totem and Taboo* (1913), *Future of An Illusion* (1927), and *Civilization and Its Discontents* (1930).[20] As Carlo Ginzburg argues, history and medicine are united by the fact that they were both conceived as sciences outside the modern scientific paradigm of Galilean physics. While Galilean science "could have taken as its own Scholastic motto *Individuum est ineffabile* ('We cannot speak about what is individual')," history and medicine were rooted in the interpretation of particular traces and clues pertaining to the individual case. "The historian," writes Ginzburg, "is like the physician who uses nosographical tables to analyze the specific sickness of the patient. As with the physician, historical knowledge is indirect, presumptive, conjectural."[21]

In his earliest psychoanalytic work, Freud had attempted to use his patients' particular symptoms and recollections to diagnose their ailments and reconstruct their case histories. Unlike Ginzburg's model physician, however, he did not simply consult nosographical tables; instead, he constructed a new nosography with accompanying standards of evidence and proof.

Somewhere between the fields of history and medicine, he developed a methodology that used admittedly meager evidence to construct historical narratives revealing the origins of his patients' illnesses. Half-remembered scenes, impressions from dreams, and finally psychoanalysis itself became the evidence upon which he founded his diagnoses. Yet as early as 1897, Freud attempted to move beyond the individual case histories to develop universal theories applicable to all of humanity.[22] Finally, in *Moses and Monotheism*, he returned to the realm of the particular. Using Biblical texts, archaeological finds, and a loose collection of traditions, he made presumptive conjectures about the history of a specific people that might reveal the origins of their one defining feature: Jewishness.

The question arises as to whether Freud's theory of Jewishness—and his theory of psychoanalysis—can be applied to other ethno-racial-religious groups. Freud's insistence on the historicity of his narratives—whether of patients or of the Jewish people—suggests that the answer to this question is *no*. A different people would have a distinct history with its own consequences and its own media of transmission. Yet since psychoanalysis (and, for that matter, Judaism) has clearly influenced people who do not identify themselves as Jewish, the answer to the question might instead be *yes*: Yes, large groups of people think in psychoanalytic terms and seem to believe that their childhood experiences shape their adult lives, that ancestors' histories matter to their present lives, and that such elements may even shape their bodily experiences. Perhaps, then, new questions are in order: Is anything about this phenomenon essentially and exclusively Jewish or psychoanalytic? Is Judaism exclusively Jewish? Is psychoanalysis exclusively Freudian? The answers to these questions, I think, can only be *no*.

In *Moses*, Freud belatedly attempted to make sense of the inexplicable remnants of analysis and the gaps in the foundations of psychoanalytic theory. Though he developed psychoanalysis as a strategy to help people "master" the past, he implicitly acknowledged that there are always leftovers—unassimilable elements that are the heart of the story. Having discovered that the individual is not master of his own psyche, Freud later acknowledged that psychoanalysis (also) could not master its own domain, let alone all the enigmas of the world. As he writes in "Analysis Terminable and Interminable" (1937), the "first step towards attaining intellectual mastery of our environment is to discover generalizations, rules and laws which bring order into chaos." Yet this step necessarily "simplifies the world of phenomena" and unavoidably results in falsification. He goes on to quote a notable satirist's "shrewd" remark: "'Every step forward is only half as big as it looks at first.' It is tempting to attribute a quite general validity to this malicious dictum. There are nearly always residual phenomena; a partial hanging-back."[23] In *Moses*, Freud took several steps back. Indeed, the sojourn to Egypt itself harkens back to the momentary euphoria (and the subsequent dismay) about his discoveries in the 1890s. Soon after presenting his work "On the Aetiology of Hysteria" to a panel of physicians in 1896, Freud wrote to his friend Wilhelm Fliess to complain about Richard von Krafft-Ebing's description of psychoanalysis as a "scientific fairy tale." "And this," Freud exclaims, "after one has demonstrated to them the solution of a more-than-thousand-year-old problem, a *caput Nili* [the source of the Nile]."[24] In *Moses*, Freud returned to the land of the Nile.

The Founding of a Theory: Establishment of a Machtbereich

MOSES AS A CASE STUDY

When Freud began his new work in August 1934 he titled it *Der Mann Moses: Ein historisches Roman* [*The Man Moses: A Historical Novel*]. In an introduction that he eventually discarded, he describes his problems composing *Der Mann Moses* as if they are entirely due to his choice of genre.[25] Well aware that he is not a typical historical novelist, he first attempts to delineate the standard models and idiosyncrasies of this hybrid form—neither history nor fiction, but a fusion of the two types of writing. Some historical novelists, notes Freud, aim to faithfully depict "the special character" of a historical period even as they admittedly invent both persons and events. Others realistically portray "historically familiar" persons, even if their main purpose is, like other novels, to "affect the emotions."[26] The two groups of novelists, he explains, are also defined by their goals: The first aims to teach their readers about the past while the second aims to entertain or emotionally engage their readers. Instead of naming his own goal, he moves on to note that *his* historical novel is shaped by the fact that, for him, "fiction and invention are easily associated with the blemish of error." Thus, he explains that what he is writing is not really a historical novel but a character study that requires reliable material as its basis, but nothing available concerning Moses can be called trustworthy. It is a tradition coming from one source, not confirmed by any other, fixed in writing only in a later period, in itself contradictory, revised several times and distorted [*entstellt*] under the influence of new tendencies, while closely interwoven with the religious and national myths of a people.[27]

With the exception of the word "tradition," Freud could very well be discussing his anxieties about his earliest case studies: There he based his narrative reconstructions almost entirely on the patients' recollections ("one source"), which were not necessarily confirmed by any other sources and were often filled with contradictions, denials, and equivocations. So too, while the Moses story was fixed in writing by any number of authors long after the events had occurred, the events in the case studies were first recalled by the patients long after they had occurred (if they had occurred at all), and only later analyzed and recorded by Freud himself.

Given that Freud thought he was writing a historical *novel*, why was he so anxious about establishing the historical truth of his work? The answer has to do with his unstated goals in writing the book. While he returned to the form and narrative of his earliest case studies, he was well past the point of believing that he could completely cure people of their persistent psychic miseries. It would be easy to conclude that Freud's purpose in exploring the nature and origins of Jewishness was to find the cure for it—to help people overcome it—just as he had hoped to find the cure for hysteria, neurosis, and psychosis.[28] Yet for many years he had recognized that certain conditions and patterns seemed entirely permanent and inexorably fated to repeat themselves, both within the individual and from generation to generation. For example, in *Beyond the Pleasure Principle* (1920) he addresses the question of why some people seem beset by "malignant fate," "demonic powers," or the "compulsion of destiny."[29] But it was not until *Moses* that he addressed the fate of being Jewish—the compulsion to believe, not in the Jewish God, but in the inalienability of one's Jewishness. Thus, in this final book, Freud was ultimately less concerned with writing an effective novel than in attempting to understand the compulsions of destiny—the facts that Jewish tradition continued to exist and that individuals continued to *be* Jewish.

While Freud was more wont to point out the gaps and contradictions in his patients' narratives, he sometimes acknowledged these peculiarities in his own texts. Indeed, throughout his oeuvre we find evidence that he revised his analyses and that his interpretations had been distorted "under the influence" of new theoretical tendencies (such as his understanding of the reality of his patients' stories).[30] For example, in a 1924 footnote added to the case study of Katharina in *Studies on Hysteria* (1893–95), he writes,

> I venture after the lapse of so many years to lift the veil of discretion and reveal the fact that Katharina was not the niece but the daughter of the landlady. . . . Distortions [*Entstellungen*] like the one which I introduced in the present instance should be altogether avoided in reporting a case history. From the point of view of understanding the case, a distortion [*Entstellung*] of this kind is not, of course, *a matter of such indifference as would be shifting the scene from one mountain to another.*[31]

Well aware that authors do not distort texts for insignificant reasons, Freud builds his case in *Moses* upon the "noticeable gaps, disturbing repetitions and obvious contradictions" in the Biblical text.[32] Indeed, he uses these textual idiosyncrasies as evidence that the authors had distorted the real history and had shifted the scene from the land of Egypt to Mount Sinai, a shift that is not, of course, "a matter of such indifference." These textual remnants are, Freud notes in *Moses*, "indications which reveal things to us which it was not intended to communicate. In its implications the distortion [*Entstellung*] of a text resembles a murder: the difficulty is not in perpetrating the deed, but in getting rid of its traces."[33] On the one hand, Freud identifies with the authors of the Biblical text, having spent a lifetime recording, analyzing, and sometimes distorting the spoken accounts of his patients. On the other hand, he sees the authors of the Biblical text as patients who have distorted their reports about the past in an attempt to repress the real traumas—the disturbing realities whose traces linger in the gaps and repetitions of their narratives. Thus the very form of *Moses* functions as both a case study and as a self-analysis with all the contradictions this implies: Self-analysis requires that one sees one's self as an Other.

HISTORICAL FICTIONS (1893–97)

To develop a standard of psychoanalytic diagnosis, Freud had to demonstrate that his patients' recollections could be used as reliable evidence, or at least as valuable clues to the mysteries of their psychic miseries. Well aware of the widespread perception that hysterics and neurotics were suspiciously regarded as deceitful malingerers, he struggled to show that his patients were not simply inventing their accounts of the past. In the

nineteenth century, hysterics and neurotics were also presumed to be hereditarily "degenerate," and, like Jews and homosexuals, they were supposedly
characterized by feminine qualities: deceit, dependence, and moral inferior-
ity.[34] To make matters worse, hysteria and neurosis were also seen as national conditions: The Germans regarded the French as particularly prone
to hysteria, and both the Germans and French regarded Jews as excessively
neurotic.[35] Since many of his early patients were Jews, Freud needed to
demonstrate that their conditions were not simply signs of degenerate familial heredity but rather traces of particular familial histories. Though he
attempted to establish his patients' memories as genuine etiological factors,
he did not altogether reject the possibility that heredity could predispose a
person to mental illness. The problem was that heredity seemed inaccessible
to analysis. In its interiority it "dazzled" physicians with its "unapproachable power," whereas external events seemed to allow the physician a point
of access.[36] By gathering evidence from the patients' symptoms, their recollections of when the symptoms began, and their memories of what life was
like before the illness, the physician could attempt to piece together a diagnostic narrative.

Freud not only had to prove that his patients were reliable sources of
evidence; he also had to establish that he was a trustworthy narrator, unaffected by the supposedly Jewish predisposition to deceit and neurosis.
Though he criticized Charcot's over-emphasis on heredity, Freud credited
his mentor with restoring dignity to the very discussion of mental illness.
Before Charcot, Freud notes, people scorned and distrusted not only the
patients but also the physicians who bothered to concern themselves with
these individuals. "*No credence* was given to a hysteric about anything" until
Charcot threw "the whole weight of his authority on the side of the *genuine-
ness and objectivity* of hysterical phenomena."[37] While Freud admits that his
case studies read like "short stories [*Novellen*]," he insists that they are "case
histories [*Krankengeschichten*]." Novels bear the traces of feminine *künstlichkeit*—artistry, artificiality, and deceit—rather than "the stamp of serious science [*des ernsten Gepräges der Wissenschaftlichkeit*]."[38] In an effort to distance
himself from such conditions, he notes that he can "console" himself "with
the reflection that the nature of the subject is evidently responsible for this,
rather than any preference of my own." In other words, the study of hysteria
practically requires one to write descriptions that we are more "accustomed
to find in the works of imaginative writers [*Dichter*]."[39] When it came time

to consider the nature of his study of *Moses*, Freud briefly considered embracing the novel, a genre that he had only hesitantly acknowledged forty years before. Now if he wanted to blame the "nature of the subject" for his novelistic artistry [*künstlichkeit*], it was unclear whether his subject was Moses, the Jewish people, or psychoanalysis itself.

Freud's oft-quoted acknowledgment of the novelistic nature of his early writing appears in the case study of Frau Elisabeth von R. in *Studies on Hysteria* (1893–95), written with Josef Breuer. Throughout this work, Freud takes special care to note that his patients are not hereditarily "tainted" and that their stories provide reliable evidence on which to found his theory. Though Elisabeth's character exhibits many features of hysteria, he explains that her illness should not be regarded as a result of "degeneracy." Indeed, he notes, "no appreciable hereditary taint, so my colleague told me, could be traced on either side of her family."[40] Here he attempts to establish his ultimate objectivity by distancing himself from the very judgment of whether his patient was hereditarily "tainted": Not Elisabeth, and not Freud, but a *colleague* is the source of information about Elisabeth's family. In describing Elisabeth, Freud remarks on those qualities which demonstrate that she is neither deceitful nor morally degenerate. Instead, he emphasizes her "giftedness, her ambition, her moral sensibility . . . and the independence of her nature which went beyond the feminine ideal and found expression in a considerable amount of obstinacy, pugnacity and reserve."[41] Drawing from her father's observations that "her mental constitution" departed "from the ideal which people like to see realized in a girl," Freud notes that Elisabeth finds consolation not from her mother or sister but from her father and her sister's husband. The father "warned her against being too positive in her judgments and against her habit of regardlessly [*schonungslos*] telling people the truth, and he often said she would find it hard to get a husband. She was in fact greatly discontented with being a girl."[42] In Freud's analysis, it is not Elisabeth's feminine nature that causes her misery but society's feminine ideal, which results in an unfulfillable expectation of a particular kind of behavior.

Yet the discovery of unfulfillable cultural expectations—some might call them prejudices—is not enough to solve the case. From Elisabeth's recollections of the onset of her illness, Freud learns that she had been particularly fond of her sister's husband and that she even "dreamt . . . of enjoying such happiness as her sister's and of finding a husband who would capture her heart like this brother-in-law of hers."[43] Apparently her symptoms emerged soon after her sister died, when Elisabeth was curiously beset by guilt for the death for which she was not responsible.[44] Having already established that his patient is a trustworthy source of evidence, Freud confidently concludes, "It was easy to *prove* to her that what she herself had told me admitted of no other interpretation." The ultimate proof that his evidence is infallible and that the girl is morally superior is that she resists his analysis. After dryly presenting the situation to her—that is, that she was in love with her brother-in-law—Freud explains that

> she made one last effort to reject the explanation: it was not true, I had talked her into it, it *could* not be true, she was incapable of such wickedness, she could never forgive herself for it. But it was a long time before my two pieces of consolation—that we are not responsible for our feelings, and that her behaviour, the fact that she had fallen ill in these circumstances, was sufficient *evidence* of her moral character—it was a long time before these consolations of mine made any impression on her.[45]

Freud's argument turns around on itself. If the reader resists his interpretation she can join Elisabeth and recognize her own "moral superiority." The analysis itself, the resistance, and the eventual acceptance of it prove the moral superiority of all parties—the analyst, the patient, and the reader— for we have already learned that Elisabeth's problem derives not from her degeneracy but from her habit of telling the truth "regardlessly [*schonungs-los*]," even when it is not pretty. Indeed, Elisabeth's problem derives at least in part from her penchant for telling the truth.

Freud would use similar terms to explain his own tendency to declare the truth even when it was inconvenient and disturbing. While he often noted that his Jewishness allowed him to face the "compact majority" of German-speaking academia, in *Moses* he declared that he was prepared to meet the resistance of his own people, that is, the Jewish people. Just as Elisabeth von R. would not refrain from telling the truth because of social niceties, Freud acknowledges that he would not be induced [*bewegen lassen*] "to put the truth aside in favour of what are supposed to be national interests; and, moreover, the clarification of a set of facts may be expected to bring us a gain in knowledge."[46] Despite the potentially ugly consequences of proclaiming these "facts," Freud resolves that he must reveal the truth about Moses to "deepen our insight into the situation."[47] The very idea that a patient or a reader would be resistant to Freud's analysis becomes proof positive that the evidence is legitimate and significant, and that the analysis is "correct."

The distinction between analysis and evidence became blurry as Freud attempted to prove the validity of psychoanalysis "on the evidence of analysis."[48] Soon after completing *Studies on Hysteria*, Freud published an essay on "Heredity and the Aetiology of the Neuroses" (1896) in which he explicitly criticized Charcot's over-emphasis on heredity. This is also the essay in which Freud makes his first published reference to psychoanalysis. Using "a new method of psycho-analysis," he writes, the physician can travel "backwards into the patient's past, step by step, and always guided by the organic train of symptoms and of memories and thoughts aroused."[49] While he describes the method as a natural process leading the physician on a trail of clues, he acknowledges that he can be easily led astray. Anticipating the reader's skeptical questions, he writes,

> How is it possible to remain convinced of the reality of these analytic confessions which claim to be memories preserved from the earliest childhood? and how is one to arm oneself against the tendency to lies and the facility of invention [*Erfindung*] which are attributed to hysterical subjects? I should accuse myself of blameworthy credulity if I did not possess more conclusive evidence.[50]

Freud was well aware that questions of evidence were inseparable from doubts about the foundations of his new theory. Rather than arguing that his predecessors' analyses of the evidence were wrong, he suggests that they had simply overlooked the clues. Charcot and his followers had missed the most important evidence, which if appropriately examined would offer no other explanation: "The precocious event has left an indelible imprint on the history of the case; it is represented in it by a host of symptoms and of special features which could be accounted for *in no other way*."[51] It seems clear that Freud began with his patients' symptoms and followed them backward in an attempt to discover their origins, but in this sentence he reverses the causality and presents the situation as a chronological sequence of events: The "precocious event" led to the imprint that led to the symptoms. Whereas Charcot regarded heredity as the cause and later sexual experiences as the "*agents provocateurs*," Freud modifies the equation: "Analysis demonstrates in an irrefutable fashion" that later sexual experiences have "a pathogenic influence for hysteria only owing to their faculty for awakening the unconscious psychical trace of the childhood event."[52] In other words, analysis is both the method of inquiry and the evidence of its efficacy.

While Freud's writings have been central to trauma studies, actual known traumas were not the starting points in any of his analyses, whether of individuals or of societies.[53] His patients came to him with symptoms, psychic miseries, and mysterious aches and pains the origins of which were *unknown*. Unlike those who study survivors of disasters (such as the Holocaust, Hiroshima, or 9/11), Freud began his case studies with only *effects* as his evidence; he had no concrete knowledge of their causes (with the exception of his brief work on war neuroses during World War I). In retrospect, he remembered that he borrowed his narrative model from the increasingly prevalent phenomenon of the railway accident in which the traveler walks away "apparently unharmed."[54] In the mid- to late nineteenth century, doctors began to notice an increase in generalized fear and "emotional shock" caused by the dangers and recurring accidents involved with railway travel. However, these cases were the subject of major controversies and legal disputes: "traumatized" travelers sued railway companies and hired doctors to support their cases; meanwhile, the railway companies hired their own medical experts to invalidate such claims.[55] In his Salpêtrière lectures in the late 1880s, Charcot discussed the railway literature, but Freud referred to it as if it were an unquestionable model of trauma without the gaps and doubts that attended his own case studies. Thus, though recent debates about the nature and definition of trauma often refer to Freud's work as an originary source, even there we find a series of borrowed and displaced narratives, full of gaps and conjectures.[56]

Historians who are prone to strict positivism in the traditions of Auguste Comte and R. G. Collingwood might criticize Freud for blending evidence and analysis as if this were an example of biased or unscientific research.[57] However, the notion that these two elements should be completely distinct reveals assumptions about what qualifies as good science (or, for that matter, good history). As Richard Lewontin explains, it is generally assumed that the best scientific experiments need no discussion of their analysis, since what makes them good is the self-evidence of the results.[58] This is, Lewontin notes, a simplified version of how science really works, but it is one that many historians have accepted unreflectively. In their attempt to transform history into a social science, some historians "attempt to lay onto history a model of science claimed by scientists and their positivist allies."[59] Thus

they overlook the fact that the very choice of evidence defines the methodology and standards of proof. "The very method which we use is itself a
form of evidence," though the connection between the method and the
evidence often remains unexamined.[60] For natural scientists, nature is the
material evidence, various experimental procedures are the methods, and
language (as well as images, graphs, and equations) is usually presumed to
be a transparent representation of the matter and the methods. For historians and literary critics, however, language usually constitutes the matter *and*
the method—it composes both the evidence and the mode of analysis.

In founding psychoanalysis, Freud struggled to establish a discipline imperfectly modeled on the structure of a physical science whose standards
were themselves in flux. Having begun his career studying the matter of
eels' gonads, he now focused on the mercurial relationships between physical matters and their linguistic representations or between psychological
turmoil and its symptomatic representation in the patients' physical ailments. Since different fields of study have different standards of proof, a
new theory that challenges the assumptions and structures of established
fields must institute new standards of proof.[61] This does not happen overnight and it does not necessarily involve deliberate choices. In Freud's case,
some of this *did* happen overnight: In the course of analyzing his own
dreams and memories, he soon realized that it was not hysterics who were
unreliable but memory itself. However, rather than rejecting memory as
irrelevant, he re-examined the very foundations of his theory.

CRACKS IN THE FOUNDATION: HISTORICAL FANTASY (1897)

From 1893 until 1897, Freud was so intent upon proving the reliability of
his patients' accounts of their pasts that he did not necessarily pay attention
to the ways in which individuals might unintentionally distort their recollections. In examining and using his evidence, he took what could be termed
a simple positivist perspective. As Ginzburg notes, "In a positivist perspective"—whether medical or historical—"the evidence is analyzed only in
order to ascertain if, and when, it implies a distortion, either intentional or
unintentional."[62] In these early years of psychoanalysis Freud attempted to
fill the gaps in his patients' narratives, but he was less sensitive to the processes that shaped the narratives themselves. During this period, he maintained an intense and intimate correspondence with Fliess, with whom he

shared his dreams and discoveries.[63] On September 21, 1897, Freud wrote what would become one of the most infamous letters in the history of psychoanalysis. Confiding in Fliess, he shares "the great secret that has been slowly dawning on me in the last few months. I no longer believe in my *neurotica*." He goes on to explain that he no longer believed that childhood seductions could be so universal as to fully account for all hysteria. Though he recounts a number of other realizations, the most famous "insight"—and possibly the most famous sentence in this letter—is his announcement that "there are no indications of reality *in the unconscious*, so that one cannot distinguish between truth and fiction that has been cathected [*besetzt*, literally "occupied"] with affect."[64]

This letter has been at the center of some of the most contentious debates about and within psychoanalysis, particularly regarding the question of whether to accept patients' narratives as representations of historical realities, fictional hallucinations, or dream-like fantasies possibly interwoven with vague references to reality. While the famous "insight" (regarding the relationship between truth and fiction) is often cited as proof that Freud abandoned all confidence in the reliability of his patients' recollections, he was in fact more circumspect about the change. While some critics portray this change as an outright rejection of scientific standards of truth and proof, others argue that such standards are out of place in what is otherwise a literary or cultural theory. When Jeffrey Masson published *The Complete Letters of Sigmund Freud to Wilhelm Fliess, 1877–1904* in 1985, he unleashed a virulent breed of Freud criticism that focused on Freud's "abandonment of the seduction theory."[65] According to this side of the "Freud Wars," though Freud briefly recognized that many children suffer from sexual abuse, he soon turned away in horror, abandoning not only the theory but also his patients since he no longer seemed to believe in the reality of their reports.[66] In Masson's words, Freud committed an "assault on truth."[67] However, in this infamous letter to Fliess in 1897, Freud does not completely abandon the reality of his patients' reports; rather, he abandons the idea that external definitions of reality can be maintained internally. By positing an "unconscious," Freud created a location—a holding space—for the elements that cannot be definitively parsed as either fact or fiction. In recognizing that his patients' reports of childhood seductions did not necessarily correspond to actual events, he did not reject them as lies; instead, he accepted them as proof of the existence of an unconscious region of the mind where fact and fiction cannot necessarily be distinguished.

What is often overlooked in discussions of Freud's famous letter is the following paragraph, in which he admits to a range of other disappointments:

> I was so far influenced [by this] that I was ready to give up two things: the complete resolution of a neurosis and the certain knowledge of its etiology in childhood. Now I have no idea of where I stand because I have not succeeded in gaining a theoretical understanding of repression [*Verdrängung*] and its interplay of forces. It seems once again arguable that only later experiences give the impetus to fantasies, which [then] hark back [*zurückgreifen*] to childhood, and with this the factor of a hereditary disposition regains [*gewinnt*] a sphere of influence [*Machtbereich*] from which I had made it my task to dislodge [*verdrängen*] it—in the interest of the illumination of neurosis.[68]

There are a number of remarkable aspects of this humble paragraph. Freud admits that he had momentarily felt confident that he could completely resolve neuroses and that he had been in full possession of the mysteries of its etiology. Now he is left without a firm place to stand since he must reevaluate the evidence upon which he had founded his theory. Repression [*Verdrängung*] is key: In the following years Freud explores the modes of censorship that the psyche uses to cover, distort, and transform the traces of events. Using the language of war, he concedes that the "hereditary disposition" may win back [*gewinnt*] control of the territory [*Machtbereich*, a word usually used to refer to regions of military control] from which Freud had tried to drive it. In an odd repetition, Freud uses the word for "repression" [*verdrängen*] to describe his attempt to *dislodge* heredity from its position in the land of psychoanalysis.

Historians of psychoanalysis have also attempted to dislodge heredity from discussions of psychoanalysis.[69] After all, Freud founded psychoanalysis as an alternative to the hereditarian (and often anti-semitic) theories of his predecessors. There is sometimes a parallel tendency to attempt to drive out heredity and biology from all discussions of Jewishness (as well as other ethno-religious-racial groups). History, culture, literature, and even religion are presented as alternatives to such narrowly deterministic and racialist thinking. It is thus surprising to recognize that Freud himself could not see a way to dislodge heredity from his theorization of history, fact, and fiction. Instead of trying to reject the role of heredity wholesale, he would eventually come to terms with its implication in history and with the ways in which our perceptions of its importance or unimportance are themselves parts of our histories, shaping our very recollections and the narratives we tell.

Imperial Expansion (1897–1914)

Even as Freud explored the vicissitudes of the dark regions of the psyche—the internal fantasies, desires, and drives that alone can cause a person to fall ill—he never completely abandoned the idea that external traumas were the ultimate cause of psychic turmoil. Though he later referred to his realization in 1897 as his "abandonment of the seduction theory," it was more of a subtle shift away from an etiological model based entirely on external traumas to "one which incorporated internal 'drives.'"[70] As Grubrich-Simitis notes, Freud exaggerated "the truly considerable difference between his two etiological conceptions into an either–or opposition." In so doing, "he created for himself an intellectual bulwark" that made it difficult to admit to the gaps in his theory, namely the impossibility of ever proving that his patients' miseries (and fantasies) originated in actual experiences in childhood.[71] Freud most explicitly exaggerated his "early mistake" regarding the reality of his patients' childhood seductions in his conversations with Jung between 1909 and 1912. As he and Jung began to collaboratively explore the parallels between mythological symbols and neurotics' fantasies, Freud began to consider going even further back, beyond the individual's past and into the realm of archaic memory. Nonetheless, he went on the defensive when he saw that Jung's interest in phylogenetic memory and mythology allowed him to disregard the reality of infantile sexuality. As the friendship dissolved, Freud attempted to shore up the foundations of psychoanalysis, insisting on the historical reality not only of individuals' memories but also of their archaic heritage.

PSYCHOANALYSIS BEYOND VIENNA (1897–1907)

Following the 1897 crisis, Freud began to move beyond medical diagnosis and toward a more general theory of the human psyche. As Grubrich-Simitis notes, "Whereas the more conventional trauma model applied to the *pathogenesis* of the relatively small number of people who had been sexually violated in childhood, the revolutionary drive model" could apply to the psychogenesis of everyone.[72] In the following months Freud attempted to emancipate himself from the particular events of individual childhoods and to develop psychoanalysis as a universal theory of humanity. Now he reported that he no longer needed to discover specific infantile traumas in his patients' pasts because he had discovered the universal existence of infant sexuality and the Oedipal complex. In his essay on "Sexuality in the Aetiology of the Neuroses" (1898)—written a few months after the infamous letter to Fliess—Freud argues that all neuroses could be traced back to everyday childhood incidents that were experienced sexually. As he was well aware, the idea that children have any sexual experiences whatsoever would be quite disturbing; if he had wanted to make his theory more palatable, he could have downplayed the shocking reality of these experiences. Instead of arguing about what did or did not happen in childhood, he also could have traced the individual's illness back beyond her own prehistory—to her ancestor's experiences—for there he would have found a "wealth of phylogenetically transferred material" to fill in the gaps in evidence.[73] Anticipating that this would be the obvious solution, he adds, "In tracing back the vicissitudes of an individual's illness to the experiences of his ancestors, we have gone too far. We have forgotten that between his conception and his maturity there lies a long and important period of life—his childhood—in which the seeds of later illness may be acquired."[74] Over the next fifteen years, Freud would continue to resist the idea that his patients' conditions could be traced back to their ancestors' experiences for this seemed to move too far away from the life history of the individual.[75]

Between 1898 and 1905, Freud published a number of works whose theories applied not only to neurotics and hysterics but to all of humanity. The next three large books were essentially collections of anecdotes, many of them gathered from his own life: *Interpretation of Dreams* (1900), *The Psychopathology of Everyday Life* (1901), and *Jokes and Their Relation to the Unconscious* (1905). Even more important, in *Three Essays on the Theory of Sexuality* (1905) he established a firm position on the question of what happened in early childhood. Whereas he had earlier proposed that sexual traumas came from adults—from outside the individual—now he proposed that the sexual experiences of early childhood were internal: Even the youngest of children had sexual desires and feelings demonstrated in their orgasmic enjoyment of sucking, rocking, and defecating. For example, in adulthood even the vibrations of a train could recall sexual feelings from childhood and could be experienced as traumatic since the memories of the earlier sexual experiences would have been repressed. Again Freud contrasts his own position with other "writers who . . . have devoted much more attention to the primaeval period which is comprised in the life of the individual's ancestors—have, that is, ascribed much more influence to heredity—than to the other primaeval period, which falls within the lifetime of the individual himself—that is, to childhood."[76] Even as he suggestively concedes that the primaeval period of the individual's life might be analogous to the primaeval period of humanity, he struggles to maintain focus on the primary realm of psychoanalytic investigation: the individual's childhood.[77]

RETURN OF THE REPRESSED: THE PROMISED LAND (1907–14)

Sometime between 1905 and 1910, psychoanalysis was transformed from a relatively obscure Viennese method to an ever-expanding movement with followers from cities around the world, including Zürich, New York, London, and Budapest. It has been widely noted that because many of his friends, followers, and patients were Jewish, Freud worried that psychoanalysis would be stigmatized as a "Jewish science," not only untrustworthy but parochial and sectarian, lacking in universal import. When Carl Gustav Jung befriended him in 1906, Freud rejoiced that he had found someone who could carry psychoanalysis beyond its Jewish ghetto. In 1908 he wrote to Karl Abraham that

> You are closer to my intellectual constitution because of racial kinship [*Rassenverwandtheit*], while he [Jung] as a Christian and a pastor's son finds his way to me only against great inner resistances [*während er als Christ und Pastorssohn nur gegen große innere Widerstände den Weg zu mir findet*]. His association [*Anschluß*] with us is then all the more valuable. I would almost have said that only his appearance has removed psychoanalysis from the danger of becoming a Jewish national affair.[78]

Even as Freud and Jung developed an intense friendship, in retrospect we can see that there were fractures in the relationship long before it fully collapsed. Many scholars have meditated on whether their friendship was doomed because of their "national" differences, evident both in Freud's suspicion that Jung was anti-semitic, and in Jung's suspicion that Freud's being Jewish (detrimentally) shaped his theories.[79] Before the two men even met, Jung declared that "even a superficial glance at my work will show how much I am indebted to the brilliant discoveries of Freud."[80] However, he also added that his acknowledgment of some aspects of Freud's theory did not "mean that I attribute to the infantile sexual trauma the exclusive importance that Freud apparently does."[81] From the very beginning of their relationship, then, Jung questioned the most important sphere of influence [*Machtbereich*]—childhood—that Freud had worked so hard to conquer.

Nonetheless, Freud delighted in the widening prospects that seemed to come with Jung's arrival on the scene. While there were early signs of discord, Freud averted his eyes and rejoiced in the founding of his new "family," with himself as the patriarch and his younger colleagues—most explicitly, Jung and Ferenczi—as his sons. In January 1909 he envisaged himself as a prophet and Jung as the leader of a new people who would carry the psychoanalytic doctrine into the future. "If I am Moses," he explained to Jung, "then you are Joshua and will take possession of the promised land of psychiatry, which I shall only be able to glimpse from afar."[82] A little over a year later, he chose a different set of father–son figures to represent the friendship. "Just rest easy, dear son Alexander," Freud writes to Jung. "I will leave you more to conquer than I could manage myself, all of psychiatry and the approval of the civilized world, which is accustomed to regard me as a savage! That ought to lighten your heart."[83] This is a remarkable letter for a number of reasons. First, while Freud identified with a number of military heroes,[84] here he puts himself in the position of the forgettable father of one of the greatest military heroes, Alexander the Great. When King Philip of Macedonia was murdered, his son Alexander was suspected of complicity since his father's death meant that the son would ascend to the kingship. Indeed, Alexander went on to conquer the entire territory from Egypt to India, effectively contributing to a "universalization" of Greek culture. In this letter, Freud anticipates his late theory about the murder of Moses, when, as on other occasions, he expresses a fear that the "son" (Jung) would kill his "father" (Freud) in order to emerge as an independent world leader. Moreover, instead of looking out over "the promised land" of psychiatry (Palestine), Freud envisions Jung conquering the entire world, distributing the gift of Greek culture (psychoanalysis) beyond its previously limited confines. Whereas psychoanalysis had been Jewish, now it was Greek (and it is no coincidence that the Oedipus complex takes its name from Greek mythology).[85] Moreover, in this same letter,

Freud moves from identifying with a displaced king to acknowledging his "savage" status, a reference that resonates with his emerging interests in mythology and anticipates his explorations of "primitive man" in *Totem and Taboo*. However, it is also a subtle acknowledgment that as a Jew, Freud would have been regarded as an outsider in both Hellenistic and Roman civilizations, as a *savage* mired in an unhealthy literality and sexuality. (I will return to this subject in the final section of this chapter.)

Before writing even the first essay of *Totem*, Freud imagined Jung as the son who would conquer the world by overtaking and possibly murdering the father. These feelings derived not from some paranoid fantasy, however, but from the very deep friendship and mutual interests that both excited and frightened Freud. Both men shared a fascination with mythology and the idea that the ancient past shaped present individuals' narratives. Their mutual interests are reflected most clearly in their writings from 1912 to 1913: Jung's *Transformations and Symbols of the Libido* is in some respects his most Freudian work (in its explorations of the concept of the libido), while Freud's *Totem and Taboo* is his most Jungian (in its emphasis on mythology rather than memory). Peter Hoffer has explored the ways in which the two men collaboratively explored "phylogenetic factors," but there were early signs that Freud was not as enthusiastic about the new territory as his younger colleague.[86] In retrospect, it is possible to see Freud's and Jung's interests in mythology and phylogenetic memory as a "common thread" linking "their respective views on the human condition,"[87] but in 1910–13 it was the province in which their differences were fully revealed.[88] As Jung became increasingly enthusiastic about his explorations in mythology and mysticism, he also began to more confidently criticize Freud's theory of the libido and his emphasis on childhood sexuality. Meanwhile, Freud followed Jung's explorations in mythology with a sort of bemused curiosity, noting, "In you the tempest rages; it comes to me as distant thunder."[89] On October 13, 1911, Freud wrote a letter to Jung in which he included a fairly long interpretation of Gilgamesh and other mythological pairs and twins.[90] As if mourning the inevitable, he concludes the letter by noting that "If there is such a thing as a phylogenetic memory in the individual, which *unfortunately will soon be undeniable*, this is also the source of the *uncanny* aspect of the 'doppelgänger.'"[91]

While Freud began to acknowledge that phylogenetic memory could shape psychic dispositions, he continued to worry that it might detract from his initial discoveries.⁹² The following month, his suspicion about the encroaching force of phylogenetic memory resurfaced at a meeting of the Vienna Psycho-Analytical Society on November 8, 1911, where the subject of the evening was "On the Supposed Timelessness of the Unconscious." The meeting began with a discussion of neurotics' tendencies to "cancel out *current reality* and to fixate on a *historical reality*."⁹³ The young analyst Sabine Spielrein then proposed a different understanding of the apparent differences in these "realities." According to the recorded minutes, she argued that "the reason why infantile experiences have such an influence and thus tend to stir up complexes lies in the fact that these experiences proceed along phylogenetic pathways."⁹⁴ Anticipating that her idea might meet with opposition from Freud's school, she prefaced her discussion by noting that she "could only approach these matters from the standpoint of her school [Jung]."⁹⁵ Sensing that she was getting at something crucial to the very structure of psychoanalysis, Freud cautiously warned the group that they should not jump to phylogenetic conclusions too quickly:

> As for the possibility of memory contents that are phylogenetically acquired (Zurich school; Spielrein), and which could explain the similarities between formations of neurosis and ancient cultures, we first have to envisage, in keeping with the procedure of "successive stage," another possibility. It could be *a matter of identical psychic conditions, which have led to identical results.*⁹⁶

Freud wanted to be sure that Spielrein and her school were not using phylogenetic memory as a way of skipping over that "long and important period" of the individual's life "between conception and maturity."⁹⁷ Moreover, as Freud noted in a letter to Jung soon after this meeting, he was troubled by Spielrein's apparent subordination of "psychological material to *bio*logical considerations."⁹⁸

In much the same way as he had attempted to overcome Charcot's overemphasis on heredity, Freud now tried to curb the Society's increasing (and increasingly alarming) interest in phylogenetic sources of psychic phenomena as opposed to ontogenetic sources in the individual's childhood experience. Having replied to Spielrein, he went on to explain his own position: While neurotics and "savages" might both believe in a sort of magic (or in "the omnipotence of thoughts"), the reason for the similarity was not that they moved along the same phylogenetic pathways. "As long as it is possible for us to explain these things by an analysis of psychic phenomena, we are not justified in coming to the conclusion that a store of memories has been carried along phylogenetically. . . . *What remains unexplained*, after this analysis of the psychic phenomena of regression, may then be regarded as phylogenetic memory."[99] After attempting to piece together the evidence of psychic conditions through psychoanalysis, there were always remnants, shards of evidence that did not fit the larger construction. While Freud had proposed the unconscious as a holding location for these materials, Jacques Lacan would go even further, ironically calling the unassimilable and inexplicable elements "the real," as if they were more real than external reality.[100] Only after the knowable realms of psychic phenomena had been thoroughly analyzed did Freud allow that heredity and phylogenetic memory could explain those residues that were otherwise inexplicable or unapproachable. As in the 1890s, again in 1911 he attempted to shore up the foundations of psychoanalysis by directing attention to the events in the individual's own life rather than in the inherited mythological history of her ancestors' lives.

By the time Freud completed *Totem and Taboo* and Jung completed *Transformations and Symbols*, the friendship was on the verge of collapse, and in the final sections of these works the two men marked out their differences. As Freud wrote the first three essays of *Totem*, he and Jung were still on speaking terms, even as there was mounting tension. Drawing on Jung's work, as well as other studies of mythology, ethnology, anthropology, and natural history, he built up a large-scale comparative study of the origins of religious traditions, neurotics' unconscious obsessions, the incest taboo, and the Oedipal complex. In a letter responding to Freud's ongoing work on the question of incest and the son's sexual feelings for his mother, Jung remarked that he was also "absorbed in the incest problem," but that he regarded it "primarily as a fantasy problem."[101] A few weeks later Jung went even further, reminding Freud that he (Freud) had originally taken "the so-called sexual trauma" literally, mistaking fantasies for realities, and that incest, too, was more of a fantasy. "Just as *cum grano salis* [with a grain of salt] it doesn't matter whether a sexual trauma really occurred or not, or was a mere fantasy, it is psychologically quite immaterial whether an incest barrier really existed or not, since it is essentially a question of later development whether or not the so-called problem of incest will become of apparent importance."[102] On May 23, 1912, Freud seemed to concede that Jung was right about his early mistake: "I value your letter for the warning it contains," he writes, "and the reminder of my first big error, when I mistook fantasies for realities."[103] However, Jung was going too far in abandoning the idea that what had "really occurred" could make all the difference. Freud noted that Jung's reference to incest and sexual trauma as "merely a fantasy" suggested a "disastrous similarity" with the work of Alfred Adler, who (according to Freud) had recently abandoned psychoanalysis, in part because of an "utter incomprehension of the unconscious."[104] Indeed, Freud had good reason to worry that Jung would disregard the literal and historical reality of sexuality; even before the two men met, Jung had publicly expressed his aversion to the entire concept of "infantile sexuality."[105] Eventually, Jung gave full vent to his distaste for Freud's emphasis on the reality of sexual and incestuous feelings in childhood. "Just as the sexualism of neuroses is not to be taken literally," he writes, "so is the sexualism of the early infantile phantasies, especially the incest problem, a regressive product of the revival of the archaic modes of function, *outweighing actuality*."[106] In other words, by following fantasies back through their phylogenetic pathways, Jung could take all of psychoanalysis "with a grain of salt." Now he was no longer mired in the reality of childhood sexuality—he had moved beyond the literal actuality of Freudian psychoanalysis.[107]

While Freud wrote the first three essays of *Totem and Taboo* as a temperate response to Jung's own studies in mythology, in the fourth (and final) essay he went in a decidedly different direction. In the first three essays he builds up a series of comparisons of neurotics and "primitives," but in "The Return of Totemism in Childhood" he traces the origins of these similarities back to a particular series of events. Specifically he claims that at some point, a primal horde of men had tired of submission to their authoritarian father. Thus they banded together and killed him, putting an end to the "patriarchal horde." As a result, they felt ambivalently triumphant, for they felt guilty about having killed the father whom they had both feared and loved.[108] This is, of course, the original murder, which would be repeated in Freud's version of the Moses story. Where he would worry about evidence to support his study of Moses, in *Totem* he does not evince this same anxiety, partly because the events in *Totem* occurred (if they occurred at all) in prehistoric time. As such, they would not have produced the kinds of evidence that would be expected of events occurring in a textual age. While Freud based his reconstruction of the primal murder on the hypotheses of

Robertson Smith (as well as Darwin and others), he did not question the evidence itself, for he generally presumed that anthropologists and natural historians were trustworthy observers who collected reliable evidence.[109] Indeed, one of the many oddities about reading the work today is the way in which he uses the ethnological hypotheses as *evidence* upon which he constructs a historical narrative that both explains and is explained by some of the most fundamental findings of psychoanalysis.[110]

Freud did not worry so much about proving the reality of the primal murder also because—contrary to general perceptions of *Totem*—the primal murder was not part of the original premise of the entire work. Having built up a series of large- and small-scale comparisons of religious and neurotic rituals in the first three essays, he reconstructed the historical narrative of their common origins almost as an after-thought in the middle of the fourth essay. In proposing a series of events that had "left ineradicable traces in the history of humanity"[111]—that is, both on individuals and on human civilization as a whole—he found himself embracing the very idea he had for so long resisted: the possibility that phylogenetically acquired memory contents "could explain the similarities between formations of neurosis and ancient cultures."[112] Here Freud suggests that the phylogenetic memory of the primal murder is the originary source not only of neurosis (and other psychic miseries) but of human civilization itself—sociality, conscience, and law.

After the crisis of 1897, Freud continued to search for the "ultimate sources" of his patients' conditions in their childhood experiences; in incorporating the idea of phylogenetic memory, he found an eternal "source" in the prehistory of all individuals. For example, in the case history of the "Wolf-Man," written in 1914, the year after the break with Jung (and simultaneously with his study of Michelangelo's statue of Moses), Freud reviews his patient's history: his dreams, his memories of his childhood, and his hereditary predisposition. In the third section, "The Seduction and Its Immediate Consequences," he traces his patient's fantasies back through various recollections to their "ultimate sources." Here he finds that the patient had been sexually seduced in early childhood by both his governess and his sister.[113] While Freud acknowledges his patient's fantasies, he insists that the "seduction by his sister was certainly not a phantasy." He goes on to establish the story's "credibility" by some other "information which had never been forgotten."[114] In his earlier case histories, Freud had been limited by whatever the patients happened to recollect in the course of analysis, supplemented by conversations with other family members (as in the case of Elisabeth or, more extensively, in the case of "Little Hans"). Now he notes that he has found the solution in "Fresh Material from the Primal Period"[115]: When significant experiences in the child's own primal history could not be discovered, the primal history of the human race could fill in the gaps. "A child catches hold of this phylogenetic experience where his own experience fails him," writes Freud. "He fills in the gaps in individual truth with prehistoric truth; he replaces occurrences in his own life by occurrences in the life of his ancestors."[116]

Partly because Freud did not share the same literary-cultural background as his Russian patient, he overlooked the fact that mythology itself provided the Wolf-Man with a narrative that shaped his phobias and life experiences.[117] A significant part of childhood is the experience of hearing stories that invoke whole fantasy worlds so sensually evocative that the fantasies are felt as more present than the present facts. Some of these narratives may not be consciously recalled later in life, but their scenes and structures no doubt shape our patterns of thought. While these stories could be categorized as a special realm of childhood experience—even sexual in their intense sensory nature—Freud did not pursue this possibility.[118] Instead, he proposed that real experiences in the distant, ancestral past were the basis for the phylogenetic memories that had compelled later individuals to generate mythological narratives and fairytales.

While Freud concedes that this solution is in agreement with Jung's hypotheses about "the existence of this phylogenetic heritage," he actually develops a very different argument about this heritage. Since Jung regarded phylogenetic heritage and mythology as the source of both individual and collective narratives of experiences, fantasies, and mythologies, he could completely pass over the question of whether any events in the phylogenetic heritage had ever really occurred. By contrast, Freud insists that real experiences were the originary source of phylogenetic memory and mythology; the patterns generated by these events then structured later experiences and filled in narrative gaps. Indeed, in his *Introductory Lectures* (1915–17), Freud goes even further and insists that

> *primal phantasies*, as I should like to call them . . . are a phylogenetic endowment. In them the individual reaches beyond his own experience into primaeval experience at points where his own experience has been too rudimentary. It seems to

me quite possible that all the things that are told to us in analysis as phantasy—the seduction of children, the inflaming of sexual excitement by observing parental intercourse, the threat of castration (or rather castration itself)—were once *real occurrences* in the primaeval times of the human family, and that children in their phantasies are simply filling in the gaps in individual truth with prehistoric truth.[119]

Now that he had completely split with Jung, Freud began to freely incorporate the concept of phylogenetic memory into the very foundations of psychoanalytic theory. However, he continued to insist upon the concerns that he had addressed in 1898 and again in 1911 at the meeting of the Vienna Psychoanalytic Society. It would be "a methodological error to seize on a phylogenetic explanation before the ontogenetic possibilities have been exhausted," he writes. "I cannot see any reason for obstinately disputing the importance of infantile prehistory while at the same time freely acknowledging the importance of ancestral prehistory."[120] By 1914, Freud no longer resisted the "undeniable" reality of the phylogenetic heritage, but he realized that "phylogenetic motives and productions themselves stand in need of elucidation, and that in quite a number of instances this is afforded by factors in the childhood of the individual."[121] While the gaps in the individual's narratives could be filled in by phylogenetic memories, there remained the problem of gaps in the phylogenetic narrative. Finally, in *Moses and Monotheism* Freud confronted this very problem: In his attempt to reconstruct the narrative of the Jewish people, he tried to fill in the gaps in the phylogenetic narrative with materials gathered from his work with individuals. But in returning to this early material, he found cracks in the foundations.

The Analogy: From the Race to the Individual and Back Again

Though Freud insists that his character study of Moses requires historical proofs, the applicability and validity of his reconstruction depends on the comparison of the origins of (collective) Jewishness with the origins of (individual) neurosis. Despite all the anxious comments about establishing the historical proof of his narrative, this analogy forms the structural foundation of *Moses and Monotheism*. Though he had compared the origins of religion to the origins of neurosis in a number of works since *Totem and Taboo*, in

Moses he introduces this comparison as if it were entirely new, even shocking.[122] "The only satisfying analogy to the remarkable course of events that we have found in the history of the Jewish religion," he writes, "lies in an apparently remote field but it is very complete, and approaches identity."[123] One might suppose that after reading through the truly surprising story of the "real" origins of the Jewish people and the Egyptian identity of Moses, the reader would not find a comparison of neurosis and religion all that surprising, especially if this reader were at all familiar with Freud's earlier works in which he had already presented this analogy.[124] The terms had already been introduced; the scene had been set. And yet, whether for rhetorical flourish or because something truly odd and discomforting is about to be discussed, Freud presents "The Analogy" as if it is something quite new and unexpected.

Like many of his contemporaries, Freud accepted the idea that the development of individuals seemed to recapitulate the development of the human race, or as Ernst Haeckel succinctly put it, "ontogeny recapitulates phylogeny." Haeckel and many other recapitulationists were primarily interested in showing how the development of the individual could be used as a model to understand the development of the (human) races. The former seemed knowable while the latter was always in the realm of speculation.[125] After Freud "abandoned" the seduction theory in 1897–98, he used Haeckel's theory to structure his synthesis of the "various organic, biogenetic, and psychological components of his previous year's thinking."[126] However, Freud's early use of the recapitulation theory was idiosyncratic: Unlike his contemporaries, he proposed that the history of the human race could be used as a model to understand the primal history [*Urgeschichte*] of the individual. In *Moses*, Freud turned his previous use of Haeckel's theory on its head: Whereas previously he had used phylogenetic development as an explanatory model for ontogenetic development, now he worked in the opposite direction, turning from his earlier theory of the individual to a theory of the (Jewish) race.

What follows Freud's announcement of "The Analogy" *is* surprising in that it is a return to the trauma theory he had both established and supposedly abandoned in the late 1890s. "We shall see," writes Freud, "that this analogy is not so surprising as might at first be thought—indeed that it is more like a postulate."[127] More than a hypothesis or a demonstration, a *postulate* is a "fundamental condition or principle, an unproved and neces-sary assumption" that supports an entire argument.[128] In other words, the analogy itself can be seen as the "clay feet" that support the "statue," the crucial evidence on which Freud's narrative is based. The material following the "surprising" analogy is perhaps more enigmatic than surprising—full of elusive references to gaps and dichotomies. However, Freud's tone is tinged with bravado, as if all these gaps had been bridged long ago—as if all para-doxes had been solved and the dichotomies overcome. Now he presents some of the most fundamental findings of psychoanalysis and acknowledges the questions that had plagued him throughout his career: "We give the name of *traumas* to those impressions, experienced early and later forgotten. . . . We may leave on one side the question of whether the aetiol-ogy of the neuroses in general may be regarded as traumatic. The obvious objection to this is that it is not possible in every case to discover a manifest trauma in the neurotic subject's earliest history."[129] Here Freud echoes the concerns that (as he discussed in the discarded introduction of 1934) were supposedly particular to the historical novel: What is the analyst to do if there is not substantial evidence to support the historical reconstruction? How can he understand the effects of events that he cannot necessarily prove actually happened? How can he reconstruct a history without trust-worthy corroborating evidence? Freud admits that "when we have nothing else at our disposal for explaining a neurosis but hereditary and constitu-tional dispositions, we are naturally tempted to say that it was not acquired but developed."[130] Freud does not follow this idea any further, since he is more interested in explaining how the Jews *acquired* their Jewishness from Moses—that is, from an external source. Thus, in the following paragraph, he restates one of the founding principles of psychoanalysis: "[T]he genesis of a neurosis invariably goes back to very early impressions in childhood." In other words, *something* must have happened in the past to produce the effects in the present; otherwise "the neurosis would not have come about."[131]

Here is the turn of the screw: To illuminate his theory of the race, Freud turns to a theory of individual development, but within this theory of the individual he turns back to a theory of race. "But the gap [*die Kluft*] between the two groups [of cases] appears not to be unbridgeable."[132] Twenty-odd pages after introducing "The Analogy" comparing the formation of the individual's neurosis to the formation of a people's character, he presents his solution to the problem as if it is entirely surprising—as if it is a step in a new direction. "When we study the reactions to early traumas," he writes, "we are quite often *surprised* to find that they are not strictly limited to what the subject himself has really experienced but diverge from it in a way that fits in much better with the model of a phylogenetic event and, in general, can only be explained by such an influence."[133] Clearly this comparison was not new or surprising: As early as 1897 Freud had used the metaphor of primal history in his search for the origins of his patients' problems. And by 1912 he had gone back to the idea of the primal history, attempting to use his discoveries in individual psychology to develop a theory of human civilization. What is new in *Moses* is that he has come full circle from the race to the individual and back to the race. Yet at the center, a gap remained.

From Mount Sinai to Egypt

Whereas Freud often referred to his early abandonment of the seduction theory, he never commented on this most remarkable change in his thinking: the idea that individuals' memories might include the experiences of their ancestors. Indeed, in *Moses* and other late works he suggests that all of psychoanalysis depends upon accepting the idea that phylogenetic memories are inherited. Why was he so circumspect about this change? If we read *Moses* as a sort of case study of psychoanalysis, a strange twist emerges. Over and over again, Freud insists that monotheism was not original to the Jews—it was imposed upon them from the outside; it was "borrowed from Egypt."[134] However, there is a secondary stage of borrowing: Not only did the Jews receive—and reject, transform, and sustain—monotheism from the Egyptian Moses. Moses also received the idea of monotheism from the pharaoh Akhenaten, but he emptied it of its most mystical elements. Where Akhenaten had proclaimed that Aten (the sun god) was a universal god whose power extended throughout the world (making Aten the perfect deity for an imperialist ruler), Moses proclaimed that the Jews' god was the *only* god, and that the Jews were this god's *only* chosen people.[135] Moses' monotheism left a "permanent imprint" on the character of the Jewish people precisely because it rejected the magical and mystical elements of Akhenaten's religion: The prohibitions against images and the rejection of human immortality meant that the people no longer had to worry about statues of the gods (which would need to be carried around) or temples or burial sites (which would tie them to particular lands). While such renunciations might have made it difficult to convince the people of the value of their new tradition, Freud notes that "their melancholy destinies and their disappointments in reality served only to intensify the survival of the Mosaic tradition."[136]

Much of the narrative seems on a par with Freud's dreamy identification with Moses, except for the question of Akhenaten. That is, in constructing his version of the story, Freud adoringly portrayed Moses as the great foreigner whose difficult precepts his own people could not accept but whose tradition would nonetheless survive. How, then, can we understand the part of Freud's narrative where he explains that Moses did not create the Mosaic tradition? If Freud saw himself as Moses, then who was his Akhenaten? If, as Freud argued, the Jewish people could not admit the foreign origins of their greatest acquisition, what was the foreign influence to which Freud could not admit? It is possible that Freud could not acknowledge the radical shift in the foundations of psychoanalytic theory—the resistance and then acceptance of phylogenetic memory—because to do so would be to admit that he had borrowed one of his most foundational (albeit late) ideas. While there is ample evidence that Freud was intensely anxious about his various appropriations (some might call it plagiarism) of others' work, there is one anecdote that is extraordinarily revealing in terms of the identity of Akhenaten. One of the major lacunae in *Moses* is any mention of the fact that Freud borrowed the very idea of the Egyptianness of Moses and the importance of Akhenaten from his younger colleague Karl Abraham.[137] In 1912, Freud and Jung engaged in a heated discussion about Abraham's recent work, but the discussion ended when Freud fell into one of his fainting spells.[138]

Like Moses, Freud may have borrowed the idea of phylogenetic memory from Jung's explorations in mythology, but he took it in a distinctly different direction. Whereas Jung's concept of the collective unconscious bordered on religious mysticism, Freud insisted that the psychoanalytic concept of phylogenetic memory remained firmly grounded in historical reality. Indeed, we might go even further: While Jung confidently saw himself as belonging to an Aryan tradition of mythology, Freud borrowed elements from a range of cultures and mythologies, including the Greeks, the Romans, and the Hebrew Bible. In Freud's account, by transforming a universalistic mystical cult into a particularist spiritual tradition, Moses was able to unite and exalt the wandering Semitic tribes, since what grounded them was not land or images, but abstract intellectual ideas. Similarly, by grounding his theory in historical reality (behind all mythology and present conditions), Freud attempted to establish a foundation for understanding the estranged citizens of the world (whether Jews or other peoples). Jung's symbolic concept of the collective unconscious is in many ways more common sense than Freud's version of phylogenetic memory. However, Freud's version of collectively inherited memory may be more compelling precisely because he insisted on something *more* grounded—more outrageously real—than any available mythologies.

Just as Mosaic monotheism had survived the murder of its founder and centuries of repression and apparent forgetting, Freud hoped that psychoanalysis would survive and develop beyond the current dismal circumstances: a dying founder, rejection of its most important discoveries, and persecution of its followers.[139] However, Freud seems to have recognized that, like Mosaic monotheism, psychoanalysis would never be universally accepted because of its difficult doctrines and its rejection of "illusions." This limitation, however, was not necessarily a defeat. By implicitly acknowledging that neither psychoanalysis nor Judaism would ever extend a universal reach, Freud may have recognized their most critical strength, the feature that distinguishes them both from their "opposites"—Judaism from Christianity, and psychoanalysis from Jungian psychotherapy. By insisting on the reality of childhood sexuality and the inheritance of real archaic memories, Freud may have limited the scope of his work, but he maintained the most difficult and most compelling element of his theory. Whereas Jung pursued the symbolic pathways and structures of the collective unconscious, Freud remained mired in the literal realm of memory and history.

Ironically, while later critics such as Masson condemn Freud's "abandonment" of reality, Jung disparaged Freud's insistence on the reality of the memories of past events, particularly sexual experiences in childhood.[140] Indeed, Jung made no secret of his disgust with Freud's emphasis on infantile sexuality and with bodily matters more generally.[141] Jung's critique is echoed by recent scholars who suggest that while Freud's grand narratives are provocative, they should not be taken literally. Thus, for example, the anthropologist and psychoanalyst Robert Paul argues that "if we read Freud's cultural books replacing his search for historical origins with a focus on such fantasy schemas—individually experienced, but also collectively shared, communicated, and transmitted as symbolic representations and as phylogenetic templates—the main arguments take on persuasive force."[142] In other words, Freud's ideas are much more palatable if we simply read them (à la Jung and Krafft-Ebing) as myths or fairy-tales.

Likewise, Yerushalmi acknowledges that while Freud's notion of inherited memory is subjectively convincing, it should not be taken *literally*.[143] Specifically, he takes Freud to task for daring to press the analogy comparing individual and collective memory to the point of an identity. As Yerushalmi writes, "As the 'life of a people' is a biological metaphor, so the 'memory of a people' is a psychological metaphor, useful, but not to be literalized."[144] Nonetheless, as Yerushalmi is acutely aware, this metaphor is one that runs throughout the Hebrew Bible, burdening each individual— past, present, and future—with the responsibility for the group's memory. Yerushalmi worries that a literal reading of the metaphor will (problematically) suggest that it is not necessary for the individual to actively remember.[145] In other words, if the metaphor is literally materialized (in the body), the individual might feel relieved of the burden of memory: The inheritance of Jewish memory would seem to suggest that there is no need for the individual to *do* anything in order to *be* Jewish. The worry, then, is that the (Jewish) individual will not practice Jewish rituals or read Jewish texts, or actively transmit the past to the future: She (and her progeny) will be Jewish whether she (or they) likes it or not.[146]

The critique of Freud's over-literalism can be understood along the lines of the classic Pauline critique of Rabbinic hermeneutics. Other scholars have argued that Freud's reasoning was Rabbinic, Talmudic, or Kabbalistic;[147] here, however, I consider Yerushalmi's (and Jung's) criticisms of Freud's logic—particularly his literalism—in light of early Christian criticisms of Rabbinic Judaism. As Daniel Boyarin notes, when the Jews were consigned to eternal carnality, a direct connection was drawn "between anthropology and hermeneutics. Because the Jews reject reading 'in the spirit,' therefore they are condemned to remain 'Israel in the flesh.'" More generally, the "failure of the Jews" was described as "owing to a *literalist* hermeneutic, one which is unwilling to go beyond or behind the material language and discover its immaterial spirit."[148] Freud was well aware of the distinctions between Pauline and Rabbinic hermeneutics and Christian supercessionist interpretations of Judaism. In *Moses*, for example, he insists that the new (Christian) religion was a "cultural regression"; what ultimately distinguished Christianity from Mosaic monotheism was the fact that Paul "abandoned the 'chosen' character of his people and its visible mark—circumcision—so that the new religion could be a universal one, embracing all men."[149] According to Freud, in relinquishing this visible mark of sublimation and intellectuality [*Geistigkeit*], Christianity could no longer maintain "the lofty heights of spirituality [*Geistigkeit*] to which the Jewish religion had soared."[150]

So too, Freud believed that Jung had abandoned the most important elements of Freudian psychoanalysis, in particular its grounding in real events experienced both physically and psychologically. In his retrospective account "On the History of the Psycho-Analytic Movement" (1914), Freud insists that to make psychoanalysis more acceptable and perhaps even appealing to the general public, Jung replaced the most difficult element of psychoanalysis with mere symbols. According to Freud, what was most troubling (for Jung and for the general public) was the notion that current conditions originate in actual sexual experiences in childhood and in real events in the primal history of the human race. By contrast, Jung intended to "eliminate what is objectionable in the family-complexes, so as to find it again in religion and ethics. For sexual libido an *abstract concept* has been substituted. . . . The Oedipus complex has a *merely* 'symbolic' meaning."[151]

Ultimately, the difference between Freud's and Jung's work may not have been so much a matter of content as one of method. According to Freud, Jung rejected infantile sexuality because he began with a theoretical concept—namely, the rejection of infantile sexuality—that he then sought to confirm by observation. By contrast, Freud asserted that *his* theory of infantile sexuality—namely, the recognition of its existence—was "obtained by the method of analysis, by pursuing the symptoms and peculiarities of neurotics back to their ultimate sources, the discovery of which then explains whatever is explicable in them and enables whatever is modifiable to be changed."[152] Instead of relegating all symptoms to the effects of universal mythologies, in his early case histories Freud insisted on the particularities of his patients' conditions and on the possibility of finding their ultimate sources. In developing a theory of Jewishness, he returned to the language of historical and scientific discovery, for he could not quite give up on the idea that there was something *real*—something grounded and particular—

that had caused later phenomena such as mythology, religion, and civilization itself. This is not simply recalcitrant positivism or racial determinism, but a belief in the work of history and medicine as fields that articulate the malleability of the world. In addition to sharing a certain methodology, both history and medicine rest on the assumption that by discovering the original sources of present conditions—mental illness, racism, or fascism, for example—it might be possible to change "whatever is modifiable" in the future. Freud refused to concede that human conditions were the result of a shared universal mythology or some sort of *a priori* biological essence, for this would leave little room for the particularity of historical circumstance and for the possibility of future transformation.

Freud's "Lamarckism" and the Politics of Racial Science

Scientific thinking does not differ in its nature from the normal activity of thought, which all of us, believers and unbelievers, employ in looking after our affairs in ordinary life.

FREUD, *New Introductory Lectures on Psycho-Analysis* (1933)

Freud Among the Evolutionary Theorists

Freud's insistence on the historical truth of his version of the Moses story may seem strange, but what is perhaps more perplexing is his insistence on the idea that the memory-traces of these events have been biologically inherited by Jewish individuals. From our own perspective in the twenty-first century, the inheritance of memory may sound not only scientifically outmoded but also regressively racist. Yet both judgments would be hasty: If we consider Freud's position in the context of political and scientific debates of the time period, we discover the limitations of our own definitions of both science and racism.

Long before writing *Moses and Monotheism*, Freud had flirted with the idea that individuals inherit an "archaic heritage" from their ancestors. It was not until this final book, however, that he explicitly insisted on the inheritance of phylogenetic memory, particularly as it related to the "character of a people

[*Volkscharakter*]."[1] Though he spends much of the book reconstructing the "real" story of the origins of Mosaic monotheism, he ultimately insists that his entire work depends upon the idea that acquired characteristics are biologically transmitted from one generation to the next. Freud acknowledges that he had "behaved for a long time as though the inheritance of memory-traces of the experience of our ancestors . . . were established beyond question." And he concedes that his position was "made more difficult by the present attitude of biological science which refuses to hear of the inheritance of acquired characters by successive generations."[2] In the published version of this paragraph, he adds a crucial sentence: "We must in all modesty confess that nevertheless we cannot do without this factor in biological evolution." It is clear that Freud struggled to articulate this confession in just the right way: While there are very few inconsistencies between the manuscript and the published text, this sentence is subtly different in the manuscript. There, in his own handwriting, we find Freud's imagination stretched to the limit: "We must in all modesty confess," he writes, "that we cannot imagine biological evolution in any other way."[3]

Freud's late acknowledgment of the current state of biological science has often been interpreted as evidence that he knew that the inheritance of acquired characters had been scientifically disproven.[4] However, it is unclear whether the question of the inheritance of acquired characters was ever purely scientific and whether such a theory can ever be definitively disproven.[5] Indeed, it is often quite difficult to distinguish the borders between scientific and political questions, and this was particularly true in regards to evolutionary and hereditary theories in Europe in the 1930s. The complicated relationship between science and politics in the 1930s extended its effects well into the '50s (and later), when many of the foundational histories of evolutionary theory and of psychoanalysis were being written. Freud was uneasy about insisting on the inheritance of acquired characters not because he knew that this idea had been scientifically disproven but because he was aware of the political implications of his position.

While Freud's initial interest in phylogenetic memory was not necessarily politically motivated, his refusal to abandon this idea in the 1930s must be understood in terms of wider debates, especially regarding the position of the Jewish people in Germany and Austria. By suggesting that individuals inherited the effects of their ancestors' experiences, Freud seemed to align himself with the Lamarckians who opposed the determinism of the neo-Darwinians' hard heredity in favor of a softer and more malleable concept of heredity allowing for the inheritance of acquired characteristics. While Lamarckism went out of fashion in the West in the 1940s, it is often forgotten that it was a major subject of scientific and political discussions well into the 1930s, if not later. In Germany, the Nazis referred to Lamarckism as the product of "liberal-Jewish-Bolshevist science" that superstitiously and foolishly supported an outmoded theory of evolution.[6] "Lamarckian" theories of Jewishness were suspiciously regarded not only by the Nazis. In the wake of the Holocaust, *any* hereditarian theory of Jewishness appeared uncomfortably similar to racist theories that had undergirded the Nazis' "final solution." However, Freud was neither the first nor the last Jewish scientist to develop a hereditarian theory of Jewishness. In asserting that the Jews inherit the memories of their ancestors, Freud developed a racial theory of Jewishness that opposed racist definitions of the Jewish people and partially (if bizarrely) explained their persistent survival despite centuries of anti-semitism and oppression.

In his classic three-volume biography *The Life and Work of Sigmund Freud* (1953), Ernest Jones explains that he could not understand Freud's "obstinacy" in insisting upon the apparently outmoded scientific theory of Lamarckism in *Moses and Monotheism*. Since then, numerous other scholars have followed Jones' lead and have remarked upon this aspect of Freud's work with bemusement and wonder: Why did he continue to insist upon the inheritance of acquired characters—particularly in the 1930s, when this idea had (supposedly) been so clearly disproven?[7] Not content to see Freud's insistence on Lamarckism as an eccentricity of old age, many historians have presented this aspect of his work as a quandary and have intensely scrutinized it with wildly differing consequences.[8] Scholars intent upon showing the fraudulence of Freud's theories have emphasized his "Lamarckism" as one of many examples demonstrating the scientifically flawed foundations of psychoanalysis.[9] Other scholars—particularly historians of psychoanalysis, many of whom are psychoanalysts themselves and therefore protective of Freud's legacy—have attempted to downplay Freud's loyalty to Lamarckian-sounding ideas for fear that all of psychoanalysis might be tainted by his idiosyncratic obstinacy.[10] In other words, they attempt to save Freud from himself. More recently, a number of historians of psychoanalysis have learned from their predecessors, and instead of downplaying

Freud's foibles they meticulously document his flaws, including his mis-guided scientific claims (such as his Lamarckism). Thus they attempt to beat the Freud-bashers at their own game and to demonstrate that psychoanaly-sis' reputation can be salvaged even if Freud's cannot.[11] While it may be possible to emancipate psychoanalysis from the power and problems of the original psychoanalyst, neither Freud nor his critics (nor any other thinker for that matter) can emancipate themselves from the historical circum-stances that shape their ideas, hopes, and fears. Finally, because Freud's "Lamarckism" emerges most explicitly in *Moses and Monotheism*, many scholars have tried to understand this aspect of his work in terms of his Jewishness, a point I will discuss in more detail.[12]

This chapter is not an attempt to show that Freud was correct or incor-rect, brilliant or flawed—he was all of these. Rather, I am interested in exploring what sorts of questions emerge if we doggedly follow his logic and its relationship to contemporary political debates which he did not always explicitly address. Recent scholarship in the history of science, particularly by Peter Bowler, Sander Gliboff, Robert Proctor, and Paul Weindling, has recast the emergence of Darwinism as a long and uneven process that can-not be disentangled from the political debates of the nineteenth and twenti-eth centuries. Drawing from this work, I recontextualize Freud's references to hereditary and evolutionary theories alongside the larger scientific and political debates of the time period. Freud's theories of Jewishness and of psychoanalysis emerge as parts of a larger conversation in which the divid-ing lines between various scientific positions—as well as between science and politics—were not so clearly established. Finally, this approach allows us to see Freud's late insistence on the inheritance of acquired characteris-tics as one among many attempts to scientifically approach the Jewish Question.

The Polemicization of Evolutionary Theory: 1890s–1930s

Many of the earliest dilemmas in psychoanalysis have direct parallels with questions addressed in debates about evolution and heredity at the turn of the twentieth century. In the founding years of psychoanalysis, Freud attempted to understand what caused individuals to change from leading healthy lives to lives beset by seemingly inexplicable maladies and mental illness. While he conceded that "the hereditary disposition" was one of the determining factors of hysteria, he asserted that the physician should explore the "other aetiological influences, of a less incomprehensible nature," and that "hysterical symptoms" could be "traced back to their origin" in "the patient's past."[13] Similarly, while Darwinian natural selection seemed to explain why certain traits and species disappeared, it could not explain why new variations emerged or how species changed even as they appeared to maintain constant identities over time.[14] One of the most convincing and long-standing solutions to this conundrum was that changes in the environment caused individuals to acquire new traits that were then inherited by the following generations.[15] Though this idea is usually identified with the French naturalist Jean Baptiste de Lamarck (1744–1829), it was common to later evolutionary theorists, including Darwin and many of Darwin's followers.[16] It was not until August Weismann proclaimed the "all-sufficiency" of natural selection that Darwinism became known as a theory that opposed (rather than extended) the environmentalism of Lamarck's initial theory of evolution.[17]

Well into the 1920s, neo-Lamarckism and neo-Darwinism were both used to support a wide range of political and social projects, including both racist and anti-racist political movements, socialist eugenics programs, and Bolshevik revolutionary activity. The inheritance of acquired characteristics suggested that the distinct characteristics of a group (such as the Jews) were the result of environmental circumstances such as poverty and social isolation; thus, if their environment were improved, their (negative) characteristics would also improve. Some assimilationist Jewish leaders used this reasoning to support their fight for increased civil rights, arguing that improved social conditions would allow Jews to change their behavior and characteristics such that they would no longer be so identifiably and "problematically" Jewish. At the same time, some non-Jewish and anti-semitic authors saw the Jews as the most dangerous group because they were particularly good chameleons—or "parasites"—who could modify their characteristics to appear like their hosts and survive undetected within their host nations. Thus, they reasoned that if racial character *was* malleable, the Jews' distinctiveness was their own fault since they had not taken action to change it.[18]

While various evolutionary and hereditary theories were used to support diverse political positions, in the 1930s—particularly in Germany and

Russia—neo-Darwinist Mendelian eugenic theories became "linked to conservative views of society," and Lamarckian theories became "linked to left-wing socialist views of society."[19] Indeed, the association of racist eugenics with Nazi Germany and Lamarckism with Communist Russia is so firmly engrained in our historical memories that it is often difficult to reconstruct the complexity of the relationships between science and politics as they emerged in the early twentieth century. As Loren Graham notes, in the 1920s the "political value implications of theories of human heredity" were widely discussed. However, the complexity of the 1920s gave way to a period in which the debates became so polemicized that we must ask whether this process was an "entirely social and political phenomenon, essentially distinct from the scientific theories under discussion," or whether "there was something intellectually inherent in each of the competing theories of heredity which supported a particular political ideology."[20] If there were inherently political elements in these theories, the "allegedly value-free nature of science" may have to be radically questioned.[21] Likewise, Freud's own use of these theories raises questions about the political nature of his science and the very definition of psychoanalysis as a science—questions to which I will return at the end of this chapter.

One of the larger questions with which theorists of evolution and race grappled was about the rate of change: How much time was required for a species or a race to change—a couple of generations or thousands of generations? If changes in the environment resulted in organisms rapidly changing forms, then the typologies of groups were not stable. Since genetic mutations were not widely understood, it was unclear how natural selection and heredity alone could result in evolutionary change. Whereas scientists interested in the dynamics of heredity generally focused on consistency from one generation to the next, those scientists who were more interested in the evolution of the species over time focused on factors of change such as natural selection and adaptation. Thus it was not until the 1950s that the phenomena of constancy *and* change were integrated in a unified theory of evolution.

Various discoveries about heredity and individual development were haphazardly and belatedly incorporated into evolutionary theories in different places at different times.[22] While it is not possible to establish exactly when one evolutionary or hereditary theory became definitively accepted, it is feasible to outline when certain theories became subjects of heated debate in particular places. For example, though Weismann proclaimed the "all-sufficiency" of natural selection in the 1880s, it was not until the mid-1890s that his work became a major subject of debate. Even then, Weismann's work did not so much disprove Lamarckian notions of evolution as it ignited a wave of anti-Darwinism: Many scientists began to proudly identify themselves as neo-Lamarckian in opposition to the Weismannians (or neo-Darwinians) who were seen as extremists for supporting a Darwinism "purged of the Lamarckian element that even Darwin himself had retained."[23] And while Gregor Mendel published his groundbreaking paper on plant breeding in 1866, it was rarely read until its rediscovery in 1900 by the Dutch plant physiologist Hugo de Vries. Even after de Vries proposed that evolution could be caused by mutation rather than by changes in the environment, scientists in America, England, Germany, and Russia continued to use Mendel's theories to support a number of opposing ideas about heredity and evolution, including Lamarckian notions of inheritance. Partly because many early embryologists were explicitly opposed to integrating embryology and evolution, it took some time before the rediscovery of Mendel's paper had a substantial effect upon evolutionary theory. Rather than integrating fields, the incorporation of Mendelian theory allowed genetics to establish itself "as a distinct branch of science by divorcing the study of heredity from embryology."[24] Indeed, the most well-known biography of Mendel was written in 1924 by Hugo Iltis, a Czech-Viennese scientist who explicitly opposed Weismann's theories and supported the inheritance of acquired characteristics.[25]

Iltis was one of many scientists who maintained positions that were not clearly Darwinian or Lamarckian and who regarded heredity as an explicitly political and moral issue. Like Iltis, many of the most outspoken scientists to combine these positions worked at Hans Przibam's Vivarium, a Viennese laboratory devoted to biological experimentation to study regeneration, embryogenesis, evolution, heredity, and adaptation. Since many of the laboratory's experiments explored how changes in the environment could affect development and heredity, these scientists were by definition open to the Lamarckian idea that organisms could acquire new hereditary characteristics. While Iltis worked at Przibam's laboratory, he also wrote a number of articles for the socialist newspaper *Die Gesellschaft: Internationale Revue für Sozialismus und Politik*, in which he argued that Lamarckism and Mendelism were not only compatible, but complementary. In his criticisms of "Race

Science and Race Delusion" (the title of a 1927 article) and other "myths of race and blood" (the title of his 1936 book), Iltis argued that Mendelism and Lamarckism needed to be combined in order to avoid the hateful "delusions" supported by Weismannian logic.[26] Specifically, he took issue with the attribution of specific mental and ethical qualities to individual races and the racial hatred inspired by such politicized science. Nonetheless, Iltis did not reject eugenics or racial hygiene, and his own science could be said to have been just as motivated by political and social concerns as the Weismannians'.

Almost all the scientists working at the Vivarium were Jewish or traveled in Jewish circles that overlapped with Freud's own social scene.[27] In "The Psychogenesis of a Case of Homosexuality in a Woman" (1920), for example, Freud approvingly mentions Eugen Steinach's attempts to surgically alter individuals' sexual identification.[28] An early endocrinologist who performed experiments demonstrating that sexuality was much more malleable than previously thought, Steinach was also famous for his "rejuvenation" operations (similar to vasectomies), one of which he performed on Freud in the fall of 1923 (to alleviate his suffering from the jaw-cancer that would eventually kill him).[29] While so-called Lamarckians attempted to show that the environment could control biological heredity, Steinach's surgeries on mammalian sexual organs and his explorations of hormones were even more radical: Many scientists argued that biological heredity controls human experience, but Steinach's work suggested that humans could directly assert control over biology.[30]

Steinach's operations became famous partly through the efforts and publications of Paul Kammerer, another Viennese Vivarium scientist.[31] While Freud admiringly quoted from Kammerer's book *The Law of the Series* in his 1919 essay on "The Uncanny,"[32] Kammerer was famous (even infamous) for his experiments on midwife toads, allegedly proving that acquired characteristics could be inherited.[33] Indeed, he is often mentioned in histories of evolutionary theory as the exemplary case showing that Lamarckism is "bad science." Kammerer is portrayed as a "pseudoscientist" at least in part because of a series of public scandals involving the falsification of evidence, a state-sponsored jaunt in Communist Russia, publications on occultism and everlasting-youth, the rejection by his lover Alma Mahler (among other lovers), and finally his suicide in 1926. However, Kammerer's case is far more complex than is suggested by various histories of pseudoscience and scientific hoaxes.[34] In his frequent public lectures, Kammerer expounded on the political implications of various kinds of Darwinist eugenics, arguing that Weismannian approaches to eugenics "only tossed the unfit aside."[35] Unlike the Weismannians, Kammerer "favored programs of human improvement through education, public health measures, and medical or even surgical intervention to make individuals *acquire* heritable physical and mental improvements. He claimed in his public lectures that these potential applications made his [Darwinism] the best form of Darwinism."[36] Kammerer was not convinced by Weismann's supposed disproof of Lamarckism; rather, he claimed that Weismann's germ-plasm idea was a veiled form of teleological "creationism" from which Mendelism needed to be freed.[37] Moreover, Kammerer argued that in their "racial fanaticism," the Weismannians overly emphasized the power of selection in order to guarantee the survival of one race over all others, whereas "race hygienists" such as Kammerer were interested in understanding adaptation in order to improve the well-being of the entire human race.[38]

While neo-Darwinism and neo-Lamarckism are often discussed as if they were opposing scientific theories, the disputes among many of these scientists were both personal and political—that is, the rhetoric and logic of personal and political animosities clearly shaped their work.[39] Kammerer did not oppose Darwinism per se; he opposed Weismann's (and Weismannians') eugenics, which were associated with neo-Darwinism. "During the First World War, Kammerer developed evolutionary arguments for international cooperation and pacifism and further reduced his estimation of the role of struggle and selection. This overt subordination of science to ideology raised hackles among his colleagues, the majority of whom supported the war, and caused his reputation to suffer further."[40] Likewise, Weismann's and others' anti-Lamarckism was often expressed through personal denunciations of individual scientists, particularly Kammerer and his "Jewish" colleagues.[41] While it is unclear whether—or how—Kammerer was Jewish, many of his opponents pointed out his Jewishness in connection with his deceitful scientific practices, his Lamarckism, and his Bolshevism.[42] Similarly, in developing his germ-plasm theory, Weismann was not necessarily motivated by anti-semitism or politics, but in later life he was known to "give vent to a more than casual anti-semitism."[43] For example, in a notebook from 1910 Weismann wrote, "Kammerer (Vienna) is a little, miserable, sticky Jew, who has proven himself on earlier occasions to be a quite unreliable worker."[44]

Though Weismann's germ-plasm theory was not initially associated with anti-semitism or racism, it was soon used as fodder in the growing discussions of "racial hygiene." The first issue of the *Archive for Racial and Social Biology* (1904) was dedicated to Weismann and Ernst Haeckel, and both were named honorary chairmen when the Society for Racial Hygiene was formed the following year.[45] These institutions were not explicitly anti-semitic or right-wing in their early years, but by the end of the 1920s they developed into robust organs of anti-semitic racism.[46] One of Weismann's students, Fritz Lenz, was an early member of the society, but he is most well-known as the author of numerous articles for the *Archive* as well as a large textbook on heredity in which he clearly delineated the political and racial implications of Lamarckism. In a 1929 article on the recent Soviet film *Falschmünzer* (or *Salamandra*), which told the story of Paul Kammerer, Lenz explained that everyone involved with Kammerer was Jewish, Bolshevik, and maliciously motivated by problematic politics. Moreover, Lenz claimed that Lamarckism was particularly representative of Jews' fantasy that "by living in the German environment and adapting to German culture, Jews could become true Germans." Small wonder, Lenz explained, that all of the notable Lamarckians happened to be Jews or "half-Jews."[47] Indeed, in his foundational book on heredity, *Foundations of Human Heredity and Racial Hygiene* (1921), he even went so far as to claim that Jews were hereditarily predisposed to support Lamarckism because it was "obviously an expression of the wish that there should be no unbridgeable racial distinctions. . . . Jews do not transform themselves into Germans by writing books on Goethe."[48]

By the 1930s, when Freud was hard at work on *Moses and Monotheism*, it was clear that the "present attitude of biological science" toward Lamarckian notions of heredity was not simply a matter of scientific proof or disproof. In his 1931 article on "National Socialism's Position on Racial Hygiene," Lenz extensively and admiringly quoted from *Mein Kampf* and trumpeted Hitler's position as the "first politician with truly great influence who recognizes racial hygiene as a mission."[49] The influence and admiration was mutual: Having read Lenz's textbook on heredity in the 1920s, Hitler incorporated the racial hygiene concepts into *Mein Kampf*. In 1937, the

Nazi Party's *Handbook for Hitler Youth* (implicitly) cited Weismann's experiments as proof that racial inheritance is "always victorious over environmental influences."[50] Meanwhile, in the Soviet Union, Weismannism was denounced as bourgeois science, Kammerer was hailed as a hero, and Lamarckian notions of heredity were eventually applied to the government-controlled agricultural projects of Trofim Denisovich Lysenko, with infamously disastrous results.[51]

Though certainly not all Lamarckians or Bolsheviks were Jews (and not all Jews or Bolsheviks were Lamarckians), Lenz's comments about this connection were not purely anti-semitic lies. Indeed, Lamarckian notions of evolution did seem to support a more malleable idea of racial character that was attractive to many German Jews in this time period. In the 1920s and '30s, many Jewish scientists turned to Lamarckism to counter racist anti-semitism, particularly as Weismannism was used more and more to support anti-semitic politics and policies. For Jews, Lamarckism seemed to support the idea that the negative characteristics and conditions associated with being Jewish were the result of malleable environmental conditions (specifically, centuries of anti-semitism) rather than of *a priori* differences perpetuated by hard-wired heredity.[52] As Lenz noted, "This enables us to understand why the Lamarckian doctrine should make so strong an appeal to the Jews."[53] In his work on Jewish social scientists in the early twentieth century, Mitchell Hart suggests that many Jewish scientists relied heavily on Lamarckian environmentalism because "it allowed them to explain the particular physical or mental traits oftentimes identified as racially Jewish as historically or socially determined."[54] Thus, while Jews were often stereotypically associated with Bolshevism, they were often drawn to it partly because of a shared logic of Lamarckian environmentalism supporting the idea that the inequities of the present were determined by historical conditions that could and should be changed in the future.

Freud's Suspiciously Bolshevik Lamarckism

It is against this background that Freud's interest in the inheritance of phylogenetic memory must be understood. Freud was clearly aware of the ongoing debates between the neo-Darwinians and neo-Lamarckians, which were widely discussed in both scientific and popular journals from the 1880s through the 1930s. Indeed, throughout his work we find the names of many scientists who were most well known for their roles in these debates and for their work on the relationships between memory and heredity.[55] As I discuss in Chapter 3, between 1912 and 1920 Freud explored the works of both Weismann and Lamarck, and he eventually concluded that individuals inherit ancestral memories. Despite his obvious association with ideas that we might now term *Lamarckian*, Freud never claimed to be a Lamarckian, even when he explored Lamarck's works. Whether he avoided describing his views as Lamarckian because of the political connotations cannot be clearly determined. Yet while the political implications of Lamarckism may not have motivated Freud's initial interest in the inheritance of phylogenetic memory, he did not turn away from this idea when the political repercussions were readily apparent. As he notes in *Moses and Monotheism*, his "position, no doubt, is made more difficult by the present attitude of biological science, which refuses to hear of the inheritance of acquired characters by succeeding generations."[56]

In 1912, before publishing *Totem and Taboo*, Freud sent a draft of the new work to his friend (and eventually his biographer), Ernest Jones. In response to Freud's proposal that the Oedipal complex could be understood as the result of phylogenetic experiences, Jones anxiously responded, "I feel that you have captured an important and far-reaching idea, in pointing to the inheritance of *Verdrängung* [repression] as the result of earlier racial experiences, but I am rather in the dark as to the relation of it to the Weismann principle of the non-transmissibility of acquired characters. I hope it can stand in harmony with this, and not in contradiction."[57] With the hindsight of later developments in evolutionary theory, Jones' remark sounds quite reasonable. Since later theorists and historians of evolutionary theory point to Weismann's germ-plasm theory as the anticipation of the later Modern Synthesis (of Darwinian natural selection and Mendelian heredity), it would seem that Freud should have heeded Jones' suggestion that the inheritance of phylogenetic experience (such as memory and repression) was not compatible with Weismann's anti-Lamarckian theory.[58] Yet Freud had ample reason to ignore Jones' comment. To begin with, Freud already suspected Jones of overzealously rejecting hereditary explanations. Upon first meeting Jones in 1908, Freud wrote to Jung, saying that Jones "is a fanatic. . . . [H]e denies all heredity; to his mind even I am a reactionary."[59] More generally, Jones' and Freud's distinct perspectives on heredity and evolution reflect the discrepancies between their scientific communities' responses to the Mendelian and Weismannian "revolutions." For example, in the English-speaking world the emergence of genetics marked the end of the credibility of the inheritance of acquired characteristics, but the same was not true in the German-speaking world.[60] As English scientists such as T. H. Morgan attempted to distinguish the new field of genetics from evolutionary theory, they also distinguished between individual and phylogenetic development much more quickly than the German scientists. Meanwhile, German scientists "refused to accept this rigid distinction and allowed cytoplasmic inheritance" to continue to shape evolutionary theory "in ways that seemed outlandish to English-speaking geneticists."[61]

In the years following the publication of *Totem and Taboo* Freud continued to explore both Weismann's and Lamarck's works without mentioning any sense of contradiction between the two. In his essay "On Narcissism" (1914), Freud explicitly referred to Weismann's germ-plasm theory (which I will discuss more in Chapter 3). And the following year he composed "A Phylogenetic Fantasy," in which he incorporated the Lamarckian idea of the inheritance of memory (but which was left unpublished until 1987). Freud sent a draft of this work, tentatively entitled "Overview of the Transference Neuroses," to his friend Sandor Ferenczi, with whom he enthusiastically shared his emerging ideas about the parallels between individual and phylogenetic development. From 1916 to 1918 Freud and Ferenczi intermittently discussed the possibility of co-writing a work about Lamarck and psychoanalysis. In December 1916 Freud wrote to Ferenczi to tell him that he had ordered "the Lamarck" from the university library. On January 1, 1917, he sent a "sketch of the Lamarck-work," a paper apparently not preserved, and reported that he had begun reading Lamarck's *Zoological Philosophy* (1809).[62]

Despite his enthusiasm for the "Lamarck-work" in the summers of 1917 and 1918, Freud never actually followed through with his plans to fill in the details of the "sketch." The problem was not that he lacked interest but rather that the difficulties presented by the volatile political situation in Europe pulled his concerns in a decidedly more practical direction. In March 1917 Freud wrote to Ferenczi about the lack of progress on the Lamarck-work: "I have not progressed either. . . . In the weeks of cold and darkness I stopped working in the evening—and have not got back to it since then."[63] By May 1917, he wrote again, despondent about the difficulties presented by the war: "I am not at all disposed to doing the work on Lamarck in the summer and would prefer to relinquish the whole thing to you."[64] As World War I and its fallout drastically affected the European economy and life in general, Freud became less interested in studying Lamarck's works than with maintaining a basic standard of living: He was far more concerned about the welfare of his sons (who were on the warfront), with acquiring basic provisions, and with maintaining psychoanalytic institutions and publications.[65] While Freud seems to have begun to doubt whether Lamarck was the solution to his theoretical problems, the main issue was that "because of the war, there were difficulties in getting the literature." As Grubrich-Simitis suggests, "Ultimately the external emergency situation, which was reaching crisis level, may also have had an inhibiting effect."[66] By the end of 1918 Freud's pursuit of Lamarck seems to have fallen by the wayside.[67]

Because of objections from the victorious powers in the autumn of 1918, the Fifth International Psycho-Analytical Congress was moved from Breslau to Budapest, home of Ferenczi. In the wake of the successful congress attended by representatives from the Austrian, German, and Hungarian governments,[68] there were two developments that are significant because they suggest that Freud moved directly from his theoretical interests in Lamarck to practical concerns that were nonetheless shaped by his interest in Lamarckism and its ties to Bolshevism. At the congress, Freud delivered his paper on "Lines of Advance in Psycho-Analytic Therapy" (1919), which he had written the summer before while he was staying with his friend Anton von Freund in a suburb of Budapest.[69] While the paper focused on "active" psychoanalytic methods (associated with Ferenczi), it also reflected the political context in which it was delivered. Freud fantasized about a "psychotherapy for the people" and proclaimed that

> at some time or other the conscience of society will awake and remind it that the poor man should have just as much right to assistance for his mind as he now has to the life-saving help offered by surgery. . . . It may be a long time before the State comes to see these duties as urgent. . . . Probably these institutions will first be started by private charity.[70]

While Freud imagined a time in which the State would assist the poor man, he recognized that such radical changes were not likely in the near future.

As for a private charity, there were rumors that von Freund considered leaving his large fortune to found just such an institution. As Abraham reported to Freud in August 1919, "things are good in our group . . . your appeal in Budapest fell on fertile ground. The polyclinic will be opened in the winter, and will grow into a psychoanalytic institute."[71] While psychoanalysis had originally been the province of well-to-do families with ample money to support such involved methods of therapy, in 1919 Freud had high hopes that its methods could be used to improve the conditions of the less fortunate and that institutions could be set up to accomplish these transformations. Like many scientists who explicitly supported Lamarckian notions of heredity, Freud believed that poverty and sickness were not permanent conditions and that they could be improved and transformed by providing therapy.[72]

The second important development in the wake of the Fifth International Congress was the meteoric rise and subsequent fall of Ferenczi, and psychoanalysis more generally, in Budapest. During the brief time in which the Bolsheviks ruled the Austro-Hungarian empire, Ferenczi became increasingly active in public life, both as a psychoanalyst and as a member of the Social Democratic Union of doctors. In a letter to Freud in November 1918, Ferenczi announced, "Your prophecy about our imminent proletarianization has come true."[73] During 1918–19 hundreds of Hungarian students signed petitions requesting that psychoanalysis be taught at the Royal Medical School at the University of Budapest. By April 1919 Ferenczi was appointed as a professor and as director of the newly established psychoanalytic clinic sponsored by the new Bolshevik state.[74] However, Ferenczi's Bolshevik honeymoon lasted only 120 days; by August 1919 the newly established Hungarian Soviet Republic was falling apart and the White Terror had begun. Jews, Leftists, Bolsheviks, and all those suspected of such "crimes" were fired from their jobs, beaten, and generally terrorized. Ferenczi was forced out of his university position, expelled from the Medical Society, and forced to abandon his projects, including the free clinic and the long-planned collaborative work on Lamarck. While it is likely that Ferenczi was fired as much for being Jewish as for being a Bolshevik, Freud evidently understood the situation in terms of politics. As he wrote to Abraham in June 1920, "Ferenczi has now been excluded from the Budapest Medical Society as a penalty for his Bolshevik professorship. As a consequence of the still existing letter censorship I could only congratulate him on the honor."[75]

The dangerous connections between Jewishness, Bolshevism, and certain dubious scientific theories (such as Lamarckism) were implicitly recognized by Ernest Jones. Though he never directly linked Freud's Lamarckism with any accusations of Bolshevism, Jones was notoriously worried about maintaining the scientific reputation of psychoanalysis and protecting it from Freud's "non-scientific" concerns. For example, in February 1926 Jones wrote to Freud asking him to publicly play down his previously private interest in telepathy because it seemed to detract from the scientific reputation of psychoanalysis, particularly in England. "In your private political opinions," writes Jones, "you might be a Bolshevist, but you would not help the spread of psychoanalysis by announcing it."[76] In response, Freud avoided direct reference to the suggestion that he was privately a Bolshevist and instead compared the situation to

> the great experiment of my life: namely, to proclaim a conviction without taking into account any echo from the outer world. . . . When anyone adduces my fall into sin, just answer him calmly that my acceptance of telepathy is my private affair like my Jewishness, my passion for smoking and many other things, and that the theme of telepathy is in essence alien [*wesenfremd*] to psychoanalysis.[77]

In addition to totally disregarding Jones' comment about Bolshevism, Freud's response is riddled with obvious contradictions. While he insists that he would not change his public convictions because of "any echo from the outer world," he goes on to note that certain things—Jewishness, smoking, and telepathy—are private affairs. Each of these is wildly different: Jewishness was (arguably) something that Freud could not change even if he wanted to, and something he often avoided discussing publicly; smoking was a habit that numerous people do give up, though with much difficulty; and telepathy was a phenomenon whose existence Freud considered plausible. While these things belong to different categories, there is a sense that they are related: There is a sense that there was no choice in these matters. It was not possible to just stop being Jewish, and it was not so easy to give up smoking or a belief in telepathy,[78] or perhaps, for that matter, Bolshevism or Lamarckism.[79] However, if they were pursued too publicly or persistently, Freud knew, they could endanger his life and work.[80]

By the time Freud wrote *Moses and Monotheism* he was excruciatingly aware of the accusation that psychoanalysis was regarded as one example of a "Jewish-Bolshevist science." In particular, Freud worried about publishing the third part of the book in which he speculates about how the "inheritance of acquired characters" shaped the Jewish people, and he waited until he was safely stowed away in England to publish this section.[81] In a letter to Arnold Zweig (and in both of the prefaces to the third section of the book), Freud explained that he feared that the new material would offend the Catholic Church, which he regarded as one of the few remaining sources of protection from the Nazis' anti-semitic policies. Specifically, he worried about a certain Pater Wilhelm Schmidt who, he notes, was

> a confidant of the Pope, and unfortunately he himself is an ethnologist and a student of comparative religion, whose books make no secret of his abhorrence of analysis and especially of my totem theory. . . . Any publication of mine will be sure to attract a certain amount of attention, which will not escape the notice of this inimical priest.[82]

While Freud clearly knew a fair bit about Schmidt, here he tells only part of the story. Schmidt was an anthropologist of international reputation who founded the journal *Anthropos* and the Anthropos Institute, both of which still exist today.[83] Like many Catholics in the 1930s, Schmidt opposed the Nazis' *racial* anti-semitism as well as their policies regarding selective breeding and eugenics.[84] While the Nazis emphasized the Jews' racial difference, Schmidt emphasized their *cultural* difference, or the "cultural concept of '*Volkstum*,'" based on a people's spiritual history.[85] While this idea understandably found favor with American anthropologists such as Franz Boas and A. L. Kroeber, it also allowed Schmidt to proclaim anti-semitic positions that, even as they were less racial, were no less virulent.[86] For example, in an article on the "Racial Principle of National Socialism," he rejects the "materialistic concept of race" and explains that "the Jews are not fundamentally racially distinct from the Aryan peoples." Instead, he argues, their difference could be found in the "very structure of their souls." Because of their rejection of Christ, the Jewish people "are a nation which in the deepest depths of their soul are uprooted. Precisely because of that, their evil and dangerous characteristics emerged which can in no way be reduced to material biological racial-concepts."[87] Thus Schmidt might have criticized Freud's racial theory of Jewishness because it suggested that the Jews' distinctions were biologically inherited.[88]

Schmidt's general abhorrence of psychoanalysis was not unrelated to his critique of racism and Bolshevism, both of which he found overly mired in the materialism of the modern world.[89] By the early 1930s, Schmidt was well known not only for his anthropological studies of race, religion, and culture, but also for his extensive and virulent attacks on psychoanalysis.[90] The two topics came together in a 1928 lecture entitled "The Oedipus Complex of Freudian Psychoanalysis and the Marriage-Ideal of Bolshevism." Here, he transfers his vitriol against "Jewish Bolshevism" onto the materialism of psychoanalytic theory. Schmidt argues that Freud's theory of the Oedipus complex is not simply wrong according to other anthropological studies, but worse: Like Bolshevism, it destroyed the institutions of marriage and the family, institutions that were central to Christian civilization.[91] In this lecture Schmidt does not directly link his attacks on Freud, psychoanalysis, or Bolshevism to the "Jewishness" of these movements, but the connections would have been readily made by Schmidt's readers. In 1920, Schmidt had presented a lecture entitled "Free Vienna from Jewish Bolshevism!" which was published in the same Catholic newspaper that later published his essays critiquing psychoanalysis.[92] By the time Freud moved to London and published the third part of *Moses*, he finally realized that the Catholic Church would not protect the Jewish people. In the second preface to the third part, written in June 1938, he notes that with the Nazis' invasion "Catholicism proved, to use the words of the Bible, 'a broken reed.'" Now Freud acknowledged "the certainty that I should now be persecuted not only for my line of thought but also for my 'race.'"[93] And he resolved to publish the final portion of his work in which he explicitly explored the relationship between his line of thought and his race.

Jones' Biography and Its Misguided Consequences

As one of the first and most vocal critics of Freud's so-called Lamarckism, Jones must have been aware of the dangers of publicly supporting a Bolshevik- or Lamarckian-sounding theory of inheritance, both in the 1930s (when Freud wrote *Moses*) and later in the 1950s (when Jones wrote his seminal biography of Freud). Indeed, in the biography he acknowledges that Freud and Marx were often lumped together as Jewish thinkers whose thought was "not only compatible but mutually complementary."[94] While he lists a number of scholars, such as Bernfeld and Simmel, who were well known for attempting to synthesize psychoanalysis with Marxism, he also includes the name of Pater Schmidt and cites Schmidt's work "The Oedipus Complex of Freudian Psychoanalysis and the Marriage-Ideal of Bolshevism."[95] However, nowhere in the biography does Jones connect psychoanalysis' associations with Bolshevism to the political connotations of Freud's Lamarckism. Rather, like many scholars after him, Jones insists that the issue of Freud's Lamarckism was purely scientific: The inheritance of acquired characters had been "scientifically" disproven, and Freud chose to disregard the evidence. Indeed, in all the secondary literature on the history of psychoanalysis, I have seen no discussion of the political implications of Freud's Lamarckism.[96]

Part of this confusion derives, I think, from Jones' 1953 biography in which he constructs a misleading and inaccurate picture of Freud's use of biological theories. While there is ample evidence that Freud rejected the idea of inherited memory until around 1912, Jones claims that "Freud remained from the beginning to the end of his life what one must call an obstinate adherent of this discredited Lamarckism."[97] Despite such statements, Jones clearly knew that Freud had earlier resisted the idea of inherited memory because in 1912 he had written Freud a letter about the extraordinary shift in *Totem and Taboo*. In the biography Jones also reports that he had had little success in finding allusions to Darwinism in Freud's work, adding, however, that Freud does refer "of course, to the doctrine of Natural Selection."[98] In fact, throughout his career Freud cited Darwin as a prominent influence, especially in *Totem and Taboo*, the work in which he began to incorporate the idea that phylogenetic memory may be inherited.[99] Indeed, in an attempt to defend Freud against such specious claims that he was a Lamarckian, Lucille Ritvo shows that Freud was overwhelmingly influenced by Darwin (rather than by Lamarck) from his days as a student in the 1870s to his final work.[100]

According to Jones, Freud's continued insistence on Lamarckian principles is the "extraordinary part of the story, which provides us with a baffling problem in the study of the development of Freud's ideas, and also in that of his personality."[101] Not only is Jones' perplexity slightly disingenuous, his internal logic is inconsistent. As proof that Lamarckism had been "completely discredited for more than half a century"—that is, since 1903—Jones quotes a passage from Julian Huxley's *1953* book, *Evolution in Action*:

> All the theories lumped together under the heads of biogenesis and Lamarckism are invalidated. . . . They are no longer consistent with the facts. Indeed, in the

light of modern discoveries, they no longer deserve to be called scientific theories, but can be seen as speculations without due basis of reality, or old superstitions disguised in modern dress. They were natural enough in their time, when we were still ignorant of the mechanism of heredity; but they have now only an historical interest.[102]

As one of the founders of the Modern Synthesis of Darwinian natural selection in the 1940s, Huxley was deeply invested in propagating the idea of a single line of theoretical development from Darwin to the Modern Synthesis. Moreover, Huxley—and, by extension, Jones—echoes the rhetoric of earlier neo-Darwinians (or Weismannians) who portrayed their Lamarckian opponents as foolishly stubborn and superstitious. For example, in 1918 one German geneticist complained that "educators, philosophers, and socialists clutch maliciously and persistently to the belief in the inheritance of acquired characters," and claimed that anyone who maintained such beliefs could only be the product of "the crudest biological ignorance" and old-fashioned "superstition."[103]

By the time Freud was writing *Moses*, Jones must have seen Freud's "insistence" on the inheritance of acquired characteristics as a major liability for the reputation of psychoanalysis.[104] As Jones recounts in the 1953 biography (with the wisdom of hindsight, of course), he "begged [Freud] to omit the passage" in *Moses* where Freud insisted on the biological inheritance of acquired characters. He goes on to recount the conversation he had with Freud regarding this particular passage:

> I told him he had *of course* the right to hold any opinion he liked in his own field of psychology, even if it ran counter to all biological principles, but *begged* him to omit the passage where he applied it to the whole field of biological evolution, since no responsible biologist regarded it as tenable any longer. *All he would say* was that they were all wrong and the passage must stay. And he documented this recalcitrance in the book with the following words: "This state of affairs is made more difficult, it is true, by the present attitude of biological science, which rejects the idea of acquired qualities being transmitted to descendants. I admit, in all modesty, that in spite of this I cannot picture biological development proceeding without taking this factor into account."[105]

In addition to the gross oversimplification of evolutionary history and the patronizing phrases ("I told him he had *of course* the right to hold any opinion he liked"), Jones actually misquotes Freud. In his bibliography Jones cites Strachey's *Standard Edition* as the source for all translations of Freud's work from which he quotes. However, in this passage he quotes from (his wife) Katherine Jones' translation of *Moses*.[106] This might be understandable if for some reason Strachey's translation seemed linguistically inaccurate (as it is known to be in many instances). However, Jones' misquotation (or rather, mistranslation) conceals the sentiment of Freud's original German, which is better retained in the *Standard Edition*'s translation. In actuality—in the German and also in the *Standard Edition*—Freud does not concede that biological science *rejects* the inheritance of acquired characteristics, but (as the *Standard Edition* translates it) that contemporary biological science "*refuses to hear of* the inheritance of acquired characters by successive generations [*biologischen Wissenschaft . . . , die von der Vererbung erworbener Eigenschaften auf die Nachkommen* nichts wissen will]"[107]—or, as a more literal translation of the German might read, "they want to hear nothing of it."

If Jones was worried about the consequences of Freud's Lamarckism in the 1930s, by the time he reconstructed the narrative in the 1953 biography he could only have been more apprehensive about this aspect of psychoanalytic theory. In the 1950s there were additional reasons why he depicted Freud's Lamarckism as the irrational obstinacy of genius rather than as a legitimate scientific position with dangerous political implications. Where Lamarckism was (ideologically and scientifically) suspect in the 1930s, by the late 1940s it was even more untenable—ridiculed and disdained—particularly in the West.[108] It is well known that from the 1930s to the 1960s Lysenko attempted to apply the Lamarckian idea of the inheritance of acquired characters to Soviet agriculture with disastrous results. Until Richard Levins and Richard Lewontin's work in the 1980s, most Western historians regarded the failures of Lysenkoism as yet another instance of the disasters that ensue when "pure" science is sullied by politics and ideology.[109] Not only was Lamarckism regarded as scientifically disproven, but it was also regarded as a prime example of "bad" (read "ideologically motivated") science. Moreover, in the 1950s, scientists and historians were beginning to come to terms with Nazis' use of biological theories to support their horrific ideological "solution," and nothing could seem worse for a scientist's reputation than to be associated with a scientific theory that appeared ideologically motivated. Jones must have been aware of the potential effects of allowing psychoanalysis to be associated with Lamarckism—a theory that was regarded not only as scientifically outmoded, but, more important, as suspiciously motivated by political (rather than purely scientific) ideals.

At the end of his chapter on Freud's use of biology, Jones seems to throw up his hands in exasperation, suggesting that maybe Freud's "Lamarckism" can be understood as a side-effect of his genius or his Jewish background. "It is not easy to account for the fixity with which Freud held this opinion and the determination with which he ignored all the biological evidence to the contrary."[110] Given Freud's belief in the omnipotence of thoughts originating in early childhood emotional experiences, Jones writes, maybe Freud's stubborn and superstitious insistence on Lamarckism can be understood as a result of his early childhood experiences with Judaism. As if such speculation were too wild to state explicitly, Jones ventures, "Was an ineffaceable mark left on his mind when he learned as a child that God visits the iniquity of the fathers upon the children, to the third and fourth generation?"[111] The idea that Freud's "Lamarckism" might be explained as an "ineffaceable mark" of Jewishness may sound preposterous, but it was not far off.

Was Lamarckism Jewish?

Freud's so-called Lamarckism can be understood as particularly Jewish not only because it was regarded as such in the 1930s, but also because of the ways in which it seems to get at the sense—shared by Jews and Gentiles alike—of the "ineffaceability" of Jewishness. Before the discovery of genetic mutation, Lamarckism was often seen as an answer to the question of how populations change over time. During the 1920s and '30s, however, the assertion of Lamarckism came to be seen as a claim that human groups were malleable, and in Germany (if not elsewhere), this suggested that Jews could lose their distinctive Jewish characteristics and become fully German, whether intentionally (through conversion or active attempts to assimilate) or unintentionally (through a gradual process of assimilation and integration). While Lamarckian heredity was described as "soft" because of its emphasis on evolutionary *change*, Weismannian heredity was referred to as "hard" because it suggested that the materials of life were permanent. Yet Freud's use of these theories was idiosyncratic (as I discuss further in Chapter 3). As he tried to better understand the "historically derived" origins of seemingly universal conflicts such as war and aggression, Freud began to reconsider the possibility of inherited memory. Ultimately, he embraced the inheritance of memory when he recognized that these conflicts were persistent and permanent. In his final book, Freud showed that the "special character of the Jewish people" was *historically* derived, but it was the *inheritance* of this character that had ensured the people's persistent survival.[112]

No less a scholar than Yerushalmi has followed Jones' suggestions that Freud's Lamarckism was both scientifically misguided and peculiarly Jewish. In *Freud's Moses*, Yerushalmi pays special attention to Freud's "stubborn" refusal to "expunge these embarrassing elements" of Lamarckism from his last book. While he admits that "the truly decisive revolutions in molecular biology and genetics were not to take place until after his death," Yerushalmi nonetheless seems perplexed that Freud insisted on Lamarckism despite the fact that he "was always aware that Lamarckism was under sharp *scientific* attack."[113] Like Jones, Yerushalmi responds to Freud's Lamarckism as if it were both surprising and surprisingly Jewish. "I find myself wondering," he writes, "whether . . . Freud's Jewishness . . . played a role in his Lamarckian predilections."[114] While Yerushalmi seems about to concede (à la Lenz) that Lamarckism might be particularly Jewish—he steps around this distasteful possibility and adds, "No, I am not implying that Lamarckism is 'Jewish.'"[115] Acutely aware of the problematic presumption that a scientific theory could be particularly Jewish, he nonetheless goes on to concede that Freud's Lamarckism might be *persuasively* Jewish, at least in "subjective" terms:

> Deconstructed into Jewish terms, what is Lamarckism if not the powerful feeling that, for better or worse, one cannot really cease being Jewish, and this not merely because of current anti-Semitism or discrimination . . . but because one's fate in being Jewish was determined long ago by the Fathers.[116]

Though Yerushalmi critiques Freud's overly literal Lamarckism, he notes that Freud's theory of Jewishness gets at "the sense that Jewishness is both inherited and indelible," a sense that is "shared equally by Jews who . . . would discard their Jewish identity if they could, as well as by Jews who passionately affirmed that identity."[117] Indeed, this sense of the indelibility of Jewishness is shared not only by both proud and self-hating Jews, but also by philo- and anti-semitic non-Jews.[118]

While Yerushalmi articulates a positive sense of the inalienability of Jewishness, the idea that Jewishness is some sort of "ineffaceable mark" has uncomfortable similarities with anti-semitic racism. It is impossible to de-termine whether Freud's sense that Jewishness was ineffaceable was the re-sult of his Jewish education (as Jones suggests),[119] or whether it was the result of his "education" in anti-semitic racism. The racialization of Jewish-ness by Jews and non-Jews, philo-semites and anti-semites, suggests that racialism is not necessarily the problem. In an odd example of historical revision, the philosopher Richard Bernstein takes *Yerushalmi* to task for sug-gesting that Freud believed in Lamarckian inheritance and, by extension, biological and racial Jewishness. Directly addressing Yerushalmi in his "dia-logue," Bernstein writes,

> you seem to be accusing Freud of the type of racism that . . . was to become the
> backbone of Nazi anti-Semitism. If there are Jewish "character traits" that are
> "transmitted phylogenetically and no longer require religion," then there is a
> biological basis for singling out Jews for extermination regardless of their pro-
> fessed religious convictions. This is why I find the claim that you keep reiterating
> so disturbing—that Freud believes Jewish acquired character traits are phyloge-
> netically transmitted by biological mechanisms.[120]

While Bernstein's reproach may be historically inaccurate, what is more interesting is that it reveals an intense discomfort with any suggestion that Jewishness is racially determined.[121] In fact, it is not only biological defini-tions that allow the "singling out [of] Jews [or any other group] for extermi-nation": biology is just one among many methods of defining a group of people. *Any* definition of a group that is used to single individuals out for extermination—whether it is self-determined identifications such as reli-gious convictions or hereditary conditions such as skin color—is equally pernicious and morally reprehensible. Thus to shift the identification of Jews or any other group from biology to self-determination does not protect against the kinds of evils that were perpetrated by the Nazis. After all, there has been a long history of anti-semitism and other forms of oppression based not on biological typology but on economic, political, and religious categories (as in the case of Pater Schmidt), and even on religious rituals (such as circumcision) meant to transfer Jewishness from one generation to the next.[122] It would be a lot easier to combat racism and anti-semitism if they were simply matters of misguided scientific understandings of race from another era.

Is Psychoanalysis a Jewish Science?

Throughout his life Freud insisted that psychoanalysis was a universal science (as opposed to a Jewish Science [*Jüdische Wissenschaft*], a phrase that explicitly refers to a field of scholarship focused on Jewish life and letters and as such suggests a limited scope for psychoanalysis). From the 1890s until the end of his life he worried that psychoanalysis would be regarded as a "Jewish national affair [*eine jüdische nationale Angelegenheit*]."[123] As Freud writes in a letter to his friend Ferenczi in 1913, "there should not be such a thing as Aryan or Jewish science. Results in science must be identical, though the presentation of them may vary."[124] While he hints at the question of whether a science that is differently *presented* is still the same science, he also implicitly recognizes the ideological nature imputed to a science that is characterized as either Aryan or Jewish. Indeed, Freud's incorporation of the inheritance of phylogenetic memory can be seen as an attempt to move beyond the ideological (religious and historical) distinctions that might separate Aryans from Jews, or Aryan from Jewish science. No longer limited by his patients' particular memories of Viennese childhoods, Freud could claim a "universal validity" for psychoanalysis as a "transcultural statement on the human condition."[125] It was not until *Moses*, however, that he turned to phylogenetic memory as a way of understanding the persistent survival of a particular people.

While Freud insisted that psychoanalysis was not a Jewish science, in the end such claims of universality ironically underscored the Jewishness of psychoanalysis. In German-speaking countries, by the 1930s it was clear that Jewish and Aryan scientists did not necessarily share the same goals, even if they concurred on certain theoretical questions. According to the logic of the Nazis, the promotion of a scientific theory as universal—or in its more coded descriptions, "international" and "trans-historical"[126]—was a form of anti-German (Jewish) conspiracy. Despite the fact that the Nazis frankly promoted their own *volkisch* ideals of science, they maintained that *their* science was free from the taint of politics and religion (of which they accused "liberal-Jewish-Bolshevist science").[127] In their attempts to unite Germany as a *Volksstaat* [nation of the people], the Nazis attempted to "replace the divisive emphasis on class by a unifying emphasis on race," and to replace the language of politics with that of science.[128] While "politics" stank of class differences and "special interests," science had been something of which Germans could be unabashedly proud. By 1933 Germany and Austria had been awarded more than one-third of all Nobel Prizes, even if many of these were awarded to scientists of Jewish descent.[129] The Nazis proudly used Nietzsche's phrase "no science without suppositions" as a slogan supporting the idea that all science—and all parts of society—should nourish and nurture the German nation.[130] As Gerhard Wagner, the head of the Nazi Physicians' League, noted in 1934, "there is no longer any *German* science without the National Socialist *Weltanschauung* as its *first* presupposition."[131] Ironically, then, both scientists *and* politicians avoided the value-laden language of politics and appealed to the supposedly neutral authority of science. While the language of science appeared value-free, the debates themselves were burdened with the political exigencies of the time period.

In the wake of World War II many scientists attempted to distance themselves from the Nazis' racist "pseudo-science" by claiming that *good* science was value-free. As Robert Proctor writes, "Value-neutrality allowed one to argue that *genuine science* could not have been implicated in the crimes of the period, despite substantial evidence to the contrary. For anti-Nazi critics, by contrast, the tragedy of German science was in having allowed itself to become politicized; German scientists had failed to remain value-neutral, and it was this failure that was responsible for the excesses of the period."[132] Similarly, many historians of psychoanalysis such as Jones and Peter Gay have attempted to protect the scientific legacy of Freud's work from his other enthusiasms and from the various claims that psychoanalysis may be a Jewish science. Particularly problematic in this context, then, is Freud's enthusiastic defense of the inheritance of acquired characteristics: It seems non-scientific both because the theory is no longer scientifically accepted,[133] and because (at least in part) it seems related to Freud's sense of his own Jewishness, if not also his politics. During Freud's lifetime, psychoanalysis was regarded as a Jewish science both because of anti-semitic accusations *and* because of Jewish ethnic pride. And, in many ways, the situation has not changed: as Yerushalmi notes, despite all attempts to the contrary, "history made psychoanalysis a 'Jewish science.'"[134]

Within the fields of science studies and history of science, it has become *de rigueur* to note that there is no science without values and that "all science is social."[135] Indeed. If, however, we simply follow Michel Foucault's claim that all science is social, we risk overlooking the most important questions that attend all forms of knowledge, whether in the sciences or the humanities. The question is not whether psychoanalysis is (or was) a Jewish science but rather what goals it served then and what our engagement with it serves now. What did Freud think he was doing in developing a "scientific" racial theory of Jewishness in the 1930s?

Even before Freud had published all of *Moses and Monotheism*, he was besieged by letters of protest "calling him to account for the enormity he had committed." As Gay recounts, "anxious scholars visited him in London to talk him out of publishing the book." Why, they wondered, had he published such a book "in a time of terrible travail, with the Nazi persecution of the Jews in Germany and Austria intensifying beyond the bounds of the most vicious czarist pogroms"?[136] Most of their protests were focused on Freud's shocking proposal that Moses was an Egyptian rather than an Israelite. Yet Freud addresses these concerns in the opening sentence of *Moses*: "To deprive a people of the man whom they take pride in as the greatest of their sons is not a thing to be gladly or carelessly undertaken, least of all by someone who is himself one of them." As if totally disregarding the letters of protest, he continues: "But we cannot allow any such reflection to induce us to put the truth aside in favour of what *are supposed to be* national interests."[137] Here Freud intimates that he actually *does* have "national interests" in mind; they are simply different from what others think they "are supposed to be."

Perhaps because of Jan Assmann's stunning book on the mnemohistory of Moses the Egyptian, or perhaps because of Edward Said's passionate lecture about Freud's identification with a non-European Moses, the proposal that Moses was an Egyptian no longer seems so shocking.[138] In the past two decades, readers have been persistently troubled by Freud's insistence on the idea that Jewishness is constituted by the biological inheritance of the memory of the murder of Moses. According to Freud, certain people are Jewish not because they believe in one god, keep kosher, circumcise their sons, or any other number of supposedly singularly Jewish beliefs, practices, or proclivities; people are Jewish *not* because they have learned about Judaism from "direct communication" or from "the influence of education."[139] Rather, people are Jewish simply because they inherit the "memory-traces of the experience of our ancestors." This is shocking stuff, particularly at a time when we are supposed to have progressed beyond such essentialist definitions of individuals' identities. Freud's theory of Jewishness is a *racial* theory of cultural memory because it insists that culture derives from race rather than the other way around. It is only when people inherit Jewishness that their belief in one god—or their circumcision of their sons, or their support of Israel, or their affection for bagels—constitutes "Jewish culture."[140] Otherwise they are simply things that historically (but not exclusively) have been associated with people who have inherited Jewishness. As Walter Benn Michaels writes, "all accounts of cultural identity require a racial component. . . . For insofar as our culture remains nothing more than what we do and believe, it is impotently descriptive."[141]

While American ideals of freedom might suggest otherwise, cultural identity is not simply a set of activities and beliefs that are individually and voluntarily chosen like some brand of toothpaste at the Superstore of Cultural Identity. Cultural identity often has as much to do with what a person does *not* do and believe and what one explicitly rejects and attempts to escape. Like race, cultural identity is often experienced as something from which one cannot escape, deriving from a number of clues that (creatively, problematically, imaginatively) refer to a person's past or genealogy. When such clues are unavailable or unclear, many people go searching for evidence through adoption agencies, genealogy societies, and, more recently, DNA testing. While DNA tests have revealed some surprising results, people often go searching for "proof" of what they already know or believe— that is, they go to specific DNA-testing services that have access to specific gene pool groups.[142] It seems undeniable that "our account of the past may be partially determined by our own identity,"[143] but the opposite is also true: Our identities are determined by our (always selective) accounts and knowledge of our pasts.

Like many other racial theories, Freud's theory of Jewishness is in no way consistent or simple. Nowhere does he insist that the mother needs to be Jewish for the child to inherit Jewish tradition; nowhere does he even specify that one (or the other) grandparent needs to be Jewish. All individuals inherit "mixtures of blood" and phylogenetic pasts: Counting back ten generations, an individual has 1,024 ancestors.[144] It is more than likely that at least one of these was someone who would be identified as something other than Jewish or, more generally, something other than the identity of the present individual.[145] This means that at any particular time there are far more people who (retrospectively, strictly genealogically) "inherit" Jewishness than there are people who call themselves Jewish. As Marc Shell suggests, the literal conceptualization of genealogical inheritance and kinship is founded upon a "key fiction, namely, that we can really know who are our consanguineous kin."[146] Freud's theory of Jewishness suggests that at some point down the genealogical line—whether literal or figural, real or fictive—the repressed will return, the memory will be "awakened," and the person will return to this "archaic" past.[147] This is not a "one-drop rule" of present identity, but a one-drop concept of future possibilities.[148]

While many Jewish leaders worry that the next generation will "forget" that they are Jewish, large numbers of people are discovering (or remembering) that they have inherited Jewish pasts.[149] The Nazis' "one-drop rule" ironically made the attempt to wipe out the Jewish people practically impossible—somewhere, at some point in time, there will be someone whose inheritance of Jewishness will be "awakened," and who will "return" to make sense of this past. Indeed, in Germany today there are widespread reports of people who previously thought that all of their grandparents were Germans who had been somehow guilty of either joining with the Nazis or quietly standing by during the Holocaust. A number of these people have recently discovered that one grandparent was Jewish (or even "half-Jewish"), and this is radically changing their perspectives on what counts as their history. No longer are they burdened with only the guilt of the perpetrator; now they are also burdened with the guilt of the victim who survives all others.[150] Likewise, *Ba'alei Teshuvah* has emerged as a full-scale movement of individuals who, having grown up in secular homes, "return" to practice an Orthodox Judaism that they never before knew. Despite the dire predictions of various social-science studies of Jewish population,[151] such "returns" to tradition continue to emerge and expand the numbers of people who willingly define themselves through their Jewish past.[152] How and why does this happen? Why do people (creatively) turn to the past to define their lives in the present?

Freud is certainly not responsible for posing these questions, but his work has provided a context and a language in which to explore these phenomena. In incorporating the idea of the inheritance of acquired characteristics, Freud developed a theory of Jewishness that accounts both for the seemingly universal compulsion to turn to our pasts to make sense of our presents, and for the particularly Jewish notion that one's Jewish identity (or lack thereof) is genealogically determined. Whereas most forms of Christianity define Christians as individuals who believe in or relate to Jesus Christ as a savior, Judaism (that is, the normative texts and traditions of Judaism since at least the fifth century) generally defines a Jew as anyone born of a Jewish parent.[153] This particularly Jewish notion emerged as a more universal concept of racialization in Europe in the nineteenth century, at least in part because of the increasing secularity of Western societies and because of the development of new scientific knowledge about heredity and evolution.[154] As Freud developed theories to explain the origins of hysteria, neurosis, sexuality, culture, and, finally, the Jewish people, he explicitly engaged with ongoing debates regarding race, heredity, and evolution. While these debates may appear strictly scientific, they were—and continue to be—shaped by the scientists' values and ideals. This is not to suggest that a person's or a society's values cannot be changed or shaped by scientific discoveries. However, the very nature of the questions we ask and the answers we seek are shaped by the societies in which we live.

THREE

Circumcision: The Unconscious Root of the Problem

In spite of all our efforts to prevent biological terminology and considerations from dominating psychoanalytic work, we cannot avoid using them even in our descriptions of the phenomena that we study. We cannot help regarding the term "instinct" as a concept on the frontier between the spheres of psychology and biology.

FREUD, "The Claims of Psycho-Analysis
for Scientific Interest" (1913)

Moses did not only give the Jews a new religion; it can be stated with equal certainty that he introduced the custom of circumcision to them. This fact is of decisive importance for our problem and has scarcely ever been considered.

FREUD, *Moses and Monotheism* (1939)

Circumcision as Counter-Evidence

Freud was well aware that there was ample evidence to suggest that acquired characteristics are not inherited. Indeed, the most paradigmatic mark of Jewishness—circumcision—would seem to be proof that acquired characteristics are not inherited since the rite must be performed in every generation for its (physical) effects to be transmitted. Not surprisingly, the subject of Jewish circumcision—and the Jewish Question more generally—often appeared in the footnotes of treatises on evolution and heredity in the late nineteenth century.[1] As Freud began to engage with the ongoing debates about race, culture, and evolution, he also began to refer to circumcision in the footnotes of his own texts. Indeed, the topic of circumcision compelled him to rethink some of the foundational ideas of psychoanalysis. More generally, circumcision compels us to pose new questions about the definitions and categories of human difference. Whereas in the early twentieth century discussions of human groups often centered on *racial* differences, in the wake of the Holocaust scholars and leaders reframed these discussions in terms of *culture*. Yet throughout the twentieth century—and perhaps even more so in the twenty-first century—these discussions have been shaped by the terms and structures of particular religious traditions and histories.[2] Circumcision forces questions of religion back into discussions that are otherwise posed only in terms of race and/or culture. It also forces questions of race and physical difference into conversations that are otherwise posed only in terms of *religion* and culture.[3]

Though Freud's late insistence on the inheritance of memory is often described as Lamarckian, there is evidence that he far more extensively engaged with the work of August Weismann, one of the most vociferous anti-Lamarckians of the late nineteenth and early twentieth centuries. While Darwin was himself agnostic about whether acquired characteristics (such as a lack of a foreskin) could be inherited,[4] in the 1880s Weismann attempted to disprove this idea once and for all. In a series of experiments that seem almost modeled on the intergenerational practice of circumcision, Weismann cut off the tails of 901 mice.[5] Since all of the five succeeding generations of mice were born with their tails intact, Weismann proclaimed that he had finally refuted the Lamarckian idea that acquired characteristics could be inherited.[6] In a footnote to his discussion of the mice, Weismann acknowledged the widespread belief that "among nations which practise circumcision as a ritual, children are sometimes born with a rudimentary prepuce," but he insisted that "this does not occur more frequently than in other nations in which circumcision is not performed."[7] Surprisingly, neither Weismann's experiments nor the general practice of circumcision convinced Freud of the implausibility of the inheritance of acquired characteristics. On the contrary, it is through his ongoing engagement with Weismann's work and with the implications of circumcision that he began to reconsider his earlier resistance to the idea that acquired characteristics could be inherited.

In 1909 Freud made his first published reference to circumcision in a footnote to a discussion of castration anxiety in the case of "Little Hans." In this footnote (which has since become the focus of many psychoanalytic discussions of anti-semitism,[8] and to which I will return at the end of this chapter), Freud notes that the "castration complex is the deepest unconscious root of anti-semitism; for even in the nursery little boys hear that a

Jew has something cut off his penis—a piece of his penis, they think—and this gives them the right to despise Jews."[9] While Freud suggests that this nursery rumor might explain the origins of anti-semitism, he avoids the question of the origins of circumcision. That is, if anti-semitism derives from the castration anxiety that is elicited by the Jew's foreskin-less penis, from what does the practice of Jewish circumcision derive and why does it persist? As Freud continued to explore the sources of castration anxiety (and by extension, circumcision), he proposed that it must have originated in phylogenetic experiences when the father *actually* punished his sons with castration. However, he could not immediately explain how the effects of these experiences could have been transmitted: If the reproductive organs had been removed, hereditary transmission would have been impossible. In proposing that circumcision was a milder substitute for castration and the root of anti-semitism, he was left with seemingly insoluble questions: First, if individuals inherited the effects of their ancestors' experiences, why weren't the effects of circumcision (that is, the lack of a foreskin) transmitted? That is, why was it necessary to perform circumcision generation after generation? Second, if circumcision was one of the origins of the "immortal hatred" of Jews, why did the Jewish people repeat the performance of this rite generation after generation? Third, how did a cultural-religious practice become the paradigmatic mark of a racially (that is, genealogically) defined group? Though Freud initially considered memory and heredity as separate factors affecting the psyche, circumcision compelled him to rethink this relationship. Whereas many scientists attempted to maintain a strict separation between the psychological and the physical fields of research, Freud attempted to trace physical symptoms back to their origins in psychical traumas. Just as the instinct emerges as "a concept on the frontier between the mental and the somatic," circumcision emerges as a concept on the frontier between the realms of memory and heredity; spirituality and physicality; and culture, religion, and race.[10] Eventually Freud developed a theory of circumcision that seemed to explain both the origins and the persistence of anti-semitism, if not also the origins and persistence of Jewishness in the face of this "immortal hatred [*unsterbliche Haß*]."[11]

Weismann, Eugenics, and Human Difference

In the 1890s Freud argued that his patients suffered from "reminiscences," that is, the effects of the individual's experiences in early childhood. Since he considered this discovery the foundation of psychoanalytic theory, he initially rejected the idea that these "effects" included the inherited effects of one's ancestors' experiences. Even if a patient's disposition was "derived from his progenitors," he maintained that he was interested only in analyzing the effects of memories derived from the individual's own childhood.[12] To carve out a space for memory, Freud needed to keep it distinct from the realm of heredity and, by extension, inherited memory. In separating the psyche's inherited material from that which was shaped in early childhood, Freud developed a theory of the psyche that resonated with Weismann's theory of the germ-plasm. According to Weismann, all organic matter could be split up into two categories of existence: first, the permanent hereditary material of the immortal [*unsterblich*] germ-plasm, and second, the malleable material of the mortal soma, or body.[13] But because Weismann was more interested in the evolution of populations than the evolving development of an individual, he was not necessarily concerned with how these parts interacted within an individual organism. Freud, on the other hand, was more interested in exploring the interaction of these parts and the multiplication of their effects within the individual's psyche. Thus, though he first insisted that heredity and experience were separate factors, he eventually reconsidered this distinction and began to explore the works of Weismann and, only later, Lamarck.[14]

From 1907 onward, Freud came into contact with Weismann's work, particularly as it shaped questions of racial and cultural difference. For example, at a meeting of the Vienna Psycho-Analytical Society in December 1907, Weismann's name was mentioned in a discussion of heredity and eugenics.[15] Christian von Ehrenfels, a Viennese eugenicist, presented a lecture on "Breeding Reform" in which he argued that monogamy was harmful for "both constitutional and cultural reasons" because it made it impossible for the individual to fulfill his sexual needs.[16] Ehrenfels noted that Freud had distinguished between "constitutional life" and "cultural life," but he (Ehrenfels) further defined it:

> We call *constitutional* those characteristics of an organism that are inborn and can be transmitted by physiological procreation. *Everything else* belongs to the *cultural* realm. This distinction was, in fact, first made by Darwin and was then defined more precisely by Weismann.[17]

It is unclear whether Darwin or Weismann actually distinguished between "constitutional" and "cultural" traits in this way. However, by the first decade of the twentieth century, Weismann's work was often cited to support the argument that individuals' characters were entirely determined by their heredity. It was also cited to bolster breeding programs: Since the hereditary (germ-plasmic) materials of humans could not be changed by modifying the environment (such as education or welfare), breeding programs were based on the idea that reproduction should be managed in order to curb the reproduction of the "unfit" elements and to encourage the reproduction of the more "fit" elements of society.[18] In the following years, Freud would continue to explore questions raised by Ehrenfels' half-hearted attempt to distinguish between those constitutional characteristics with which an individual is born and the "everything else" that belongs to the cultural realm: How is this cultural realm formed? Does it change over time, or is it equally resistant to change? Is there just one cultural realm of humanity, or are there many? Can a person define his own cultural realm, or does it define him?

While Freud was persuaded by some of Ehrenfels' arguments, he went in a decidedly different direction regarding the distinction between constitutional and cultural characteristics of a people. Following Ehrenfels' presentation in Vienna, Freud briefly discussed eugenics in his essay "'Civilized' Sexual Morality and Modern Nervous Illness" (1908), which he published in Ehrenfels' new periodical *Sexual Problems*.[19] In the opening paragraphs, he approvingly cites Ehrenfels' work on "modern nervous illness,"[20] and he notes the comparison of "the innate character of a people with their cultural attainments."[21] Instead of pursuing this idea any further, however, he refers the reader to Ehrenfels' work for "a more extensive consideration of this significant line of thought."[22] Despite his apparent approval of Ehrenfels' arguments in favor of breeding, Freud subtly argues against Ehrenfels' emphasis on heredity. Whereas Ehrenfels argued that "nervous illness" is "innate" and transmitted only "by inheritance," Freud explains that "close inspection shows that it is really a question of the effect of powerful infantile impressions."[23] The increase in "nervous illness" in modern times, argues Freud, can be better understood by investigating the ways in which "civilized" morality imposes intolerable restrictions on the satisfaction of individuals' sexual needs.[24] While he suggests that the sexual restrictions of "civilized" morality are responsible for the spread of "nervous illness," he defends civilization's "achievements," such as the institutions of marriage and the family: "Even if the damage done by civilized sexual morality is admitted, it may be argued . . . that the cultural gain derived from such an extensive restriction of sexuality probably more than balances these sufferings, which, after all, only affect a minority in any severe form."[25] This is the earliest of Freud's discussions of the tension between the preservation of the self and the preservation of society (or between instinctual life and civilization). This tension might be better described as a power dynamic between the individual and the group (whether species, race, society, or civilization): While individuals attempt to preserve themselves, they must work against society's powerful attempts to preserve itself. Likewise, as individuals attempt to control society, society exerts its control over individuals. The question is, can individuals define their society (or civilization), or does society always define individuals? Do individuals "live off" of the group, or does the group live off the creative energies of its individuals? Does history determine individuals' lives in the present, or do individuals in the present determine history? Such questions are central to understanding Freud's theorization of Jewishness and psychoanalysis.

During his 1909 trip to America, Freud had a number of opportunities to discuss both Lamarck's and Weismann's work, especially as they shaped debates about the definitions of race and culture. During his time in Worcester, Massachusetts, Freud stayed at the home of G. Stanley Hall, an eminent psychologist and the president of Clark University, who had organized the event to celebrate the twentieth anniversary of the school. Hall was famous for his work with adolescents and for comparing "primitive" cultures to the "primitive" stages of human development in childhood and adolescence. He was also committed to the ideas that the development of the individual was a recapitulation of the development of the human race and that acquired characteristics could be inherited. For example, the year before Freud visited, Hall wrote that "only Lamarckianism in its most extreme form can explain the evolution of races, species and their every diversity, great and small," even as he acknowledged that "Weismann is essentially right that net results of individual life upon germ plasm are minimal or naught, the past determining everything."[26] Like many other scientists of the time-period, Hall did not see a contradiction between a Lamarckian understanding of racial difference and the Weismannian theory of the germ-plasm, for according to both, the past determines everything.[27]

Also at Clark to deliver a celebratory lecture and to accept an honorary degree was Franz Boas, who presented a lecture on "the laws of hereditary stability and of environmental variability of the human body."[28] Specifically, he insisted that these "laws" could be derived from "the historical changes that the bodily appearance of man has undergone in the course of time, and in his displacement from one geographical or social environment to another."[29] At the time, Boas was engaged in a series of investigations (1908–10) for the United States Immigration Commission.[30] While the Commission was quite sure that the "American type" was stable (a fixed racial—white, European—type), Boas attempted to demonstrate that the descendants of immigrants had been able to change their "type" within one or two generations. Through changing their environment (by moving to America), these immigrants had transformed themselves from their various national types (Irish, Italian, Jewish, German) and had become "American." By studying a series of mental and physical measurements of eighteen thousand descendants of immigrants, Boas tried to show that the individuals had changed in response to the environment and that these changes had been transmitted to the next generation. As such, he concluded, human types and abilities were not "permanent and stationary," as the Commission had previously presumed.[31] In his report to the Immigration Commission, Boas tried to prove that (certain) human types could be transformed depending on the environment in which the individuals lived. While he focused on bodily characteristics in his report to the Commission, he was most famous for his anthropological work exploring the cultures of the world. It is significant that his report referred only to *white* European immigrants whose nationalities (according to Boas) were being erroneously discussed as if they were racial types. Indeed, Boas' report to the Immigration Commission and his later work can be seen as attempts to show that race applies only to permanent physical distinctions while other kinds of typologization (such as nationality, religion, and culture) were malleable. For example, in his essay on the "Mind of Primitive Man" (1911), he would insist that "there is no close relation between race and culture,"[32] an argument that has come to define many post–World War II debates about the relationship of these two terms (about which I will say more later in this chapter).[33] In other words, for Boas and for many others, race should be used only to refer to permanent physical characteristics, whereas culture (as well as nationality, religion, and culture) should be used to refer to malleable characteristics and practices. However, these distinctions do not necessarily work in all times and places. It is difficult to say whether Freud actually attended Boas' lecture. Nonetheless, it is likely that, in the course of the celebrations, Freud would have heard about Boas' current work on immigrants and racial types.[34]

Soon after returning from his trip to America in 1909, Freud acquired and read at least part of a book entitled *The Race Problem, with Particular Consideration of the Theoretical Foundations of the Jewish Race Question* by the Jewish scientist Ignaz Zollschan.[35] While much of the book is a defense of the Jewish people—their cultural and economic worth—it is also a meditation on the very definition of the Jewish people: "Is there a homogeneous Jewish Race," asks Zollschan, "and has it always been marked by the same particular characteristics—historically and for all eternity?"[36] For Zollschan, as for many of his contemporaries, the question of the existence of a Jewish race was separate from the question of whether the Jewish people had always been defined by the same fixed characteristics. In his chapter "On the Subject of Heredity as It Is Important for the Racial Problem," Zollschan presents two opposing approaches to this question: "Regarding character-types in the whole organic world, the Weismannian school asserts *fixity* [*Starrheit*], while their opponents assert that there is *malleability* [*Modifika-bilität*]."[37] While Zollschan accepts the Weismannian concept of the hereditary germ-plasm, he rejects the idea that psychological or intellectual [*geistigen*] characteristics of a race were permanent. Thus, citing Eduard von Hartmann, he notes that "it proves nothing that amputated arms and legs and mutilations like circumcision are, for the most part, not inherited, for in the typical idea of the species, the concepts are too base and palpable [*zu grobe und handgriffliche Eingriffe*] to expect their realization in the children."[38] In the remainder of the chapter, Zollschan uses Richard Semon's concept of the *engramme* to explain how elements that are first acquired by individuals can *become* hereditary characteristics. The lack of a foreskin might not be hereditary, Zollschan argues, but other characteristics—the impalpable, the intangible, and intellectual—were acquired, modified, and maintained such that they became seemingly fixed elements of the Jewish racial character.[39]

Freud's Lamarckian Weismannism

By the time Freud published the fourth (and final) essay of *Totem and Taboo* in 1913, he had begun to incorporate the idea that individuals needed to contend with the effects not only of their own experiences but also of their ancestors' experiences. Individuals seemed to be reacting to memories of events that they did not themselves experience: threats of castration, primal scenes, omnipotent fathers, and sexy mothers. While Freud would briefly explore Lamarck's work in 1917–18, he first (and more explicitly and extensively) explored Weismann's work and its implications for psychoanalysis.[40] In the opening of his essay on "The Dynamics of the Transference Neuroses" (1912), he explains that these repeated behaviors can be understood as "stereotype plates" that are "constantly repeated—constantly reprinted afresh—in the course of a person's life." He begins by emphasizing that these repeated behaviors are "certainly not entirely insusceptible to change in the face of recent experiences";[41] in other words, psychoanalysis might be able to alleviate the individual's symptoms. However, he adds a long footnote in which he acknowledges that there might be certain conflicts that are unalterable. It is here that Freud first (publicly) reconsiders his earlier resistance to the idea that heredity and memory are entirely distinct. With a blustery tone of over-protestation, he notes, "We refuse to posit any contrast in principle between the two sets of aetiological factors . . . one might venture to regard constitution itself as a precipitate from the accidental effects produced on the endlessly *long chain of our ancestors*."[42] An irreconcilable tension emerges: The individual must contend not only with the effects of his own childhood, but also with the effects of being a link in an "endlessly long chain of our ancestors." Psychoanalysis might reduce a patient's symptoms, but he would still have to contend with that "endlessly long chain of our ancestors," a chain that could not so easily be broken or modified.

In his 1914 essay "On Narcissism," Freud extends his meditations on the "long chain of our ancestors" as he explores the dynamics of transference and the seemingly endless repetition of the past in the present.[43] Drawing from Weismann's germ-plasm theory, he proposes that the individual carries "on a twofold existence: one to serve his own purposes and the other as a *link in a chain [als Glied in einer Kette]*."[44] In this passage (as in the passage in "The Dynamics of Transference"), Freud quietly—perhaps even unconsciously—seems to allude to the "Chain of Tradition [*Traditionskette*]," a phrase colloquially used to refer to the genealogical chain of Jewishness. Each Jew is a link in this Chain of Tradition, which stretches all the way back to Abraham. In Jewish literary history, the Chain of Tradition also refs to the unbroken sequence of transmission of an *acquired* property: "Moses received Torah from Sinai and delivered it to Joshua, and Joshua to the Elders, and the Elders to the Prophets, and the Prophets delivered it to the Men of the Great Synagogue."[45] In the essay "On Narcissism," Freud goes on to explain that each individual serves this chain "against his will, or at least involuntarily. . . . He is the mortal vehicle of a (possibly) immortal [*unsterbliche*] substance—like the inheritor of an entailed property, who is only the temporary holder of an estate which survives him."[46] It is not clear to what Freud is referring when he explains that every individual is a "mortal vehicle of an immortal substance"—is the immortal substance some sort of human disposition? Is it civilization as a whole, or is it a specific culture, religion, or genealogical chain? Moreover, if each individual is a temporary carrier of some sort of immortal substance, how did the individual *acquire* this material? How did this *stuff* become the permanent property of the individual?[47]

These questions linger in Freud's discussions of castration anxiety and circumcision, first in the case of "Little Hans," and then more explicitly in texts written around the same time such as "On Narcissism." While Freud did not explicitly explore the particularity of Jewish circumcision until *Moses and Monotheism*, his brief explorations of circumcision and castration are intertwined with his earlier discussions of the relationship between heredity and experience. For example, in the case history of the "Wolf Man" (written in 1914–15) he notes that the boy's fear of castration derived not only from his own childhood experience but from the fact that "he had to fit into a phylogenetic pattern."[48] In the boy's own experience, the *mother* threatened him with castration as punishment for masturbating, but "in this respect," notes Freud, "heredity triumphed over accidental experience; in man's prehistory it was unquestionably the father who practised castration as a punishment and who later softened it down into circumcision."[49] Freud was clearly interested in the connection between castration and the father–son relationship, but throughout these discussions he gestures toward the occluded mother: Over and over again he claims that the childhood memory is of an experience with a mother while the ancestral chain of memory is made up of fathers. Instead of simply focusing on the father–son relationship, Freud actively displaces the mother. This is part of his idiosyncratic inversion of Jewish tradition (which I discuss in more detail in Chapter 5): Whereas Jewishness is traditionally transmitted through the mother's body (that is, through matrilineage), Freud suggests that the important ancestral memories invoke the father. Similarly, in his interpretations of the complicated meanings of Jewish circumcision, anthropologist Eric Kline Silverman suggests that neonatal circumcision allows men to reclaim the power and prominence of the female's body and to usurp the symbols of fertility and procreation in the days following the birth. Where Gilman, Boyarin, and Geller have focused on the ways in which Freud drew from anti-semitic images of Jewish circumcised men as feminine, weak, impotent, and homosexual, Silverman's analysis of the practice suggests a more dynamic perspective on the power-plays involved in the ritual: Rather than only emphasizing the man's impotence, circumcision demonstrates and documents his recovery of power from the birth mother. These inversions are reflected in Freud's own discussions of the relationships between mothers and fathers and between individuals and their "ancestral chains." In Silverman's words, circumcision is "a 'cultural' transcendence over, or re-creation of, the 'natural' world. . . . [C]ircumcision celebrates an eternal covenant and the creation of a community whose existence transcends any particular life."[50] In Freud's Weismannian terminology, circumcision sustains the "endlessly long chain of our ancestors" by making the Jewish male body a "mortal vehicle of a (possibly) immortal substance."[51]

Soon after composing the case history of the "Wolf Man," in July 1915 Freud sent Ferenczi a draft of his "Phylogenetic Fantasy," which he provisionally entitled "Overview of the Transference Neuroses." Drawing together his meditations on both the narcissistic and transference neuroses, Freud tries to solve the question of how these patterns become permanently imprinted such that they are incessantly repeated, not only within an individual's lifespan but from one generation to the next. As he reconstructs the story of the primal murder that he had first explored in *Totem*, he adds far more details, particularly about what caused the sons to rebel and kill the father (rather than continuing to live under his authoritarian rule). According to Freud, in response to particular climactic changes that threatened the survival of the human hordes, the primal father not only *threatened* the sons with castration, but he actually robbed "them of their manhood." After millennia, the effects of these events were fixed as "dispositions" to these two types of neuroses. Since neurosis was acquired in response to changes in the environment, Freud explains that "it is therefore a *cultural* acquisition."[52] Here we can see a slippage between the terms "culture" and "race":

Neurosis begins as a cultural acquisition, but as its effects and patterns become imprinted they become seemingly permanent attributes of the genealogical chain. The inheritance of acquired characteristics suggests that culture is transmuted into race when seemingly fleeting impressions become immortal [*unsterblich*] characteristics of ourselves, of our families, and of the societies in which we live.

Soon after receiving the manuscript of the "Phylogenetic Fantasy," Ferenczi wrote a letter to Freud in which he pointed out that there was a major problem with Freud's logic: If the sons were robbed of "their manhood" through castration, they would have no way of hereditarily transmitting these dispositions. "The castrated ones cannot have reproduced and fixated their condition phylogenetically," notes Ferenczi, "therefore you must surely mean the fixation of castration *anxiety*."[53] In other words, Freud could solve the problem of phylogenetic inheritance by recognizing that it was not necessarily the physical effects of castration that were transmitted, but rather its psychological effects. Even so, notes Ferenczi, if the castration anxiety derived from a real castration, it could not be hereditarily transmitted. In response, Freud added a concluding section to the draft in which he acknowledged "the difficulty" of explaining "how the brutal father . . . reproduced himself."[54] Noting that neurosis is obviously "acquired under conditions that exclude heredity,"[55] Freud presents a couple of solutions that he ultimately finds unconvincing: Perhaps there was a younger son who was "not castrated himself, but knows the fate of his older brothers and fears it for himself." Or perhaps "there may remain a chain of others, who . . . can propagate the [vicissitudes of the male sex] as dispositions."[56] Finally, Freud acknowledges that he cannot quite make sense of "how the dispositions produced by the father's oppression spread to women."[57] "A Phylogenetic Fantasy" concludes not with a solution to any of these problems but with plans for future work. "There remains room for new acquisition and for influences with which we are not acquainted," Freud writes. "In sum, we are not at the end, but rather at the beginning, of an understanding of this phylogenetic factor."[58]

Left unpublished until 1987, the draft of "Overview of the Transference Neuroses" has often been presented as proof that Freud was a Lamarckian,[59] though he did not actually mention Lamarck in any (extant) correspondence until after he had written this essay and sent it off to Ferenczi. As Freud writes, "A Phylogenetic Fantasy" was not the "end" of his explorations of the "phylogenetic factor," but rather "the beginning," and it was *after* he finished the draft that he turned to Lamarck's works.[60] Six months later, in a letter to Ferenczi on January 6, 1916, Freud speculates about the "conditions of artistic endowment": "First the wealth of phylogenetically transferred material, as with the neurotic; second, a good remnant of the old technique of modifying oneself instead of the outside world (see Lamarck, etc.)."[61] This is the first mention of Lamarck's name in all of Freud's published works, drafts, and correspondence (though it is impossible to know what correspondence or notes have not yet been found or what the sealed archives may hold).[62]

Over the next two years, Freud and Ferenczi feverishly corresponded about the possibility of co-writing a work about Lamarck and psychoanalysis. While their work may not have taken off because of the political exigencies (discussed in Chapter 2), they were briefly caught up in the excitement of new possibilities. In December 1916, Freud ordered "the Lamarck" from the university library.[63] On January 1, 1917, he reported to Ferenczi that he was beginning to read Lamarck's *Zoological Philosophy* (1809) and he enclosed a "sketch of the Lamarck-work" (a manuscript that was apparently not preserved or has not yet been discovered).[64] By November of that year, Freud was apparently so caught up in the burgeoning work that, in a letter to his friend Karl Abraham, he asked, "Have I really not told you anything about the Lamarck idea?" He continues:

> The idea is to put Lamarck entirely on our ground and to show that the "necessity" that according to him *creates and transforms organs* is nothing but the power of unconscious ideas over one's own body, of which we see remnants in hysteria, in short the "omnipotence of thoughts." Purpose and usefulness would then be explained psychoanalytically; it would be the completion of psychoanalysis. Two great principles of change or progress would emerge: one through (autoplastic) adaptation of one's own body, and a later (heteroplastic) one through transmuting the outer world.[65]

Whereas in "A Phylogenetic Fantasy" Freud could not explain how the neuroses would have been transferred (since the sons had been castrated, effectively making hereditary transmission impossible), in his letter to Abraham he explains that he has found the solution: According to Lamarck, it was actually possible for humans to adapt their own bodies—to regenerate lost limbs and create new organs! Indeed, in *Beyond the Pleasure Principle*

(1920), Freud notes that "the power of regenerating a lost organ by growing afresh a precisely similar one extends far up into the animal kingdom."[66] Thus tails, testicles, fingers, and foreskins might all be cut off, but with the "power of unconscious ideas" they might actually be restored!

Freud's comments about the potential regeneration of organs seem not only outrageous, but also outside the purview of psychoanalysis. Yet they reveal the ways in which the psyche is never completely separate from the body. As Thomas Laqueur writes, culture—consisting of both conscious and unconscious ideas and actions—"represents itself in bodies, forges them, as on an anvil, into the required shape."[67] Indeed, with the help of various medical procedures, it *is* possible to create and transform organs, to reshape bodies (from male to female, from darker skin to lighter skin, and so on). Rather than trying to determine the relative importance of heredity and experience (or race and culture), Freud's late work illuminates the ways in which "the authority of nature" is "rhetorically appropriated to legitimize the creations of culture."[68] Like sex-change and skin-altering procedures, circumcision is not simply a matter of rhetoric but an actual physical transformation that calls into question the boundaries between race and culture.

In his short-lived exploration of Lamarck, Freud was briefly optimistic about the potential of humans to transform themselves. Yet while various scientists and eugenicists argued that evolution—whether by natural selection or Lamarckian inheritance—progressively worked toward weeding out the lower elements of the organic world, Freud ultimately rejected the most mechanical and teleological elements of these theories.[69] "There is unquestionably no universal instinct towards higher development observable in the animal or plant world," he writes in *Beyond the Pleasure Principle*. And even if there is some "higher development and involution" he explains that it must be understood as "the consequences of adaptation to the pressure of external forces."[70]

In *Beyond the Pleasure Principle* Freud returns to Weismann's germ-plasm theory and to the question of how the "immortal property" became permanent. In an extension of the "far-fetched speculation" of "A Phylogenetic Fantasy," he notes that certain "excitations coming from the external world" enter consciousness and "leave permanent traces behind . . . which form the foundation of memory."[71] While the "compulsion to repeat" may be the result of "organic striving," Freud explains that such "behaviour is only to a very slight degree attributable to mechanical causes, and the historical explanation cannot accordingly be neglected."[72] Over and over again Freud insists on the primacy of history and the environment in determining organic hereditary material: The instincts are "historically determined," and even "the phenomenon of organic development must be attributed to *external* disturbing and diverting influences."[73] In reaction to changes in the environment, the organism struggles to preserve itself and to preserve the species—that is, it struggles with two conflicting instincts: the self-preservative life instinct and the species-preservative sexual instinct. To further explore this tension, Freud cites Weismann's germ-plasm theory, which (in Freud's mind) proposed

> a division of living substance into mortal and immortal parts. The mortal part is the body in the narrower sense—the "soma"—which alone is subject to natural death. The germ-cells, on the other hand, are potentially immortal [*unsterbliche*], in so far as they are able, under certain favourable conditions, to develop into a new individual, or, in other words, to surround themselves with a new soma. (Weismann, 1884)[74]

As in the essay "On Narcissism," here Freud speculates about the relationship of the individual to something eminently grander and more permanent than his bodily life—the "potentially immortal" and "endlessly long chain" that he "involuntarily" serves. While he virtually quotes from Weismann's work, his emphasis of certain words and turns of phrase raises questions that he would implicitly continue to explore in *Moses and Monotheism*. For example, he repeatedly hesitates before the word "immortal": The substance is "(possibly) immortal [*vielleicht—unsterblich*]"; the germ-cells are "potentially immortal [*potentiell unsterblich*]." Are these hesitations evidence that he wished that such properties and patterns (like neurosis and anti-semitism) were *not* so persistent, or was he not sure whether such properties (as Judaism) are truly so persistent as to survive forever? (Or is there something about immortality that runs counter to Freud's thought?[75]) What are the "favourable conditions" under which this material might become "immortal"? How is this "immortal part" perpetuated? How does it "surround" itself with a new body without losing its permanent characteristics?

Though he briefly considered the possibility that organs and bodily parts might magically be regenerated, Freud eventually recognized that—unlike the scientists from whose work he drew—he did not have to remain tethered to the bodily realm.[76] From the beginning, he had been interested in the relationship between the physical and the psychical realms, and in 1915, he theorized that the instinct was "a concept on the frontier between the mental and the somatic."[77] Ultimately he abandoned his short-lived interest in morphological questions of regenerated organs and bodily parts and instead focused on their representations in the psyche. As he notes in *Beyond the Pleasure Principle*, Weismann regarded "living substance morphologically" and focused on the description of external shapes and forms, including the transmission (or non-transmission) of modifications of external body-parts (particularly excised tails and circumcised penises). "We, on the other hand," Freud notes, "deal . . . not with the living substance but with the *forces* operating *in* it."[78] In shifting the emphasis from castration to castration anxiety, Freud moved away from the question of how castration and circumcision had permanently shaped the body's physical form; instead, he focused on how their effects had become permanently imprinted on the *psyche*, creating *forces* that were perpetuated from one generation to the next. In arguing that castration anxiety derives from real physical experiences in the ancestral past, Freud suggests a different relationship between race and culture: It is not simply that culture derives from race, but that cultural forces are shaped by our physical (racialized) bodies, which are themselves shaped by cultural experiences such as circumcision. Culture produces race produces culture.

Freud's Final Cut

In *Moses and Monotheism* Freud returned to the questions he had first mentioned in the case of "Little Hans" and that he had explored with the help of Weismann's theory of the immortal germ-plasm. By insisting that Jewishness is the result of phylogenetic experiences that are biologically transmitted, Freud seems to develop a racial theory of Jewishness. However, the figure of circumcision complicates our understanding of the concept of race. Why would Jews continue to circumcise their sons, particularly if it arouses the castration complex, "the deepest unconscious root" of anti-semitism, and as such may jeopardize their chances for survival? What is the relationship between the immortality [*Unsterblichkeit*] of anti-semitic hatred and of the Jewish people?[79]

In *Moses* Freud insists that he cannot do without the idea that acquired characteristics are inherited, but he goes on to acknowledge that he is still left with two important questions, both of which gesture toward the role of circumcision. First, he asks, "under what conditions does a memory of this kind enter the archaic heritage? Secondly, in what circumstances can [the memory] become active—that is, can it advance to consciousness from its unconscious state in the id, even though in an altered and distorted shape?"[80] The answer to the first question, Freud writes, is that "the memory enters the archaic heritage if the event was important enough, or repeated often enough, or both." In answer to the second question, he writes, "What is certainly of decisive importance, is the awakening of the forgotten memory-trace by a recent real repetition of the event."[81] In Freud's chain of Jewish tradition, circumcision could be the missing link: It seems to fulfill the conditions that make a memory enter the archaic heritage. It is both important and repeated in each generation, leaving such deep impressions that its effects might be felt for generations to come regardless of whether these generations are themselves circumcised. And yet, even with the transmission of these effects, there must be something to "awaken" the memory, to remind the person that he is Jewish. Because circumcision is repeated in every generation, it could be said to "awaken" the phylogenetic past. If Jewish tradition is hereditarily transmitted, circumcision seems to confer and confirm this inheritance.

I am not entirely satisfied with these answers to Freud's questions. If Jewishness is an inherited tradition—one that is transmitted beyond direct communication—it is not clear how the young Jew comes to know that he is Jewish. It is also not clear how a Jewish boy comes to know that he was circumcised since he does not remember life before the circumcision or the act of circumcision itself.[82] In other words, how does the young boy realize that his penis looked different when he was born? How does he come to know that a piece of his penis had been cut off? In the infamous footnote in the case of "Little Hans" (and also in a footnote in *Totem and Taboo*), Freud emphasizes not the act or trauma of circumcision but its status as a *rumor*: Little boys do not consciously experience circumcision; they *hear* about it.[83] It seems reasonable to assume that the circumcised boy does not automatically know that a part of his penis has been cut off; like the non-circumcised boys in the nursery, at some point the Jewish boy must also "hear that a Jew has something cut off his penis." Like the mark itself, the knowledge of circumcision is usually acquired before the age of conscious memory. Children hear that the Jew has something cut off his penis, but the question of when or why this happens is not addressed. Are Jews born with something cut off their penis? Who cuts off a piece of their penis? And why?

Freud's infamous footnote has often been read as an attempt to occlude Jewish identity—both his own and his patient's.[84] Indeed, common sense would suggest that only gentile uncircumcised boys would need to *hear* about the Jew's circumcision, whereas little Jewish circumcised boys would *already know* about it (since all they would have to do is look down).[85] However, this interpretation overlooks the most curious aspect of Jewish circumcision: the fact that the Jewish boy does not necessarily always already know about his difference—his difference from others, and his difference from his uncircumcised seven-day-old self. Freud explains that hearing about circumcision gives little boys "a right to despise Jews," since the circumcision seems to remind them of the apparently very real possibility that their penises could be entirely cut off.[86] Thus he suggests that such negative feelings about circumcision would apply equally to Jews and non-Jews and could partially explain both the "immortal hatred" of anti-semitism and the feelings of self-hatred that Gilman has so extensively documented.[87] Instead of an attempt to cover up Jewishness, then, Freud's famous footnote alludes to questions that lurk in the minds of individuals who are aware of the fact that they are racially—that is, physically and permanently—marked. Individuals are marked by the facts of circumcision even when they are not circumcised, just as individuals are also affected by the Jewish Question even when they believe that they are not Jewish.

This reading of Freud's footnote is anticipated by Frantz Fanon's memory of his initial recognition of racial difference, which he describes in *Black Skin, White Masks* (1967). Though Fanon does not explicitly refer to the case of "Little Hans," he draws from psychoanalytic theory as he explores the processes of racialization and its effects on the subject. Fanon recounts hearing a child say to her mother, "Look, a Negro!"[88] Though the term *Negro* begins as an "external stimulus that flicked over me as I passed by," it impresses itself upon Fanon's bodily ego. Forced to recognize that the girl is speaking about *him*, Fanon writes that this "epidermalization" made him "responsible at the same time for my body, for my race, for my ancestors."[89] Interestingly, Fanon evokes the terms of circumcision, but one that has gone terribly wrong: "What else could it be for me but an amputation, an excision, a hemorrhage that spattered my whole body with black blood?"[90] The term *Negro* impresses itself *upon* the body even as it intrudes *into* the body and potentially dismembers that body; it is translated from signifier to signified, an inert physical feature to which meanings are assigned and internalized. While Fanon notes that the "anti-semite is inevitably anti-negro,"[91] he acknowledges that there are obvious differences between Jewish and Negro racialization: "the Jew can be unknown in his Jewishness. He is not wholly what he is . . . He is a white man, and, aside from some rather debatable characteristics, he can sometimes go unnoticed."[92] Whereas the Jewish male may carry the marks of his circumcision on his usually concealed member, the Negro's "whole body" is "spattered" with the castrating effects of racialization.

While the Jew has been portrayed as physically different, this singular mark of difference is found only on male bodies, and it is usually hidden beneath clothing. More important, in some historical circumstances the mark is not actually different. Just as the Negro surrounded by other Negroes does not necessarily recognize any Negro particularities, the Jewish boy surrounded by other circumcised boys (as in Muslim countries or in America since the mid–twentieth century) may not know that his mark has anything to do with his Jewishness.[93] More interestingly, perhaps, is the fact that in Freud's Vienna, and in his own family, many boys were still regarded as Jewish—even physically so—without this mark of difference.[94] We can assume that such boys might "hear" that the Jew has had something cut off his penis without immediately understanding the significance. Thus the uncircumcised Jewish boy may be left with additional unanswerable questions: Would this mean that (as a Jew) he too would eventually have something cut off his penis? Or would it mean that since the Jew has had something cut off his penis, he was not actually a Jew? Such questions would understandably intrude into the calm of a child's psyche, compelling him to ask questions about his own sexual and racial identities, identities that are sometimes perceived and portrayed as self-evident matters.[95]

In all his works before *Moses and Monotheism*, there is a sense that Freud was himself a bit horrified by circumcision. His comparisons of circumcision to castration and his exploration of the "compulsion to repeat" have given ample fodder to anti-circumcision activists who are pleased to have Freud on their side.[96] While I would not go so far as to say that Freud would have joined the fight to abolish circumcision, for most of his life he showed no interest in supporting the continued performance of the rite. Moreover, he was mildly critical of the odd logic that was driving Anglo-Americans to practice circumcision regardless of their religious affiliation—namely, the idea that circumcision reduced boys' desires to masturbate.[97] However, in his final book, Freud greatly expanded upon his earlier discussions of circumcision such that a very different understanding of the messy relationships between psychoanalysis, circumcision, anti-semitism, and Jewishness emerges.

If "the castration complex is the deepest unconscious root of anti-semitism,"[98] Freud suggests that circumcision is the deepest root of Jewishness, something that cannot be pulled out, cut off, or erased. In *Moses* he explains that circumcision is a "key-fossil" attesting to the survival of the Jewish chain of tradition.[99] Indeed, it is *the* symbol of the Jews' sacred consecration, the sign of their supreme intellectual spirituality [*Geistigkeit*].[100] Over and over again, Freud notes that by imposing the custom of circumcision, Moses made his people "holy." As in his earlier works Freud suggests that circumcision may make "a disagreeable, uncanny impression [*unliebsamen, unheimlichen Eindruck*]" because it recalls "the dreaded castration and along with it a portion [*Stück*, piece] of the primaeval past which is gladly forgotten."[101] And yet, as any good Freudian knows, there is nothing under the sun—or in our pasts—that can so simply be "forgotten." Even when Mosaic monotheism seemed to have been forgotten, its traces remained, albeit in a repressed and distorted form. Thus, while the people rejected the strict ideals of Mosaic monotheism, Freud explains, they "would not renounce this *mark* [*Zeichen*] of their holiness"; they retained "at least the external *mark* of the religion of Moses—circumcision."[102] In *Moses*, then, Freud suggests that circumcision is what marks the Jew as both holy (from the inside) and disagreeable (from the outside); it is also the key to the contradiction between the non-materiality of Jewish abstract intellectuality [*Geistigkeit*] and the physical materiality needed to sustain such intellectual abstraction.

Even more bizarre than this paradoxical symbolism of circumcision is the fact that circumcision serves as Freud's key evidence for his theory about the Egyptian origins of Mosaic monotheism. Since circumcision was a "generally popular custom in Egypt," Freud explains, the Jews must have acquired this custom from Moses, an Egyptian who "was himself circumcised."[103] In order to make the Semites into a "superior substitute" for the

Egyptians he was leaving behind, Moses introduced the custom of circumcision.[104] The logic here is nothing if not confusing and surprising, for Freud
suggests that the mark of Jewish difference was in fact originally a universal
condition of the Egyptian people among whom the Jews (or proto-Jews)
lived. In other words, this paradigmatic mark of Jewish difference is in fact
a *residue* of sameness. Indeed, Freud seems to suggest that when the Jews
began to practice circumcision, it was (perhaps) their first attempt to fit
in with the people among whom they lived; circumcision thus recalls the
unfulfillable desire to assimilate, to be like everyone else. It was only once
the people left Egypt that circumcision became a sign of Jewish difference.
From that time on, Freud explains, they were "isolated" by this "sign
[*Zeichen*]," which kept them "apart from the foreign peoples among whom
their wanderings would lead them, just as the Egyptians themselves had
kept apart from all foreigners."[105] Thus, while circumcision began as a folk-
custom of the Egyptians, it became the visible mark of the Jews' "consecration," which proved their particular *Geistigkeit* and their "submission" to a
burden of memory.

It is not entirely clear how *Geistigkeit*—the incorporeal quality of the
Jews' intellectual spirituality—could be represented by any sort of physical
mark, let alone the mark of circumcision. It is also not clear, as Freud acknowledges, why "an advance in intellectuality [*Geistigkeit*]" and a rejection
of so-called sensuality should be valued as something "sacred [*heilig*]" and
thereby "raise the self-regard both of an individual and of a people."[106]
These questions are partially answered by recognizing the importance of
the "renunciation of instinct." In the development of an individual, part of
the process of becoming an adult involves internalizing external restrictions
such as parental rules and regulations. In the development of a people,
Freud explains, "one of the most important stages of hominization [*Mensch-
werdung*, becoming human]" involves the triumph of "higher intellectual
processes" over sensory perceptions.[107] Ultimately, Freud identifies this
"prolongation of the will of the primal father" as *sacredness* [*Heiligkeit*]:
"Hence come the strength of its emotional tone and the impossibility of
finding a rational basis for it."[108] As the "symbolic substitute" of castration,
then, circumcision symbolizes the submission to an "absolute power,"
whether one's parents or God, and forms the basis of ethics: the regulation
of the relationships between the individual and society.[109] Thus, in submit-
ting to a god that is unrepresentable—"untouchable" and unnameable—the

Jews became supremely sacred, and the visible mark of their supreme holiness is none other than circumcision. Thus, circumcision both substantiates the abstract intellectuality [*Geistigkeit*] and ensures the survival of the Jewish intellectual tradition.

Freud suggests that the phenomena of anti-semitism and philo-semitism—or the parallel phenomena of self-hatred and ethnic pride—ultimately originate from the same source. As he explains, "Those who do not practise [circumcision] look on it as very strange and are a little horrified by it, but those who have adopted circumcision are proud of it. They feel exalted by it, ennobled, as it were, and look down with contempt on others, whom they regard as unclean."[110] Here Freud zeroes in on a more general paradox: People often feel most strongly about customs and characteristics over which they have no control. In other words, you can pick your friends and you can pick your clothes, but generally, you can't pick your mother or your mother-tongue, and you also can't choose whether you were circumcised as an infant. Anti-semitism is not so much "a disease of the uncircumcised," as Gilman suggests,[111] but a curious expression of the conflicts and differences that precede our entrance into a world of memory. Anti- and philo-semitism are not opposites, then, but part of a single phenomenon of identifying one's self as distinct from Others.[112]

One of the glaring omissions in Freud's discussions of circumcision is any discussion of the fact that, unlike many other peoples who practice circumcision, the Jewish people circumcise their sons when they are just eight days old.[113] At this age, the boy can neither make any decisions for himself nor prove his dedication to the group. In other cultures, such as the Ndembu in Africa, where the males are circumcised at the age of puberty, circumcision functions as an obvious symbol of fertility and of the lineage which the boy will soon produce.[114] In the Hebrew Bible, Abraham is commanded to circumcise himself and all his sons as a way to seal God's promise of fertility. However, after Abraham, Jewish males are supposed to be circumcised long before they are fertile—the birth of the boy is proof of the *father*'s fertility. The circumcision confirms that the genealogical chain of tradition has not been broken. The fact that a boy is circumcised at a time of his life that (almost certainly) will not be remembered—at least not consciously—means that the boy may perceive the mark as something with which he was born. In this respect, then, circumcision may be experienced as an inherited memory—an archaic experience that marks a Jewish male for his entire life,

minus the first eight days, whether he likes it or not (de-circumcision operations aside).[115]

Freud did not simply forget to mention that Jewish circumcision is performed soon after the boy's birth, but his avoidance of this fact is emblematic of the tensions the rite elicits. Circumcision is an artificial inscription
upon the body, but it suggests the seeds of a past that the Jewish boy inherits
inside the body. What is artificial is experienced and transformed into what
is natural and vice versa. As Howard Eilberg-Schwartz notes, circumcision
functions as the symbol of intergenerational continuity and fertility, as "a
rite which simultaneously confer[s] and confirm[s] one's" descent.[116] Circumcision gestures toward the paradigmatic paradox of Freud's theory of
Jewishness in that it is "physical yet not physiological, genealogical but not
genetic,"[117] a divine prescription that requires human inscription. The fact
that Jews are often defined as Jewish by their genealogy is also a matter of
human agency—a prescription and an inscription—devised and sustained
both by individuals who wrote Jewish literature and by individuals who
wrote anti-Jewish treatises from the first to the twenty-first centuries of the
Common Era. Circumcision does not *make* people Jewish, but it reminds
certain men that they were *born* Jewish. While many people are regarded as
Jewish simply because they were born to a Jewish parent, the performance
of circumcision reminds us that this so-called racial definition of Jewishness
is neither biological nor permanent (nor God-given).[118]

Like other racial markings such as skin, hair, eyes, body shape, and so
on, circumcision is not usually something individuals choose for themselves.
However, unlike other racial markings, circumcision requires Jewish parents to choose whether to transmit this particular mark of Jewishness to
their sons. Oddly enough, this aspect of circumcision is often overlooked in
discussions of Jewish identity and its racialization. For example, in a number
of discussions of George Eliot's *Daniel Deronda*, literary critics have joked
that, for the first three quarters of the eight-hundred-page book, Daniel
must have avoided "looking down," since if he had looked down he would
have seen the evidence revealing his "true" (Jewish) identity.[119] While Eliot
repeatedly alludes to the "indelible mark" of circumcision, she never explicitly names it. Yet when Daniel finds his birth-mother, it becomes evident
that she attempted to *not* transmit the marks of difference to her son, even
going so far as to arrange that he be brought up by someone other than her
and, notably, someone not like her (that is, not Jewish). We could assume,

then, that Daniel's mother would not have had her baby son circumcised (though of course, the question remains open).[120] Nonetheless, she fails to stop the transmission of a Jewish past, for by the end of the novel, Daniel "returns" to his Jewish identity. Circumcision can function as a physical and cultural reminder of racial identity, but it is still a human intervention, a material marker of a forgotten past, a "time immemorial" that cannot be re-covered except by further human inventions.[121]

The Root But Not the Solution

Recent historiography on the rise of racism in the early twentieth century often focuses on the novel emphasis on biological heredity in the late nineteenth century. Yet this supposedly new form of racism was powerful only because it was based on long-established cultural differences. Thus the post–World War II rejection of "race" in favor of "culture" was in many ways a return to the roots of racism.[122] In his work on the inflections of race, nation, and class, Etienne Balibar describes the ways in which anti-semitism was itself a cultural tradition based not on biological or physical differences but on the notion of irreducible spiritual difference. "Admittedly," writes Balibar, "bodily stigmata play a great role in its phantasmatics, but they do so more as signs of a deep psychology, as signs of a spiritual inheritance rather than a biological heredity."[123] While Balibar alludes to the religious roots of "culturalist racism," he sidesteps the historical derivations of the relationship between heredity and culture. The notion that the body shows signs of spiritual inheritance is itself a product not of sixteenth-century Spain or nineteenth-century Germany but of the first five centuries of the Common Era.[124] In this time period, the Rabbis established guidelines for performing Jewish rituals including circumcision, and they eventually insisted on the primacy of the body in determining membership in the Jewish community.[125] By contrast, Paul rejected circumcision of the body and asserted that membership in the community should be based on spiritual distinctions rather than on bodily or genealogical particularities. These distinct approaches to the definitions of community continue to shape contemporary discussions of race, culture, and religion, including discussions of Freud's final book. Central to these discussions is the Jewish practice of neonatal male circumcision. While Freud suggests that circumcision is the "deepest unconscious root of anti-semitism," it is not the solution to the questions of why anti-semitism refuses to die and why Judaism continues to survive.

This is demonstrated in the recent work of Franz Maciejewski and in his ensuing debate with Jan Assmann. According to Maciejewski, "the reality of circumcision" is the "central traumatic experience of Jewish socialization and ethnogenesis"; it is the historical event that gave rise both to monotheism (centuries before the Common Era) and to psychoanalysis (in the twentieth century).[126] In response, Assmann argues that both Freud and Maciejewski over-emphasize the importance of the body:

> With his phylogenetic constructions, Freud underestimated the effectiveness of cultural transmissions, for example the ritual of neonatal circumcision; perhaps, however, [Maciejewski] for his part underestimates the power of writing. There is monotheism also without infant-circumcision; yet monotheism is unthinkable without a canon of sacred writing which is foundational to life. In the Jewish tradition, circumcision is a "sign" which is written on the body and which, through the study of the Torah, is continued and completed as a "circumcision of the heart."[127]

In his interpretation of circumcision's function, Assmann registers a discomfort with the bodily definition of Jewishness. Specifically, he argues that circumcision functions as a sign of *anticipation* (of the boy's life) rather than a sign of *confirmation* of what has already occurred (the boy's birth and his genealogical inheritance of Jewishness). According to Assmann, the continuation and completion of the sign are achieved through the study of the Torah ("circumcision of the heart"). In privileging the "circumcision of the heart" (as the ultimate goal of circumcision of the body), Assmann ironically echoes Paul's interpretations of circumcision and of community. While he does not entirely ignore the body, he avoids the notion that circumcision *confirms* the Jewishness of a boy who is born Jewish and *continues* to mark him as Jewish regardless of whether he ever studies the Torah.

While "circumcision of the heart" appears in Deuteronomy and in Jeremiah (that is, in the Hebrew Bible), its significance emerges much more clearly in Paul's letters. For example, in his Letter to the Romans, we find an emphasis on the continuation and completion of circumcision:

> Circumcision indeed is of value if you obey the law; but if you break the law, your circumcision becomes uncircumcision. So, if a man who is uncircumcised

keeps the precepts of the law, will not his uncircumcision be regarded as circumcision? Then those who are physically uncircumcised but keep the law will condemn you who have the written code and circumcision but break the law. For he is not a real Jew who is one outwardly, nor is true circumcision something external and physical. He is a Jew who is one inwardly, and real circumcision is a matter of the heart, spiritual and not literal. His praise is not from men but from God. (2 Romans: 25–29)[128]

Like Assmann, Paul does not entirely disregard the importance of circumcision, but he shifts the emphasis away from the body by interpreting the sign of circumcision as provisional, a potential portent of what is yet to come. Paul and Assmann resist the notion that circumcision functions as a testimony to what has already occurred, evidence of a covenant that has already been cut, connecting the individual body of the boy to God and to the bodies of his ancestors. This interpretive schism runs counter to what is perhaps the greatest divide between Judaism and Christianity: Where Judaism continues to wait for the Messiah, Christianity holds that the Messiah has already arrived, precisely in the form of a human body.

Oddly, throughout their debates, Assmann and Maciejewski remain mired in the Hebrew Bible, as if two millennia of Jewish and Christian (if not also Muslim and secular) interpretations had not shaped our own understandings of these texts and traditions. For example, in drawing out the distinctions between his own position and that of Maciejewski, Assmann notes that their disagreement is foreshadowed in the Hebrew Bible. According to Assmann, Maciejewski's position is Abrahamic: "Circumcision and genealogy ('Abraham's seed') are the decisive criteria." By contrast, Assmann insists that he follows the "Mosaic-Deuteronomic position: beyond genealogy and circumcision what is decisive is the following of the Law [*Befolgung des Gesetzes*]."[129] Yet in Jewish tradition, the following of the Law entails both genealogy and circumcision.[130] Instead of presenting his disagreement with Maciejewski in terms of a split between Rabbinic and Pauline (or Jewish and Christian) hermeneutics, Assmann presents it as a difference contained within the Hebrew Bible. While he does not go as far as Paul to argue that physical circumcision does not matter, he takes a particularly Pauline perspective on the sequence of circumcision's symbolization—that is, how it functions as a sign of the Jewish people.[131] For Assmann and Paul, circumcision anticipates a spiritual fulfillment; for Rabbinic Judaism it confirms and seals a covenant.

While Assmann and Maciejewski go back and forth regarding their interpretations of circumcision and its relationship to the origins and survival of
the Jewish people, they avoid the terms of Jewish definition that have been
primary for at least the past fifteen centuries. That is, in focusing on the
importance of the originary trauma of circumcision (Maciejewski) and of
cultural mnemotechnologies (Assmann), they pass over the particularly Jewish mnemotechnology of genealogy that circumcision embodies and invokes.[132] Circumcision functions as the sign of what *has already occurred*: it
is the sign of an inheritance; it is a sign that the father has achieved a "completion" (of his own circumcision) by sustaining the genealogy of Abraham.
Though the Rabbis insisted that Jewish genealogy is matrilineal, circumcision calls upon the father to take responsibility for the boy's circumcision;
the ritual itself shifts the focus from the mother's body to the father's body.
His seed is perpetuated through his son, whose own seed-bearing organ is
fully revealed through the ritual.[133] Circumcision is a sign of an inherited
obligation to sustain the Jewish past (genealogy, tradition, and memory) in
the future, but whether this obligation will or can ever be fulfilled remains
open. Circumcision thus functions as a sign of community membership, a
reminder of the burdens and responsibilities of membership in the community, and of the sacrifices that one must perform to preserve the community
itself.[134]

Circumcision forces us to break down the dichotomies between body and
text, between cultural and biological transmission, and between conscious
and unconscious memory. As a "cultural mnemotechnology" or as an "art
of memory," circumcision recalls not only the genealogical definition of the
Jewish people, but also the Biblical text that is itself an art of memory.[135]
Yet it is unclear whether these arts of memory document or create the past:
Which came first, the Biblical description of God's command to Abraham
to circumcise himself and all his descendants (which eventually resulted in
the Jewish practice of circumcision), or the general practice of circumcision
(whose existence was documented in the Biblical text)? Did the text result in
the bodily practice or does the text document what was already a widespread
practice?[136]

While circumcision does not produce the Jew, as a cultural practice it
sustains the genealogical definition of Jewishness. For the past fifteen centuries, only a Jewish woman could "produce" a Jew: Only a child born of a
Jewish woman (that is, either a convert or a woman who was herself the

daughter of a Jewish woman) is unquestioningly counted as a member of the Jewish community.[137] This is the missing link in many discussions of circumcision that are (not surprisingly) focused on males and their members. Why would Jewish women care about circumcision when it seems like one more example of a conversation that is pertinent only to men obsessed with their penises? Why would Jewish women want to maintain a rite that re-iterates patriarchal power and privilege? The answer, I think, has nothing to do with penis envy or some vague notion that women want to castrate men. Rather, circumcision emphasizes the role of the body as the site of the production of Jewishness, and for more than fifteen centuries, only the female's body has had the power to produce Jews.

It is no accident, then, that the importance of circumcision may derive from the historical moment at which genealogy became the primary definition of membership in the Jewish community. Before the fourth century there were probably a large range of people who were known as Jews but who were not necessarily circumcised or descended from a Jewish mother or father: They were individuals who read the Jewish texts, who practiced Jewish rituals, who followed Jewish dietary regulations, or they were people who married and socialized with such people. Part of Paul's critique of Judaism was that so-called Jews didn't necessarily *act* very "Jewish" in an ethical and spiritual sense. If people were going to refer to the Law as the defining feature of Judaism, Paul insisted that they needed to fulfill the spirit of the Law rather than remain tethered to the material letter of the Law. Where Paul charged that the Rabbis over-valued the more materialistic aspects of the Law (such as circumcision), the Rabbis insisted that these rituals and regulations were foundational, and they composed and redacted texts that emphasized the material performances and practices. Thus in the first centuries of the Common Era, they established that "the offspring of a gentile mother and a Jewish father is a gentile, while the offspring of a Jewish mother and a gentile father is a Jew."[138] By the beginning of the fifth century, "at the stage of the 'definitive' formulation of Rabbinic Judaism in the Babylonian Talmud," the Rabbis rejected the idea that "to be a Jew is to 'believe such and such' or to 'practice so and so.'" Instead, they proposed "the distinct ecclesiological principle: 'An Israelite even if he [sic] sins, remains an Israelite [one remains a part of a Jewish or Israelite people whether or not one adheres to the Torah, subscribes to its major precepts, or affiliates with the community].'"[139] Regardless of the originally intended meaning of this sentence, it has been interpreted to mean that a Jew remains a

Jew regardless of apostasy; this would also suggest that a Jew remains a Jew regardless of circumcision. Even now that the Reform Movement has argued in favor of counting patrilineage as well as matrilineage, the decisive criterion remains lineage, not circumcision or Torah study.

Circumcision may *remind* a person of his inheritance of Jewish obligations—to study the Torah, to maintain the traditions, to sustain the Jewish genealogy—but it does not necessarily guarantee such continuation or completion. As Freud notes, the Jews' ethical ideas "possess the characteristic—uncompleted and incapable of completion—of obsessional neurotic reaction-formations."[140] Judaism is "open to the future"—the Messiah has *not yet* come.[141] In his meditations on the uncanny, Freud repeatedly suggests that circumcision is an uncanny reminder of castration; "Everything is uncanny [*unheimlich*] that ought to have remained secret and hidden but has come to light."[142] As a physical trace of a process that is otherwise "secret and hidden," circumcision enacts a transference that is both bodily and textual, mystical and violent, and powerful and scary in its implications. In the next chapter, I pursue the "secret" inclinations of Freud's theories: the occulted aspects of psychoanalysis, the dangerous fantasies of the psychoanalyst, and the uncontrollable transmissions from the past to the present and vice versa. While circumcision brings us to the frontiers between race, culture, and religion, psychoanalysis leads us toward the margins of scientific rationality.

Secret Inclinations beyond Direct Communication

I know that you are not without a secret inclination toward occult matters.

F R E U D , letter to Sandor Ferenczi, July 21, 1915

If one regards oneself as a sceptic, it is a good plan to have occasional doubts about one's scepticism too. It may be that I too have a secret inclination towards the miraculous which thus goes half way to meet the creation of occult facts.

F R E U D , *New Introductory Lectures on Psycho-Analysis* (1933)

To urge the patient to suppress, renounce or sublimate her instincts the moment she has admitted her erotic transference would be, not an analytic way of dealing with them, but a senseless one. It would be just as though, after summoning up a spirit from the underworld by cunning spells, one were to send him down again without having asked him a single question. One would have brought the re-pressed into consciousness, only to repress it once more in a fright. Nor should we deceive ourselves about the success of any such proceeding. As we know, the passions are little affected by sublime speeches. The patient will feel only the humiliation, and she will not fail to take her revenge for it.

F R E U D , "Observations on Transference-Love" (1915)

The Psychoanalyst as Prophetic Patient

The relationship between Freud and his younger colleagues was structured like an analysis: Freud was the father-analyst, and Carl Gustav Jung and Sandor Ferenczi were his "sons." Though he had explored the notion of transference [*Übertragung*] as early as 1905 in the postscript to the case of "Dora," in 1909–11 he saw that the situation was alarmingly repeating it-self. What was most worrisome about these repetitions was that it was not only the patients who were slipping and falling into transferential patterns, but Freud's star disciples. Where the patient (Dora) had fallen in love with the analyst (Breuer), now the analysts were falling for their patients. In the midst of intense exchanges with Jung and Ferenczi, Freud began to consider the possibility that repetitive transferential patterns might be akin to tele-pathic transmissions and may occur as the result of phylogenetic memories. Indeed, as he was privately dealing with his disciples' "secret inclinations," he made his first extensive attempts to incorporate phylogenetic memory into psychoanalytic theory in his essays on transference written from 1911 to 1915.[1] Throughout these discussions, there is an uneasy sense that such phenomena are beyond the individual's control: Transmissions from the past—impulses, fantasies, desires—fill up the present until it almost over-flows from the pressure. Finally, in *Moses and Monotheism*, Freud suggests that the Jewish subject is one whose psyche is overflowing with transmis-sions from a Jewish past; to be Jewish is to recognize a transference of Jew-ishness in one's self.

From 1907 until 1920, Freud advised his two "sons" about their danger-ous intimacies with certain young female patients. Jung's complicated affair with his patient (and analyst-in-training) Sabine Spielrein threatened to overwhelm the scientific veneer of psychoanalysis, and Ferenczi's budding affairs with his patients Gizella Pálos and her daughter Elma were almost too complicated and perverse to follow. As in any analysis, however, there were times when the structure of Freud's relationships with his "sons" was inverted, eliciting anxieties about the dangerous intimacies of letter-writing, analysis, and transference. While Ferenczi confided in Freud about his vari-ous secret inclinations, he also allowed Freud to confide in him about his own anxieties and fantasies about prophecies and telepathic communica-tions. As World War I began, Freud sent Ferenczi letters in which he fret-fully considered the possibility that he had received telepathic transmissions from the future, foretelling his own death and the death of his son. During World War I, Freud's sons Martin and Ernst were posted on the Russian warfront, and Freud waited for communications from them—hopefully only letters since anything else (such as a soldier on the front step, a telegram, or a telephone call) would announce the message of death.[2] During this anxious time, he sent Ferenczi letters almost daily, sometimes chiding him for not responding quickly or extensively enough. On July 10, 1915, Freud reported to Ferenczi that the previous night he had had "a prophetic dream which very clearly" foretold the deaths of his sons. He then attempted to rationally explain away the dream as a "bold challenge to the occult pow-ers" in response to a book (on the occult) that he had been reading earlier that day.[3] Yet even as he "rationally" clarified the dream, he did so self-consciously and ironically, boldly challenging the very powers in which he supposedly did not believe. Freud's challenges and clarifications could not conceal the fact that he could not stop thinking about this dream in the following weeks.

It was during this restless period that Freud composed "A Phylogenetic Fantasy" (or "Overview of the Transference Neuroses," its provisional title), in which, he explained to Ferenczi, he was "dealing with fantasies that disturb me and that will hardly be suitable for public expression."[4] In admitting these fantasies, he gestured toward the other secrets (fantasies or nightmares) that were then disturbing his sleep. Indeed, Freud's meditations on the inheritance of memory were deeply enmeshed with his thoughts on other mysterious processes: the transmission of thoughts and images between two individuals without any direct communication, the uncanny anticipations of the future in the present, and the disturbing ways in which roles could be reversed and exchanged. Such phenomena were beyond the realm of sensory perception and scientific proof. They also complicated questions of belief, since they could occur regardless of whether an individual believed in the phenomena of telepathy, or in the inheritance of memory, or in the existence of transference. Freud's meditations on transference [*Übertragung*] and telepathic thought-transference [*Gedankübertragung*] anticipate and illuminate his late theory of Jewishness: a theory that depends upon the inheritance of memory but that also insists upon the mysteriousness and non-materiality of such inheritance. Yet the reverse is also true: His theory of Jewishness retrospectively illuminates his earlier writings on transference and on telepathy.

During this intense period of correspondence, Freud fell into deeply transferential relationships. Even as he played the analyst ("how are your private relations?" he asks Ferenczi), he also played the role of the patient-son, desperate for his father-analyst's letters and critiques. Additionally, Freud compelled Ferenczi to play the role of his absent sons whose letters he anxiously awaited. When Ferenczi wrote back about his own phylogenetic speculations on the Ice Age, Freud quickly replied, evidently annoyed: "Would like to have heard more critique about the phylogenetic fantasy."[5] Two days later, on July 20, 1915, Freud writes again, remarking on the "coincidence" of Ferenczi's own thoughts on phylogenetic patterns.[6] Freud closes the letter, "I hope to hear from you soon, as well as how your private relations are taking shape."[7] The following day, before Ferenczi had a chance to respond to this letter, Freud sent another letter to Ferenczi: "You will marvel that I am now bombarding you this way with letters." Whereas Ferenczi had often sent Freud long letters full of speculative fantasies, now Freud sent his younger colleague long and anxious letters, hopeful for some reassuring response to his phylogenetic fantasy. In the July 21 letter, Freud continues, reminding Ferenczi that he knows about his younger friend's "secret inclination for the occult," but he goes on to speculate further about his own inclination: his possibly "prophetic" dream of July 8/9. Having just received a letter from his son Martin dated July 7, he concludes that "the prophecy has already failed. So, we are certainly not dealing with such crude things."[8] The letter reported that Martin's arm had been grazed by a Russian bullet, and so Freud reasoned that "since he himself is writing, it really can't have been something worse. . . . He doesn't indicate a date [of the bullet's grazing his arm]." Freud continues, speculating about the time of day and the increased sensitivity to such prophetic transmissions at night. Nonetheless, he overlooks the (obvious) fact that Martin's letter of July 7 could not serve as evidence that the prophecy had failed (and that Martin was still alive) because the date of the letter was the day *before* the night (July 8/9) on which Freud had the dream about Martin's death.

Freud considered the possibility that the dream was truly prophetic and telepathic as if this act of consideration would itself boldly challenge the occult powers and the angel of death. While this series of letters and events could be interpreted as proof of Freud's "ambivalent" feelings toward the occult, it is also evidence of a negative prophetic logic. As he explains in *The Psychopathology of Everyday Life*, "prophetic" dreams and signs are by no means meaningless, even when they do not "come true." Where the "superstitious person" projects his motivations onto the external world, Freud insists that—as a psychoanalyst—he "looked within."[9] In this case, Freud was both the analyst and the superstitious person, and as such he was simultaneously engaged in both processes: He looked within *and* projected his wishes onto the external world in a sort of self-replicating mirroring process. By entertaining the possibility of the prophetic potential of dreams and the uncanny prophecies of chance events, Freud hoped to keep these prophecies (such as the death of his son or his own death) from coming true.[10] And yet, by considering the prophecy, he acknowledged its potential.

The question is not whether Freud believed in the reality of telepathic thought-transference or any other occult mysteries, or even whether such phenomena are actually real. Whereas he was concerned about the "truth" of his patients' accounts of their past, he never expressed any doubt about the influence of the past on the present or about the phenomenon of transference. According to Freud, transference occurs both inside and outside psychoanalysis; it is unstoppable if not inevitable.[11] The challenge, then, is how to take control of these transmissions and repetitions before they take control of you. "Transference arises spontaneously in all human relationships just as it does between the patient and the physician," Freud writes. "The less its presence is suspected, the more powerfully it operates. So psycho-analysis does not create it, but merely reveals it to consciousness and gains control of it in order to guide psychical processes towards the desired goal."[12] These transmissions could seize control of the psychoanalyst and the patient, and, before you know it, the situation could explode: Prophecies could come true; patients might analyze their analysts, or worse, marry them. However, if the analyst could recognize the phenomena before they spin out of control, he might be able to make the transference "the true vehicle of therapeutic influence."[13]

Freud's anxieties about the potential of transference invoke paradoxes and images at the heart of the Jewish Question. Transference occurs not only in psychoanalysis, but between individuals every day. So, too, the Jewish Question confronts not only "real" Jews,[14] but everyone who has an image, sense, question, or feeling about Jews, Jewishness, or Judaism; the transference of Jewishness (and the questions it raises) occurs not only in Jewish communities or families but between individuals every day. There is a sense that transference is the key to psychoanalysis, to the invocations of the past which overwhelm the present. The individual herself becomes a sort of test tube where the present and the past, the living and the ghosts, are mixed together, creating potentially explosive reactions. If these mixtures are left to their own devices, they can drive a person crazy. Freud attempted to name these invisible forces—they were ghostly transmissions from the past that took up residence in the individual's psyche and found a home in the unconscious. But in naming these forces, psychoanalysis might also heighten their effects. Likewise, the recognition of a Jewish past (real or imagined) may create an extra "catalytic ferment" in the test tube.[15] It is unclear what causes such a transferential reaction. It may be solid, liquid, or gas; it may be a matter of chemistry or history; or, it may be the circuitry of genealogy, shock-waves transporting us into the past, present, and future, condensing the matter of the moment.

If to be Jewish is to be caught in an interminable process of transference, it is highly likely that a person can be Jewish without being conscious of it. As Freud writes of transference, "the less its presence is suspected, the more powerfully it operates."[16] Similarly, in his "Address to the Society of B'nai B'rith" in 1926, he explains that what made "the attraction of Jewry and Jews irresistible" were the "many obscure emotional forces, which were *the more powerful the less they could be expressed in words*."[17] The less one suspects that one is Jewish—the less one suspects "its presence"—the more powerfully the Jewish Question impresses its shapeless content, its "obscure forces." Indeed, it is possible that the most rabid anti-semites (certain of their own non-Jewishness) are those who can find no other way of expressing their suspicions about the presence of something "obscure," something uncanny and strange in themselves. The distinction between anti-semitism and Jewish ethnic pride becomes a matter of repression or expression.

Mysterious Heredity

The previous chapters argued that Freud's late insistence on the inheritance of memory was not exceptional in the context of his earlier work or in the context of his contemporaries' thoughts on questions of heredity and evolution. Nonetheless, in *Moses and Monotheism* he tarries a while before turning to heredity as an explanation for why and how the traces of the Mosaic tradition have been infallibly transmitted over so many generations. It is only after he first considers the possibility that the tradition could have been transmitted through oral and written communication that he concludes that these forms of "direct communication" are insufficient to explain its persistence. "When I spoke of the survival of a tradition," he writes, "I had mostly in mind an *inherited* tradition of this kind and *not one transmitted by communication*."[18] Freud turns to the medium of heredity as if it were familiar, but he makes it mysterious by insisting on its most obvious quality: the fact that it functions outside the realm of communication, outside representation, language, images, or customs—in short, without the participation of sensory perception. Freud's theory of Jewishness derives from his earlier explorations of other mysterious phenomena (such as telepathy and trans-ference) that occur in an extra-sensory realm, beyond language, beyond ges-ture, beyond representation. Jewish tradition emerges as a persistent process of transference; to be Jewish is to be caught up in this process, interminably and sometimes unconsciously.

Freud makes what we believe we know under the name of heredity and Jewishness enigmatic. In his essay "Freud and the Scene of Writing," Jacques Derrida argues that Freud "does not simply use" metaphors "for di-dactic ends." While Derrida focuses on Freud's use of scriptorial metaphors to illuminate the psychoanalytic concept of memory, his interpretation of these metaphors suggests a productive way of reading Freud's discussions of hereditary transmission. "If to manipulate means to make of the known an allusion to the unknown," Derrida writes, Freud does not manipulate metaphors of writing; rather, "he makes what we believe we know under the name of writing enigmatic." Freud's metaphors are "indispensable" not because they illuminate memory but "because they illuminate, inversely the meaning of a trace in general."[19] Likewise, his metaphors of heredity and Jewishness are indispensable because they illuminate "inversely" the nature of transmission, subjectivity, and modernity. Though Freud founded psy-choanalysis upon ideals of conversation and communication, he "inter-rupts" our confidence in these ideals. Instead, he suggests that pre- or extra-linguistic forms of transmission, such as heredity or telepathy, are always in the background, silently and subtly controlling the more palpable transmis-sions such as writing and talking. Precisely because they are ungraspable, heredity and telepathy may be more potent; unlike that which is sensorially apprehended or physically graspable, such phenomena "seize" the psyche, compelling the imagination to conjure mysteries beyond belief. If to see is to believe, invisible phenomena such as telepathy, transference, and Jewish-ness (both the character and the invisible/unnameable Jewish god) stretch the boundaries of rational belief even as they define rationality itself.

The Victorian and Modernist periods were marked by intense debates about "ghosts in the machine," the occult haunting of rationality and mo-dernity.[20] Discussions about telepathy and ghostly communication were in-extricably linked to the "wider reconceptualizations of the borders of individual consciousness and emerge together with new communication technologies such as the telephone and the telegraph."[21] Because of the new permeability of geographic borders, many Eastern European Jews (like members of Freud's own family) were able to immigrate and attempt to integrate with Christian Western-European society. Thus, as Freud developed theories of transference and of the inheritance of memory, he was haunted by the imagery, logic, and anxieties of the occult, and these were themselves haunted by the Jewish Question.

Telepathy and Jewishness emerge as processes of transmission whose potential failures are tied up with the "inevitability of communicative leakage."[22] Both telepathic communication and Jewish tradition linger as archaic remnants and as prophetic ghosts of a future past. These images play into two seemingly opposed refrains about the future of Jewishness in the early twentieth century: On the one hand, Jewish leaders worried about ensuring the future of *Judentum*—the Jewish people, Jewish traditions, and Judaism.[23] They worried about the transmission of Jewishness from one generation to the next; they worried that Judaism *would not arrive at its destination* in the future. On the other hand, the persistent image of the Wandering Jew—uncanny and eternal—suggests that Jewishness cannot help but be transmitted to the future; if it is repressed (oppressed, forgotten), it will return. If it is expelled, it will flourish elsewhere. Of course, the Wandering Jews' uncanny survival was not only a positive prophecy about the future: In the anti-semitic imaginary, the Wandering Jew had long been a part of the Christian portrayal of the Jews as disembodied, spectrally traveling the earth as a consequence of their rejection of Jesus Christ. Anti-semitic literature depicted the Jews as disease-ridden—cancerous and contagious—both internally developing and externally acquired.[24] As Susan Shapiro writes in her study of "the uncanny Jew," "the success of the Jew in mimicking the German further threatened the German's ability to define himself as, precisely, not a Jew, ironically making 'jewification' (in a logic of 'contagion') both more pervasive and threatening because [it was] invisible, unlocatable and, thus, uncontainable."[25] In attempting to describe the nature of the unconscious, telepathic transmissions, and transferential reactions, Freud turns to images that implicitly evoke the "uncanny" position of the Jews in Western Europe. So too, in his meditations on the Jewish Question, he invokes the very same images and logic that "haunt" his earlier explorations of transference, telepathy, and the unconscious.[26]

While numerous scholars have explored the relationships between Freud's texts on the occult with his more "properly" psychoanalytic works, there has been little discussion of how these matters are intertwined with his attempts to confront the Jewish Question.[27] Freud worried that psycho-analysis would be regarded as a Jewish science and, as such, less than purely scientific, but his texts on Lamarckism, telepathy, and transference have also raised suspicions about the scientific nature of psychoanalysis. More specifically, each of these elements has elicited doubts about Freud's scientific credentials, his authority, and his ability to objectively observe his subject matter.

The idea that Freud's earlier discussions of telepathy and transference anticipate and illuminate his late theorization of Jewishness—and vice versa—is itself caught up in a logic of transference. Alan Bass has suggested that this "subversion of what is usually taken as a fixed sequence" is a central concern of Jacques Derrida's, particularly in his book *The Post Card.* But this "subversion" is not original to Derrida; rather, it is central to those aspects of Freud's work from which Derrida draws inspiration. As Bass writes, "What if the usual and seemingly fixed sequence were reversible? What if each term of the sequence contained within itself the principle that subverts the usual progression? What could there be between each term and itself that would operate this subversion?"[28] Freud's conceptualizations of transference and inheritance are not so much "sequences" but constant processes of transmission, unpredictably moving back and forth between individuals, generations, and genera. There is a compression of time: The past overwhelms the present, even as the present pushes toward the future and calls upon an absent past, present only insofar as it can be imagined. This logic is at the heart of Freud's meditations on the "timelessness of the unconscious";[29] it is also at the heart of God's covenant with the Jewish people: "Not with you alone do I make this covenant and this oath, but with him who stands here this day before the Lord, and also with him who is not here with us this day" (Deuteronomy 29: 14–15). Transference and telepathy suggest that the human subject (and perhaps particularly the Jewish subject) is caught up in a process in which the present is never just the present: Each moment overflows with the past, driving it toward the future.

Such concepts of compressed time and overwhelming influence resonate with the literary critic Harold Bloom's theory of the anxiety of influence. Literary authors are forever anxious about being overly influenced by their precursors and about establishing the originality of their own voices. Bloom reverses the sequence: Authors are actually influenced by their *successors*, their interpreters, and perhaps even their plagiarizers. For example, the

Bible is belatedly "influenced" by Shakespeare because, when we read it, we hear the echoes of Shakespeare. So, too, Shakespeare realizes Freud's notions of the family romance, the Oedipal complex, and the compulsion to repeat. The poetic predecessor is fathered by his successor. The son discovers (or invents) a father whom he loves, hates, envies, and worships. The son may sustain his father's legacy or he may be compelled to "kill" the father in order to become a father himself. Bloom re-produces Freud's concept of the family romance as an analogue for "the revisionary ratios that govern intra-poetic relations."[30] Such revisions—transformations of sons into fathers and vice versa—also govern intra-generational relations in their re-inventions of tradition. There is a sense that poets are never content with "second chances," but continually strive for a "vision of immortality." Poets (and sons) must go further than their predecessors.[31] Instead of a clear sequence in which one generation influences the next, the transmission and transformation goes backward and forward in time. Sons do not simply sustain or destroy their father's legacies; they transform them. "Influence," writes Bloom, ventriloquizing Oscar Wilde, is "a transference of personality, a mode of giving away what is most precious to one's self, and its exercise produces a sense, and, it may be, a reality of loss. Every disciple takes away something from his master."[32] The disciple masters and rewrites the master; the two individuals trade places, over and over, such that it is unclear who is the predecessor and who is the successor.[33]

A Theory of Jewish Transference

In a zoology class at a large European university, the students are assigned to write a paper on elephants. The French student writes a treatise on "The Sexual Behavior of Elephants"; the German puts together "A Comprehensive Bibliography of Everything About The Elephant"; and the Jewish student composes a study of "The Elephant and the Jewish Question."

The joke assumes that the listener knows and believes in national typologies, but the humor of the joke resides in the way that the Jew is defined by her very preoccupation with typology.[34] Eric Santner presents a version of this joke in his discussion of Philippe Lacoue-Labarthe, Jean-Luc Nancy, and Slavoj Žižek's reflections on the self-reflexive logic underlying national typologization, particularly that which underlies anti-semitism.[35]

According to Žižek, anti-semitism derives not from a hatred of the Jewish type per se but from the realization that there is no Jewish type. In the words of Alfred Rosenberg, Hitler's chief ideologue, "All European nations possess a well-defined 'spiritual shape' [*Gestalt*] which gives expression to their ethnic character—and this 'spiritual shape' is precisely what is missing in Jews."[36] For Žižek, this "very 'shapelessness' is the constitutive feature of subjectivity" that underlies "the Judaeo-democratic concept of 'abstract universalism.'"[37] Ironically, the "shapelessness" of Jewishness allows the Jewish people both to embrace "abstract universality" and to claim that the Jewish people are specially chosen by a god who is abstract (or shapeless) and universal. Similarly, Freud suggests that America's sense of itself as "God's own country" is supported by the shapelessness of its content ("Americanness").[38]

By contrast, Santner argues that the Jewish people are defined by a "too-muchness," a "*jew-essence*" that overflows all attempts to define the Jewish type.[39] Where Jacques Lacan uses the word *joiussance* to refer to a kind of intense pleasure that is almost too much to bear, Santner suggests that *jew-essence* is an "uncanny secretion of *jouissance*."[40] If all humans experience *jouissance*, why would some people overflow with *jew-essence*? (Would a "half-Jewish" person also overflow with such *jew-essence*, or are such questions too real, too earthly, too physical? And if so, why?) In Santner's words, the human psyche is psychoanalytically "defined by the fact that it includes more reality than it can contain, is the bearer of an excess, a too much of pressure that is not merely psychological."[41] How, then, do we make sense of his description of *jew-essence* as the defining feature of the Jewish subject? What is this "essence" that overflows all attempts to define the subject? Is there a *jew-essence* that defines *all* human subjects? Is such a quality particular to the Jewish psyche? Or is the Jewish psyche defined as Jewish precisely because it overflows with this "essence" whereas non-Jewish psyches are able to contain it without allowing it to overflow? Is the Jewish Question simply an intensified version of the conundrum that underlies all attempts to define and come to terms with modern subjectivity?

Santner interprets *Moses and Monotheism* as Freud's attempt to understand the enigma of his own "essential nature" as a Jew by recovering the memory of a previously unnamed trauma. For Santner, this "essential nature" is a "compulsive hermeneutic drive" to decode, or what he calls "*Jewish transference*, i.e. the unconscious transmission of the cultural patterns and values—of *essence*—that make a Jew a Jew."[42] While he alludes to the unconsciousness of this process, he ultimately reads Jewishness as a conscious activity of interpretation and translation. Santner sees an occult logic haunting the margins of Freud's discussions of Jewishness and its transmission. However, he argues that the "prospect of engaging in a kind of spiritism is in part what pushed Freud to his Lamarckian hypothesis: better controversial science than occultism."[43] While Santner distinguishes between controversial science, interpretation, and hermeneutic drives on the one hand, and occultism, telepathy, and spiritualism on the other, for Freud these realms were not mutually exclusive. Freud's science is controversial precisely because it attends to the occult nature of the unconscious, the uncontrollable forces that shape the question of subjectivity in general and of the Jewish subject in particular. Freud's "Lamarckian hypothesis" about the hereditary transmission of Jewishness is an extension of his earlier explorations of telepathy and transference, both of which were explicitly marked by the Jewish Question. Freud's theories of transference and Jewishness (as well as *Jewish transference*) were controversial precisely because they accentuated the occult leanings of his science, the magic of the hermeneutic drive, and the mysteries of heredity.

In discussing transference and telepathy, Freud not only uses images that implicitly refer to the position of the Jewish people in Europe, he employs a logic that drips with the anxieties of a Jewish person attempting to answer the Jewish Question.[44] While this anxiety may be seen as a matter of one's Jewishness, it is not limited to Jews, since to confront the Jewish Question is to be a part of the study: to be wrapped up in its distinctions, positions, and consequences, to take up a position of influence or of being influenced. Indeed, part of what emerges from reading Freud's theory of Jewishness as a theory of transference (and vice versa) is the idea that such positions—Jew and non-Jew, disciple and master, analyst and patient, father and son, self and Other—are not entirely stable or irreversible, and this is what imbues the relationships with a surplus of anxiety in anticipation of the trauma of transference. As I discussed in Chapter 1, Freud's early discussions of the etiology of hysteria were shaped by his attempts to maintain an authoritative scientific position, objectively distinct from the suspiciously creative [*künstlich*] inclinations of his (mostly Jewish) patients.[45] However, as he established transference as central to the psychoanalytic process, he implicitly recognized that he could not so easily separate himself from his subject matter or its tendencies. Both the analyst and patient were subject to transferential reactions, transmissions from their pasts that crowded and controlled the present. While he attempted to distinguish paranoid reasoning and spiritualist explorations from "properly" psychoanalytic investigations, he was well aware of the similarities and interactions between the activities.[46] Reading through his correspondence, we find him seriously considering the possibility that the future might be prophesied by signs and letters in the present, and that these transmissions may be archaic traces of an ancient past. Like the transferential processes of psychoanalysis proper, Jewish transference emerges as a process that can operate without individuals' participation or agreement, even if its presence is more or less suspected (acknowledged or avoided) at any particular moment in the present.

Pseudoscientific Metaphors: Believing the Consequences

In reading heredity, telepathy, transference, and Jewishness as metaphors, I do not mean to suggest that they should be read *only* as metaphors—like writing, they are *real* and their realities are nowhere more clear than in their consequences. While discussions of Freud's "position" on these matters have often focused on the question of his belief (in the reality of telepathy, in the existence of God) or his feelings (positive or negative, proud or ashamed to be Jewish), Freud was sensitive to the fact that it ultimately made no difference what he believed or felt. Similarly, in the matter of transference, he might have wished that he needed to deal with only the patient's feelings for the analyst, but he soon realized that the analyst's own feelings could subtly, sexually, and disastrously shape the patient's own transference. Freud avoided publicly discussing this phenomenon of "counter-transference" for it suggested that the analyst was not in control of the situation: Ghosts, transmissions, thoughts, and feelings could escape one's body, enter another's body, and cause chemical explosions.

In confronting the vicissitudes of transference, telepathy, and Jewishness, Freud recognized that it was impossible to maintain a purely objective view on these matters. While much has been made of his attempt to maintain a rational scientific stance, recent scholarship suggests that the question of Freud's belief or disbelief in occultism is irrelevant because "psychical research is not an occult practice like Spiritualist séances or mediumistic prophecies, requiring belief; nor is it a paranormal experience like forebodings or superstitions, again requiring belief; it is, rather, the *disinterested* investigation of occult practices and paranormal experiences."[47] Despite the scientific ambitions of psychical and psychoanalytical researchers, it was impossible to remain detached: In dealing with transference, Freud recognized that he was caught up in the processes he was trying to describe. Likewise, he did not attempt to completely deny the possibility of telepathy; instead, he imagined the possibilities—both fantastic and nightmarish—that might ensue if it occurred. The fantasy was that these transmissions might be controllable; the nightmare was that the wrong people might seize control. Finally, in the matter of Jewishness, Freud was acutely aware that as a Jewish scientist, anything he said would be regarded as suspiciously non-objective. Thus he often noted that it was not Jews who should speak against antisemitism but rather non-Jews, since non-Jews had a better chance of convincing other non-Jews that their positions were objectively true.[48]

What emerges in each of these cases is a sense that Freud was explicitly toying with the margins of science—not so much with demystifying seemingly mystical experiences, but with integrating experiences of the unknown and unknowable into the very practice and theorization of psychoanalysis. Though his earliest and latest psychoanalytic works suggest parallels between psychoanalysis, medicine, and history (as I argued in Chapter 1), in his discussions of transference and telepathy, Freud turns to comparisons with other forms of science, particularly chemistry and telecommunication. On the surface, chemistry might seem a more rational model of science than psychoanalysis, but it was itself historically associated with alchemy, "cunning spells," and other mystical modes of transformation.[49] Chemistry "blurs the identity of what we call rationality"; it is a "hybrid creation: half science, half technique."[50] Similarly, while telecommunicative technologies may seem more concretely tethered to the realities of the physical world than the mercurial exchanges of psychoanalysis, they began as futuristic fantasies, shrouded in the mists of spiritual communion with those who were dead or too distant for "normal" direct communication. Thus, in his attempts to concretely and scientifically demonstrate psychoanalytic technique, Freud veers into territories that yet again threaten the scientific veneer of his project.

It is thus not surprising that Ernest Jones unsuccessfully tried to convince Freud to change his tune about the two matters on either side of transference: the "controversial science" of Lamarckism and the "occultism" of telepathy.⁵¹ Freud's considerations of intergenerational transmission, transference, and telepathy are inextricably linked not only by Jones' anxieties about these matters, but by a series of linguistic, historical, and conceptual resonances. *Linguistic* because Freud uses the same root word—*Übertragung*—to refer to transference, telepathic thought-transference, and intergenerational transmission. *Historical* because Freud's meditations on these three forms of transmission were concurrent: In the very same letters in which he confronts the problems and questions of transference and the inheritance of memory, he also considers the possibilities of telepathy and prophecy. *Conceptual* because the images and anxieties are interwoven, repeated, and transformed: Explosive chemical reactions, telephones, foreign bodies, and alien guests haunt Freud's writing not only on these three forms of transmission but also on the unconscious and its symptoms.

Übertragung: *Linguistic Traces in the Background*

At the end of *Totem and Taboo*, Freud acknowledges that he is left with the question of how the memory of the primal murder could have survived over so many generations. Specifically, he asks, "What are the ways and means employed by one generation in order to *hand on* [*übertragen*] its mental states to the next one?"⁵² While the *Standard Edition* translates *übertragen* as "hand on," the German word is the verb form of *Übertragung*, the word that Freud uses to refer to the psychoanalytic concept of transference. In "Analysis Terminable and Interminable" (1937), Freud suggests that "the psychological peculiarities of families, races and nations . . . and even particular psychical contents, such as symbolism, have no other sources than hereditary transmission [*erbliche Übertragung*]," which have left their traces in "the archaic heritage."⁵³ Finally, in *Moses and Monotheism*, in the course of a long discussion of the vicissitudes of the recording and transmission of the memory of Moses' murder, he writes that the "trustworthiness" of the tradition "suffered from the fact that it was less stable and definite than the written account and exposed to numerous changes and alterations when it was *handed on* [*übertragen*] from one generation to another by oral communication."⁵⁴ The term is repeated as he tries to understand how the tradition "had been *handed on* [*übertragen*] from grandfather to grandchild."⁵⁵ In retracing Freud's earlier discussions of the *transference* [*Übertragung*] of memories, thoughts and ideas—the ways in which they are handed on [*über-tragen*]—it becomes clear that his repeated choice of the word *übertragen* is not simply a matter of coincidence. (He could have written that the memory-traces were *inherited* [*geerbt* or *ererbt*] or *passed on* [*weitergegeben*].) Yet Freud assumes that beyond all the distortions of "direct communication" there are memory-traces that have been infallibly *transferred* through some other medium.

In *Totem and Taboo*, Freud presents two possible solutions to the question of intergenerational transmission. Asserting that "direct communication and tradition . . . are not enough to account for the process" of transmission between generations, he turns to the possibility that the memory-traces of the primal murder were biologically transmitted.[56] "A part of the problem," he writes, "seems to be met by the inheritance of psychical dispositions."[57] However, he goes on to attempt to solve the *other* part of the problem by further exploring the transmissive possibilities of traditions. Though people may have attempted to ruthlessly suppress the violent memories, Freud explains that "an unconscious understanding . . . of all the customs, ceremonies and dogmas left behind by the original relation to the father may have made it possible for later generations to take over their heritage of emotion."[58] When Freud was nearly finished writing *Totem*, he sent it to his friend Sandor Ferenczi. Ferenczi was aware that Freud had been trying to keep phylogenetic memory from forcing its way into the foreground of psychoanalysis.[59] Thus he wrote to Freud to say that his "idea of transmission by means of *unconscious understanding* . . . forces the phylogenetic theories into the *background*."[60] However, neither Freud nor Ferenczi could make the phylogenetic memories stay in the background for long. Indeed, Freud was on the verge of exploring the possibility that phylogenetic theories were not necessarily alternatives to theories of "unconscious understanding" but possibly part of the same process of uncanny transmission.

In the following years, Freud came to see the biological inheritance of phylogenetic memory as an explanation for the "unconscious understanding" that works in the background, moving between generations and between individuals beyond any forms of "direct communication." Likewise, as he attempted to describe telepathic transmissions, he used similar terms, noting that telepathy might have been an archaic form of communication that, even after the invention of language, had persisted "in the background."[61] Eventually, in *Moses and Monotheism*, he would attend to the particular forces that had operated in the "background" of the Jewish people and that had persistently defined them. As he explains, despite the Israelites' murder of Moses and their subsequent repression of his memory, "this tradition of a great past . . . *continued to work in the background*," and "gradually gained more and more power over men's minds, and . . . finally succeeded . . . in calling back to life the religion of Moses which had been established and then abandoned long centuries earlier."[62] Tradition lingers behind the scenes, conveying secret messages, haunted by global conspiracies and spectral cryptographies.[63] Freud's attention to these forces was not an exceptional excursion into non-psychoanalytic realms; it was of a piece with his earliest work in which he explored how these "background forces" (the unconscious, the memory-traces, and their vicissitudes) shape the foreground (the conscious, the present, the future).

Transferential Transformations: Psychoanalysis and the Chemistry of Love

Following their trip to America in 1909, Freud anxiously corresponded with Jung and Ferenczi about the possibilities of transference [*Übertragung*] and telepathic thought-transference [*Gedankübertragung*]. Throughout this correspondence, he attempted to maintain control of psychoanalysis and to protect it from his colleagues' questionable interests. Specifically, both Ferenczi and Jung increasingly explored phenomena that were regarded as occult—mythology, prophecies, and telepathy. While Freud advised Jung and Ferenczi to keep quiet about their "secret inclinations" for the occult, he was obviously far more concerned about their secret inclinations for certain young female patients.[64] Indeed, neither Jung's nor Ferenczi's interests in the occult had ever been secret: Ferenczi's first published paper in 1899 was on mediumship, and Jung's doctoral dissertation was "On the Psychology and Pathology of So-called Occult Phenomena" (1902).[65] Thus, while Freud worried about their secret inclinations for their patients, he expressed this discomfort by advising them on their not-so-secret inclinations for the occult.

Freud's first extensive discussion of transference appears in his "Five Lectures" (presented at Clark University in Massachusetts in 1909 and published in 1910), but many of his most revealing comments about the subject appear in his correspondence with Jung and Ferenczi from this same time period. As Jung's affair with his patient Sabine Spielrein reached its climax,

Freud knew that he needed to deal with the messy situation. To Jung, he gave circumspect but pointed advice: These experiences "help us to develop the thick skin we need and to dominate 'counter-transference,' which is after all a permanent problem for us."[66] Obviously, Freud had ample reason to be worried about the "permanent" possibility that psychoanalysts would continue to fall into transferential love relationships with their patients, but in the "Five Lectures," he makes almost no mention of the analyst's transference. Nonetheless, his anxieties about transference and its counter-phenomenon bubble to the surface in these lectures: Borrowing an analogy from chemistry, he notes that "it is only in the raised temperature of [the patient's] experience of the transference that [his symptoms] can be resolved and reduced to other psychical products." Thus the physician "plays the part of a catalytic ferment which temporarily attracts to itself the affects liberated in the process."[67] In this passage, Freud portrays the transferential reaction not as a chemist's carefully controlled experiment in a test tube but as a naturally occurring phenomenon. Here is where the analogy breaks down: If "transference arises *spontaneously* in all human relationships just as it does between the patient and the physician," there is no need for the physician to serve as a catalyst.[68]

Ultimately, Freud maintained a more studied silence on the matter of counter-transference than he did on the matter of telepathy and the occult. As the complications of Jung's affair with Spielrein became clearer, Freud advised his colleague, "We must never let our poor neurotics drive us crazy. I believe an article on 'counter-transference' is sorely needed; of course we could not publish it, we should have to circulate copies among ourselves."[69] Freud suggests that the matter of counter-transference—like the matter of telepathy—is a deep, dark family secret, one that must be controlled from within. Indeed, the secret article on counter-transference was apparently never written, while "secret" articles on telepathy *were* written and were, in fact, circulated among the "secret" psychoanalytic committee (and later published).[70] Freud goes so far as to blame Jung's difficulties on the very project of psychoanalysis. Again using one of his many analogies with chemistry, he tells Jung to

> remember Lassalle's fine sentence about the chemist whose test tube had cracked: "With a slight frown over the resistance of matter, he gets on with his work." In view of the kind of matter we work with, it will never be possible to

avoid little laboratory explosions. Maybe we didn't slant the test tube enough, or we heated it too quickly. In this way we learn what part of the danger lies in the matter and what part in our way of handling it.[71]

While Freud pictures the analyst as the chemist, it is not entirely clear what the "matter" is—is it the patient's feelings for the physician, or is it the physician's feelings for the patient? Is it her symptoms or is it psychoanalysis itself?

It is significant that Freud's first published reference to counter-transfer-ence appears in an essay titled "The Future Prospects of Psycho-Analytic Therapy" (1910), for what ultimately made him concerned about transfer-ence was the fact that now "a considerable number of people are practising psychoanalysis and exchanging their observations with one another."[72] In other words, with clear prospects for both expansion and a future, Freud realized that he could not necessarily control how his ideas would be inter-preted, applied, and disseminated. In this essay, he acknowledges only that counter-transference arises in the psychoanalyst "as a result of the patient's influence on his unconscious feelings, and we are almost inclined to insist that he shall recognize this counter-transference in himself and overcome it."[73] Freud seems to almost (but not quite) blame the patient for influenc-ing the analyst, but he avoids the obvious question: How could she *not* in-fluence the analyst? If it is the analyst's job to listen, to be influenced by the patient, how can he remain neutral, like a surgeon who cannot let his feel-ings dictate the course of his knife,[74] or like a chemist who merely frowns over his test tube? This could be an explosive situation if the patient acts as a catalyst for the analyst's transference and vice versa. Freud was well aware that the analyst's unconscious reactions influence the patient's reactions, but to admit to the interactive form of transference would be far too danger-ous. Even so, he hesitates in his recommendations: "we are *almost* inclined"—but not entirely decided—that the psychoanalyst should "recog-nize . . . and overcome" the counter-transference. Whereas Ferenczi would later follow this strand of thought much further in his development of mu-tual analysis, Freud continued to treat the matter with utmost caution.[75]

Technologies, Nightmares, Dreams, and Occultism

While Freud experimented with modeling psychoanalytic technique on chemistry, he recognized that the psychoanalyst could not exert complete control over the analytic relationship any more than an individual can control his or her inheritance. In "Recommendations to Physicians Practicing Psychoanalysis" (1912), Freud paraphrases his oft-quoted advice that the patient should say whatever comes to mind. Here, however, he gives advice not to the patient, but to the physician, who "must put himself in a position to make use of everything he is told for the purposes of interpretation and of recognizing the concealed unconscious material without substituting a censorship of his own for the selection that the patient has forgone."[76] Whereas previously Freud warned that the transference was "ordained to be the greatest obstacle," now he worries that the analyst himself can impede the transference and the cure. He explains the matter in a succinct "formula":

> He must turn his own unconscious like a receptive [*empfangendes*] organ towards the transmitting unconscious of the patient. He must adjust himself to the patient as a telephone receiver is adjusted to the transmitting microphone. Just as the receiver converts back into soundwaves the electric oscillations in the telephone line which were set up by sound waves, so the doctor's unconscious is able, from the derivatives of the unconscious which are communicated to him, to reconstruct that unconscious, which has determined the patient's free associations.[77]

Freud's "formula" transforms the unconscious into an inanimate (non-human) technology, an apparatus designed for receiving and sending. This is a strange model of the psychoanalytic conversation: In this passage, the analyst does not simply hear the sounds of the patient's voice; rather, his unconscious receives the entire contents of the patient's unconscious. The psychoanalytic conversation anticipates and models a telephone conversation, for while the physician and the patient sit in the same room, the distance between the unconscious apparatuses of the two people is heightened by the fact that the patient does not look at the physician sitting behind his or her reclining body. As in a telephone conversation, there are obstacles to complete communication. (An actual telephone would not improve the situation since there would be static, missed connections, misunderstood words, and delays in transmission.) Freud imagines a virtual (imaginary, futuristic) telephone that might allow one unconscious to receive the vibrations—feelings, memories, thoughts—of the other. Mysterious transmissions through a virtual telephone might even lead to a new form of intimacy.[78]

Such descriptions begin to sound like fairy tales or prophecies. Indeed, Freud was quite aware that the new transmitting tele-technologies—railways, telegraphy, and telephony—had adjusted our "mutual relations" and changed the way we communicate.[79] "With every tool," he writes in *Civilization and Its Discontents* (1930), "man is perfecting his own organs, whether motor or sensory, or is removing the limits to their functioning."[80] Along with extending the human sensory apparatus, then, these new technologies made it possible for rational scientific minds to believe in realities that *sounded* like fairy tales, myths, or ancient prophecies. "With the help of the telephone," Freud writes, man can now "hear at distances which would be respected as unattainable even in a fairy tale."[81] The new reality of hearing the actual voice of a person who was physically miles away made it not unreasonable to expect that one could at least sense the thoughts of a person who was only feet away. Indeed, in some respects, telepathy begins to sound almost more reasonable than telephony. This is not a completely technologically deterministic argument—people had imagined telephony and television long before such tele-technologies became commonplace reality in the late nineteenth and early twentieth centuries. Indeed, the wishful imagination of such super-natural possibilities—in science fiction, myths, or dreams—is no doubt in some way a prerequisite for the development of the actual technologies.[82] Telepathy and transferential technologies are separated by only a thread of rationalization: "the interpretive claims of psychoanalysis make the analyst resemble the fortune teller."[83]

In his lecture on "Dreams and Occultism" (1933), Freud returns to the image of the telephone to describe the "technology" of telepathic transmission. In an attempt to describe an example of the telepathic process, he turns to the telephone, but he fumbles with the technological comparisons: "It is as if she had been informed by telephone," he explains, quickly adding, "though such was not the case; it is a kind of psychical counterpart to wireless telegraphy."[84] The technological metaphor begins to disintegrate for the telephone is a *material* form of communication, in some ways not so different from language itself: Thought is transformed into sounds, which are then translated back into meaning by the listener. With the telephone, this process is further abstracted: Speech is transduced into electrical impulses along a wire and retransduced into sound and sent to the receiver. By moving to telegraphy, Freud at once moves into a realm both more and less material: Messages travel along mysterious wireless routes, but they are transformed into another linguistic code of inscription such that the result is a series of marks that are static in place and time.

Lurking beneath the surface of Freud's technological descriptions is an unspeakable violence. For example, in "Dreams and Occultism," he makes an odd non-detour as he moves from "the subject of dreams and telepathy" to other "events" that may be described as "occult." As if he is about to introduce something other than dreams and telepathy, he introduces his next step: "There is, for instance, the phenomenon of thought transference [*Gedankübertragung*], which is *so close* to telepathy and can indeed *without much violence* be regarded as the same thing."[85] Why does he point out that there is not "much violence" in this proximity of terms? He goes on to describe telepathic thought-transference as something explicitly beyond language:

> Mental processes in one person—ideas, emotional states, conative impulses [*Willensimpulse*]—can be transferred [*übertragen*] to another person through empty space without employing the familiar methods of communication by means of words and signs. You will realize how remarkable [*merkwürdig*], and perhaps even of what great practical importance, it would be if something of the kind really happened.[86]

There is a bubbling excitement in this passage, but one wonders who would use this new method of communication? Psychoanalysts? Politicians? Religious leaders?

Freud seems to have thought that describing the telepathic process—making it "graspable [*habhaft*]"—might allow people to harness its powers and to control it. Indeed, the issue of control is central to understanding the concomitant fantasies and anxieties, the dreams and nightmares that attend both telepathy and Jewish transference. He continues his lecture with a lengthy and spectacular series of metaphors, discussing the "transformations" that occur in the telepathic process: "The analogy with other transformations, such as occur in speaking and hearing by telephone, would then be unmistakable. And only think if one could get hold of this physical equivalent of the psychical act! [*Und denken Sie, wenn man dieses physikalischen Äquivalents des psychischen Akts habhaft werden könnte!*]."[87] Freud fantasizes about the possibility that describing a phenomenon will allow a person to control it, to channel its powers for greater purposes. Such fantasies are not so surprising in light of the technologies to which Freud refers. Though scientists had known about the existence of radio waves since at least 1873, it was not until 1895 that Guglielmo Marconi was able to control the waves to use them for long-distance communication through radio and wireless telegraphy. Through his contact with the Society for Psychical Research, Freud might have heard about Sir Oliver Lodge, an Oxford physicist who, after attempting to harness radio waves for wireless telegraphy in the 1890s, turned his attention to other forms of transmission, like telepathy and communication with the dead.[88] By 1932, it had become quite common for journalists to remark that with the invention and expansion of telegraphy, telephony, and television (in 1927), the next step was transmission of thoughts without the use of speech or writing.[89] Freud believed that psychoanalysis had special access to harnessing—if not also *producing*—telepathic communication, since "by inserting the unconscious between what is physical and what was previously called 'psychical,'" it had "paved the way for the assumption of such processes as telepathy. If only one accustoms oneself to the idea of telepathy, one can accomplish a great deal with it—for the time being, it is true, only in imagination [*Phantasie*]."[90]

Though he sounds quite hopeful—even wishful—about the possibilities of telepathic thought-transference, he also reveals a not-so-subtle anxiety about such prospects. Telepathy promises to fulfill a dream of universal and timeless communication for if it were real there would be no need for language, travel, telephones, telegraphs, and televisions. Indeed, Freud continues as if spinning out the fantasy:

> It is a familiar fact that we do not know how the common purpose comes about in the great insect communities: possibly it is done by means of a direct psychical *transference* [*Übertragung*] of this kind. One is led to a suspicion that this is the original, archaic method of communication between individuals and that in the course of phylogenetic evolution it has been replaced by the better method of giving information [*Mitteilung*] with the help of signals [*Zeichen*, signs] which are picked up by the sense organs. But the older method might have persisted *in the background* and still be able to put itself into effect under certain conditions—for instance, in passionately excited mobs [*leidenschaftlich erregten Massen*]. All this is still uncertain and full of unsolved riddles; but there is no reason to be frightened by it [*kein Grund zum Erschrecken*].[91]

Here the dream of perfect communication morphs into a nightmare of uncontrollable and dehumanized masses. Freud protests a little too much that "there is no reason to be frightened by it." The image of an insect community recalls other swarming mobs, pogroms, and lynchings—herds and masses moving as one. "Crowd-consciousness infects identity with an exteriority that is at once social, historical, and—Freud's phylogenetic speculations suggest—potentially inhuman."[92]

While Freud yearningly fantasizes about the prospects of being able to grasp this other form of communication, there is a latent anxiety about what would (or *could*) happen if it were seized by the wrong person. The problem with modern medical discoveries and technological inventions is that as much as they enable fantastic new wonders, they can also enable fantastically archaic horrors. Both are described as "unimaginable," but while horrific results are not always expected, new realities often begin as imagined fantasies. The human imagination is horrifyingly enormous and includes futures both wondrous and wondrously horrible. While the former are often called dreams and the latter nightmares, both can be prophetic. Indeed, Freud's descriptions of insect communities are oddly prophetic (or reminiscent) of two interconnected sets of images: On one screen, we see the Nazis stepping in formation, controlled by some invisible force, moving with precision and decision, powered by anti-semitic fear and repressed rage; on the opposite screen, we see the Nazis' image of the Jews swarming the homeland [*Heimat*], spreading like a cancerous tumor or a contagious disease. Though Jews were often pictured as swarms of rodents—as in the infamous propaganda film *Der Ewige Jude* [*The Eternal Jew*] (1940)—more generally they were pictured as vermin that had to be "exterminated."[93] Freud's image of insects communicating through some archaic medium is uncannily prophetic in more ways than one. If one is inside or in control of such a community, this form of extra-sensory transmission might be exciting. But there is never just one community; there is always an outside.

Psychoanalysis: Occulted beyond Sensory Perception

Despite his protestations about maintaining the distinctions between psychoanalysis and the occult, Freud was well aware of the inextricability of these pursuits. "What, after all, could be more occulted at the time than the Freudian unconscious, this dynamic, structural thing, founded on the mechanism of sexual repression and 'outside,' in a way still inconceivable to his contemporaries, the consciousness?"[94] Just as Freud's meditations on the Jewish Question extend far beyond the works in which he explicitly addressed it, so, too, his meditations on the occult can be found far beyond the essays in which he explicitly confronted the questions of telepathy and the relationship of psychoanalysis to the occult.[95] Significantly, Freud published his essay on "The Unconscious" (1915) in the *Proceedings for the Society of Psychical Research*, and it is this context that compelled him to distinguish his theory of the unconscious from the non-physiological theories of psychology associated with some of the society's researchers, such as William James and Frederic Myers. Though many of the people interested in occultism were admittedly seeking confirmation of religious beliefs, the Society's researchers insisted that their work was scientific.[96] In attempting to devise rational and psychological explanations for occult phenomena, they not only conducted controlled experiments, they also investigated mediums who were known to be spurious in the hopes of learning more about human psychology and trickery.[97] Freud's concern about the association of psychoanalysis with the Society of Psychical Research was not that it would detract from its scientific reputation, but that the theories of the Society's researchers were "more orthodox, more rigorously close, to the dominant psychology" that suspiciously regarded Freud's thought.[98] In "The Unconscious" and throughout his career, Freud showed a familiarity with the Society's methods, procedures, and definitions, particularly regarding telepathy.[99] For example, when Frederic Myers coined the term *telepathy* in 1882, he noted that it referred to "all cases of impression received at a distance without *the normal operation of the recognized sense organs*."[100] Similarly, Freud observed that various mysterious phenomena such as telepathy and unconscious communication seemed to occur without the participation of human sense organs. There is an extension of the human body through new and future technologies. "Man has become a kind of prosthetic God," he writes in *Civilization and Its Discontents*. "When he puts on all his auxiliary organs he is truly magnificent; but those organs have not grown on to him and they still give him much trouble at times."[101]

Like the psychical researchers who went to lengths to prove the existence of telepathic transmissions imperceptible to "the recognized sense organs," Freud struggled to prove the existence of his concept of the unconscious. "In its innermost nature," he writes, the unconscious "is as much unknown to us as the reality of the external world, and it is as incompletely presented by the data of consciousness as is the external world by the communications of our sense organs."[102] The unconscious could only be proven by its *consequences*, "ideas and impulses which emerge one knows not whence."[103] Likewise, Freud explains that Moses could prove the existence of his abstract deity only by appealing to consequences: "The fact must also be *proved* to them in some way if they are to believe it and to draw consequences from the belief. In the religion of Moses the Exodus from Egypt served as the proof; God, or Moses in his name, was never tired of appealing to this evidence in his favor."[104] Indeed, Freud explains that this "triumph of intellectuality over sensuality" was the defining feature of Mosaic monotheism. Echoing Myers' definition of telepathy, he writes, "The new realm of intellectuality [*Geistigkeit*] was opened up, in which ideas, memories and inferences became decisive in contrast to the lower psychical activity which had *direct perceptions by the sense-organs* as its content."[105]

Something odd happens when we compare Freud's proof of the unconscious to his description of Moses' proof of the existence of God. In a discussion of the unconscious, Freud explains that the symptoms invade the individual like the aforementioned foreign bodies or "like all-powerful guests from an alien world, immortal beings intruding into the turmoil of mortal life."[106] On the one hand, these "immortal beings" are simply another name for ghosts ascending from the unconscious netherworld where they populate the archaic heritage, the burden of the past in the present.[107] On the other hand, these same images gesture toward the position of the Jews as "alien guests" who not only "intruded" into "the turmoil of mortal life," but were also blamed for causing this turmoil. In the anti-semitic imagination, Jews were figured as "all-powerful" guests invading the body politic of Western Europe. In *Moses and Monotheism*, Freud links the fantasy of omnipotence to the emergence of monotheism: The Pharaoh's world-empire was transformed into universal monotheism, which in turn sustained the Jewish people by giving them pride in being a "chosen" people.[108] While the Jews had long ago abandoned the "wishful phantasy" of "world dominion," their enemies continued to believe in the Jewish conspiracy of the Elders of Zion.[109] This delusion of omnipotence is fostered by the image of Jews as "spectral, disembodied spirits lacking a national home and, thus, as unwelcome guests and aliens wandering into and within other people's homes, disrupting and haunting them, making them *Unheimliche* [uncanny]."[110] However, it is not only the Jews who are uncanny, but the very *existence* of Jewishness that compels others to recognize the uncanniness of the human subject, the alien strangeness within each individual. As Santner notes, "What makes the Other *other* is not his or her spatial exteriority with respect to my being but the fact that he or she is *strange*, is a *stranger*, and not only to me but also to him- or herself, is the bearer of an internal alterity . . . against this background, the very opposition between 'neighbor' and 'stranger' begins to lose its force."[111]

While Freud avoids explicitly referring to Jews in his discussions of the unconscious and the uncanny, he uses language and imagery that invoke the Jewish Question. For example, in "The Unconscious," he attempts to explain the place of fantasies in the psychoanalytic structure of the psyche. Fantasies may derive from the unconscious, he explains, but their ultimate place in the psyche is unclear: They "qualitatively belong" to the preconscious system, even as they "factually belong" to the unconscious. Unable to find a firm location for the fantasies, Freud ultimately turns the question around—now the question is not their derivation but their fate: "Their origin is what decides their fate." Here, in the midst of a technical discussion of the systems of the psyche, he inserts a surprising analogy: "We may compare them [the fantasies] with individuals of mixed race who, taken all round, resemble white men, but who betray their coloured descent by some striking feature or other, and on that account are excluded from society and enjoy none of the privileges of white people."[112] The individual's features are "striking" only because the person's descent is supposedly "known"—otherwise it could not be "betrayed." But what if this origin is itself a fantasy? How do we distinguish between the one drop of reality and the one drop of fantasy? Where do these fantasies originate? How and why are they sustained? If the "origin is what decides the fate" of both fantasies and individuals, how can we distinguish between real and fantasized origins? And what decides the individual's fate: the real origin or the fantasy-origin?

Boyarin notes that Freud's comments on race—here and elsewhere—have elicited what appear to be two diametrically opposed interpretations: On the one hand, Freud is portrayed as the white man who secures his position of power in contrast to women and "dark" colonized peoples.[113] On the other hand, he uses "white" and "black" as "barely disguised ciphers for Aryan and Jew," indeed as displacements for the tensions between these terms.[114] Like Boyarin, I read these two approaches to Freud's racial discourse as reflections of one phenomenon. But where Boyarin sees this phenomenon as a reflection of the "European Jew's racial anomalousness" as "white/not quite,"[115] I see it as a reflection of the anomalousness of racial certitude in general. The Jew is "uncanny" precisely because he demonstrates that such definitions—of whiteness, of maleness, of Aryanness—are *always* "not quite." While the condition of doubled consciousness seems to mark particular subjects who "know" that they are Jews (or "not quite" whites), Freud would suggest that all individuals are marked by such doubling. The psyche always contains more than it can bear.

Haunted by the Ghosts of Freud and Derrida

Freud's meditations on the occult have been extensively explored and documented, particularly in response to Derrida's essay "Telepathy" (1987). Derrida and other scholars have attended to the ways in which transference, telepathy, and intergenerational transmission are related within Freud's oeuvre, but they have oddly put aside the question of how these matters relate to the Jewish Question.[116] While Derrida does not comment on the connection between telepathy and Jewishness, his curatorial choices suggest that he was aware (even if only unconsciously) of an ongoing relationship: a pattern of influence, if not exchange. Before turning to Derrida, I will first introduce the material from which he draws in "Telepathy," namely the chapter on occultism in Ernest Jones' biography of Freud. As with Freud's "obstinate" belief in the inheritance of memory, Jones tried to blame Freud's eccentric interest in the occult on the quirks of genius and on mystical remnants of Jewishness.[117] In Jones' account, Freud's willingness to entertain the reality of occult phenomena emerges as structurally similar to his position as a "godless Jew." Jones recalls a late-night conversation in which he had asked Freud "where such beliefs" in the occult would end: "If one could believe in mental processes floating in the air, one could go on to a belief in angels. . . . 'Quite so,'" replied Freud, "even *der liebe Gott* [even dear God].'" Jones goes on to remark that though this was all said in a "jocular tone," it suggested a "more serious undertone as well."[118] Jones was clearly worried that by entertaining such idiosyncratic notions, Freud would seriously endanger the reputation of psychoanalysis as a science. To make this point, Jones cites his own letter to Freud: "In your private political opinions, you might be a Bolshevist, but you would not help the spread of psychoanalysis by announcing it." In response, Freud apologized to Jones for his "apparent inconsistency" on the matter and reported that certain recent experiences with his daughter and with Ferenczi had presented "such a convincing force for me [Freud] that the diplomatic considerations on the other side had to give way."[119] Freud's famous reply, of course, weaves all these concerns together and practically demonstrates the concept of negation:

> I was once more faced with a case where on a reduced scale I had to repeat the great experiment of my life: namely, to proclaim a conviction without taking into account any echo from the outer world. So then it was unavoidable. When any-one adduces my fall into sin, just answer him calmly that conversion to telepathy is my private affair like my Jewishness, my passion for smoking and many other things, and that the theme of telepathy is in essence alien to psychoanalysis.[120]

Let us remember that Freud often noted that his Jewishness allowed him to face the "compact majority," to be intellectually independent without worrying about "any echo from the outer world." Here, however, he insists that his "conviction" is private. Quite obviously, he doth protest a bit too much. As Derrida remarks in response to this passage, "Who would be satisfied with such a declaration coming from him?"[121]

Cutting and pasting Freud's letters to Jones in between his own post-cards, Derrida follows Freud's lead and uses a language that mimics, mirrors, and contorts the language that was used to describe the position of Jews in Germany and other Western European nations in the first decades of the twentieth century. He suggests that telepathy is itself a "foreign body," haunting the borders of psychoanalysis, something that is "closely bound up with psychoanalysis, but with which psychoanalysis cannot come to terms."[122] "'The theme of telepathy,' he [Freud] will say in a letter to Jones, 'is in essence alien [*étranger*] to psychoanalysis.'" This is Derrida quoting Freud: Telepathy is alien. "Foreign bodies" permeate the subject. But Derrida demurs, leaving the elephant in the corner. While Derrida emphasizes the speciousness of Freud's rhetoric, noting that "this letter is contradictory from start to finish," he does not stop to note the letter's coherence.[123] Quite obviously, none of these things (Bolshevism, telepathy, Jewishness, and smoking) were simply Freud's "own affairs": This is what is most frustrating about being a social being and, even more so, about being a spokesperson for your own creation. After reminding Freud of his "private political opinions," Jones writes, "You also forget sometimes in what a special position you are personally. When many things pass under the name of psycho-analysis our answer to inquirers is 'psycho-analysis is Freud,' so now the statement that psa [psychoanalysis] leads logically to telepathy, etc., is more difficult to meet."[124] In other words, nothing Freud did—nothing Freud *was*—was simply a private affair. Not even smoking was private, since (in addition to second-hand smoke) Freud's penchant for cigars was at least partially responsible for the jaw cancer that was beginning to make him dependent on his family, particularly Anna (whom he mentions in the letter to Jones).

Freud contends that telepathy is like his Jewishness—private and "foreign [*fremde*]" to the project of psychoanalysis. But in reality, Jewishness had never been a completely private affair, irrelevant to psychoanalysis. It was constantly posing problems—but also opportunities, as he was fond of noting—for the position of psychoanalysis. Telepathy and Jewishness were "foreign bodies" that could not be easily integrated, but whose presence was vital to the organism's life. As Freud notes in *Civilization and Its Discontents*, "the Jewish people, scattered everywhere, have rendered most useful services to the civilizations of the countries that have been their hosts": As "alien guests," they have provided an outlet for their hosts' aggressive tendencies.[125]

If only in its literary imagery, this "haunted" theory of transmission seems far more Derridean than Freudian, since Freud gingerly danced around the possibilities of such uncanny transmissions while Derrida could be said to have made a career out of such dancing. Indeed, in Derrida's very textual practice (as well as the various theorists who have extended and clarified his philosophical poetry)[126]—he incorporates the ghost of Freud, most explicitly in "Telepathy" and *The Post Card*. In these works, Derrida weaves tapestries out of quotations from Freud's letters and texts and his [Derrida's] own speculations and letters to ghosts. Thus, in many sections, it is almost impossible to distinguish Derrida's text from Freud's, his thoughts from those of the spirits whom he channels, presence from absence, text from erasure. Here is a telling example, reproduced with its typographical idiosyncrasies:

15 July 1979

a terrifying consolation. Sometimes I also approach Telepathy as if it were an assurance finally

　Instead of muddling everything up, or complicating the parasitism, as I told you and as I believe, I hope for complete presence from it, fusional immediacy, parousia to keep you, at a distance, in order to keep myself within you, I play pantheism versus separation, so you are no longer leaving, you can no longer even confront me with your 'determination', nor I

　Fort: Da, *tele*pathy against tele*pathy*, distance against menacing immediacy, but also the opposite.[127]

This passage calls for an extensive interpretation, but I will only mention a few points (or questions, as it were). First, the identities of "I" and "you" are unclear: Is this Derrida speaking *to* or *through* Freud (or Freud speaking through Derrida)? Will the "parousia" bring back Freud or Derrida (now that he, too, has entered the realm of ghosts)?[128] Who or what is here (*fort*) and who is there (*da*)? (Derrida's style is itself contagious, forcing a reader to engage in speculative cycles of playing with words whose linguistic chains threaten to self-replicate indefinitely.) Who is involved in the *parasitism*? Is Derrida the parasite to Freud's body of work, or has Freud been transformed into a parasite that lives through Derrida's playful interpretations? Or can we see the parasitism as part of a larger collection of allusions to the Jewish Question, to the question of how Jewishness is or is not "foreign" to psychoanalysis, to Europe, and to all humanity?

　These questions also echo the question of how to distinguish the "private" and familiar [*heimliche*] from the "alien," strange [*fremde*], and uncanny [*unheimliche*]. Is it possible to distinguish between the diverse elements lurking within one body: the foreign from the self, that which we have acquired from that which we have developed, the genealogical strands from the environmental influences? While these questions were being pursued in the realm of evolutionary theory, they were central to Freud's attempt to establish a theory of subjectivity. At the end of his lecture on "dreams and occultism," Freud presents a story that he had heard from Dorothy Burlingame in which a "mother's childhood memory . . . *bursts* in on the following generation (her son, aged 10, brings her a gold coin for her to put by on the same day she had talked about it in analysis)."[129] Derrida places this story within his own essay on "Telepathy," suggesting that the transmission between generations is telepathic. While Freud explains that "the action had forced its way that day into the child's life like a *foreign body*," the person who is most surprised by the interaction is the mother: It is only the mother who is aware of the foreign body, whereas the child experiences the event as if it is something entirely new.[130] While many of Freud's stories about intergenerational transmission are between fathers and sons, the story that he quotes from Burlingame is about a mother and a son. The "foreign body" refers not only to memory or telepathy, but also to the fact of motherhood. It is only the expulsion of the foreign body (the fetus) that makes telepathy possible, that produces a "distance [*tele-*]" at which one can experience the other's thoughts, feelings, and memories [*-pathos*]. With proper care, one self becomes an other.

Freud began to worry about the effects of telepathy and counter-transference on psychoanalysis not because they were *a priori* external to his work, but because he began to realize he no longer had control over the body of psychoanalytic thought: It had become "foreign," distinct from himself. In the same year in which he published "Future Prospects for Psychoanalytic Therapy," he acknowledged that Ferenczi's reports "seem to me finally to shatter the doubts about the existence of thought transference. Now it is a matter of getting used to it in your thoughts and losing respect for its novelty, and also *preserving the secret long enough in the maternal womb*, but that is where the doubt ends."[131] Yet contrary to the requirements of nature, history suggests that there are some things that are never expelled from the womb.

Phantom Letters

In many discussions of transmission and Jewishness, the question of what (specifically) is transmitted is often left quite ambiguous. While Freud developed a theory of Jewishness, nowhere does he set out to explain what this Jewishness *is*—it is neither a physical nor a psychological characteristic or "essence," nor is it simply the memory of the murder of Moses. Indeed, Freud's description of Jewishness is not a *thing* (or collection of things) that can be transmitted, but rather the very *process* of transmitting, awakening, and responding to the memory-traces of Moses. The condition of being Jewish may in fact be simply a state of "remembering" that one is Jewish, even if this "remembering" is unconscious, rejected, or refused. This logical conundrum can be compared to Edgar Allan Poe's story "The Purloined

Letter," in which an apparently very important letter changes hands a number of times. While the reader of Poe's story knows that the letter is important—and that it may contain a secret—the reader never learns the contents of the letter.[132] As Barbara Johnson explains, "The letter, then, acts as a signifier *not* because its contents are lacking, but because its function is not dependent on the knowledge or non-knowledge of those contents."[133] In other words, the condition of being Jewish is not an empty condition, but it functions independently from the knowledge or non-knowledge of what it means to be Jewish.

Within the discipline of literary criticism, Poe's story is well known as the object of Jacques Lacan's and Jacques Derrida's opposing interpretations and discussions of Freudian logic. In the final sentence of his "Seminar on the 'Purloined Letter,'" Lacan states, "The letter always arrives at its destination."[134] Johnson notes that this sentence can be "simply pleonastic or variously paradoxical": Among other things, it can mean that "wherever the letter is, is its destination," "the repressed always returns," and "we all die."[135] Thus the letter is meaning, or death—the death letter that we all someday receive. Derrida responds that Lacan errs in overlooking "the possibility of sheer accident, irreversible loss, unappropriable residues, and infinite divisibility, which are necessary and inevitable in the system's very elaboration."[136] Indeed, it is the possibility of such accidents—resulting in forgetting, oblivion, or worse, death and destruction—that drives people to write, send, and save letters. This is one form of *archive fever*: a drive to recall life from dead matter.[137]

According to Derridean logic, there is no guarantee that a letter will arrive at its destination. Neither genealogical inheritance nor telepathic transmission (nor any combination thereof) can guarantee that the letter will be received by the intended addressee. What would it mean if we *could* guarantee that the letter would arrive, that the traces in the archive would be deciphered, that Jewishness would survive to the next generation, if not eternally? "The ultimate naïvety," writes Derrida, "would be to allow oneself to think that Telepathy guarantees a destination which 'posts and telecommunications' fail to provide."[138] It is unknown whether the letter always arrives at its destination. There is an ethical hesitation, a refusal to enter the business of fortune telling. Only at the end of time—and possibly not even then—can any such judgments be made.

The process of transmission is powered by an illusion, an oversight of its performative dimension.[139] In one of his many glosses of Lacan and Derrida's impasse, Žižek reveals the circular logic that makes it possible for one's origins to decide one's fate:

> When I recognize myself as the addressee of the call of the ideological big Other (Nation, Democracy, Party, God, and so forth), when this call "arrives at its destination" in me, I automatically misrecognize that it is this very act of recognition which *makes me* what I have recognized myself as—I don't recognize myself in it because I'm its addressee, I become its addressee the moment I recognize myself in it. *This* is the reason why a letter always reaches its addressee: because one becomes its addressee when one is reached.[140]

But what happens when a person rejects the "call"? Is it possible to hear the call, to know that it is addressed to you, and to turn away from it? "The letter always arrives at its destination" suggests that the letter's destination was preordained. But to insist (with Derrida) that "it is unknown whether the letter always arrives" suggests that it was sent to a specific destination. As Žižek notes, "it makes sense only insofar as I presuppose that I can be its addressee *before* the letter reaches me—in other words, it presupposes the traditional teleological trajectory with a preordained goal."[141] When the older generation worries about whether the next generation will "receive" the "letter" and whether they will transmit it to the following generations, they mistakenly assume that transmission travels in only one direction. Time expands and collapses, sending the future into the past and the past into the future. "Not with you alone. . . ."[142]

The illusions of transmission are multiplied by *phantom cryptology*. Nicolas Abraham and Maria Torok propose that family secrets are received by individuals who are entirely oblivious to their receipt. In Abraham and Torok's work, the "concepts of crypt and incorporation denote the individual's forcible creation of a psychic tomb, arising from his or her inassimilable life experiences, while the phantom concerns the unwitting reception of a secret which was someone else's psychic burden."[143] The individual is haunted by the secrets of an Other. Whereas Derrida holds the "phantom" as a sort of epistemological category—that which *cannot* be spoken, that which is *yet* to be spoken—Abraham and Torok suggest that the phantom can and *must* be apprehended: "to stage a word—whether metaphorically, as an alloseme, or as a cryptonym—constitutes an attempt at exorcism, an attempt, that is, to relieve the unconscious by placing the effects of the phantom in the social realm."[144] Corporeal matters are hidden away in one body, only to re-emerge in another as incorporeal phantoms, other-worldly beings burdening the psyche. Should these foreign bodies be expelled or assimilated? Is this the Jewish Question?

Phantoms call the individual to fulfill a debt to a particular past: the obligation to one's parents, or the memory of one's parents or the memory of one's parents' parents, or the guilt of having murdered Moses, or the covenant with God: "Not with you alone . . ." What happens when a person only senses (or *suspects*) this debt but cannot quite express it? Does it become more powerful "the less it can be expressed in words"? What happens when, for example, a person who does not "know" that he "is" Jewish receives a letter (out of the blue) that says his mother was Jewish, and that, as such, he too is Jewish? Does the person need to "stage" this secret socially? Does he need to "come out" as Jewish, or can he just put the letter in a drawer and forget about it? Are these the only choices? Would a person be "cured" of his Jewish "problem" if he "staged" his (secret) Jewishness and "returned" to a life of Jewish ritual? Would such "social practices" expel the phantom? Or would such a staging sustain its effects? Could such a staging allow the person to get better (feel better, perhaps even at peace) or would he feel the same or worse (haunted, miserable, discontented)? Would this be for better (for the survival of the Jewish tradition) or for worse (for the survival of anti-semitism)? And are these alternatives to one another, or parts of one phenomenon of human existence?

While it might be reasonable to think that the "phantom effect" would progressively fade "during its transmission from one generation to the next and that, finally," it would disappear, "this is not at all the case." Instead, phantoms seem to gain more power the longer they persist, particularly "when shared or complementary phantoms find a way of being established as social practices along the lines of *staged words*."[145] How does one stage words? In psychoanalysis? In a public lecture? In a letter?

In his "Notes on the Phantom," Abraham presents two cases of the phantom effect. In the first, we meet an "enthusiastic young scientist" who studies genealogy in his spare time. After not seeing each other for a long while, the two men meet and the young scientist immediately insults Abraham: "I was of low birth . . . Devoid of religious sentiment . . . I was indifferent to my origins; neither did I care that his be known and publicized."

Right away, the scientist "excessively" apologizes and tries to take it all back. "His own father is a free-thinker. He hates genealogical inquiries. . . . Why delve into the past? This however did not stop his father from marrying an aristocrat. . . ."[146] Without stopping to comment, Abraham continues the story: the man tells of his father's mother and her other sons, but he notably skips over his father's father: "It was all on account of my father's beliefs," the man says. "The family on his side deserted us." By the end of the story, the man reports that he was convinced he "was the child of his female analyst and her prestigious colleague."[147] Abraham deciphers the story: his father had been a bastard, and to cover up the "degrading fact," he had told his son that he was of "aristocratic origins." The father's *own* secret, "alive in the father's unconscious," was *transferred* to the son's unconscious. The scientist, then, is living with the phantom of the father's own encrypted secrets.

This case poses many questions about the relationship between the patient and his phantoms. How did the phantom make its way from the father to the son? Abraham and Torok insist that it is not inherited. The phantom, Abraham explains, is "nothing but an invention of the living . . . in the sense that the phantom is meant to objectify, even if under the guise of individual or collective hallucinations, the gap produced in us by the concealment of some part of a love object's life . . . what haunts are not the dead, but the gaps left within us by the secrets of others."[148] There is the question, then, whether the son has *invented* the "fact" of his father's "illegitimate" birth. Does the man *need* this gap to explain the gaps in his own life, the secrets that he cannot share with himself, let alone with his analyst? Does he create one fiction to conceal others: repressed or unfulfillable desires, inadmissible secrets of an other order? Is this not part of the co-existence of the desperate wish to tell everyone about a crime and the anxiety that someone might find out about it?

In the second case of the phantom effect, Abraham tells the story of an amateur geologist who spent his weekends "breaking rocks," using them to catch butterflies, which he then killed in a can of cyanide. In fact, Abraham explains, the man was poetically re-enacting a secret: His mother's beloved (his father?) had been "denounced by the grandmother (an unspeakable and secret fact). He was sent to 'break rocks' [*casser les cailloux* = do forced labor]. . . . he later died in the gas chamber."[149] As in the first case, the father's secret is unconsciously transferred to the son. But again, there are more questions: Why did the grandmother denounce the mother's beloved? Why was he "sent away"?

Despite the fact that Abraham and Torok's cryptological theory of transgenerational haunting implicitly refers to the inheritance of traumas and the anxieties associated with unknown genealogies, they do not ever (as far as I can tell) explicitly refer to Jewishness or to the Holocaust. This is particularly odd since their theories have significantly shaped recent scholarship on Jewish messianism, on the Holocaust, and on Derrida's own "theories of Jewishness."[150] Indeed, their very language of "intergenerational haunting" is itself haunted by Freud's theory of Jewishness in *Moses and Monotheism*: An inherited trauma burdens generation after generation precisely because it is "unsuspected," unaddressed, and therefore repressed.

In the introductions to their two classic works *The Wolf Man's Magic Word* (1976) and *The Shell and the Kernel* (1978), their editor-translator Nicholas Rand notes that Abraham and Torok left Hungary in the 1930s and '40s to settle in France.[151] While it is certainly not necessary to know which "side" they would have been on during this time, such questions are difficult to avoid. Their names alone might make some people presume that they were Jewish,[152] but such questions are never mentioned by them, or by Rand. Is this not a phantom in itself? Nowhere do they tell us of their own involvement in the story: Was Abraham also obsessed with genealogies? Was he encrypting secrets about his own genealogy? Was he also in danger of being sent to the camps? Was Abraham's interpretation of his patient's story haunted by his own (firsthand? secondhand?) experience of haunting?[153] Was he haunted by family traumas, untimely deaths that, though not witnessed, were experienced as inherited narratives, compulsions to repeat, patterns that had to be staged?[154]

It is significant that Freud's meditations on the inheritance of memory and on the potential reality of telepathy have been taken most seriously— not as a historical or psychoanalytic anomaly, and not as a literary flirtation with mysticism—by scholars whose primary work is not in the realm of cultural or literary theory but in the clinic, specifically with children of Holocaust survivors. For these scholars, the inheritance of memory is inextricable from a notion of telepathy that is not only spectral or metaphorical but also bodily experienced. In the book *Generations of the Holocaust* (1982), the psychoanalyst James Herzog draws from Dorothy Burlingame's writings on telepathy in order to make sense of cases in which patients seem traumatized by their parents' experiences in the camps. Unlike some psychoanalysts who were uncomfortable with incorporating telepathy in their practices, Burlingame explored how parents and children seemed to share unconscious material through an uncanny and almost bodily medium of transmission akin to telepathy.[155] Likewise, in the clinical context, Grubrich-Simitis describes "contemporary attempts to understand transgenerational transmission of trauma":

> When the primary object has been so severely traumatized that the trauma cannot be assimilated by the psychic metabolism, it is then unconsciously passed on to the next generation in order to be mastered—implanted, as it were, like a *foreign body*. The transmission seems to occur along primitive paths of communication that are as yet little understood, from unconscious to unconscious, through archaic transferences and countertransferences—scarcely on the level of mental ego but more on that of the *body ego*. This happens with such *oppressive inevitability and so close to the soma, that the idea of hereditary transmission of acquired characters easily comes to mind.*[156]

Similarly, in her study of Freud's *Moses*, Grubrich-Simitis suggests that while the "objective disadvantage" of Freud's Lamarckism is that it is "scientifically untenable," it "does not dispose of the fundamental questions" that it raises. Namely, "how are we to understand and indeed explain the undeniable phenomenon of the return of the repressed in accordance with certain rhythms, or the *silent*—that is, not manifestly verbal—transmission of traumatizations from one generation to the next? These are questions of the greatest importance not only clinically but also collectively, and psychoanalysts are still searching for answers to them today."[157]

It is somehow surprising when phantasmagoric visitors don't just drift away even as they are re-produced as fantasies and science fictions.[158] Freud's haunted theory of Jewish transference suggests that tradition (whatever it may be) does not simply get passed down from one generation to another. Rather, it meanders, drifts, and veers backward and forward in time and space. Years after their deaths, Spinoza is re-embraced as a Jew, Karl Marx is both admired and reviled for his Jewishness, and it is discovered that even Christopher Columbus may have been Jewish. What makes these historical individuals Jewish is a current revival of the idea that one's genealogical descent determines one's Jewishness (not that this idea had ever disappeared).[159] In America, it may be possible to insist that "the history we study is never our own; it is always the history of people who were in some respects like us and in other respects different."[160] However, this line of reasoning holds only if we regard the present as absolutely distinct from the past. If we allow ourselves to fantasize about time travel, the argument falls apart: What if *I* had been there? What if now were then, and then were now? Would I have been able to choose my history, or would it have been imposed upon me—by my parents, by the judges, by some slip of the tongue? Is it possible to control the transmissions that issue from the past, haunt and invade the present, and, in the process, redefine the world as we thought we knew it?

FIVE

Immaterial Materiality: The "Special Case" of Jewish Tradition

> In mental life nothing which has once been formed can perish—everything is somehow preserved and in suitable circumstances . . . it can once more be brought to light.
>
> F R E U D , *Civilization and Its Discontents* (1930)

> Among the precepts of the Moses religion there is one that is of greater importance than appears to begin with. This is the prohibition against making an image of God—the compulsion to worship a God whom one cannot see . . . if this prohibition were accepted, it must have a profound effect. For it meant that a sensory perception was given second place to what may be called an abstract idea—a triumph of intellectuality over sensuality or, strictly speaking, an instinctual renunciation, with all its necessary psychological consequences.
>
> F R E U D , *Moses and Monotheism* (1939)

Material Memory and Diasporic Identity

In the last twenty years, an extensive discussion of the concept of memory has emerged across the disciplines. Historians, literary theorists, and psychologists have demonstrated that memory is malleable, utterly open to creative reconstruction, never pure, never absolute.[1] Ironically, while individuals and nations consistently call upon memory in their attempts to construct a stable sense of identity, the reason they turn to memory is that it is just as plastic as identity. And yet, across a diverse set of historical and geographical contexts, people seem to fantasize about memory as if it were something stable—something more concrete and indestructible than objects, archives, and physical sites of memory. Indeed, this seems even more pronounced in our own era of global diaspora since it is clear that all identities are compound: built upon sundry shards of histories, memories, and traditions. Edward Said suggests that by recognizing the shared brokenness of identity, historically antagonistic communities might be able to over-come their apparent differences and move toward a peaceful future. In one of his final lectures, "Freud and the Non-European," Said recuperates Freud's *Moses and Monotheism* as just such a reconfiguration of the ruins of Jewish identity.[2] In reading Freud's assertion that Moses was an Egyptian as an "opening out of Jewish identity towards its non-Jewish background,"[3] Said emphasizes the openness not only of Jewish identity, but of all di-asporic identity. Nonetheless, Said acknowledges that Freud's narrative sug-gests something that does not necessarily accord with his hopeful thesis: According to Freud, the Israelites' murder of Moses resulted in an indelible memory that has persistently and singularly defined the Jewish people.

In contrast to Said, I argue that Freud's last book is an attempt to unearth the reasons for the perplexing fixity of identity, perhaps most particularly that which is not firmly established upon a land of its own. While many historically antagonistic communities cling to shattered pasts scattered throughout their lands, diasporic communities struggle to hold onto non-material memories scattered throughout the world. In the case of the Jewish people, this concept of memory has been transmitted not only through texts and rituals but also through the belief in the power of genealogy; that is, for at least fifteen centuries, certain individuals have been defined as Jewish because of the belief that they have genealogically inherited Jewishness. Here we come upon an apparent contradiction: On the one hand, Judaism is often embraced as an ethical ideal, a collection of spiritual and intellectual principles, including devotion to an unrepresentable deity. On the other hand, Jewishness is experienced as utterly material, as a commitment to physical rituals and bodily proscriptions, and as a weight that is schlepped around the world wherever Jewish bodies go. In his final book, Freud sug-gests that these aspects of Jewishness are not necessarily at odds; rather, he reveals an inextricable link between the conceptualization of *Judentum* as a body of abstract intellectual ideals and as a genealogical chain of material bodies.

Two decades before writing *Moses and Monotheism*, Freud had become interested in the idea that memory could be inherited, but in no other work did he explicitly connect this idea to a particular people, culture, or religion. Given that the genealogical definition of Jewishness distinguishes Judaism from other religious traditions (most specifically, Christianity), it should not be surprising to find that Freud argues that the Jewish tradition is genealogically inherited. What *is* surprising is that he does not particularly emphasize this difference; instead, he places the key statement regarding the inheritance of memory almost as an after-thought.[4] Perhaps in part because he knew that this notion of heredity was contentious, he gave far more rhetorical emphasis and textual space to the "intellectual-spiritual" particularities of Judaism. According to Freud, while "primitive" religions were defined by the performance of rituals and ceremonies, the Jewish tradition was defined by its supreme *Geistigkeit*—a highly specific word that in the *Standard Edition* is variably translated as "intellectuality" or "spirituality."[5] While he was well aware of the historic specificity of this term in German Idealist philosophy and the range of meaning it could suggest—from "spirit" to "ghost" to "breath," which in Hebrew is the same word (*ruach*) as "soul"[6]—he refashioned the term to describe what he saw as the most important distinction of Mosaic monotheism. In a section entitled "The Advance in Intellectuality [*Fortschritt in der Geistigkeit*]," he explains that the Jewish tradition had reached the heights of "ideal abstraction" and had survived in a realm beyond sensory perception.[7] As such, its survival could not be explained by the material media of culture—not "direct communication" nor "the influence of education by the setting of an example," not rituals and not texts.[8] The survival and transmission of Jewish tradition required a medium "beyond sensory perception," and ultimately this medium was biological heredity.

Since it has been some time since I presented the plot of *Moses and Monotheism*, let me repeat the basic outline as it pertains to this chapter. According to Freud, the Jewish tradition originated when an Egyptian priest named Moses chose a band of Semites upon whom he imposed a strict monotheism based on the abstract ideals of intellectual-spirituality [*Geistigkeit*]. By rejecting the most material and magical elements of "primitive" religions, Mosaic monotheism became supremely spiritual [*geistig*]: It condemned "magical" ceremonies, denied the existence of an afterlife, and prohibited material representations of the deity.[9] Whereas "primitive" religions proved their power through material evidence ("magical" ceremonies, material representations of the deities, etc.), the power of Mosaic monotheism was always a "hypothesis," since it could not be perceived through human sensory organs. Unable to tolerate "such a highly spiritualized [*Vergeistigte*] religion,"[10] the band of Semites killed Moses (repeating the prehistoric murder of the primal father described in Freud's *Totem and Taboo*) and apparently forgot about the episode. Through a complicated series of events, and over many years, the original band of Semites joined up with other groups from Midian and Kadesh who worshipped a volcano god named Yahweh and whose leader was also named Moses. The multiplicities were covered over: The groups, gods, and leaders were unified into one narrative, one people, one god, and one leader. The reason these events were not recorded in the Bible, Freud explains, is that the people repressed the memory of the murder and composed a text that covered up its traces. Nonetheless, the memories continued to exert their influence. Because the traces are genealogically transmitted, they eternally compel the people to sustain the Jewish tradition—to preserve the abstract ideals of intellectual spirituality [*Geistigkeit*].

In defining the Jewish tradition by both its supreme spirituality and its genealogical transmission, Freud seems to construct an irresolvable paradox.[11] On the one hand, he insists that the Jewish tradition is above all defined by its rejection of materiality: The prohibition against making an image of God and the avoidance of "magical abuses" meant that its survival could not depend on ceremonies, ritual objects, or other forms of "direct communication." On the other hand, he insists that the Jewish tradition is genealogically transmitted through the most material of media: the body.[12] In Freud's theory of Jewishness, these two elements are inseparable: The *Geistigkeit* of the Jewish tradition *requires* biological transmission for its survival, while the biological transmission *confirms* the supreme spirituality [*Geistigkeit*] of the tradition. Freud suggests that the Jewish tradition has survived precisely because it is genealogically transmitted from generation to generation. Indeed, Freud's final book can be seen as an attempt to address the "special case" of Jewish tradition, specifically why and how it is transmitted from generation to generation even when parents attempt to repress their Jewishness by not practicing Jewish rituals or by converting and raising their children as non-Jews.[13] Unlike children of Christians or Muslims, who may choose to no longer be "counted" as Christian or Muslim, children of Jewish parents are "counted" as Jewish by both Jews and non-Jews, regardless of individual experiences or choices.[14] As Theodor Reik put it in his book on *Jewish Wit*, "once a Jew always a Jew."[15] While the genealogical transmission of Jewishness may seem to suggest that it is a race rather than a religious faith or cultural practice, genealogy functions as a link between these terms. For those who "return" to practice Judaism, Jewishness is often conceived of as something that they had already inherited; thus, they *return* to fulfill their obligations to a body of spiritual and intellectual ideals that are grasped (if only partially) through texts, rituals, and practices.

Most scholars who have addressed these aspects of Freud's final book have focused on either his insistence on the biological transmission of memory or his emphasis on Jewish *Geistigkeit*. While their projects are very different, Jan Assmann and Daniel Boyarin both read Freud's spiritualization [*Vergeisterung*] of Judaism as an ironic and defensive inversion of Christian anti-Jewish images of the Jewish people as mired in the materiality of text and flesh.[16] By contrast, Yerushalmi and Gilman have each attended to Freud's peculiar insistence upon a "Lamarckian" notion of heredity, and hence upon a racial definition of Jewishness—the idea that a person inherits Jewishness for better and for worse and regardless of her own feelings, beliefs, or practices.[17] In his seminal 1991 work *Freud's Moses*, Yerushalmi interprets Freud's insistence on this idea as a dangerous separation of Jewishness (the ethnic-racial condition of being Jewish) and Judaism (the religion sometimes practiced by Jewish people). If Jewishness can be transmitted "'independently of direct communication and education by example,'" he writes (quoting Freud), "then that means that 'Jewishness' can be transmitted independently of 'Judaism,' that the former is interminable even if the latter be terminated."[18] For Yerushalmi, the emphasis on the (often discomforting) bodily definitions of Jewishness seems to detract from the appreciation of the more noble and precious ideals of Judaism. Whereas Yerushalmi and Gilman each concentrate on Freud's ethnic-racial definition of Jewishness, Assmann and Boyarin focus on his construction of the intellectual-spiritual ideals of Judaism. I argue that in his final book, Freud attempts to make sense of the counter-intuitive connections between Jewishness and Judaism and suggests that the spiritual [*geistig*] ideals of Judaism are inseparable from the physical survival of the Jewish people. Freud insists on an idiosyncratic version of intellectual-spirituality [*Geistigkeit*] not to deny the body (as Boyarin claims) but to make sense of the special case of bodily definition within Judaism.

In the ongoing debate about Freud's relationship to *Judentum*, one of the major questions has been whether he positively regarded it as a religion

(Judaism) based on spiritual-intellectual ideals, or negatively as a racial-ethnic identity (Jewishness) based on internalized anti-semitism. For example, while Richard Bernstein addresses both the biological and the spiritual [*geistig*] elements in Freud's last book, he insists that they cannot coexist: "Freud explicitly denies the importance of biological transmission and *positively* asserts the importance of an 'ideal factor' in Jewish survival."[19] Jacques Le Rider goes so far as to suggest that a racial definition of Jewishness is a psychological problem that "Freud radically overcame," forgoing the "temptation of falling back into 'biological,' 'hereditary,' and 'racial' representations of Jewish identity."[20] However, if the racialization of *Judentum* is a sort of psychological problem, it is one that continuously returns, even after it has been seemingly "overcome."[21] In January 1935, Lou Andreas-Salomé wrote a letter to Freud, responding to his description of his burgeoning work: "What particularly fascinated *me* is a specific characteristic of the 'return of the repressed,' namely, the way in which *noble and precious* elements return despite long intermixture with every conceivable kind of material."[22] While this sentence has been repeatedly quoted as evidence that Freud's last book can be read as a positive evaluation of *Judentum*,[23] it seems instead to raise the question as to why an individual or a people would repress elements that were so "noble and precious." The importance of Freud's last book derives, I think, not from solving the problem of whether *Judentum* is a religion, race, or culture (as if such a problem were solvable), but from exploring its most problematic and paradoxical aspects without knowing whether their return will be noble or otherwise.

The "Special Case" of Jewish Tradition

Central to the relationship of Jewish intellectual-spirituality [*Geistigkeit*] and Jewish genealogy is the concept of tradition in the "special case of Jewish history."[24] Twenty years earlier, Freud had explored the nature of "primitive" traditions in *Totem and Taboo*, but in *Moses and Monotheism* he redefines tradition as something that is both supremely *geistig* (ideally immaterial, beyond sensory perception) and undeniably material (genealogically inherited in the body, beyond individual experience). Freud's insistence on the genealogical transmission of Jewish tradition can be better understood by comparing his use of the word "tradition" in *Moses and Monotheism* with his earlier use of the word in *Totem and Taboo*. Throughout the earlier work, he explores the nature of traditions—specific customs, rituals, and ceremonies—that had preserved the memory of the murder of the primal father and guaranteed its transmission to future generations. From the very first sentence of *Totem and Taboo*, he addresses the question of transmission and the role of tradition in this process. "Prehistoric man," he writes, "is known to us through the *inanimate monuments* and implements which he has left behind, through the information about his art, his religion and his attitude towards life which has come down to us either *directly* or by way of *tradition* handed down in legends, myths and fairy tales, and through the relics of his mode of thought which survive in our own *manners and customs*."[25] Here, Freud refers to tradition as one among many "inanimate" media that transmit the past into the present: from "monuments" to "myths" to "manners." As he explores the nature of these media in the four essays of *Totem and Taboo*, he narrates a history of religion from the origins of "primitive" man's totemic rituals to the development of Christian communion, but he completely passes over the development of Mosaic monotheism. Though he briefly mentions the early sacrifices of the Semitic peoples, a discussion of Jewish monotheistic tradition is nowhere to be found in *Totem*.[26]

In the following years, Freud began to reconsider his initial resistance to the idea that phylogenetic memory could be inherited, but it was not until *Moses and Monotheism* that he explicitly insisted on the genealogical transmission of a religious tradition.[27] Likewise, it was not until *Moses and Monotheism* that he addressed the question of the "special case of Jewish history." Though he defensively asserts that *Moses and Monotheism* contains no new arguments,[28] it obviously contains new materials and more specific arguments than those that had appeared in *Totem and Taboo*. Most particularly, in the later book he revises the definitions of "tradition" and the solutions to the questions of its transmission. In *Moses and Monotheism*, he notes that he intends to explore

> what the real nature of a tradition resides in, and what its special power rests on
> . . . what sacrilege [*Frevel*] one commits against the splendid diversity of human
> life if one recognizes only those motives which arise from *material* needs [*aus
> materiellen Bedürfnissen*], from what sources some ideas (and particularly religious
> ones) derive their power to subject both men and peoples to their *yoke* [*unter-
> jochen*]—to study all this in the *special case* [*Spezialfall*] of *Jewish history* would be
> an alluring task.[29]

While Freud begins the passage by referring to "the real nature of tradition" as if it were something universal, he concludes that the present work was driven by his desire to explore the "special case of Jewish history"—how it was that Jewish tradition had "subjected" generations to its "yoke," not through fulfilling material needs but through something else as yet unmentioned. In the shift from the universal case of tradition to the particular case of Jewish tradition, Freud distinguishes his study of tradition from that which "recognizes only those motives which arise from material needs"—the latter, he notes, commits a sacrilege "against the splendid diversity of human life." Such a distinction could apply to much of Freud's work: As opposed to the fields of anthropology, ethnology, and sociology, psychoanalysis focuses not on how people satisfy their material needs—food, water, shelter—but on how and why they are driven to satisfy non-material needs, how they are "subjected" to powers that have no political or legal currency, no ramifications in the material world.[30] In the rest of the book, Freud explores how the Jewish tradition subjects the Jewish people to its yoke through such abstract powers and ideas. The transmission and power of Jewish tradition, he suggests, rise above the realm of material needs and physical satisfactions.

In *Moses and Monotheism*, Freud explicitly distinguishes Jewish tradition from "primitive" traditions such as those he had discussed in *Totem and Taboo*, as well as Egyptian polytheism and Christianity. To begin with, Moses established a tradition of abstract intellectual [*geistig*] monotheism, distinguished by its explicit rejection of the "magical and ceremonial acts, charms and amulets" that had shaped "primitive" religions, and that would return with the development of Christianity.[31] Since the "primitive" religions (in *Totem and Taboo*) had existed in a prehistoric and hence pre-textual age, their transmission depended upon customs and ceremonies. By contrast, Mosaic monotheism could be transmitted through a number of textual, oral, and other documentary media. Freud repeatedly uses *tradition* to refer to various documentary sources and media of transmission that could account for the survival of the traces of the "real" origins of Moses and his monotheism. There is the Biblical tradition, but also "traditions other than the Biblical one."[32] Yet tradition is not only a medium of transmission; it is the kernel of truth that has been infallibly transmitted despite tendentious purposes: "The Jews possess a copious literature apart from the Bible," he writes, including "legends and myths" that might contain "fragments of a trustworthy tradition [*Stücke guter Tradition*] for which no room was found in the Pentateuch."[33] Thus, by "Jewish tradition," Freud means not only traditions—"customs, ceremonies and dogmas" or oral and written literature—but something beyond these physical entities, something far more encompassing and complex.

Tradition emerges as a key term that both resists and surpasses definition but which holds the contradictions of Freud's theory of Jewishness within it. While he is obviously aware of the "standard" definitions of tradition—broadly referring to "oral" traditions but also more generally to pre- or extraliterary lore[34]—in *Moses* he uses the term so insistently and repeatedly that it becomes saturated almost to the point of nonsense. Throughout his career, Freud imbued everyday words with complex psychoanalytic meanings—*das Es* [translated as "the id," but literally "the It"] or *Besetzung* [translated as "cathexis," but literally "occupation"] such that the words themselves became the "conceptual equipment" of psychoanalysis, the tools that contain and reveal contradictory aspects of human nature.[35] In *Moses*, he employs the word "tradition" as a specialized term requiring constant re-definition and qualification. In one of the more dizzying passages, he suggests that the tradition of Moses had been orally transmitted such that it emerged as a more faithful remainder of the past than any cultural or religious materials, such as texts, customs, or rituals. As he explains,

> A discrepancy [*Gegensatz*] was able to grow up between the written record [*schrift-lichen Fixierung*] and the oral transmission [*mündlichen Überlieferung*] of the same material [*desselben Stoffes*]—tradition. What had been omitted or changed in the written record might very well have been preserved intact [*unversehrt erhalten geblieben*] in tradition. Tradition was a supplement [*Ergänzung* (completion, complement)] but at the same time a contradiction [*Widerspruch*] to historical writing. It was less subjected to the influence of distorting purposes and perhaps at some points [*in manchen Stücken* (in some *pieces*)] quite exempt from them, and it might therefore be more truthful than the account that had been recorded in writing [*der Schriftlich fixierte Bericht*]. Its trustworthiness, however, suffered from the fact that it was less stable and definite than the written account and exposed to numerous changes and alterations when it was handed on from one generation to another by oral communication. A tradition of such a kind might meet with various sorts of fate. What we should most expect would be that it would be *crushed* [*erschlagen*] by the written account, would be unable to stand up against it, would become more and more shadowy [*schattenhafter*] and would finally pass

into oblivion. But it might meet with other fates: one of these would be that the tradition itself would end in a written record, and we shall have to deal with yet others as we proceed.[36]

Freud begins by posing tradition as the oral complement to historical writing, but, in the course of the passage, it becomes clear that tradition is more than just a synonym for oral transmission. Tradition is not equivalent to oral tradition because, as he explains, "it was handed on from one generation to another *by* oral communication." Tradition emerges as that which is (mysteriously) transmitted; it is the medium and the message. Freud uses exceedingly physical imagery to describe this tradition: It is "fixed" in writing, it is something that can be "delivered" orally, it is material "*stuff* [*Stoffes*]" that can be "preserved intact [*unversehrt erhalten*]"; it can be broken into "pieces [*Stücken*]," such that we should probably expect it to be "crushed [*erschlagen*]" or at least for it to disappear into the shadows. Tradition seems almost palpable, but precisely because it is not only physical, it cannot be crushed. It is both the "completion [*Ergänzung*]" and the "contradiction [*Widerspruch*]" of "historical writing." By the end of the passage, tradition emerges as far more than an oral medium of transmission for while it might result in another "written record," there are other possibilities.

The counter-intuitive density of Freud's concept of tradition emerges most clearly in the section entitled "Difficulties." Though he seems to have already thoroughly explained the survival of tradition through its oral transmission, he admits that he is still left with the question of "what form the operative tradition in the life of peoples is present."[37] Here again he turns to the possibility that the tradition was "based on conscious memories of oral communications [*mündliche Mitteilungen*] which people then living had received from their ancestors only two or three generations back who had themselves been participants and eye-witnesses of the events in question."[38] However, now he explicitly acknowledges that he is not satisfied with this explanation: "it is no longer possible to say . . . who the people were who preserved this knowledge and handed it on [*übertragen*] by word of mouth" or whether the tradition is still based on "knowledge communicated in a *normal* way . . . from grandfather to grandchild."[39] If the tradition were possessed by only "a few people" (rather than being "public property [*Volksgut*]"), explains Freud, this wouldn't "explain its effect," its "lasting emotion in the masses," and its "power to deeply *seize* them [*die Massen so nachhaltig zu ergreifen*]."[40] Here is where it becomes clear that by tradition, Freud does not simply mean oral tradition, the "opposite" of historical writing, but something else beyond all forms of "direct communication." Freud concludes that "there must have been something present in the ignorant masses, too, which was in some way akin [*verwandt*] to the knowledge of the few and went half way to meet it when it was uttered."[41] What was this "something"? How did the tradition survive, not only in the elite individuals who respectfully transmitted it through "normal" means of communications, but also in all those people who could not read the texts or did not want to listen to their grandparents' stories?

This, then, is the problem that drives Freud to insist on some other form of transmission for Jewish tradition, something beyond the "normal" forms of direct communication [*direkter Mitteilung*], whether oral, written, or ritual. Whereas "primitive" religions could be transmitted through an "unconscious understanding" of "customs, ceremonies and dogmas," Mosaic monotheism could not be transmitted in this way, since part of what defined it was an explicit rejection of "magical" ceremonies.[42] With Mosaic monotheism, a "new realm of intellectuality [*Geistigkeit*] was opened up, in which ideas, memories and inferences became decisive in contrast to the lower psychical activity which had direct perceptions by the sense-organs as its content."[43] The Jewish tradition could not have been transmitted through the usual forms of material culture, whether customs and ceremonies, texts, oral communications, or education, because

> a tradition that was based *only* on communication [*Mitteilung*] could not lead to the compulsive character [*Zwang*] that attaches to religious phenomena. It would be listened to, judged, and perhaps dismissed, like any other piece of information *from outside*; it would never attain the privilege of being liberated from the constraint [*Zwang*] of logical thought.[44]

While Freud first refers to "compulsion [*Zwang*]" as the power of tradition (or religion) to subject a people to its yoke, he then uses the same word—*Zwang*—to refer to the "compulsion [*Zwang*—the second time Strachey translates it as "constraint"] of logical thought." It is almost as if Freud is trying to understand how the compulsion of tradition can override his own compulsion to explain everything through the logic of scientific rationality. Since biological transmission is not from the "outside," it could not be logically rationalized, documented, or observed, and, as such, it could "attain the privilege of being liberated" from the solid and empirical world. When the Semites killed Moses, they acquired memories that could never be completely erased, repressed, or repudiated; instead, the traces of this history would be eternally transmitted to each successive generation. Thus Freud insisted that he could not "do without" the idea of the inheritance of phylogenetic memory.[45] Jewish tradition was a "special case" precisely because it had survived (at least in part) through biological transmission, persistently compelling its people to *be* Jewish, regardless of logical thought. Thus, Freud not only needed the biological factor itself; he needed to deal with its place in the special case of Jewish history.

Geistigkeit *and Its Inversions*

Like many Jewish thinkers before and since, Freud reinterprets what has often been regarded as a problematic particularity of the Jewish people: the fact that Jews are Jewish not because of religious beliefs, cultural practices, linguistic abilities, or citizenship in a particular land, but because they have apparently inherited Jewishness in their bodies.[46] While the bodily definition of Jewishness has been a source of racist anti-semitism since at least the fifteenth century,[47] it can be traced to Jewish and Christian texts from the first centuries of the Common Era. Since Paul, much of Christian anti-Judaism has centered on the idea that, while Christianity has apparently ascended to the heights of abstract spirituality [*Geistigkeit*], the Jewish people remain mired in the materiality of the flesh and of the text.[48] As Assmann writes,

> Freud was fully and perhaps even ironically aware of what he was doing in using such a Christian topos. For this Christian concept constitutes . . . a centerpiece of Christian anti-Judaism. This is precisely the Christian reason for the abolition of the law. St. Paul's critique of the law argues in terms of "spirit" (*pneuma*) and "flesh" (*sarx*) or "spirit" and "letter" (*gramma*). The spirit animates, the letter kills (2 Cor. 3, 6). Halacha is abolished as external and material. The law is opposed by the principal of faith, based neither on sensual evidence nor on reason. In the eyes of the Christians, the Jews remained within the bounds of the flesh: *Israel carnalis*. Only the exodus from the realm of the law opens access to the realm of the spirit.[49]

In this essay, "The Advance in Intellectuality," and in his more recent work, Assmann attends to the ways in which Freud foregrounds the Mosaic distinction by inverting one of the standard tropes of Christian anti-Judaism.[50] This is a revision of his earlier thesis, advanced in *Moses the Egyptian* (1997), where he argues that Freud participated in an Enlightenment discourse attempting to supercede the age-old Mosaic distinction between "true" and "false" religion (as well as between such dichotomies as Israel–Egypt, Jew–Gentile, and culture–nature). Similarly, Grubrich-Simitis argues that in *Moses*, Freud envisioned that the boundaries between Jew and Gentile might be overcome; "perhaps . . . [he] had even imagined, in the register of a daydream, that his own theory of culture might help to facilitate this collective process of self-healing."[51] While these utopian interpretations are attractive, they are marked by a particular Christian universalism that Freud did not entirely share. Freud's last book is not an attempt to overcome the persistent boundaries (or, in Grubrich-Simitis' phrase, the "paranoid split") between Jew and Gentile, or to make Judaism less carnal. In appropriating the Christian trope of spirituality [*Geistigkeit*], Freud attempts to make sense of the most material and bodily aspects of Jewish definition and its relationship to the persistence of Jewish tradition. While the materiality of genealogy may seem to weigh down the supreme spirituality [*Geistigkeit*] of Jewish tradition, Freud suggests that the bodily transmission of Jewishness confirms its spiritual supremacy. Because of its spirituality, Jewish tradition *requires* a medium of transmission that functions beyond the realm of sensory perception, beyond individual judgments, choices, or experiences. Less spiritual traditions could be transmitted through material media, such as texts, objects, rituals, or lands, but (according to Freud) Jewish tradition is different. (Indeed, such material things may be dangerous since they can be transformed into idols of worship, thereby displacing the emphasis on pure spirituality.) Jewish tradition has survived through a material medium—genealogy—that is nonetheless spiritual [*geistig*], since it requires no "direct perceptions by the sense organs."[52]

In insisting upon both the non-material idealism of intellectuality [*Geistigkeit*] and the materiality of biological inheritance, Freud addresses longstanding questions of Jewish embodiment. As Howard Eilberg-Schwartz suggests, throughout history, "Jewish bodies" have been "doubly damned." On the one hand, Jews were "inadequately embodied"—pictured as weak, feminine men with small or foreshortened penises, excessively interested in "feminine" concerns such as books, study, and the family.[53] On the other hand, they were considered overly embodied: pictured as grotesque, hairy, smelly women; and too mired in the flesh: clinging to bodily rituals such as circumcision, *mikvah* (ritual immersion) and genealogical (rather than spiritual) definitions of the community. Over time, two general strategies for countering these charges emerged. The first was to "pursue embodiment," exemplified most clearly by certain Zionists such as Max Nordau in his fantasy of the "Muscle Jew" but anticipated by the Maccabees' pursuit of Greek ideals of fitness and bodily perfection.[54] The second strategy was to "flee embodiment through the spiritualization of the tradition," as with various Jewish scholars' attempts to redefine Judaism as the most spiritual [*geistig*] of religions along Kantian lines.[55] Likewise, the popular designation of the Jewish people as the "People of the Book" has often privileged certain disembodied "dimensions of Jewish experience at the expense of others."[56] While Freud's emphasis on the Jews' "Advance in Spirituality [*Fortschritt in der Geistigkeit*]" seems to similarly privilege the textual and intellectual [*geistig*] aspects of Judaism, it is complicated by his insistence on the genealogical transmission of Jewishness. By refiguring the materiality of Jewish genealogy as proof of its supreme spirituality [*Geistigkeit*], Freud seems like those Jewish scholars and leaders who insist that Judaism is not a race but a spiritual or ethical tradition.[57] However, by insisting on the genealogical transmission of Jewishness, he seems more in line with those Jewish scientists who have attempted to prove that the Jews are a race, united by genes or genealogies rather than by cultural or intellectual ideals.[58] Ultimately, Freud refuses to make a choice between the two possibilities: Instead, he develops a theory of Jewishness that incorporates both the racial materiality and the ideal intellectuality [*Geistigkeit*] of the Jewish tradition.

If Moses' "dematerialization of God" was the initial advance in *Geistigkeit*, how have "the Jews *retained* their inclination to intellectual interests"? How have they preserved their "ideal factor"? The answer is that, in killing Moses, the originator of the "ideal factor," the Jews acquired a memory that could never be completely repressed or erased and that would be inexorably transmitted from generation to generation.[59] In *Totem and Taboo* and *Civilization and Its Discontents*, Freud had explained that the sociality of all civilization was initiated by an originary act of violence.[60] As Jacqueline Rose writes, "monotheism, together with the 'advance in intellectuality' that is said to accompany it, takes hold only because of the bloody deed which presided over its birth." The "underlying thesis" is that "there is no social-ity without violence, that people are most powerfully and effectively united by what they agree to hate. What binds the people to each other and to their God is that they killed him."[61] Indeed, it is this act of violence that ultimately makes the Jews Jewish, for it is the memory of this act that causes the Jewish people both to repress *and* to return to the Mosaic religion. After killing Moses, Freud explains,

> the Jewish people had abandoned the Aten religion brought to them by Moses and had turned to the worship of another god who differed little from the Baalim [local gods] of the neighboring peoples. All the tendentious efforts of later times failed to disguise this shameful fact. *But the Mosaic religion had not vanished without leaving a trace; some sort of memory of it had kept alive—a possibly obscured and dis-torted tradition.* And it was this tradition of a great past which continued to oper-ate (from the background, as it were), which gradually acquired more and more power over people's minds and which in the end succeeded in changing the god Yahweh into the Mosaic god and in re-awakening into life the religion of Moses that had been introduced and then abandoned long centuries before.[62]

It is only through the complicated processes of the repression and the re-awakening of the memory of murder that the Jewish tradition ultimately ascends to the heights of "ideal abstraction," initiated by Moses' aniconic prohibitions. While the Jewish people have not "harmonized" their *Geistig-keit* with physical activity (like the Greeks), their *Geistigkeit* originates from the transcendence of a brutal and physical act of violence and the eventual acceptance of the transcendent monotheism that drove them to commit that act.

Oddly, while Freud builds his entire narrative around this originary mur-der, in the section "The Advance in Intellectuality [*Geistigkeit*]," he does not directly refer to this violent act or to its memory. Instead, he refers to the violence of other peoples, and explains that the Jews "retained their inclination to *geistig* interests" at least in part because of the violence of others. "The nation's political misfortune taught it to value at its true worth the one possession that remained to it—its literature."[63] Indeed, he goes on to note that the "Holy Writ and the intellectual concern with it" not only "held the scattered people together," it also "helped to check the brutality and the tendency to violence which are apt to appear where the develop-ment of muscular strength is the popular ideal."[64] Here, Freud seems to argue that it is the *text* that defines the Jewish people, though he has spent pages and pages speculating about how the Jewish tradition—the memory-traces of the murder of Moses—has survived over innumerable generations, despite and beyond the tendentious textual distortions, through some means *other than direct communication*. Has Freud momentarily repressed the originary brutal act of murder and replaced it with the brutal and violent tendencies of *others* who cause the Jews their "political misfortune"? Though the text may have remained the most valuable possession of the Jewish people, this should not be confused with that which compelled them to preserve their tradition, including the text. Nonetheless, it is not the texts that make Jews Jewish. Rather, it is the permanent imprint of the Mosaic tradition: inscribed, distorted, repressed, preserved, and revived such that Jews continue to feel compelled to turn to these texts, to awaken the memory-traces that have been transmitted beyond sensory perception.

Genealogy and Its Apparent Incongruities

In what follows, I attend to three incongruities that emerge in Freud's theorization of Jewishness as both genealogically defined and as supremely abstract [*geistig*]. First, if Moses was an Egyptian, the question arises as to how and why Mosaic monotheism became Jewish. When and with whom did the genealogical chain of Jewish tradition begin? Second, Freud's racial theory is complicated by the fact that he openly acknowledges that there have always been "mixtures of blood." How do we make sense of this apparent contradiction in his racial reasoning? Third, and perhaps most important, how does he make sense of the base materiality of genealogy and biology without giving up on the "ideal" *Geistigkeit* of Jewish tradition?

EGYPTIAN MOSES, JEWISH MONOTHEISM

If Moses was an Egyptian, how did Mosaic monotheism become Jewish? Freud provides a partial explanation for this apparent inconsistency. While Moses and his monotheism were originally Egyptian, Freud explains that "there arose from among the midst of the people an unending succession of men who were *not linked* to Moses in their origin [*nicht durch ihre Herkunft mit Moses verbunden*] but were enthralled [*erfaßt*] by the great and mighty *tradition* which had grown up little by little in obscurity: and it was these men, the Prophets, who tirelessly preached the old Mosaic doctrine."[65] As in a number of other instances, Strachey's translation stumbles over the weird physicality of Freud's construction. Looking more carefully at the German text, it becomes evident that once these men arose, they could not tear themselves away [*nicht mehr abreißende*] from the chain of tradition that gripped [*erfaßt*] them. Moreover, while *abreißen* suggests a spatial relation, *nicht mehr* suggests a temporal one; Freud's construction of the "unending succession" is both physical and temporal, and, as such, eternally physical and physically eternal.[66] While the "seed of monotheism may have been Egyptian," he explains, it "failed to ripen in Egypt."[67]

Freud's claim that Moses and his monotheism were originally Egyptian has given rise to a number of anxious responses that represent a more general discomfort with certain aspects of Jewish definition. Indeed, Freud knew that denying the Jewish people "the man whom they take pride in as the greatest of their sons" would be interpreted as an insensitive defamation, particularly considering the political situation in which he wrote the book.[68] Though the idea that Moses was an Egyptian was certainly not original to Freud, a number of scholars have argued that his interest in this notion suggests a discomfort with—if not an outright renunciation of—his own Jewishness.[69] To counter such interpretations, other scholars have emphasized the abundance of moments—both in *Moses* and in his private correspondence—in which Freud evinces ethnic pride in his Jewishness.[70] While he may have made Moses an Egyptian, they argue, Freud insists that it was the *Jews* who sustained this "great and mighty tradition."[71] As Yerushalmi writes, "Would an Egyptian Moses make Freud any less a Jew? Does the assertion as Marthe Robert insists, 'declare a whole people illegitimate?' The Jews have never claimed descent from Moses, and Abraham, from whom they do claim it, was originally a Chaldean. Whether God or Moses made the Jews, they have been Jews ever since."[72] Yet the idea that the Jews "have been Jews ever since" leads one to ask, ever since *when?* In a letter to Andreas-Salomé, Freud noted that his last book began with "the question as to what has really created the particular character of the Jew, and [had] come to the conclusion that the Jew is the creation of the man Moses. Who was this Moses and what did he bring about?"[73] While Freud reconstructed a story of the creation of the Jewish character, he was less clear about how and at what moment the band of Semites become Jews such that they would be Jewish *eternally*.

Freud insists on the Egyptianness of Moses not to condemn *or* to commend the Jewish people; rather, he refuses to simplify the intricate paradoxes of Jewishness. If Moses was Egyptian *and* the Jews were those who sustained his monotheistic tradition, it would seem (ipso facto) that if one followed Moses' monotheistic tradition, one would be defined as a Jew. Even if the "old Mosaic doctrine" was preached by an unending succession of prophets, Freud ultimately insists that the Jewish tradition was transmitted and sustained through inheritance, not (only) by direct communication.[74] If individuals inherit Jewishness—regardless of whether they consciously remember the old Mosaic doctrine and regardless of whether they practice Jewish traditions and customs—they remain eternally Jewish. The Egyptianness of Freud's Moses does not make the Jews any less Jewish, but it does point to the complexity of the relationship between Jewishness and Judaism. While Judaism is defined by a body of texts, histories, customs, and rituals, it persists only because Jewish people continue to interpret this body of knowledge and practices, one of which is the genealogical definition of Jewishness.

The continuing discomfort with this aspect of Judaism is evident in the scholarly displeasure with Freud's insistence on the heritability of Jewishness. While Yerushalmi grants that it supposedly makes no difference if Moses was "originally" Egyptian, he nonetheless tries to argue against Freud's idea. "What's in a name?" he asks. "*An Egyptian delivered us out of the hand of the shepherds*, which simply means that in speech, dress, and manner, he *appeared* to them to be an Egyptian."[75] In other words, even if Moses appeared *culturally* Egyptian, he could still be *genetically* Jewish. What worries Yerushalmi is the idea that "'Jewishness' can be transmitted independently of 'Judaism.'"[76] Like many Jewish leaders and scholars, Yerushalmi worries that Jewishness will be *only* an ethnic-racial identity—an identity based on loosely understood cultural stereotypes—rather than a vital living practice of reading texts and observing traditions handed down from generation to generation.[77] While he is willing to grant that Moses and his "monotheism [were] genetically Egyptian," he insists that monotheism "has been *historically* Jewish."[78] However, Freud's insistence on *both* the genetic and historical Egyptianness of Moses and his monotheism points to the

particular connection between genealogy and history for the Jewish people.[79] Freud's reconstruction of the origins of Jewish monotheism is important precisely because it articulates the inextricability of genealogy and
history.

PURE *GEISTIGKEIT*, MIXED BLOOD?

How can we make sense of Freud's emphasis on the pure spirituality [*Geistigkeit*] of the Jewish tradition alongside his acknowledgment of the "mixtures of blood" in Jewish genealogical history? While the Jewish tradition
has been sustained by (some) Jews, it has also incorporated the offspring
of intermarriage and intermixing; how, then, has the tradition remained
spiritually Jewish (or Jewishly spiritual)? Freud notes that the Jews

> survived by keeping apart from others. *Mixtures of blood* interfered little with this,
> since what held them together was an *ideal factor*, the possession in common of
> certain intellectual and emotional wealth [*bestimmter intellektueller und emotionel-
> ler Güter*]. The religion of Moses led to this result because (1) it allowed the
> people to take a share in the grandeur of a new idea of God, (2) it asserted that
> this people had been chosen by this great God and were destined to receive
> evidences of his special favour and (3) it forced upon the people an advance in
> intellectuality [*Fortschritt in der Geistigkeit*] which, important enough in itself,
> opened up the way, in addition, to the appreciation of intellectual work [*intellek-
> tuellen Arbeit*] and to further renunciations of instinct [*Triebverzichten*].[80]

The mere articulation of the phrase "mixtures of blood" might be enough
for some readers to hastily proclaim that Freud was simply reciting proto-
Nazi notions of race and peoplehood. Bernstein, however, cites this passage
as proof that "Freud explicitly *denies* the importance of biological transmission."[81] Thus he argues that Freud had no use for the "disproven" Lamarckian theory of evolution and that he had nothing to do with pseudo-scientific
racial theories. I read the above passage differently: Freud acknowledges
that "mixtures of blood" did not interfere with the transmission of Jewish
tradition only because he also insists that Jewishness is genealogically transmitted. There would be no need to note that "mixtures of blood" did not
interfere with the survival of the Jewish people *unless* this survival depended
(at least in part) upon hereditary transmission.

Freud was one of many Jewish scientists (anthropologists, biologists, doctors) who concerned themselves with the definition of the Jewish people.

Many of these scientists began with the question "what are the Jews?" This question in turn led to a number of other questions: "Do the Jews constitute a single, stable racial type, or are they made up of many races? Are [their] . . . dispositions . . . hereditary or environmental?"[82] Freud straddles both sides of these either–or questions. First, according to Freud, the Jews came from at least "two groups of people who came together to form the nation."[83] He notes that the "Jewish type was finally fixed" by the reforms that "took seriously the regulations that aimed at making the entire people holy; their separation from their neighbours was made effective by the prohibition of mixed marriages."[84] While he is open to the idea that the Jews were originally made up of many different peoples, he insists that the many generations of "separation" from other peoples resulted in a *fixed* Jewish racial type that is nonetheless defined by its *ideal* factor of intellectual spirituality [*Geistigkeit*]. According to Freud's reasoning, then, the Jewish people can be a single stable racial type but nonetheless remain unaffected by "mixtures of blood."

SUPREME SPIRITUALITY, DEBASED BIOLOGY

Most important, how do we make sense of the supreme intellectual spirituality [*Geistigkeit*] of the Jewish tradition alongside the base materiality of genealogy that is biologically conceived? To account for this apparent contradiction, Freud refigures Jewish genealogy as a medium that requires no sensory perception. While he refers to the *Geistigkeit* of Jewish tradition throughout *Moses*, he most extensively defines what he means by this term in the section "The Advance in Intellectuality [*Fortschritt in der Geistigkeit*]" and in the following section, "Renunciation of Instinct [*Triebverzicht*]." In addition to the specific Mosaic prohibitions and renunciations (which I discussed earlier), he repeatedly notes that the "new realm of intellectuality [*Geistigkeit*]" was defined by the fact that "ideas, memories and inferences [*Schlußprozesse*] became decisive in contrast to the lower psychical activity which had direct [*unmittelbare*] perceptions by the sense-organs as its content."[85] Part of the "advance in intellectuality [*Geistigkeit*]," he explains, was the transition from matriarchy to patriarchy:

> This turning from the mother to the father points in addition to a victory of intellectuality [*Geistigkeit*] over sensuality [*Sinnlichkeit*]—that is, an advance in civilization [*Kulturfortschritt*] since maternity [*Mutterschaft*] is proved by the evidence of the senses while paternity [*Vaterschaft*] is a hypothesis [*Annahme*], based

on an inference [*Schluss*] and a premiss. Taking sides in this way with a thought-process in preference to a sense [*sinnliche*] perception has proved to be a momentous step.[86]

Whereas Assmann argues that Freud "knowingly and ironically" inverts the Christian concept of *Geistigkeit* to identify what is most remarkable about the Jews, I see this inversion extending even further.[87] Freud also knowingly and ironically inverts the "matrilineal principle" of Jewish definition to establish a "masculinist *Geistigkeit*" which *incorporates* the body.[88] According to the matrilineal principle, if the mother is Jewish, the child is also Jewish, whereas if she is non-Jewish (even if the father is Jewish), the child is regarded as non-Jewish.[89] Though rabbinic family law is almost entirely patrilineal, in determining the status of the offspring of mixed marriages it is *matrilineal*. There are many explanations for this particular legal aspect of Jewish definition,[90] but the most common—and the most commonsense—explanation is that the mother's identity can be "proved by the evidence of the senses," while the father's identity is always "a hypothesis, based on an inference and a premiss."[91] Thus Freud masculinizes the most feminine aspect of Jewish bodily definition. However, he does this not to rewrite Jewishness as Aryan (as Assmann suggests) or to reject carnality (as Boyarin argues),[92] but to make sense of the specificity of the bodily definition of Jewishness. Thus, while Freud insists that Jewish tradition is biologically transmitted, he masculinizes Jewish genealogy so that it can remain in a realm beyond sensory perception.[93]

By inverting the matrilineal principle, Freud produces a theory of Jewishness that is scientific, yet beyond the criteria of scientific evidence and proof which were then becoming standard. In the 1930s, as new technologies were developed for documenting observations and for controlling experimental conditions, scientific standards began to be defined by the quality of material evidence and controlled experimentation.[94] Throughout his career, Freud drew on developing biological and evolutionary theories, and he regularly expressed an aspiration that psychoanalysis would be regarded as a science, based on actual observations.[95] Yet if psychoanalysis was a science, it was one that had almost no access to material evidence and whose theories could not be "proved by the evidence of the senses." Psychoanalytic theory was (like paternity) always "a hypothesis, based on an inference and a premiss." Nonetheless, Freud could see—or at least was convinced he could see—that (like Mosaic monotheism) psychoanalysis subjects people to its power by presenting its hypotheses to its patients rather than by working with physical materials or by fulfilling material needs. Likewise, Freud observed that Jewish tradition is defined first and foremost by the fact that it does not require material evidence to subject the people to its *yoke*. Rather, what subjects them is the hypothesis that they have inherited *something* (Jewishness) defined not by "sensory perceptions" but by "abstract ideas," "memories and inferences."[96] Freud's theory of Jewishness could be considered scientific in the sense that it is a hypothesis based on observations of the "special case" of Jewish history. Yet it is in a different realm—a more abstractly intellectual [*geistig*] realm—than those scientific attempts to prove the genetic unity of all Jews (or at least all priestly males) using material evidence that, though microscopic, depends upon sensory perception.[97] According to Freud, the biological inheritance of Jewishness does not detract from its abstract ideals as long as it remains a "hypothesis." Thus he refigures the materiality of Jewish genealogy as a purely intellectual matter.

The Future of Fixity

Freud's approach to the problem of Jewish embodiment has parallels with certain statements of his contemporary Franz Rosenzweig.[98] Though they were working within different disciplines (Freud within science and history, Rosenzweig within philosophy and Jewish studies), both spiritualize [*vergeisten*] the Jewish religion *and* insist on a bodily—if not also racial—definition of the Jewish people. While Freud insists that the Jewish tradition is biologically transmitted, Rosenzweig notes that the Jewish people are a "community of blood."[99] Both suggest that this somewhat racial definition of the Jewish people is what allows the Jewish tradition to maintain its spiritual [*geistig*] ideals and to survive in a realm beyond sensory perception, or, as Rosenzweig put it, "beyond the external life."[100] According to both, the Jews became a people precisely when they departed from the material-social world (of national politics rooted in land, language, and history). Freud explains that "after the destruction of the Temple in Jerusalem by Titus, the Rabbi Jochanan ben Zakkai asked permission to open the first Torah school in Jabneh. From that time on, the Holy Writ and the intellectual concern [*geistige Bemühung*] with it were what held the scattered [*versprengte*] people together."[101] Though the destruction of the Second Temple—as well as the subsequent loss of land and the dispersion of the people—are often identified as the source of an originary "brokenness" of the Jewish people, here we can see that this diasporic condition is partly responsible for sustaining the Jewish tradition. For Freud and Rosenzweig, the survival of the Jewish people is linked to the sense that they maintain an intellectual [*geistig*] "home" beyond the grounded materiality of physical land.

The fact that both Freud and Rosenzweig identify this brokenness as endemic to the modern Jewish condition has something to do with the historical situation in which they both found themselves—that is, the moment when German-speaking Jews were once again threatened with the loss of their *Heimat*, albeit this time the homeland was not the Land of Israel, but rather Germany or Austria. With the diffusion of the Jewish people throughout the world and with the possibilities for assimilation afforded by political emancipation in the nineteenth century, there was a sense (if only briefly) that Jews could establish their homes within the various nations in which they resided. However, Freud and Rosenzweig both recognized (in their own ways) that the Jews are a "radically deterritorialized" people.[102] As Pierre Nora has suggested, with the breakdown of stable *milieux de memoire* (environments of memory), people search for and usually find other *lieux de mémoire*, places where memory can stably reside.[103] In the case of the Jewish people, the most enduring *lieu de mémoire* has been the body. For better *and* for worse, Freud insists that the Jewish people originated and were defined by a decisive disruption—the incorporation of a foreign religion (Egyptian monotheism) and a violent trauma (the murder of Moses). Since then, Jewish tradition has survived in a realm beyond sensory perception: within each Jewish body in each new generation.

Like Rosenzweig, Freud suggests that the Jews are a uniquely eternal people. "As we know," he writes, "of all the peoples who lived round the basin of the Mediterranean in antiquity, the Jewish people is almost the only one which still exists *in name* and also *in substance*."[104] It is not clear why Freud qualifies the extraordinary exclusivity of this statement with the word "almost." Perhaps he hesitates in the face of the extraordinariness of the Jewish claim to exclusive uniqueness. Derrida, I think, rightly problematizes this "logic of election": the idea that the experience of "the promise (the future) and the injunction of memory (the past)" is unique to the Jewish people is traumatic in itself.[105] This singular "name" (Jewish?) and this particular "substance" (Judaism? Jewishness?) insistently refer to one another, compelling the Jewish people to return to Judaism such that Judaism (the religion and its traditions) is defined by the Jewish people. The fact of genealogical Jewishness *compels* a person to define and redefine the nature of Judaism; Judaism exists only as a religion of the people. Or, as Rosenzweig put it, the "longing" for the eternal holy land "compels" the Jewish people to

> concentrate the full force of its will on a thing which, for other peoples, is only one among others yet which to it is essential and vital [*eigentlichen und reinen Lebenspunkt*]: the community of blood [*der Blutsgemeinschaft*] . . . the will to be a people dares not cling to any mechanical [*totes*, literally *dead*] means; the will can realize its end only through the people itself. *Das Volk ist Volk nur durch das Volk.* [The people is a people only through the people.][106]

For Freud, it is not education, texts, or rituals that make Jews Jewish but rather the biologically inherited memory of events (multiple, violent, messy, as well as peculiarly ideal) that constitutes Jewish tradition and that compels Jews to be Jewish (and to sometimes practice Jewish traditions). This logic is not so different from the tobacco companies' contention that smoking does not cause lung cancer. Rather, the tobacco companies insist, it is the genetic predisposition to lung cancer that causes people to smoke. In other words, it is not an individual's feelings that cause him or her to feel Jewish and to turn to Judaism. Rather, it is the inheritance of Jewishness (and the subsequent identification of the person as Jewish) that compels a person to *be* Jewish and to do, practice, and have an affinity for particular things that are (then) understood as Jewish.[107] As Žižek repeats after Lacan, "there is no repression prior to the return of the repressed."[108]

While there are converts to Judaism—people who join the "community of blood"—for the majority of Jews, it is the genealogical inheritance of Jewishness that compels them to practice, repress, repudiate, or return to this tradition. The possibility of conversion to Judaism might seem to disprove the purely genealogical injunction to *be* Jewish, but the process of conversion emphasizes this logic: The "convert is adopted into the [Jewish] family and assigned a new 'genealogical' identity," by receiving a new Jewish name whose ending is "ben Avraham" or "bas Avraham" (son or daughter of Abraham).[109] Thus he or she is regarded as a descendant of Abraham, the first convert to Judaism. Likewise, when a person (who was previously non- or not so observant) begins to intensely practice Judaism, that person is referred to as a *hozer bi'teshuvah*—that is, one who has "returned," as if she has returned to her own past (even, or most particularly, one which she did not know).[110] According to Freud, repressions and repudiations are evidence of transmission (acknowledgments that there is a presence and that the tradition has been inherited). How can one repudiate Jewishness if it is not present? Indeed, the logic of conversion itself makes conversion away from (or out of) Judaism impossible. As Assmann writes, "Conversion defines itself as the result of an overcoming and a liberation from one's own past which is no longer one's own. Remembering their disowned past is obligatory for converts in order not to relapse."[111] Since remembering the Jewish past in some way constitutes *being* Jewish, the act of conversion from Jewishness ironically confirms one's Jewishness.

At least since the Holocaust, there has been a strong desire from within Jewish communities to repudiate and repress the racial definition of Jewishness because it seems too close to externally imposed anti-semitic definitions. For this reason, a number of scholars have attempted to reduce or remove this troubling element both from Freud's definition and from Jewish communities' self-definitions.[112] Until quite recently, scholars and community leaders have understandably shied away from any discussions hinting of race and have applauded the scientific community's rejection of race as a useful category.[113] Indeed, it seems as if certain notions of race may become part of the past. In particular contexts and for particular communities, it is quite possible to argue that genealogy is not the same as race or ethnicity, let alone culture, religion, or community.[114] These terms are historically determined and are different for different groups in different times. It may be true that we are moving toward a non-genealogical, non-racial definition of Jewishness, for as Shaye Cohen has convincingly noted, "the nexus of religion, ethnicity, and nationality [and I would include race in this list] was not revealed to the people of Israel by Moses at Mount Sinai but [was] created by historical Jews living in historical time."[115] It may be possible that the racial definition of Jewishness is something that is better forgotten and will some day slip away into the mists of oblivion.

While some might wish for the historical invention (or resuscitation) of a non-genealogical, non-racial definition of Jewishness, we should, however, be careful what we wish for. When a portion of the painful past "returns from oblivion," explains Freud, it "asserts itself with peculiar force, exercises an incomparably powerful influence on people in the mass, and raises an irresistible claim to truth against which logical objections remain powerless."[116] Throughout his life, Freud argued that the return of the repressed is inevitable. In his final book, he extended this argument to suggest that the Jewish people will survive, despite all reforms, rejections, repudiations, and repressions. However, as shocking as this may sound, such a future is not necessarily hopeful, since it also suggests that the "fixity of identity"—racial fever and the violence that is so often legitimated by it—is inescapable.

Rather than repressing the racial elements of Jewish definition, Freud suggests that a vigilant scrutiny of these elements is crucial if there is to be any hope of controlling these "peculiar" forces rather than being controlled by them. Historically antagonistic communities may not ever overcome their differences. However, the continued analysis of their differences—and this includes both the presence and absence of racial fever—may reduce the likelihood that these differences will be used in the service of violence or oppression. The discomfort and strength of Freud's theory of Jewishness is the notion that, when the repressed returns, we cannot predetermine whether the return will be for better or for worse. We can, however, take historical and human actions to anticipate and work through these returns and to sustain the more noble and precious elements in the future.

Belated Speculations: Excuse me, are you Jewish?

On most Friday afternoons, a Chassidic man stands on a street corner. He searches the crowd, hoping to find individuals who know they are Jewish and who can easily trace their matrilineage to women whom he immediately (magically?) recognizes as Jewish. But in asking the question, he disseminates it, strewing its effects throughout the crowd. Each person of whom he asks the question is touched by the process. Yet it is not only the Chassid who poses the question. The burdens of Jewishness are transferred to anyone who has ever considered whether she is Jewish (or why she is not Jewish, or why it might matter); it hails people regardless of their religious beliefs or their sense of belonging. "It 'recruits' subjects among the individuals (it recruits them all), or 'transforms' the individuals into subjects (it transforms them all). . . . 'Hey, you there!' "[1] the man calls. 'Are you Jewish?' "

Common-sensically, it is only the Jewish person who feels hailed by the call from behind—from her past, as it were. Yet anyone who hears the call—and recognizes it as something that matters or that might matter—has been "recruited" into the system. "Excuse me, are you Jewish?" The question opens the door to others who may suspect something lurking within themselves or within others, within their past or future. "No, I'm not Jewish . . ." but what if I were? Generations compress, time expands: What if I had been there? What if it happens again? Where will I have been when the repressed returns? This ideological "calling" resonates with the "calling" to God that some people hear. The distinction between these calls is that it is fairly easy to assert that one does not believe in God, but it is nearly impossible to maintain that one does not believe in Jews: God may not exist, but Jews do.

Psychoanalysis similarly hails all of us who have ever used the words "unconscious" or "ego," or "Freudian slip." It's easy to assert that you don't believe in the efficacy of a treatment that calls itself psychoanalytic, or that you don't believe that what Freud (or any other psychoanalyst) writes is true, but it is difficult to assert that you don't believe in psychoanalysis, at least in its existence as a historical-cultural phenomenon. Haunting the history and practice of psychoanalysis is the question of whether Freud discovered the phenomena of transference, the unconscious, and so on, or whether he created these phenomena, like the God of Genesis who called the Heaven and Earth into being, or like the writers of the Bible who called God into being. In developing a racial theory of Jewishness, did Freud reveal a process already at work, or was he complicit in sustaining this illusion?

Writing of transference, Freud notes, "The less its presence is suspected, the more powerfully it operates."[2] However, in a case of protesting too much, he also insists that "psychoanalysis does not create it, but merely reveals it to consciousness and gains control of it in order to guide psychical processes towards the desired goal."[3] Certainly, the word "transference [*Übertragung*]" existed prior to the founding of psychoanalysis—indeed, it existed at least in part as a description of telepathic transferences, of overly intimate and immoral influences. Yet there is a larger danger that Freud quietly acknowledges: Revealing a phenomenon is not necessarily enough—the psychoanalyst must "gain control" of it. The question remains unanswered as to how the processes of revealing and controlling are related. It is not clear that revealing the transference necessarily allows you to control it—it may actually unleash its powers so that precautions will be necessary. For example, you might want to see a psychoanalyst who may be able to gain control of the situation.

Psychoanalysis reveals how we are all already trapped in various structures—of family, language, society, culture, race, religion, and tradition. However, it is unclear whether (or rather, how) psychoanalysis may be complicit in the perpetuation of these structures. What happens if the questions of belief are shifted from God to race? What would it mean to insist that you don't believe in race? On the one hand, a refusal to believe in race can be seen as a willfully naive disregard of the reality that race constitutes and shapes the experience of all people (whether black, brown, or white, Jewish or non-Jewish). Indeed, to believe in race may be a necessary step in the processes of recognizing and eradicating racism. However, to insist that one does not believe in race is also an attempt to empty the concept of its power and to put an end to the oppressive use of racial categories. Unfortunately, simply insisting that one does not believe in God or race does not eradicate the violence perpetrated in the name of God or race. The question then, is how—and whether—one can talk about racial fever without being complicit in its perpetuation.

INTRODUCTION

1. Which half? Top or bottom? Right or left? Such questions are met with quizzical looks. Apparently, the only appropriate answers are "my mother" or "my father."

2. While moving beyond the color line is deeply important to overcoming seemingly irreconcilable differences between human groups, it will not move us beyond the other kinds of lines (political, genealogical, historical, cultural, socioeconomic, religious) that race often represents. Indeed, my book is an attempt to counterintuitively think about race as a concept already beyond the color line. See Paul Gilroy, *Against Race: Imagining Political Culture Beyond the Color Line* (Cambridge: Harvard University Press, 2000).

3. It is no coincidence that I became interested in these questions while living in Germany, a country that in the last twenty years has seen an enormous growth of Jewish museums, Jewish organizations, Jewish archives, and perhaps most interestingly, Jewish communities. This is not simply because of a rising birth-rate among German Jews. First, with the fall of Communism, there was a huge wave of post-Soviet Jewish immigration to Germany. Second, many Germans have discovered that one or more grandparents were Jewish, perhaps even just "half-Jewish"; this has (partially) motivated many to convert or "return" to Judaism. See Barbara Kessel, *Suddenly Jewish: Jews Raised as Gentiles Discover Their Jewish Roots* (Hanover: University Press of New England, 2000).

4. On the curious history of archives and definitions of Jewishness in Germany, see Deborah Hertz, *How Jews Became Germans: The History of Conversion and Assimilation in Berlin* (New Haven: Yale University Press, 2007), 1–16. Though I learned of Hertz's work long after proposing my exhibit to the Jewish Museum, there is an uncanny resonance between the logic displayed in the actual *Judenkartei* that Hertz stumbled upon and in the chart that I imagined.

5. Particularly in the 1980s and '90s, there were good economic reasons to attempt to prove one's Jewish identity in Germany. If immigrants to Germany could prove that they were Jewish, they were eligible for various state benefits

and financial assistance. This aspect of the Jewish Question added a new reason for some people to feel suspicious about their new "brethren." See Larissa Remennick, "'Idealists Headed to Israel, Pragmatics Chose Europe': Identity Dilemmas and Social Incorporation among Former Soviet Jews Who Migrated to Germany,'" *Immigrants & Minorities* 23.1 (2005).

6. The irony, of course, is that one of the most inclusive definitions of Jewishness was established by the Nuremburg Laws of 1935. While I had a very positive first meeting with the curatorial committee, when I introduced this aspect of the exhibit (at the second meeting), I received an icy reaction. "Why do you want to complicate things?" the curator asked. "Why not choose *normal* Jews, *real* Jews, people we *know* are Jewish?!" The questions persist, particularly in Israel where Jews with even the most "normal" Jewish biographies are asked to prove their Jewish matrilineage. See Gershom Gorenberg, "How Do You Prove You're a Jew?," *New York Times*, March 2, 2008.

7. Jacques Derrida, *Archive Fever: A Freudian Impression*, trans. Eric Prenowitz (Chicago: University of Chicago Press, 1996), 91.

8. Ibid., 68.

9. See Harold Bloom, *The Anxiety of Influence: A Theory of Poetry* (New York: Oxford University Press, 1997).

10. Freud, *Moses and Monotheism*, 103.

11. Yosef Hayim Yerushalmi, *Freud's Moses: Judaism Terminable and Interminable* (New Haven: Yale University Press, 1991), 2.

12. Ibid., 9–10. Yerushalmi derives his notion of the Psychological Jew from Philip Rieff, *Freud: The Mind of the Moralist* (New York: Viking Press, 1959).

13. Yerushalmi, *Freud's Moses*, 11.

14. Ibid., xvii.

15. Thus, where Freud ironically denied knowing what a *menorah* was and asserted that he knew no Hebrew, Yerushalmi finds that Freud was far "more" Jewish than he let on: not only was his mother tongue probably Yiddish, he also knew a fair amount about particular Jewish holidays, rituals, and historic figures. Yerushalmi, *Freud's Moses*, 64–79.

16. Thus Yerushalmi dedicates his book *Zakhor: Jewish History and Jewish Memory* to "the memory of my father Yehuda Yerushalmi for the loving gift of a living past and to my son Ariel who brings joy to the present and past into future." Yosef Hayim Yerushalmi, *Zakhor: Jewish History and Jewish Memory* (Seattle: University of Washington Press, 1996), v.

17. Interestingly, Yerushalmi does not mention his training or brief position as a rabbi in his books or in his "autobiographical study" in "Yerushalmi, Yosef Hayim (1932–)," *Contemporary Authors Online*, The Gale Group (2002).

18. Yerushalmi and Frédéric Brenner, *Marranes* (Paris: Editions de la Différence, 1992), 44. Quoted in Derrida, *Archive Fever*, 70.

19. Peter Schäfer argues that "Yerushalmi's attempt to fetch him [Freud] home to the Jewish fold can probably be termed a failure." In particular, he

takes issue with Yerushalmi's presumptuous use of Jakob Freud's presentation of a Hebrew Bible to his son, Sigmund, as the key piece of evidence. Yerushalmi and other scholars have seen the Hebrew dedication in *melitzah* (a form of poetry composed entirely in allusive Hebrew quotations) as the key evidence proving that, contrary to Sigmund's protestations, he could probably read Hebrew and was more Jewish than he let on. Schäfer argues that there is no evidence that Sigmund could actually read the dedication: Jakob wrote the dedication in Hebrew "just because such dedications were traditionally written in Hebrew." See Peter Schäfer, "The Triumph of Pure Spirituality: Sigmund Freud's *Moses and Monotheism*," *Jewish Studies Quarterly* 9 (2002), 384. In my work, such debates are irrelevant: Perhaps Sigmund learned Hebrew, perhaps he did not. Perhaps some Hebrew words looked or sounded familiar, perhaps they did not. What is more important, or rather more interesting, is Freud's own circuitous explorations of what *does* make a person Jewish and how this Jewishness has survived despite all odds.

20. I am resisting the temptation to interrupt this discussion with excursive acknowledgments of my own situation. Most explicitly: As neither a son nor a father nor a rabbi, I am aware that I am breaking into a sort of sacred chain of homosocial transference and transmission, both Jewish and psychoanalytic. Where Freud, Yerushalmi, and Derrida wrote their seminal books (*Moses and Monotheism*, *Freud's Moses*, and *Archive Fever*, respectively) after establishing their scholarly reigns and producing both biological and non-biological sons, is it not somewhat outrageous for a young woman to explore these matters as a first foray in the world of scholarship, Judaism, and psychoanalysis? The question of whether a daughter can speak in her own name is raised by both Yerushalmi and Derrida: *Freud's Moses*, 100; *Archive Fever*, 43. These questions are echoed (or anticipated?) by Liliane Weissberg: "How should we position ourselves as readers . . . vis-à-vis the figure of . . . Freud, if we are circumcised, not yet circumcised, or worse—a woman?" Weissberg, "Introduction: Freudian Genealogies," *The Germanic Review* 83.1 (2008), 10.

21. Throughout this book, I refer to Freud's final book as *Moses and Monotheism* (the English title of the 1939 translation by Katherine Jones and of James Strachey's version in *The Standard Edition*). A literal translation of Freud's German title would be *The Man Moses and the Monotheistic Religion: Three Essays*.

22. Freud, "The Dynamics of Transference," 99n92.

23. Like most jokes, the origins of this joke are unknown. Freud is reported to have discussed it with Otto Rank sometime before 1908. Rank incorporated the question of Moses' origins into his *Myth of the Birth of the Hero*, which (though not cited by Freud) is an explicit forerunner of Freud's theory about Moses' origins. Freud later presents the joke in his *Introductory Lectures on Psycho-Analysis* (161), but he most fully explored its contours twenty years later in *Moses and Monotheism*. Finally (though who can say what "finally" will be?), Yerushalmi presents this joke in the first paragraph of the first chapter of *Freud's Moses*.

24. Jan. 6, 1935, Freud and Andreas-Salomé, *Letters*, trans. William and Elaine Robson-Scott, ed. Ernst Pfeiffer (New York: Harcourt, Brace, Jovanovich, 1972), 204.

25. All quotations in this paragraph are from Freud's letter of Jan. 6, 1935, ibid., 204–5.

26. June 28, 1938, Freud and Zweig, *The Letters of Sigmund Freud and Arnold Zweig*, trans. Elaine Robson-Scott and William Robson-Scott (New York: Harcourt Brace & World, 1970), 135.

27. Freud, *Moses and Monotheism*, 7.

28. Coincidentally, in her 1939 novel *Moses, Man of the Mountain*, Zora Neale Hurston also proposed a mysterious and complicated birth-story suggesting that Moses was originally an Egyptian prince. The idea that Moses and monotheism were originally Egyptian has been important to Afro-centric authors of the twentieth and twenty-first centuries. See, for example, the vast body of work by Cheikh Anta Diop and Molefi Kete Asante, as well as the extensive discussions of Martin Bernal's *Black Athena*.

29. Freud's interest in the Egyptian pharaoh Akhenaten is part of a relatively recent cultural phenomenon that began with the archaeological discoveries in the early to mid–nineteenth century and the museum exhibitions soon thereafter. Since then, a huge range of artists and authors have embraced the figure of Akhenaten as, for example, a proto-Nazi, an Afro-centric hero, the first gay man, the patron saint of pedophiles, and the "first individual in history." See Dominic Montserrat, *Akhenaten: History, Fantasy, and Ancient Egypt* (New York: Routledge, 2000).

30. Jan Assmann, *Moses the Egyptian: The Memory of Egypt in Western Monotheism* (Cambridge: Harvard University Press, 1997), 2. One could argue that in the *Midrash Rabbah* the rabbis briefly speculate about whether Moses might have been an Egyptian (that is, born to an Egyptian mother). The question is why Pharaoh charged *all his people* [rather than only the Hebrews] to cast their sons into the river. The rabbis respond that the astrologers told Pharaoh, " 'The mother of Israel's savior is already pregnant with him, but we do not know whether he is an Israelite or an Egyptian.'. . . It does not say 'every son who is an Israelite,' but '*every son*,' whether he be Jew or Egyptian. But they would not agree, saying: 'An Egyptian son would not redeem them; he must be an Hebrew.' " Freedman and Simon, *The Midrash Rabbah*, trans. H. Freedman and Maurice Simon, vol. 2, *Exodus* and *Leviticus* (New York: The Soncino Press, 1977), 25. For extensive documentation of the Moses and Exodus narratives in a wide range of historical, cultural, and religious contexts, see Brian Britt, *Rewriting Moses: The Narrative Eclipse of the Text* (New York: T&T Clark, 2004); and Scott Langston, *Exodus Through the Centuries* (Malden: Blackwell, 2006).

31. Freud, *Moses and Monotheism*, 99–100, my emphasis.

32. For example, Jan Assmann reads Freud's hesitations as indicative of his "involvement in the discourse about Moses the Egyptian and its hidden

agenda." Assmann, *Moses the Egyptian*, 147–48. See also Michel de Certeau, *The Writing of History*, trans. Tom Conley (New York: Columbia University Press, 1988), 309–28.

33. A meticulous description of the manuscripts is included in Ilse Grubrich-Simitis, *Back to Freud's Texts: Making Silent Documents Speak*, trans. Phillip Slotkin (New Haven: Yale University Press, 1996); and *Early Freud and Late Freud: Reading Anew Studies on Hysteria and Moses and Monotheism*, trans. Philip Slotkin (New York: Routledge, 1997).

34. Freud, *Moses and Monotheism*, 103.

35. On Zweig's and Freud's correspondence and the "choice between psychoanalysis and fascism," see Jacqueline Rose, *The Last Resistance* (New York: Verso, 2007), 17ff. I did not see Rose's study until after I had completed this manuscript, but the resonance (and even at times near coincidence) of our arguments suggests that the questions raised by psychoanalysis and its relationship to fascism, racism, and nationalism continue to be of utmost importance in these early years of the twenty-first century.

36. Arnold Zweig, *Bilanz der Deutschen Judenheit 1933. Ein Versuch* (Leipzig: Reclam-Bibliothek, 1991).

37. Thomas Mann's 1933 historical-Biblical novel, *The Tales of Jacob*, undoubtedly shaped Freud's own approach to the genre.

38. Sept. 30, 1934, Freud and Zweig, *The Letters of Sigmund Freud and Arnold Zweig*, 91. "Immortal hatred" is my own translation of "*unsterbliche haß*"; Robson-Scotts' translation is "undying hatred."

39. May 8, 1932, ibid., 41.

40. The scholarship on Freud's Jewish identity is immense. The key biographical works from which I draw include the following: Sander Gilman, *Freud, Race, and Gender* (New York: Verso, 2007); Moshe Gresser, *Dual Allegiance: Freud as a Modern Jew* (Albany: State University of New York Press, 1994); Emanuel Rice, *Freud and Moses: The Long Journey Home* (Albany: State University of New York Press, 1990); and Yerushalmi, *Freud's Moses*. In addition, there are invaluable documentary sources included in Marianne Krüll, *Freud and His Father*, trans. Arnold Pomerans (New York: Norton, 1986).

41. Freud, "Autobiographical Study," 7.

42. Krüll, *Freud and His Father*, 240. Though Freud never explicitly refers to his own circumcision, a number of recent studies have meditated on the possibility that this "scar" was the original trauma or trace in the history of psychoanalysis. See Derrida, *Archive Fever*; Franz Maciejewski, *Psychoanalytisches Archiv und jüdisches Gedächtnis: Freud, Beschneidung und Monotheismus* (Vienna: Passagen Verlag, 2002).

43. Sigmund Freud, "Letter to the Editor of the *Jewish Press Centre in Zurich*," 291.

44. Freud, "Address to the Society of B'nai B'rith," 273–74, my emphasis.

45. Freud, *Totem and Taboo*, xv.

46. Jan Assmann, "Sigmund Freud und das Kulturelle Gedächtnis," *Psyche* 58.1 (2004).

47. Daniel Boyarin, *Unheroic Conduct: The Rise of Heterosexuality and the Invention of the Jewish Man* (Berkeley: University of California Press, 1997), 248.

48. I am indebted to Jay Geller's work for its detailed documentation and synthesis of the enormous scholarship on Freud, Jewishness, and anti-semitism. Since his book was published after I completed the manuscript, I refer mostly to his previously published essays. See Geller, *On Freud's Jewish Body: Mitigating Circumcisions* (New York: Fordham University Press, 2007).

49. Assmann, *Moses the Egyptian*. Assmann's emphasis on Akhenaten and the notion of the "Mosaic distinction" resonates with an Egyptian historical novel published almost simultaneously with *Moses the Egyptian*: see Naguib Mahfouz, *Akhenaten, Dweller in Truth*, trans. Tagreid Abu-Hassabo (New York: Random House, 1998).

50. Assmann, *Moses the Egyptian*, 7.

51. Ibid., 8.

52. Ibid., 6, 21–22.

53. Though Assmann's (English) subtitle evokes missionary language, I would not go as far as Schäfer, who practically indicts Assmann for such careless (if not also supersessionist and anti-semitic) wording. See Peter Schäfer, "Geschichte und Gedächtnisgeschichte: Jan Assmanns *Mosaische Unterscheidung*," *Memoria—Wege jüdischen Erinnerns, Festschrift für Michael Brocke zum 65. Geburtstag*, eds. Birgit Klein and Christiane E. Müller (Berlin: Metropol Verlag, 2005), 36.

54. While this idea was popular among both Jews and non-Jews, the non-Jewish version has often been interpreted as anti-semitic because it seeks to do away with Jewishness (and hence, the Jews). An example of this conflict can be seen in an essay by Ernest Jones (Freud's biographer and disciple), in which he expresses support for the idea that the Jewish Question could be solved by assimilation. While Jones attempts to demonstrate that he is not anti-semitic (with varying degrees of success), his essay has (nonetheless) been read as "anti-Jewish bigotry." See Ernest Jones, "The Psychology of the Jewish Question," *Essays in Applied Psycho-Analysis*, vol. 1 (London: Hogarth Press and the Institute of Psycho-Analysis, 1951); and Yerushalmi, *Freud's Moses*, 54–55.

55. Jan Assmann, "Der Fortschritt in der Geistigkeit. Sigmund Freuds Konstruktion des Judentums," *Psyche* 2.56 (2002), 167–68.

56. Ibid., 169. Assmann takes Freud to task for insisting upon the phylogenetic inheritance of memory at least in part because of Assmann's discomfort with the racial tones of Freud's theory of Jewishness. Assmann's discomfort reflects a much larger discomfort with acknowledging any persistent link between Jewishness and race, particularly in Germany.

57. This is not to suggest that race or Jewishness are completely invisible or beyond physical representation. Indeed, the concept of human difference that I

am developing can be contrasted with the concept of "invisible religion" developed by Thomas Luckmann. According to Luckmann, the individual selects beliefs and values from various religious, political and cultural belief systems; religion is the universal term to describe the means by which the human organism transcends biological nature. See Karel Dobbelaere, "Some Trends in European Sociology of Religion: The Secularization Debate," *Sociological Analysis* 48.2 (1987), 111. By contrast, my interest is in how (some) people feel that Jewishness is not something that they selected for themselves but rather something that was selected for them long before they were born and that was somehow invisibly imprinted in or on their bodies.

58. Grubrich-Simitis, *Early Freud and Late Freud*, 77, 61–62.

59. Ibid., 77–78.

60. See, for example, Schäfer, "The Triumph of Pure Spirituality."

61. Eric L. Santner, *On the Pscychotheology of Everyday Life: Reflections on Freud and Rosenzweig* (Chicago: University of Chicago Press, 2001), 5. Edward Said develops a similar thesis about the "shared brokenness" defining all communities, though he poses his argument in political rather than philosophical terms. See Edward Said, *Freud and the Non-European* (New York: Verso, 2003).

62. Santner, *On the Psychotheology of Everyday Life*, 5.

63. Ibid., 6–7.

64. Ibid., 7.

65. Grubrich-Simitis, *Early Freud and Late Freud*, 4–5.

66. Nonetheless, whether we have actually *read* Freud's work or not, there is a sense that we have all already incorporated psychoanalytic terms and structures of thought.

67. This includes the work of Grubrich-Simitis, Nicolas Abraham, Maria Torok, and Nicholas Rand.

68. In her explorations of "those aspects of Jewish texts and culture not intended for public consumption," Naomi Seidman directly confronts this problem. Ultimately, she argues that (*pace* Gershom Scholem) scholars of Jewish studies no longer have to limit ourselves to "apologetic research." While I completely agree, the loss of Jewish languages that Seidman notes—as well as the forces of assimilation and intermarriage—also means that we now live in a time in which the distinctions between insiders and outsiders (Jews and Gentiles) are no longer so clear. See Naomi Seidman, *Jewish-Christian Difference and the Politics of Translation* (Chicago: University of Chicago Press, 2006), 277–78.

69. Grubrich-Simitis, *Early Freud and Late Freud*, 2. Most recently, see Jerry Adler with Anne Underwood, "Freud Is (Not) Dead," *Newsweek*, March 27, 2006.

70. The very use of the term *unsterbliche* to refer to anti-semitic hatred gestures toward other, more common usages of this adjective to describe both love (as in "immortal love") and the Jews (as an "eternal," "undead," and "wandering people").

71. On the non-equivalence of monotheism and Judaism, see for example Schäfer, "Geschichte und Gedächtnisgeschichte." On the relationship between monotheism and religious hatred, see Jan Assmann, *Of God and Gods: Egypt, Israel, and the Rise of Monotheism* (Madison: University of Wisconsin Press, 2008); Regina Schwartz, *The Curse of Cain: The Violent Legacy of Monotheism* (Chicago: University of Chicago Press, 1997).

72. Jay Geller, "*Atheist* Jew or Atheist *Jew*: Freud's Jewish Question and Ours," *Modern Judaism* 26.1 (2006), 1; and "Identifying 'Someone Who Is Himself One of Them': Recent Studies of Freud's Jewish Identity," *Religious Studies Review* 23.4 (1997).

73. The question of how to translate various terms designating Jewishness is not limited to the German–English context, but extends back to antiquity. Shaye Cohen argues that before the second century B.C.E., the Greek *Ioudaios* (pl., *Ioudaioi*), Latin *Iudaeus* (pl., *Iudaei*), and Hebrew *Yehudi* (pl., *Yehudim*) were originally ethno-geographic terms, "designating the eponymous inhabitants of the land of *Ioudaia/Yehudah.*" Even as the most distinctive of their defining characteristics was the "manner in which they worshipped their God, what we would today call their 'religion,'" for both ancient Greeks and contemporary social scientists, "'religion' is only one of many items that make a culture or a group distinctive. Perhaps, then we should translate Ioudaïsmos not as 'Judaism' but 'Jewishness.'" Shaye J.D. Cohen, *The Beginnings of Jewishness: Boundaries, Varieties, Uncertainties* (Berkeley: University of California Press, 1999), 7, 69.

74. Even if we do harbor secret agendas, we must be aware that our work (and our translations) may "betray" us in that what we write can always be used for agendas that may be radically opposed to our own. For example, the website www.tribalreview.com cites, links, and catalogues many Jewish publications (both academic and popular) to demonstrate the "evil" influence of Jewish power and wealth (despite the website's assertions that it is not anti-semitic). Indeed, I half-expect *this* book to be cited as evidence that the Jews are to blame for racism, an argument that I would not support! Of course, such a (racist) statement ("The Jews are responsible for racism") *does* raise a question that is at the heart of this book: "Who are the Jews?"

75. When speaking of Jewishness in the twentieth century, the term *ambivalence* has often been used to refer to the self-conscious wavering between self-hatred and ethnic pride. For example, characters in Woody Allen's films and in Philip Roth's novels have often been described as ambivalent about their Jewishness.

76. Freud, "Autobiographical Study," 9.

77. May 3, 1908, Freud and Carl Gustav Jung, *The Freud/Jung Letters: The Correspondence between Sigmund Freud and C.G. Jung*, ed. William McGuire, trans. R.F.C. Hull and Ralph Manheim (Princeton: Princeton University Press, 1974), 145.

78. May 3, 1908, Freud and Karl Abraham, *A Psychoanalytic Dialogue: Letters of Sigmund Freud and Karl Abraham, 1907–1926*, trans. Bernard Marsh and

Hilda C. Abraham, eds. Hilda C. Abraham and Ernst L. Freud (New York: Basic Books/Hogarth Press, 1965), 34.

79. Freud maintained a sort of protective secrecy not only about "Jewish" matters, but also about certain potentially dangerous aspects of psychoanalysis, such as telepathy, counter-transference and the occult. See my discussion of these topics in Chapter 4.

80. June 8, 1913, Freud and Sandor Ferenczi, *The Correspondence of Sigmund Freud and Sandor Ferenczi*, trans. Peter T. Hoffer, eds. Eva Brabant, et al. (1993–2000), I: 491.

81. See Yosef Hayim Yerushalmi, *Assimilation and Racial Anti-Semitism: The Iberian and the German Models* (New York: Leo Baeck Institute, 1982).

82. John M. Efron, *Defenders of the Race: Jewish Doctors and Race Science in Fin-de-Siècle Europe* (New Haven: Yale University Press, 1994); Eric Goldstein, *The Price of Whiteness: Jews, Race, and American Identities* (Princeton: Princeton University Press, 2006). See also Lynn Davidman and Shelly Tenenbaum, "It's in My Genes: Biological Discourse and Essentialist Views of Identity Among Contemporary American Jews," *The Sociological Quarterly* 48.3 (2007). On the "co-constitution of race and religion," see Henry Goldschmidt, *Race and Religion: Among the Chosen Peoples of Crown Heights* (New Brunswick: Rutgers University Press), 26–35.

83. Goldstein, *The Price of Whiteness*; John Stratton, *Coming Out Jewish: Constructing Ambivalent Identities* (New York: Routledge, 2000).

84. See Adrian Piper, "Passing for White, Passing for Black," Adrian Piper Research Archive (2004).

85. Amy Harmon, "Seeking Ancestry in DNA Ties Uncovered by Tests," *New York Times*, April 12, 2006.

86. See Marc Shell, *Children of the Earth: Literature, Politics and Nationhood* (New York: Oxford University Press, 1993).

87. For commentary on this phenomenon, see Lewis Gordon, "Foreword," *In Every Tongue: The Racial and Ethnic Diversity of the Jewish People*, eds. Diane Tobin, Gary Tobin, and Scott Rubin (San Francisco: Institute for Jewish & Community Research, 2005).

88. Daniel Boyarin, "The Christian Invention of Judaism," 22. There is much debate as to when lineage (and then specifically matrilineage) became the primary definition of Jewishness, but it seems that the fifth century is the latest. See Cohen, *The Beginnings of Jewishness*, 263–307.

89. Contrary to Boyarin, Denise Buell convincingly argues that early Christian self-definitions were equally filled with "ethnic reasoning" and that the categories of religion and race continued to be permeable even after the fourth century. See Buell, *Why This New Race?: Ethnic Reasoning in Early Christianity* (New York: Columbia University Press, 2005), 169, 232. While scholars continue to search for the origins of racial thinking—finding it often in Jewish and Christian texts from the first five centuries of the common era, in medieval texts

from the Iberian peninsula, or in nineteenth-century scientific discourse—I do not believe that the discovery of any particular origin will itself lead to the discovery of the solution to ending racism. Rather, it is through tracing the paths of these discourses that we may become more conscious of the ways in which racial language continues to shape our everyday realities and the ways in which we shape and employ this discourse every day.

90. For a broader exploration of the idea that, in the twentieth century, various Jewish particularities became more generalized, see Yuri Slezkine, *The Jewish Century* (Princeton: Princeton University Press, 2004).

91. As Slavoj Žižek argues, it was "at the very moment when the Jews were deprived of their specific properties which made it easy to distinguish them from the rest of the population, that their 'curse' was inscribed into their very being." Žižek, *The Parallax View* (Cambridge: MIT Press, 2005), 289–90.

92. I discuss this in more detail in Chapter 4. See also Janet Oppenheim, *The Other World: Spiritualism and Psychical Research in England, 1850–1914* (London: Cambridge University Press, 1985), 1.

93. Laura Otis paints a broad picture of "organic memory" (that is, the integration of heredity and memory), particularly at the turn of the twentieth century. However, she almost exclusively emphasizes the obvious racist rhetoric of this phenomenon. See Otis, *Organic Memory: History and the Body in the Late Nineteenth and Early Twentieth Centuries* (Lincoln: University of Nebraska Press, 1994). See also Daniel L. Schacter, *Forgotten Ideas, Neglected Pioneers: Richard Semon and the Story of Memory* (Philadelphia: Psychology Press, 2001).

94. Freud, "Five Lectures on Psychoanalysis," 51; "Address to the Society of B'nai B'rith," 273–74.

1. FREUD'S *MOSES* AND THE FOUNDATIONS OF PSYCHOANALYSIS

1. Jan. 6, 1935, Freud and Andreas-Salomé, *Letters*, 204–5.

2. Freud, *Moses and Monotheism*, 52. Grubrich-Simitis argues that Freud conceived only the first and second of the three essays as a historical novel. Grubrich-Simitis, *Early Freud and Late Freud*, 93.

3. Freud, *Moses and Monotheism*, 99.

4. Ibid., 100, my emphasis.

5. While the correspondence began in 1906, the two men did not meet until 1908. See William McGuire's introduction to Freud and Jung, *The Freud/Jung Letters*, xviii–xix.

6. Freud is known to have borrowed ideas from Johann Wolfgang von Goethe, Jean-Martin Charcot, Wilhelm Fliess, Carl Gustav Jung, Karl Abraham, Sandor Ferenczi, and Arnold Zweig, to name just a few.

7. Eric L. Santner, "Freud's *Moses* and the Ethics of Nomotropic Desire," *October* 88 (1999), 7.

8. Ibid., 6.

9. Grubrich-Simitis, *Early Freud and Late Freud*, 61.

10. Ibid., 9.

11. Freud, *Moses and Monotheism*, 16.

12. Ibid., 17, my emphasis.

13. Ibid.

14. Dec. 16, 1934, Freud and Zweig, *The Letters of Sigmund Freud and Arnold Zweig*, 98. While the statue is simply a common figure of speech, Freud's recurring use of this image to describe his work on *Moses* conjures the image of Michelangelo's *Moses*, about which Freud had written an essay twenty years before. Since the apparent subject of the new work was also Moses (and monotheism), it seems clear that the statue to which he refers in these passages must be Moses. However, if Freud worried about the "clay feet" supporting his work, he worried about the very foundations of psychoanalysis: The statue is not only Moses but psychoanalysis itself. For more meditations on the image of the statue, see Assmann, *Moses the Egyptian*, 148; and Yerushalmi, *Freud's Moses*, 22.

15. Marthe Robert is just one of many who read the exceptional style of Freud's last book as symptomatic of his life-long ambivalence regarding his Jewish identity. See Marthe Robert, *From Oedipus to Moses: Freud's Jewish Identity*, trans. Ralph Manheim (London: Routledge & Kegan, 1977). For a thorough treatment of historians (up to 1991) who read Freud's *Moses* as evidence of Freud's ultimate rejection of his Jewish identity, see Yerushalmi, *Freud's Moses*, 115–116n125.

16. Yerushalmi, *Freud's Moses*, 21.

17. De Certeau, *The Writing of History*, 310. De Certeau emphasizes the novelistic aspects of Freud's last book and suggests that the process of creative reconstruction may be intrinsic to all historical writing, not just Freud's.

18. Yerushalmi, *Freud's Moses*, 21. Similarly, Assmann notes that Freud "began by writing a historical novel and ended up by using almost juridical forms of authentification to present his historical evidence." *Moses the Egyptian*, 148.

19. Grubrich-Simitis, *Early Freud and Late Freud*, 10.

20. In these intervening theoretical texts (*Totem and Taboo, Future of an Illusion*, and *Civilization and Its Discontents*), Freud did not worry about establishing the "historical truth" because there was not any historical evidence that could prove or disprove his theory. It is this "non-falsifiable" aspect of psychoanalysis that, Karl Popper argues, makes it "non-scientific." Yet as Richard Lewontin notes, in "an ironic reversal of the Popperian claim," the more general the argument, the more it is protected against the claims of counter-evidence. Lewontin, "Facts and the Factitious in Natural Sciences," *Questions of Evidence: Proof, Practice, and Persuasion across the Disciplines*, eds. James Chandler, Arnold I. Davidson, and Harry Harootunian (Chicago: University of Chicago Press, 1991), 482. While Popper is often cited as the theorist who proved that psychoanalysis was unscientific (and hence, less valuable), he was actually more circumspect about what its status as non-science meant. Indeed, he notes that all

theories "originate from myths," and even those theories that are non-scientific are not "unimportant, or insignificant, or 'meaningless,' or 'nonsensical.'" See Karl Popper, *Conjectures and Refutations: The Growth of Scientific Knowledge* (New York: Routledge, 2002), 50–51.

21. Carlo Ginzburg, *Clues, Myths, and the Historical Method* (Baltimore: Johns Hopkins University Press, 1992), 106.

22. That is, by abandoning the seduction theory Freud moved from an explicit and simple connection between individual narratives and etiology to a grander and more universal framework in which he derived larger patterns from distinct narratives.

23. Freud, "Analysis Terminable and Interminable," 228.

24. Apr. 26, 1896, Freud and Wilhelm Fliess, *The Complete Letters of Sigmund Freud to Wilhelm Fliess, 1877–1904*, ed. Jeffrey M. Masson (Cambridge: Harvard University Press, 1985).

25. I quote from the English translation and the original German printed in Yerushalmi, *Freud's Moses*, 17, 101–3. This introduction remained unpublished until 1979, when it was first printed in Italian: Pier Cesare Bori, "Una pagina inedita di Freud: la premessa al romanzo storico su Mosè," *Rivista di storia contemporanea* 7 (1979).

26. Freud's categorization of the two forms of historical novels align with two of the more common models of this genre, some of which aim to dutifully portray entire eras (such as Sir Walter Scott's *Waverly*), others of which use the biography of particular persons as their jumping-off point (such as Scott's *Napolean*). Freud also was familiar with Thomas Mann's 1933 historical novel *The Tales of Jacob* (the first part of his Joseph trilogy), which others have suggested may have served as a model for Freud's own historical novel. See Yosef Hayim Yerushalmi, "Freud on the 'Historical Novel.'": From the Manuscript Draft (1934) of *Moses and Monotheism*," *International Journal of Psycho-Analysis* 70 (1989).

27. Freud, "Introduction to the Manuscript Draft (1934) of *Der Mann Moses*."

28. Schäfer, "The Triumph of Pure Spirituality."

29. Freud, *Beyond the Pleasure Principle*, 21, 23.

30. Freud, "Introduction to the Manuscript Draft (1934) of *Der Mann Moses*."

31. Freud and Breuer, *Studies on Hysteria*, 134, my emphasis.

32. Freud, *Moses and Monotheism*, 43.

33. Ibid. The German here is important, for as the editor notes, "*Stelle* means 'a place', and '*ent-*' is a prefix indicating a change of condition" (43n3). In other words, a distortion [*Entstellung*] is a change of location, like moving a scene from one mountain to another.

34. Sander Gilman has extensively documented the related stereotypes of Jewishness, mental illness, and homosexuality (among other conditions) in the

late nineteenth and early twentieth century, particularly in relationship to Freud's work. See, for example, Sander L. Gilman, *Difference and Pathology: Stereotypes of Sexuality, Race, and Madness* (Ithaca: Cornell University Press, 1985); *Jewish Self-Hatred: Anti-Semitism and the Hidden Language of the Jews* (Baltimore: Johns Hopkins University Press, 1990); *The Jew's Body* (New York: Routledge, 1991); and *Freud, Race, and Gender*. See also Geller, *On Freud's Jewish Body*.

35. Hannah S. Decker, "The Medical Reception of Psychoanalysis in Germany, 1894–1907: Three Brief Studies," *Bulletin of the History of Medicine* 45 (1971).

36. Freud, "Heredity and the Aetiology of the Neuroses," 145–46.

37. Freud, "Charcot," 19, my emphasis.

38. Freud and Breuer, *Studies on Hysteria*, 160.

39. Ibid.

40. Ibid., 161.

41. Ibid.

42. Ibid., 140.

43. Ibid.

44. This theme re-emerges in both *Totem and Taboo* and in *Moses and Monotheism* as Freud attempts to discover the reasons why people regularly feel guilty for an act (such as murder) they did not commit.

45. Freud and Breuer, *Studies on Hysteria*, 157.

46. Freud, *Moses and Monotheism*, 7.

47. Freud, *Moses and Monotheism*, trans. Katherine Jones (New York: Vintage Books, 1939), 3.

48. Freud and Breuer, *Studies on Hysteria*, 168.

49. Freud, "Heredity in the Aetiology of the Neuroses," 151.

50. Ibid., 153.

51. Ibid., my emphasis.

52. Ibid., 155.

53. See, for example, Cathy Caruth, ed., *Trauma: Explorations in Memory* (Baltimore: Johns Hopkins University Press, 1995); Shoshana Felman and Dori Laub, *Testimony: Crises of Witnessing in Literature, Psychoanalysis, and History* (New York: Routledge, 1992).

54. Freud, *Moses and Monotheism*, 67; and Freud and Breuer, *Studies on Hysteria*, 213. In fact, the early reference in *Studies on Hysteria* to the railway accident as a model of trauma is not Freud's but Breuer's.

55. See Ralph Harrington, "The Railway Accident: Trains, Trauma and Technological Crisis in Nineteenth-Century Britain" (2004).

56. See, for example, Cathy Caruth, *Unclaimed Experience: Trauma, Narrative, and History* (Baltimore: Johns Hopkins University Press, 1996), 1–24.

57. See R. G. Collingwood, *The Idea of History* (New York: Oxford University Press, 1994).

58. Richard Lewontin, "Facts and the Factitious in Natural Sciences," 479.

59. Ibid., 480.

60. Lewontin, "A Rejoinder to William Wimsatt," *Questions of Evidence: Proof, Practice, and Persuasion across the Disciplines*, eds. James Chandler, Arnold I. Davidson, and Harry Harootunian (Chicago: University of Chicago Press, 1991), 504.

61. In his study of the emergence of statistical thinking in the early twentieth century, Ian Hacking notes that "A new kind of 'objective knowledge' came into being, the product of new technologies for gaining information about natural and social processes. There emerged new criteria for what counted as evidence for knowledge of this kind." Interestingly, while statistics emerged as one method for "taming chance," Freud rarely mentioned statistics; instead, he developed a discipline to "tame" the narrative chances of heredity and history. See Ian Hacking, *The Taming of Chance* (New York: Cambridge University Press, 1990), vii.

62. Carlo Ginzburg, "Checking the Evidence: The Judge and the Historian," *Questions of Evidence: Proof, Practice, and Persuasion across the Disciplines*, eds. James Chandler, Arnold I. Davidson, and Harry Harootunian (Chicago: University of Chicago Press, 1991), 294.

63. For example, in the famous letter of September 21, 1897, Freud admits that "The expectation of eternal fame was so beautiful, as was that of certain wealth. . . . Everything depended upon whether or not hysteria would come out right. Now I can once again remain quiet and modest, go on worrying and saving." Freud and Fliess, *The Complete Letters*, 266.

64. Ibid., 264.

65. Ibid. See also J. M. Masson, *The Assault on Truth: Freud's Suppression of the Seduction Theory* (New York: Harper Perennial, 1992).

66. The criticism is not limited to questions of "proof" and "truth." The original publication of the Freud–Fliess letters (edited by Freud's most loyal followers, most significantly his daughter), omitted important phrases that complicate the questions of whether Freud truly abandoned the seduction theory (and, according to Masson, also his patients), or whether he hesitantly turned away from it. See Freud and Fliess, *The Origins of Psycho-Analysis*, eds. Marie Bonaparte, Anna Freud, and Ernst Kris (New York: Basic Books, 1954), 215–16; Freud and Fliess, *The Complete Letters*, 264–65.

67. According to Jeffrey Masson's interpretation, "what matters for Freud are the psychological effects, and these effects, Freud states, are no different where the event is a real one or imagined." Masson, *The Assault on Truth*, 133. Numerous scholars have amended Masson's extreme critique of Freud's abandonment of the seduction theory. See, for example, Ilse Grubrich-Simitis, "Trauma or Drive—Drive and Trauma: A Reading of Sigmund Freud's Phylogenetic Fantasy of 1915," *The Psychoanalytic Study of the Child* 43 (1988), 12; and Nicholas Rand and Maria Torok, *Questions for Freud: The Secret History of Psychoanalysis* (Cambridge: Harvard University Press, 1997), 228n3.

68. Sept. 21, 1897, Freud and Fliess, *The Complete Letters*, 265.

69. See, for example, Larry Stewart, "Freud Before Oedipus: Race and Heredity in the Origins of Psychoanalysis," *Journal of the History of Biology* 9 (1976).

70. Grubrich-Simitis, "Trauma or Drive—Drive and Trauma," 11.

71. Ibid.

72. Grubrich-Simitis, *Early Freud and Late Freud*, 63.

73. In 1916 Freud would excitedly write to Ferenczi that "the wealth of phylogenetically transferred material" could explain the origins of "artistic endowment" as well as the "transference neuroses" and castration anxiety. Jan. 6, 1916, Sigmund Freud and Sandor Ferenczi, *The Correspondence of Sigmund Freud and Sandor Ferenczi*, II: 101. I discuss the Freud–Ferenczi correspondence in more detail in Chapters 3 and 4.

74. Freud, "Sexuality in the Aetiology of the Neuroses," 280.

75. Freud's resistance to and later acceptance of archaic memory could be compared to Elisabeth's resistance to Freud's analysis. His initial resistance to the idea would ultimately "prove" its viability.

76. Freud, *Three Essays on the Theory of Sexuality*, 173.

77. In these years Freud embraced Haeckel's recapitulation theory—"ontogeny recapitulates phylogeny," or the individual's development recapitulates the development of the human race. However, he resisted the related idea that individuals inherit phylogenetic memories (or an archaic heritage, as he would later call it).

78. May 3, 1908, Freud and Karl Abraham, *A Psychoanalytic Dialogue*, 34.

79. See, for example, John Kerr, *A Most Dangerous Method: The Story of Jung, Freud, and Sabina Spielrein* (New York: Knopf, 1993); Aryeh Maidenbaum and Stephen A. Martin, *Lingering Shadows: Jungians, Freudians, and Anti-Semitism* (Boston: Shambhala, 1991); and Yerushalmi, *Freud's Moses*, 41ff.

80. Jung, *The Psychology of Dementia Praecox* (1906), *Collected Works*. Vol. 3 (Princeton: Princeton University Press, 1953–77), 3.

81. Ibid., 4.

82. Jan. 17, 1909, Freud and Jung, *The Freud/Jung Letters*, 196–97. Ten years before, Freud had referred to a vision of "the promised land" from afar in *Interpretation of Dreams*. There, however, he identified with Hannibal rather than Moses, and the "promised land" was Rome rather than Palestine. Timparano (and many others) discuss Freud's life-long identification with various military figures (many of them failed) and his ambivalent feelings toward Rome. See Robert, *From Oedipus to Moses*; Timpanaro, "Freud's Roman Phobia" *New Left Review* 1.147 (1984); and Silas L. Warner, "Freud the Mighty Warrior," *Journal of the American Academy of Psychoanalysis* 19.2 (1991).

83. Mar. 6, 1910, Freud and Jung, *The Freud/Jung Letters*, 300.

84. On Freud's image of himself as a great leader of a religion, movement, and people, see Erich Fromm, *Sigmund Freud's Mission* (New York: Harper, 1959); and Robert, *From Oedipus to Moses*.

85. On the tensions between Hellenism and Hebraism in Freud's work, see Jean-Joseph Goux, *Symbolic Economies: After Marx and Freud*, trans. Jennifer Curtiss Gage (Ithaca: Cornell University Press, 1990).

86. In 1909 both Jung and Freud spoke of their interests in mythology as preceding the other's. For example, Jung wrote to Freud about his interests in mythology and symbolism as early as October 14, 1909, if not earlier. A month later, however, after Jung wrote another letter about his ongoing mythological studies, Freud suggested that he had been working on mythological questions (by himself) for longer than Jung. "I was delighted to learn that you are going into mythology. A little less loneliness. I can't wait to hear of your discoveries. I hope you will soon come to agree with me that in all likelihood mythology centers on the same nuclear complex as the neuroses." Nov. 11, 1909, Freud and Jung, *The Freud/Jung Letters*, 260. See also Jung's letters on Oct. 14, 1909 and Nov. 8, 1909.

87. Peter T. Hoffer, "The Concept of Phylogenetic Inheritance in Freud and Jung," *Journal of the American Psychoanalytic Institution* 40.2 (1992), 520–21.

88. Sulloway also shows how Jung's interest in the "archaic heritage" was a way for him to deemphasize sexuality and childhood etiology. However, he does not comment on the differences between Freud's and Jung's views regarding the "reality" of the phylogenetic past. See Frank J. Sulloway, *Freud, Biologist of the Mind: Beyond the Psychoanalytic Legend* (New York: Basic Books, 1979), 434–35.

89. Feb. 13, 1910, Freud and Jung, *The Freud/Jung Letters*, 298.

90. In this letter Freud mentions Remus and Romulus; according to the myth, Romulus killed Remus so that he could have the city (Rome) named after him (Romulus). Freud would later compare Romulus' birth-story to Moses' birth-story. See Freud, *Moses and Monotheism*, 11, 13.

91. Oct. 13, 1911, Freud and Jung, *The Freud/Jung Letters*, 449, my emphasis of "unfortunately will soon be undeniable," Freud's emphasis of "uncanny." Interestingly, Hoffer quotes this same sentence but he leaves out the phrase "which will soon be undeniable" and replaces it with ellipses. See Hoffer, "The Concept of Phylogenetic Inheritance in Freud and Jung," 520.

92. See, for example, Freud's letter in October 1911 to Else Voigtländer in which he defends himself against the charge that he had over-estimated the importance of "accidental influences on character formation." Explaining that she had unnecessarily polemicized the relationship between heredity and experience, he rhetorically asks, "Why should there be an antithesis, since constitution after all *is nothing but* the sediment of experiences from a long line of ancestors; and why should the *individual* experience not be granted a share alongside the experience of ancestors?" *The Letters of Sigmund Freud*, trans. Tania and James Stern, ed. Ernst L. Freud (New York: Basic Books, 1960), 284, my emphasis.

93. Wilhelm Stekel, quoted in Herman Nunberg and Ernst Federn, *Minutes of the Vienna Psycho-Analytical Society, 1906–1915*, trans. M. Nunberg (New York: International Universities Press, 1962–1975), III: 299, my emphasis.

94. Ibid., 302.

95. Ibid., square brackets in original. Sabina Spielrein was not only Jung's budding pupil and analysand; she was also deeply in love with Jung and maintained fantasies of producing a perfect synthesis of Freud's Jewishness with Jung's Aryanness by having her own Jewish egg fertilized by Jung's Aryan seed. See Aldo Carotenuto, *A Secret Symmetry: Sabina Spielrein Between Freud and Jung*, trans. Aldo Pomerans, John Shepley, and Krishna Winston (New York: Pantheon, 1982); and Kerr, *A Most Dangerous Method*.

96. Nunberg and Federn, *Minutes of the Vienna Psycho-Analytical Society*, III: 307, my emphasis.

97. Freud, "Sexuality in the Aetiology of the Neuroses," 280.

98. Nov. 30, 1911, Freud and Jung, *The Freud/Jung Letters*, 469.

99. Nunberg and Federn, *Minutes of the Vienna Psycho-Analytical Society*, III: 307, my emphasis.

100. Jacques Lacan, *The Four Fundamental Concepts of Psychoanalysis*, ed. Jacques-Alain Miller, trans. Alan Sheridan (New York: Norton, 1998), 54ff.

101. Apr. 27, 1912, Freud and Jung, *The Freud/Jung Letters*, 502.

102. May 17, 1912, ibid., 506.

103. May 23, 1912, ibid., 507.

104. See Michael Vannoy Adams, "'It Was All a Mistake': Jung's Postcards to Ernest Jones and Kipling's Short Story 'The Phantom Rickshaw,'" (2006). Alfred Adler abandoned not only psychoanalysis; he also abandoned his Jewishness (by converting to Protestantism in 1904).

105. Jung, *The Psychology of Dementia Praecox*, 3ff.

106. Carl Gustav Jung, *Psychology of the Unconscious: A Study of the Transformations and Symbolisms of the Libido* (1911–12), ed. William McGuire, trans. Beatrice M. Hinkle (Princeton: Princeton University Press, 1953–1977), 396.

107. Jung seems to have hoped that Freud would follow suit and give up on the idea that conditions in the present derived from childhood sexuality and traumas. Thus, for example, Ferenczi wrote to Freud about the imminent Fourth Psychoanalytic Congress (the last to be attended by Jung) and his plans to "discuss Jung's false assumption that you *have given up* (and not just expanded) the trauma theory." Aug. 5, 1913, Freud and Ferenczi, *The Correspondence of Sigmund Freud and Sandor Ferenczi*, I: 503. See also Grubrich-Simitis, *Early Freud and Late Freud*, 74.

108. Freud, *Totem and Taboo*, 141–43. As others have noted, Freud had long joked about Jung's wishful fantasies of killing the father (Freud himself). In narrating a story about the band of brothers who kill the primal father, Freud articulated his anxieties about his position as the father of psychoanalysis, always threatened by a band of brothers who want to destroy the authoritarian patriarchal power. See Ilse Grubrich-Simitis, "Metapsychology and Metabiology," trans. Axel and Peter T. Hoffer, *A Phylogenetic Fantasy: Overview of the Transference Neuroses, by Sigmund Freud* (Cambridge: Harvard University Press, 1987), 99n37.

109. See, however, Freud's note in *Totem and Taboo* in which he acknowledges the difficulties that observers encounter when trying to document their savage subjects (102n1). Of course, the position of the anthropologist as a trustworthy and objective observer is no longer taken for granted. The radical questioning of the anthropologist's position in relation to his subject can, in fact, be traced to the work of certain anthropologists, such as Michel Leiris, Bernard Malinowski, and Claude Lévi-Strauss, whose approaches were shaped by their (often critical) reading of Freud's works. See Celia Brickman, *Aboriginal Populations in the Mind: Race and Primitivity in Psychoanalysis* (New York: Columbia University Press, 2003), 10–11; and James Clifford, *The Predicament of Culture: Twentieth-Century Ethnography, Literature, and Art* (Cambridge: Harvard University Press, 1994), 22. While Clifford suggests that the "breakup of ethnographic authority" was a result of the "redistribution of colonial power" after 1950, John Efron argues the anthropologist's position was in question from at least the late nineteenth century, when many Jews began to use the language of science as a way of resisting the dominant structures of power. These Jewish scientists were confronted with the fact that the observer's position is never completely objective. See Efron, *Defenders of the Race*, 2–3.

110. What is odd is not the interdisciplinary nature of *Totem* but its structure of evidence and proof. Indeed, the mix of genres and topics is not so strange when one compares Freud's work to that of Francis Galton, who in one work would cover horse breeding, photography, creativity, literature, immigration, and racial science, to name just a few of the subjects in his *Inquiries into Human Faculty and Its Development* (1893).

111. Freud, *Totem and Taboo*, 155.

112. Nunberg and Federn, *Minutes of the Vienna Psycho-Analytical Society*, III: 307.

113. Freud, "From a History of an Infantile Neurosis (Wolf-Man)," 19ff.

114. Ibid., 21.

115. Ibid., 89ff.

116. Ibid., 97.

117. Carlo Ginzburg, "Freud, the Wolf-Man, and the Werewolves," *Clues, Myths, and the Historical Method* (Baltimore: Johns Hopkins University Press, 1992).

118. Jan Assmann argues that this disregard of cultural memory (in favor of phylogenetic memory) was Freud's blind spot. Assmann, "Sigmund Freud und das Kulturelle Gedächtnis," *Psyche* 58.1 (2004).

119. Freud, *Introductory Lectures on Psycho-Analysis*, 370, my emphasis.

120. Freud, "From a History of an Infantile Neurosis (Wolf-Man)," 97.

121. Ibid.

122. For example, Freud compared the origins of religion and neurosis in *The Future of an Illusion* (1927) and in *Civilization and Its Discontents* (1930).

123. Freud, *Moses and Monotheism*, 72.

124. While Freud compared the rituals performed by neurotics and religious individuals as early as 1907, it was not until 1912 that he made the explicit comparison between the origins of neurosis, religion, and civilization. After that, however, this analogy became commonplace in his writings. See Freud, "Obsessive Actions and Religious Practices"; Freud, *Totem and Taboo*; Freud, *The Future of an Illusion*; and Freud, *Civilization and Its Discontents*.

125. Though Haeckel's recapitulation theory is very often associated with the Lamarckian idea of the inheritance of acquired characteristics, they are not in fact corollaries of one another. Indeed, as I have noted, until 1912 Freud resisted the idea that individuals inherit phylogenetic memory because this seemed to move too far away from the particularities of the individual's own experience.

126. Sulloway, *Freud, Biologist of the Mind*, 200. See also 293–94, 199–204.

127. Freud, *Moses and Monotheism*, 72.

128. *Oxford English Dictionary Online*, s.v. "postulate."

129. Freud, *Moses and Monotheism*, 72.

130. Ibid., 73.

131. Ibid.

132. Ibid.

133. Ibid., 99, my emphasis.

134. Ibid., 85.

135. Ibid., 85–88. In *Future of an Illusion*, Freud suggests that the belief in chosenness is another illusion that derives from the singularity of God. "Now that God was a single person, man's relations to him could recover the intimacy and intensity of the child's relation to his father. But if one had done so much for one's father, one wanted to have a reward, or at least to be his only beloved child, his Chosen People" (19). Similarly, in *Ancient Judaism*, Max Weber claims that while other monotheistic cults had existed before Jewish monotheism, by proclaiming their god as the universal god the Jewish people became "chosen" for exclusivity and particularity.

136. Freud, *Moses and Monotheism*, 86.

137. Karl Abraham, "Amenhotep IV (Ichnaton): Psychoanalytische Beiträge zum Verständnis seiner Persönlichkeit und des monotheistischen Atonkultes," *Imago: Zeitschrift für Anwendung der Psychoanalyse auf die Geisteswissenschaften* I (1912); and Leonard Shengold, "A Parapraxis of Freud in Relation to Karl Abraham," *American Imago* 29 (1972).

138. Ernest Jones, *The Life and Work of Sigmund Freud* (New York: Basic Books, 1953–1957), II: 147. Though the anecdote is *just an anecdote*, it suggests a series of transferential transformations: If Freud identified with Moses, he might have been initially disturbed by the idea that Moses was not the inventor of his own religion. On the occasion of the fainting spell in 1912, Freud may have quickly recalculated a genealogy for Mosaic monotheism: If Akhenaten/Jung was the source of Mosaic monotheism/psychoanalysis, perhaps Freud momentarily imagined that he was Akhenaten's father. Thus when Jung argued

that Abraham had made too much of Akhenaten's death wishes against the father, Freud may have seen this as the ultimate proof of Jung's own death wishes against his "father" (Freud). At the same time, Freud might have briefly imagined himself as the son (Moses) to Jung (Akhenaten), in which case he would be dealing with his own death wishes. Indeed, in Jung's version of the story, after Freud fainted, Jung picked him up and carried him to another room; "I shall never forget the look he cast at me," writes Jung. "In his weakness he looked at me as if I were his father. Whatever other causes may have contributed to this faint—the atmosphere was very tense—the fantasy of father-murder" was definitely a factor. Obviously this is a piece of intense imaginative reconstruction, but the intellectual exchanges between Freud and his colleagues (or followers) were the source of intense anxieties for Freud. See Jones, *The Life and Work of Sigmund Freud*, II: 147; Carl Gustav Jung, *Memories, Dreams, Reflections*, ed. Aniela Jaffé, trans. Richard and Clara Winston (New York: Vintage Books, 1965), 156ff; and Yerushalmi, *Freud's Moses*, 60.

139. Grubrich-Simitis, *Early Freud and Late Freud*, 61–62.

140. In November 1912 Jung excitedly reported on his recent trip to America, where he had presented lectures at "the University of Fordham" (*sic*) in New York. "I found that my version of psychoanalysis won over many people who until now had been put off by the problem of sexuality in neurosis." Nov. 11, 1912, Freud and Jung, *The Freud/Jung Letters*, 515. This critical distinction between Freud's and Jung's concepts of phylogenetic memory has been extended by Jungians such as Lilian Frey-Rohn, who writes, "When referring to inherited dispositions, Freud by no means had in mind systems of predetermined channels or pathways (Jung) but 'memory-traces of the experience of earlier generations.' By thinking *only in concrete terms*, Freud went so far as to ascribe such memory-traces to the after-effect of prehistoric events." See Frey-Rohn, *From Freud to Jung: A Comparative Study of the Psychology of the Unconscious*, trans. Fred E. Engreen and Evelyn K. Engreen (New York: Putnam, 1974), 127, my emphasis.

141. For example, during a stint as a physician on the warfront, Jung wrote a letter to Freud in which he noted that he was surrounded by "the constant spectacle of *odious corporeality*." However, he notes "something can be gained even from its more indelicate aspect, to wit, from what is known as the 'short-arm inspection' [*sogenannte Schwanzvisite*]." Jung goes on to describe his examination of the penises of five hundred conscripted men: "At this phallic parade of 500 soldiers 14% had phimosis. Here we have the biological incentive to circumcision. The commonest abnormality seems to be a tendency to hypospadias. It looks positively female." Such comments suggest that it might be interesting to further explore Jung's own theory of circumcision. Oct. 4, 1911, Freud and Jung, *The Freud/Jung Letters*, 444.

142. Robert Paul, "Freud's Anthropology: A Reading of the 'Cultural Books,'" *The Cambridge Companion to Freud*, ed. Jerome Neu (New York: Cambridge University Press, 1991), 268. Paul argues that we must "reject the literal

historicity of the primal crime, as well as the idea of the history of civilization being like maturation from infancy on through stages comparable to those in an individual life." However, he adds that "our rejection of these aspects of Freud's cultural thought should not lead us to ignore the fact that the parallels he cites are highly persuasive, indicating that the fantasies, impulses, defenses, and symbolisms observed clinically in obsessional personalities, and culturally in the rites, symbols and traditions of our civilization are closely related if not identical" (284).

143. What does it mean to take something literally? On the one hand, to take something literally is to take a statement as a representation of physical reality. Thus, for example, Yerushalmi, Robert Paul, and others seem concerned that Freud's "phylogenetic fantasy" may be misunderstood as a matter of fact. However, to take something literally may also mean that one strictly adheres to the primary irreducible meaning of a word or text. Indeed, it is never quite clear whether Freud's works—*Moses* in particular—should be read as scientific attempts to accurately represent reality or as literary texts (to be approached *as texts*). A third way of approaching Freud's texts, however, is to focus on their consequences. What happens if we take his speculations as realities with repercussions in the real world?

144. Yerushalmi, *Freud's Moses*, 87–88. See also Yosef Hayim Yerushalmi, "Reflections on Forgetting," *Zakhor: Jewish History and Jewish Memory* (Seattle: University of Washington Press, 1996), 109.

145. Yerushalmi, "Reflections on Forgetting," 109. This anxiety resonates with Dominick LaCapra's uneasiness about the blurred effects of "secondary witnessing," whereby the historian over-identifies with his subject (the witness), thereby making the "real" witness irrelevant or unnecessary. See, for example, LaCapra, *Writing History, Writing Trauma* (Baltimore: Johns Hopkins University Press, 2000), 97ff. See also LaCapra, *Representing the Holocaust: History, Theory, Trauma* (Ithaca: Cornell University Press, 1994); and LaCapra, *History in Transit: Experience, Identity, Critical Theory* (Ithaca: Cornell University Press, 2004).

146. This problematically assumes that individuals will naturally transmit the past to the future by biologically reproducing.

147. For an interpretation of Freud's logic as particularly Rabbinic, see Susan Handelman, *The Slayers of Moses* (Albany: State University of New York Press, 1982). For an interpretation that sets Freud's work in the Jewish mystical tradition, see David Bakan, *Sigmund Freud and the Jewish Mystical Tradition* (Princeton: Van Nostrand, 1958). At various times, Freud both embraced and rejected the idea that psychoanalysts might be compared to Talmudists. For example, in *Moses* he writes that "it did not seem attractive to find oneself classed with the schoolmen and Talmudists who delight in exhibiting their ingenuity without regard to how remote from reality their thesis may be" (17). On the other hand, he happily accepted Abraham's comment about the Talmudic

structure and logic of *Jokes and Their Relation to the Unconscious* (1905) as a compliment. May 11, 1908, Freud and Abraham, *A Psychoanalytic Dialogue*, 36.

148. Daniel Boyarin, *Carnal Israel: Reading Sex in Talmudic Culture* (Berkeley: University of California Press, 1993), 8.

149. Freud, *Moses and Monotheism*, 88.

150. Here I use Katherine Jones' translation: *Moses and Monotheism*, 112.

151. Freud, "On the History of the Psycho-Analytic Movement," 62. This was, of course, *Freud's* view of things, and should not be misunderstood as an objective view of the differences between the two men's theories. However, many Jungians and Freudians seem to agree on this distinction. See Adams, "It Was All a Mistake"; and Frey-Rohn, *From Freud to Jung*, 127.

152. Freud, "On the History of the Psycho-Analytic Movement," 18–19.

2. FREUD'S "LAMARCKISM" AND THE POLITICS OF RACIAL SCIENCE

1. Freud, *Moses and Monotheism*, 100.

2. Ibid.

3. Here I present my own translation of the published German text, which reads as follows: "Aber wir gestehen in aller Bescheidenheit, daß wir trotzdem diesen Faktor in der biologischen Entwicklung nicht entbehren können." Freud, *Gesammelte Werke*, XVI: 207. The manuscript differs only slightly: "Aber wir gestehen in aller Bescheidenheit, daß wir uns trotzdem die biologische Entwicklung auf keinem anderen Weg vorstellen können." The manuscript of *Der Mann Moses und die monotheistische Religion* is in Reel 5, Box OV 11, Sigmund Freud Papers, Sigmund Freud Collection, Manuscript Division, Library of Congress, Washington, DC.

4. As I will discuss later in this chapter, part of this misunderstanding may be due to the fact that Ernest Jones uses Katherine Jones' translation of this passage, which is slightly misleading. The original German reads "biologischen Wissenschaft . . . , die von der Vererbung erworbener Eigneschaften auf die Nachkommen *nichts wissen will*." In Katherine Jones' translation, Freud acknowledges that biological science "*rejects* the idea of acquired qualities being transmitted to descendants" (128). The translation in the *Standard Edition* is closer to the German: "Biological science *refuses to hear of* the inheritance of acquired characters by successive generations" (100).

5. Recent work in the field of epigenetics shows that epimutations in response to the environment may be hereditarily transmitted and suggests that Lamarck might have been a "little bit right." See, for example, Michael Balter, "Genetics: Was Lamarck Just a Little Bit Right?" *Science*, April 7, 2000; Eva Jablonka and Marion Lamb, *Epigenetic Inheritance and Evolution: The Lamarckian Dimension* (New York: Oxford University Press, 1995); and Edward Steele, Robyn Lindley, and Robert Blanden, *Lamarck's Signature: How Retrogenes Are Changing Darwin's Natural Selection Paradigm* (Reading: Perseus, 1998).

6. Robert Proctor, "Nazi Medicine and the Politics of Knowledge," *The "Racial" Economy of Science*, ed. Sandra Harding (Bloomington: Indiana University Press, 1993), 350.

7. For example, Emmanuel Rice suggests that the central weakness in Freud's theory is his "seemingly irrational dependence on Lamarck's theory of inheritance of acquired characteristics" (146). Since Rice could not make sense of why "Freud, the scientist, would accept this hypothesis without question, hesitation or doubt," he argues, "We must look to Freud the man for an explanation." Rice, *Freud and Moses: The Long Journey Home*, 152. See also Stephen Jay Gould, *Ontogeny and Phylogeny* (Cambridge: Harvard University Press, 1977), 155ff.

8. The key source in discussions of Freud's use of biological theory is Sulloway, *Freud, Biologist of the Mind*.

9. Richard Webster writes in a review of Frederick Crews' *The Memory Wars* and John Forrester's *Dispatches from the Freud Wars* that "the picture of Freud which has gradually emerged . . . is of a man so deeply ensnared in the fallacies of Lamarck, Haeckel, and late-nineteenth-century evolutionary biology, and so engulfed by the diagnostic darkness of turn-of-the-century European medicine, that he led an entire generation of gifted intellectuals deeper and deeper into a labyrinth of error from which our intellectual culture as a whole is still struggling to emerge." Richard Webster, "The Bewildered Visionary," *Times Literary Supplement* (May 16, 1997). See also Webster, *Why Freud Was Wrong: Sin, Science and Psychoanalysis* (New York: Basic Books, 1995), 236, 240.

10. The clearest example of this argument can be found in the work of Lucille Ritvo, who goes to extraordinary lengths to show that Freud's belief in the inheritance of acquired characteristics was not Lamarckian but Darwinian. See Ritvo, *Darwin's Influence on Freud: A Tale of Two Sciences* (New Haven: Yale University Press, 1990). Similarly, Dennis Wrong groups Freud's Lamarckism alongside other embarrassing elements such as the death instinct and the primal crime, which many psychoanalysts have tried to keep from contaminating psychoanalysis proper. Wrong, *The Problem of Order: What Unites and Divides Society* (New York: The Free Press, 1994), 122. For a critique of Wrong, see Howard L. Kaye, "Was Freud a Medical Scientist or a Social Theorist? The Mysterious 'Development of the Hero,'" *Sociological Theory* 21.4 (2003), 379.

11. Patricia Kitcher argues that Freud drastically misunderstood many scientific concepts because he attempted to be interdisciplinary. Thus she remarks that when Lamarckism had become "highly controversial," Freud was not able to "free himself from such dubious entanglements when he had the chance" (178). Ironically, it seems that Kitcher's work lacks an interdisciplinary element that would have allowed her to see the larger context of the controversies regarding Lamarckism during Freud's lifetime. See Kitcher, *Freud's Dream: A Complete Interdisciplinary Science of Mind* (Cambridge: MIT Press, 1992), 174ff.

Similarly, after applauding Kitcher for chastising Freud for his misguided understandings of evolutionary science, Peter Rudnytsky notes that the "emancipation from [Freud's] oppressive influence is at the same time an expression of loyalty to what is noblest in his spirit . . . it is necessary to let go of Freud to preserve psychoanalysis." Rudnytsky, *Reading Psycho-Analysis: Freud, Rank, Ferenczi, Groddeck* (Ithaca: Cornell University Press, 2002), 218.

12. Rice, *Freud and Moses*, 146. See also Richard J. Bernstein, *Freud and the Legacy of Moses* (New York: Cambridge University Press, 1998); José Brunner, *Freud and the Politics of Psychoanalysis* (New Brunswick: Transaction Publishers, 2001); Gilman, *Freud, Race, and Gender*; and Yerushalmi, *Freud's Moses*.

13. Freud, "Heredity and the Aetiology of the Neuroses," 151.

14. For example, how was it possible to refer to humans as a constant group if they had evolved from apes, changing physical and mental characteristics until they came to resemble present-day human beings? Such questions were also posed about racial and linguistic groups: How was it possible to identify both the constants of Aryans or Semites while taking into account the idea that peoples and languages changed over time?

15. On the historical emergence of the cultural idea of the "generation," see Sigrid Weigel, *Genea-Logik: Generation, Tradition und Evolution zwischen Kultur- und Naturwissenschaften* (Munich: Fink, 2006).

16. Because the belief in the inheritance of acquired characters has been associated with anti-Darwinism since the end of the nineteenth century, and because such a belief has long gone out of favor, there has been much confusion about whether this idea was antithetical to Darwinian natural selection. Darwin himself was convinced that "variations of all kinds and degrees are directly or indirectly caused by the conditions of life to which each being, and more especially its ancestors, have been exposed." Charles Darwin, *The Variation of Animals and Plants under Domestication* (London: Murray, 1868), 240–41.

17. Peter J. Bowler, *The Non-Darwinian Revolution: Reinterpreting a Historical Myth* (Baltimore: Johns Hopkins University Press, 1988), 117.

18. Where *racial character* is often used to designate that which cannot be modified, in this time period (if not also since then), it could include elements that are modifiable, that is, what we might today commonly categorize as "cultural."

19. Loren R. Graham, "Science and Values: The Eugenics Movement in Germany and Russia in the 1920s," *The American Historical Review* 82.5 (1977), 1134.

20. Ibid.

21. Ibid.

22. See Jonathan Harwood, *Styles of Scientific Thought: The German Genetics Community, 1900–1933* (Chicago: University of Chicago Press, 1993).

23. Bowler, *The Non-Darwinian Revolution*, 116–18.

24. Ibid., 117–18.

25. Hugo Iltis, *Gregor Johann Mendel: Leben, Werk und Wirkung* (Berlin: J. Springer, 1924).

26. "Rassenwissenschaft und Rassenwahn," *Die Gesellschaft: Internationale Revue für Sozialismus und Politik* (1927); Hugo Iltis, *Der Mythus von Blut und Rasse* (Vienna: R. Harand, 1936). See also Iltis, *Volkstümliche Rassenkunde* (Jena: Urania-Verlagsgesellschaft, 1930). Loren Graham suggests that Iltis "saw in Lamarckism a way of softening the hard facts of genetics, and in that way he helped forge the links between leftist politics and Lamarckism that were growing in the 1920s." Graham, "Science and Values," 1142.

27. For a more extensive discussion of the Vivarium's overlapping social and scientific circles, see Deborah Coen, "Living Precisely in Fin-de-Siècle Vienna," *Journal of the History of Biology* 39.3 (2006).

28. Freud, "The Psychogenesis of a Case of Homosexuality in a Woman," 171–72. Though today sexuality and gender are often discussed as distinct (though related) categories, in this historical context "sexual identification" would include both terms.

29. Peter Gay, *Freud: A Life for Our Time* (New York: Norton, 1988), 426; Jones, *The Life and Work of Sigmund Freud*, III: 98. There is other evidence that Freud was quite friendly with Steinach. For example, in an interview on the occasion of his one hundredth birthday, the sexologist Harry Benjamin recalled that his mentor Steinach had arranged a meeting with Freud; this suggests that Steinach was close enough to Freud to arrange such things. See Erwin J. Haeberle, "The Transatlantic Commuter: An Interview with Harry Benjamin on the Occasion of His 100th Birthday," *Sexualmedizin* 14.1 (1985).

30. See Chandak Sengoopta, "Glandular Politics: Experimental Biology, Clinical Medicine, and Homosexual Emancipation in Fin-de-Siècle Europe," *Isis* 89.3 (1998); and Sengoopta, *The Most Secret Quintessence of Life: Sex, Glands, and Hormones, 1850–1950* (Chicago: University of Chicago Press, 2006).

31. Paul Kammerer, *Rejuvenation and the Prolongation of Human Efficiency: Experiences with the Steinach-Operation on Man and Animals* (New York: Boni and Liverlight, 1923).

32. Freud, "The Uncanny," 238. Freud cites Kammerer's book *The Law of the Series* [*Das Gesetz der Serie*], in which he argues that "uncanny" coincidences can be explained by the law of the series. But the citation is itself uncanny: It appears in the context of Freud's discussion of coincidental numbers that may prophecy a person's date of death (a subject that Freud often discussed). Seven years later, Kammerer committed suicide on September 23, 1926; Freud died exactly thirteen years after Kammerer, on September 23, 1939. Coincidence? Uncanny? Prophecy? Chapter 4 contains more meditations on these sorts of questions.

33. On Kammerer's midwife toad experiments, see Arthur Koestler, *The Case of the Midwife Toad* (London: Hutchinson, 1971).

34. See, for example, Robert K. Merton, *On Social Structure and Science* (Chicago: University of Chicago Press, 1996), 295. Sander Gliboff shows that the

reasons for Kammerer's downfall were not only that he apparently falsified his evidence. In addition to general anti-semitic accusations, Kammerer was also widely criticized for his general showman style (which only added to the perception of him as a charlatan and confirmed anti-semitic accusations that he was deceitful). See Gliboff, "The Pebble and the Planet: Paul Kammerer, Ernst Haeckel, and the Meaning of Darwinism," PhD dissertation, Johns Hopkins University, Baltimore, 2001"; and Gliboff, "The Case of Paul Kammerer: Evolution and Experimentation in the Early 20th Century," *Journal of the History of Biology* 39.3 (2006), 527.

35. Gliboff, "The Pebble and the Planet," 209.

36. Ibid., my emphasis.

37. Ibid., 219–20. Then, as now, "creationism" was often used as a euphemism for anti-scientific religious positions that supported theological teleology and rejected Darwinian natural selection.

38. Cheryl Logan, "Overheated Rats, Race, and the Double Gland: Paul Kammerer, Endocrinology and the Problem of Somatic Induction," *Journal of the History of Biology* 40.4 (2007).

39. As Paul Weindling notes, most critics of racism and racial hygiene were also "committed to biologistic solutions for social problems." Weindling, *Health, Race, and German Politics Between National Unification and Nazism, 1870–1945* (New York: Cambridge University Press, 1989), 331. This does not mean, however, that Darwinism or Mendelism *led* to the Nazi horrors. In an interesting turn of the historiographic screw, Richard Weikart has extensively (and sometimes convincingly) argued that Darwinian evolutionary theories made possible (or thinkable) the Nazis' general lack of ethics and their racist genocide. But Weikart implicitly supports the idea that Darwinism and evolution without God lead to evil and that intelligent design is gentler and better. It is no coincidence that Weikart received research funding for his book *From Darwin to Hitler* (2004) from the Center for Science and Culture (CSC) and that he is listed as a fellow of the Discovery Institute, a Christian organization that promotes various religious agendas, most specifically the idea of intelligent design.

40. Gliboff, "The Pebble and the Planet," 209.

41. There is some debate about whether Iltis and Kammerer should be considered Jewish scientists, since it is difficult to find evidence that they identified themselves as Jewish. On the one hand, they traveled in Jewish circles and they were labeled as Jews by their political and scientific enemies. On the other hand, there is some twisted logic at work when historians and museum curators refer to individuals as Jews just because their (anti-semitic) enemies had called them Jews. In her dissertation on Jewish racial scientists, Veronika Lipphardt includes only those scientists who identified themselves as Jewish; therefore she does not focus on Iltis or Kammerer. (This mode of self-identification equates the scientist's "self" with whatever limited traces of one's "self" can be found in the archives.) Lipphardt, "Biowissenschaftler mit jüdischem Hintergrund und

die Biologie der Juden: Debatten, Identitäten, Institutionen (1900–1935)," PhD dissertation, Humboldt Universität, Baltimore, 2006.

42. Fritz Lenz, "Der Fall Kammerer und seine Umfilmung durch Lunatscharsky," *Archiv für Rassen- und Gesellschaftsbiologie* 21 (1929); and Lenz, Erwin Baur and Eugen Fischer, *Human Heredity* (New York: The Macmillan Company, 1931), 674–75.

43. Nick Hopwood, "Book Review: August Weismann's *Ausgewählte Briefe und Dokumente*, ed. Frederick B. Churchill and Helmut Risler," *Bulletin of the History of Medicine* 76.2 (2002), 384.

44. Quoted in Gliboff, "The Pebble and the Planet," 187n314. "*Klebrig* [sticky]" was a common anti-semitic epithet at this time, suggesting that Jewishness was contagious and that Jews were parasites who would "stick" to other people and suck out the lifeblood. I thank Lipphardt and Gliboff for clarifying this phrase.

45. Robert Proctor, *Racial Hygiene: Medicine Under the Nazis* (Cambridge: Harvard University Press, 1988), 33. The German name of the publication was *Archiv für Rassen- und Gesellschaftsbiologie*.

46. In its early years, the *Archive* published a wider range of articles, including some by scientists who self-identified as Jewish, Lamarckian, and/or anti-racist. See Paul Weindling, "The Evolution of Jewish Identity: Ignaz Zollschan between Jewish and Aryan Race Theories, 1910–1945," *Jewish Tradition and the Challenge of Darwinism*, eds. Geoffrey Cantor and Marc Swetlitz (Chicago: University of Chicago Press, 2006).

47. Lenz, "Der Fall Kammerer und seine Umfilmung durch Lunatscharsky," 316–17.

48. The German title of Lenz's book was *Grundriss der menschlichen Erblichkeitslehr und Rassenhygiene* (1927); Lenz's remarks are here quoted from the later English edition: Lenz, Baur, and Fischer, *Human Heredity*, 674–75. Lenz directly accuses Kammerer of being a Jew, a Lamarckian, and a Bolshevik, all of which he assumes are correlated: "For instance, it is extremely characteristic that Kammerer, who was himself both a Jew and a Lamarckian, should write that 'the denial of the racial importance of acquired characteristics favors race hatred'" (674). While Kammerer saw connections between the biological theory of the inheritance of acquired characters and his political stance against racial and social inequality, it seems dubious that he ever actually said the words attributed to him by Lenz. Moreover, Kammerer did not necessarily see himself as either a Lamarckian or a Jew, but by the 1920s both of these labels were used as much as accusatory epithets as descriptive classifications.

49. Fritz Lenz, "Die Stellung des Nationalsozialismus zur Rassenhygiene," *Archiv für Rassen- und Gesellschaftsbiologie* 25 (1931), 308. In 1933 Lenz became head of the department of heredity and eugenics at the Kaiser-Wilhelm Institute for Anthropology in Berlin-Dahlem, "replacing the former director who was dismissed for political reasons. He also had his share in shaping the 'Law

for the Prevention of Hereditary Disease in Posterity' dated 1933." See Center for Holocaust and Genocide Studies, "Histories and Narratives: Documentary Evidence" (Regents of the University of Minnesota, 2008).

50. Quoted in Proctor, *Racial Hygiene*, 37–38.

51. See Richard Lewontin and Richard Levins, "The Problem of Lysenko-ism," *The Dialectical Biologist* (Cambridge: Harvard University Press, 1985).

52. Many scientists continued to integrate various positions that could be described as Mendelian, Weismannian, Darwinian, *and* Lamarckian. As Lipphardt shows, there was not a neat division between scientists who adhered to nature, neo-Darwinism, and determinism (on the one hand), and those who supported nurture, Lamarckism, and anti-determinism (on the other). Moreover, there were many Jewish "race" scientists who gravitated toward the first "nature" category. Lipphardt, "Biowissenschaftler mit jüdischem Hintergrund und die Biologie der Juden," 21.

53. Quoted in Proctor, *Racial Hygiene*, 55. See also Gliboff, "The Pebble and the Planet."

54. Mitchell Bryan Hart, *Social Science and the Politics of Modern Jewish Identity* (Stanford: Stanford University Press, 2000), 12.

55. For example, in 1893–94, *Contemporary Review* featured a year-long debate between Weismann and Herbert Spencer (a neo-Lamarckian) regarding the causes of evolutionary change. In his first edition of the *Interpretation of Dreams* (1900), Freud referred to Spencer's work on the meaning of dreams "in pre-historic times by primitive races of man" (2). In 1906, at a meeting of the Vienna Psycho-Analytical Society, he sharply critiqued Richard Semon's work on the "mneme"—a concept that integrated memory and heredity (and that has more recently reemerged in a slightly altered form in Richard Dawkins' study of *The Selfish Gene*). In *Introductory Lectures on Psycho-Analysis* (1916–17), Freud notes the work of Darwin, A. R. Wallace, "and their predecessors" that met with "the most violent contemporary opposition" (285). See also Nunberg and Federn, *Minutes of the Vienna Psycho-Analytical Society*, I: 48–51. On Semon's concept of the "mneme," see Schacter, *Forgotten Ideas, Neglected Pioneers*.

56. Freud, *Moses and Monotheism*, 100.

57. Aug. 7, 1912, Freud and Jones, *The Complete Correspondence of Sigmund Freud and Ernest Jones*, ed. Andrew Paskauskas (Cambridge: Harvard University Press, 1993), 150. Interestingly, though Jones regularly quotes from his correspondence with Freud in the biography, he does not include this letter in his discussion of Freud's "Lamarckism." In Chapter 3 I explore Freud's use of Weismann's theories in more detail.

58. On the Modern Synthesis, often referred to as the Modern Evolutionary Synthesis, see Ernst Mayr, *The Growth of Biological Thought: Diversity, Evolution and Inheritance* (Cambridge: Harvard University Press, 1982), 706.

59. May 3, 1908, Freud and Jung, *The Freud/Jung Letters*, 145.

60. Bowler, *The Non-Darwinian Revolution*, 104.

61. Ibid., 123–25. See also Harwood, *Styles of Scientific Thought*.

62. Grubrich-Simitis, "Metapsychology and Metabiology," 94.

63. Mar. 2, 1917, Freud and Ferenczi, *The Correspondence of Sigmund Freud and Sandor Ferenczi*, II: 186.

64. May 29, 1917, ibid., II: 210. Indeed, within a few years Ferenczi would explicitly incorporate Lamarck's work (as opposed to Darwin's) in his book, *Thalassa*. He writes, "The more psychological concept of Lamarck, which concedes a role in phylogenesis to impulses and instincts as well, is nearer to the heart of the psychoanalyst than is that of the great English naturalist [Darwin] who would attribute everything to variation alone and thus in the last analysis to chance." Sandor Ferenczi, *Thalassa: A Theory of Genitality* (1924), trans. Henry Alden Bunker (London: Karnac, 1989), 50.

65. May 29, 1917, and Jan.–Feb. 1918, Freud and Ferenczi, *The Correspondence of Sigmund Freud and Sandor Ferenczi*, II: 259–63.

66. Grubrich-Simitis, "Metapsychology and Metabiology," 94.

67. In other words, Freud never explicitly repudiated or rejected Lamarckism; instead, he seems to have simply become less interested in reading Lamarck's works. Though he continued to insist on the inheritance of acquired characteristics, he would not necessarily have regarded this idea as specifically *Lamarckian*.

68. While the politicians were explicitly Bolshevik, they seem to have been interested in psychoanalysis because it could potentially alleviate the "war neuroses." Freud's, Ferenczi's, and Simmel's recent work on the war neuroses suggested that soldiers suffering from the effects of war could, with the help of psychoanalysis, recover and return to the front. See Jones, *The Life and Work of Sigmund Freud*, II: 197–98.

69. Freud, "Lines of Advance in Psycho-Analytic Therapy," 158, editor's note.

70. Ibid., 167.

71. Aug. 3, 1919, Freud and Abraham, *A Psychoanalytic Dialogue*, 402. The private charity was never established, partly because of the war and the difficulties in transferring money, but also because von Freund died the following year before he could arrange all the specifics.

72. On the subject of Freud's and other psychoanalysts' social activism and support of clinics for the poor, see Elizabeth Ann Danto, *Freud's Free Clinics: Psychoanalysis and Social Justice, 1918–1938* (New York: Columbia University Press, 2005).

73. Nov. 7, 1918, Freud and Ferenczi, *The Correspondence of Sigmund Freud and Sandor Ferenczi*, II: 308.

74. Michelle Moreau-Ricaud, "The Founding of the Budapest School," *Ferenczi's Turn in Psychoanalysis*, eds. Peter L. Rudnytsky, Antal Bókay, and Patrizia Giampieri-Deutsch (New York: New York University Press, 1996), 53–54. See also André Haynal, "Introduction," *The Correspondence of Sigmund Freud and Sandor Ferenczi*, II: xxix–xxx.

75. June 21, 1920, Freud and Abraham, *A Psychoanalytic Dialogue*, 313.

76. Feb. 25, 1926, Freud and Jones, *The Complete Correspondence of Sigmund Freud and Ernest Jones*, 592–93.

77. Mar. 7, 1926, ibid., 596–97. Peter Gay emphasizes that Freud's use of the word *"wesenfremd"* is proof that "Judaism was *inessential*, not to Freud, but to his creation, psychoanalysis." In focusing on only the religious, faith-based aspects of Judaism (rather than the broader condition of *being* Jewish), Gay overlooks the inescapable conditions that Freud had to confront in creating psychoanalysis—he had no choice but to be a Jewish scientist. Gay's statement that Freud "was a Jew but not a Jewish scientist" is both historically impossible during Freud's lifetime and retrospectively false. Peter Gay, *A Godless Jew: Freud, Atheism, and the Making of Psychoanalysis* (New Haven: Yale University Press, 1987), 148. On the question of whether psychoanalysis is a "Jewish science," see Yerushalmi, *Freud's Moses*, 98.

78. Or more to the point, if telepathy were a real phenomenon, it would not be possible to stop the flow of telepathic transmissions by refusing to believe in it.

79. In Chapter 4 I discuss the intimate connections between Freud's interest in telepathic transmission, his ideas about intergenerational transmission, and his theorization of transference.

80. Freud was well aware of the dangers that both smoking and Jewishness posed to his life: Three years earlier (in 1923) he had been diagnosed with jaw cancer, most probably caused (at least in part) by his cigar-smoking habit. During World War I, as he was contemplating the "Lamarck-work," he bitterly complained in letters to Ferenczi both of the difficulty of living without a constant cigar supply and of coping with the rise of anti-semitic violence. See Haynal's introduction to *The Correspondence of Sigmund Freud and Sandor Ferenczi*, II: xxxiii–xxxiv.

81. Freud, *Moses and Monotheism*, 100, 57–58.

82. Sept. 9, 1934, Freud and Zweig, *The Letters of Sigmund Freud and Arnold Zweig*, 92. See also Freud, *Moses and Monotheism*, 55, 57.

83. My biographical information on Schmidt is drawn from the following sources: Thomas Hauschild, "Christians, Jews, and the Other in Germany Anthropology," *American Anthropologist* 99.4 (1997); Joseph Henninger, *P. Wilhelm Schmidt S. V. D., 1868–1954: Eine biographische Skizze* (Freiburg: Paulusdruckerei, 1956); Wilhelm Koppers, "Obituary of Pater Wilhelm Schmidt," *Mitteilungen der Anthropologischen Gesellschaft in Wien* 83 (1954); Schmidt, "Blut-Rasse-Volk," *Kirche im Kampf*, ed. Clemens Holzmeister (Vienna: Seelsorger Verlag, 1936).

84. See Etienne Lepicard, "Eugenics and Roman Catholicism, An Encyclical Letter in Context: *Casti connubii*, December 31, 1930," *Science in Context* 11.3–4 (1998).

85. Ritchie Robertson, "'My True Enemy': Freud and the Catholic Church, 1927–39," *Austria in the Thirties: Culture and History*, eds. Kenneth Segar and John Warren (Riverside: Ariadne Press, 1990), 334.

86. Both Boas and Kroeber were Jewish, and they both signed on to the list of seventy-six anthropologists honoring Schmidt on his sixtieth birthday in Wilhelm Koppers, ed., *Festschrift P. W. Schmidt: 76 sprachwissenschaftliche, ethnologische, religionswissenschaftliche, prähistorische und andere Studien* (Vienna: Mechitharisten-Congregations-Buchdruckerei, 1928).

87. Wilhelm Schmidt, "Das Rassenprinzip des Nationalsozialismus," *Schönere Zukunft* 7 (1931–32), 999. All translations of Schmidt's work are my own.

88. In fact, if Schmidt had not been so negatively predisposed toward Freud, he might have seen a certain resonance between his own perspective and that of Freud's, since ultimately Freud insisted that the Jews' racial distinction is spiritual [*geistig*]. I discuss Freud's emphasis on Jewish spirituality [*Geistigkeit*] in more detail in Chapter 5.

89. Wilhelm Schmidt, *Rasse und Volk: eine Untersuchung zur Bestimmung ihrer Grenzen und zur Erfassung ihrer Beziehungen* (Munich: J. Kösel & F. Pustet, 1927); and Schmidt, "Eine wissenschaftliche Abrechnung mit der Psychoanalyse." *Das Neue Reich* 11 (1928–29).

90. See, for example, Wilhelm Schmidt, *The Origin and Growth of Religion: Facts and Theories*, trans. H. J. Rose (London: Methnon, 1935); Schmidt, "Blut-Rasse-Volk"; and Schmidt, *The Culture Historical Method of Ethnology: The Scientific Approach to the Racial Question*, trans. S. A. Sieber (New York: Fortuny's, 1939).

91. Wilhelm Schmidt, "Der Ödipus-Komplex der Freudschen Psychoanalyse und die Ehegestaltung des Bolshewismus," *Nationalwirtschaft* 2 (1928), 401–36.

92. Schmidt, "Befreiung Wiens vom jüdischen Bolshewismus! Eine Katholikentagsrede von Professor Dr Wilhelm Schmidt S.V.D.," *Das Neue Reich* 3 (1920). Though Schmidt published regularly in this explicitly Catholic-interest journal (later continued under the name *Schönere Zukunft* [*Better Future*])— including essays titled "The Jewish Question" (1933–34) and "The Racial Principle of National Socialism" (1931–32)—he published the lecture on "The Oedipus Complex of Freudian Psychoanalysis and the Marriage" in a less specifically Catholic journal, *Nationalwirtschaft*.

93. Freud, *Moses and Monotheism*, 57.

94. Jones, *The Life and Work of Sigmund Freud*, III: 344.

95. Ibid., III: 344, 518n341.

96. Neither of the two classic works on Freud's use of biological theory mentions any of the general associations between Lamarckism, Bolshevism, and Jews. See Ritvo, *Darwin's Influence on Freud*; and Sulloway, *Freud, Biologist of the Mind*. Grubrich-Simitis alludes to the facts that neo-Lamarckism was used as the scientific basis for T. D. Lysenko's Soviet Marxist agriculture program and

that Freud would have been peripherally aware of the debates about Kammer-er's work. But she does not develop these connections any further. See "Meta-psychology and Metabiology," 98–99n36, 99n38.

97. Jones, *The Life and Work of Sigmund Freud*, III: 311.

98. Ibid., 309–10. Jones also notes that Freud had certainly "read the neo-Darwinian books by Weismann, Haeckel and others," as if Freud's *reading* of either of these scientists would automatically result in his embracing their positions.

99. The *Concordance* lists thirty-four mentions of Darwin in the *Standard Edition* alone. See Guttman, et al., *The Concordance to the Standard Edition of the Complete Psychological Works of Sigmund Freud*, 2nd ed. (New York: International Universities Press, 1984).

100. Ritvo, *Darwin's Influence on Freud*.

101. Jones, *The Life and Work of Sigmund Freud*, 310.

102. Ibid., 310–11.

103. Hermann Siemens, quoted in Proctor, *Racial Hygiene*, 34.

104. As far as I can tell, there has been no mention in the scholarly literature that Jones' worries about Freud's Lamarckism were intensified by the political and social connotations of this idea—whether in the 1930s or in the 1950s.

105. Jones, *The Life and Work of Sigmund Freud*, III: 313, my emphasis.

106. Freud, *Moses and Monotheism*, trans. Katherine Jones, 127–28. I have not found any explanations or discussions as to why Jones selectively quoted from Katherine Jones' translation rather than the cited *Standard Edition*.

107. Freud, *Moses and Monotheism*, 100.

108. Graham, "Science and Values." See also Joravsky, "Soviet Marxism and Biology before Lysenko," *Journal of the History of Ideas* 20.1 (1959).

109. Lewontin and Levins, "The Problem of Lysenkoism."

110. Jones, *The Life and Work of Sigmund Freud*, III: 313.

111. Ibid.

112. Freud, *Moses and Monotheism*, 123.

113. Yerushalmi, *Freud's Moses*, 31, my emphasis.

114. Ibid., 31.

115. Ibid.

116. Ibid.

117. Ibid., 32.

118. On the ways in which philo-semitism and anti-semitism seem to "sup-ply and comply with each other in strange and disconcerting ways," see Steven Connor, "Some of My Best Friends Are Philosemites," Paper presented at a panel marking the publication of *The Jew in the Text: Modernity and the Construc-tion of Identity*, ed. Tamar Garb and Linda Nochlin, Institute of Contemporary Arts, London, UK, 1995.

119. Yerushalmi amply demonstrates that Freud's knowledge of Judaism was much broader than Freud liked to publicly proclaim. See Yerushalmi, *Freud's Moses*.

120. Bernstein, *Freud and the Legacy of Moses*, 112–13.

121. Whether the definition of "who's a Jew" is racist depends on how and why the definitions are being used. While it is obvious that Nazi definitions of Jewishness were racist, it is less clear whether Jewish definitions of Jewishness should also be considered racist. On the one hand, late-twentieth-century Jewish organizations have retrospectively made numerous individuals into Jews based on their genealogical Jewishness and on the fact that they were regarded as Jewish by the Nazis. However, if Jewish definitions are coupled with political and economic power, the resulting policies of exclusive race-based citizenship or benefits would certainly seem to qualify as racist.

122. This is not to suggest that these categories are completely distinct. The problems of (physical and anthropological definitions of) race and (economic, educational) class in America are, for example, difficult to separate.

123. May 3, 1908, Freud and Abraham, *A Psychoanalytic Dialogue*, 34.

124. June 8, 1913, Freud and Ferenczi, *The Correspondence of Sigmund Freud and Sandor Ferenczi*, I: 491.

125. Grubrich-Simitis, "Metapsychology and Metabiology," 99.

126. These were the terms used by Gerhard Wagner, head of the Nazi Physicians' League, in a 1934 speech to the Gesellschaft Deutscher Naturforscher [Society of German Scientists]. Quoted in Robert Proctor, *Value-Free Science? Purity and Power in Modern Knowledge* (Cambridge: Harvard University Press, 1991), 171.

127. Proctor, "Nazi Medicine and the Politics of Knowledge," 350.

128. Proctor, *Racial Hygiene*, 294.

129. Ibid.

130. Proctor, *Value-Free Science?*, 171.

131. Quoted in ibid.

132. Ibid., 175, my emphasis.

133. Nonetheless, Lamarckian notions of inheritance continue to rear their heads in the field of epigenetics, for example. See note 5 in this chapter.

134. Yerushalmi, *Freud's Moses*, 98.

135. Proctor, *Value-Free Science?*, x–xi.

136. Gay, *A Godless Jew*, 149.

137. Freud, *Moses and Monotheism*, 7.

138. See Assmann, *Moses the Egyptian*; and Said, *Freud and the Non-European*.

139. Freud, *Moses and Monotheism*, 99.

140. See Michael P. Kramer, "Race, Literary History, and the 'Jewish Question,'" *Prooftexts* 21.3 (2001). Kramer argues that the matter of a writer's "extraction" (290) is the solid ground, the "facticity" (291) and "fundamentum" (302) that quietly props up all discussions of Jewish literature. When I began writing this book, I was entirely sympathetic to Kramer's argument. After eight years of thinking about *racial fever*, however, I have realized that matters of "extraction" are anything *but* solid.

141. Walter Benn Michaels, "Race into Culture: A Critical Geneaology of Identity," *Critical Inquiry* 18 (1992), 682.

142. See, for example, the recent *New York Times* article discussing various individuals' search for ethnicities that would give them not only a sense of their heritage but also access to benefits for particular minorities, including affirmative action and Israeli citizenship. Amy Harmon, "Seeking Ancestry in DNA Ties Uncovered by Tests," *New York Times* (April 12, 2006).

143. Michaels, "Race into Culture," 682.

144. Freud, *Moses and Monotheism*, 123. I discuss the phrase "mixtures of blood" more extensively in Chapter 5.

145. Indeed, there are a number of stories of (Jewish) Holocaust survivors who (even after the Holocaust) continued to believe that they were arrested because of their Communist associations rather than their Jewishness. Thus, even if their children or grandchildren identify as Jewish (having inherited the burden of memory from the survivor), the survivors may continue to consider themselves as something other than Jewish. I explore this conundrum in more detail in Chapter 4.

146. Marc Shell, *Children of the Earth: Literature, Politics and Nationhood* (New York: Oxford University Press, 1993), 4.

147. "What is certainly of decisive importance, however, is the *awakenening* of the forgotten memory-trace by a recent real repetition of the event." Freud, *Moses and Monotheism*, 101, my emphasis.

148. Erin Aubry Kaplan suggests that while the one-drop rule of racial identification in America was developed because of racism, its effects have allowed African Americans to consolidate a sense of identity and community: "By forcing blacks of all complexions and blood percentages into the same boat, the law ironically laid a foundation of black unity that remains in place today." Kaplan, "Black Like I Thought I Was," *L.A. Weekly* (Oct. 7, 2003).

149. See Emma Klein, *Lost Jews: The Struggle for Identity Today* (New York: St. Martin's Press, 1995). Many individuals in Africa have reclaimed their Jewishness in the past hundred years; see Edith Bruder, *Black Jews of Africa: History, Religion, Identity* (New York: Oxford University Press, 2008). See also the increasing body of work on "crypto-Jews" occasioned in part by the media coverage around the five hundredth anniversary of the Spanish Inquisition in 1992, for example Janet Liebman Jacobs, *Hidden Heritage: The Legacy of the Crypto-Jews* (Berkeley: University of California Press, 2002).

150. Along these lines, a recent article describes a large number of people (at least three hundred) who were children of Nazis (with no known Jews in their genealogical pasts) and who as adults have converted to Judaism and moved to Israel. Apparently, a sizable number of these individuals have prominent positions as academics in Jewish Studies. Most spectacularly, there are reports that this group includes descendants of Hitler, Himmler, and Göring. See Yitta Halberstam, "Choosing Judaism: Light in All the Dark Places," *Jewish Action* 5766 (2006).

151. Bernard Wasserstein, *Vanishing Diaspora: The Jews in Europe Since 1945* (Cambridge: Harvard University Press, 1996).

152. There is an emerging body of scholarship on new Jewish identities in Europe and elsewhere. See, for example, Zvi Gitelman, Barry Kosmin, and András Kovács, eds., *New Jewish Identities: Contemporary Europe and Beyond* (New York: Central European University Press, 2003); and Jonathan Webber, *Jewish Identities in the New Europe* (London: Littman Library of Jewish Civilization, 1994).

153. While Rabbinic Judaism uses only matrilineage to determine a person's Jewishness, in both pre-Rabbinic Judaism and some forms of contemporary Reform Judaism a person is defined as Jewish if either the father or mother is Jewish. On the historical derivation of matrilineal and patrilineal definitions of Jewishness, see Cohen, *The Beginnings of Jewishness*. On conversion and its relationship to Jewish genealogy, see Boyarin, *A Radical Jew: Paul and the Politics of Identity* (Berkeley: University of California Press, 1994), 240–41.

154. See Yuri Slezkine, *The Jewish Century* (Princeton: Princeton University Press, 2004).

3. CIRCUMCISION: THE UNCONSCIOUS ROOT OF THE PROBLEM

1. Circumcision was also central to debates about the political and ritual authority of Jewish communities in Germany and Austria during the late nineteenth and early twentieth centuries. See Robin Judd, *Contested Rituals: Circumcision, Kosher Butchering, and Jewish Political Life in Germany, 1843–1933* (Ithaca: Cornell University Press, 2007).

2. See, for example, Marcia Ian, "'Invisible Religion': The Extimate Secular in American Society," *Jouvert: A Journal of Postcolonial Studies* 3.1–2 (1999); and Lisa Lampert-Weissig, "Race Periodicity, and the (Neo-)Middle Ages," *MLQ: Modern Language Quarterly* 65.3 (2004).

3. Circumcision is central to debates not only about Jewish difference, but also to debates about Muslim-Hindu co-existence and to debates about health reforms involving various communities in Africa (some of which already practice male and/or female cutting for ritual purposes, others of which are being encouraged to begin practicing male circumcision for health reasons). See Dibyesh Anand, "Anxious Sexualities: Masculinity, Nationalism and Violence," *British Journal of Politics and International Relations* 9.2 (2007).

4. In *The Variation of Animals and Plants under Domestication* (1868)—a book that Freud had in his library—Darwin notes that "With respect to Jews, I have been assured by three medical men of the Jewish faith that circumcision, which has been practised for so many ages, has produced no inherited effect." Yet he also notes that "In some cases the effects of injuries or mutilations apparently are inherited," and that "in Germany Jews are often born in a condition rendering circumcision difficult, so that a name is there applied to them signifying

'born circumcised.'" Charles Darwin, *The Variation of Animals and Plants under Domestication* (London: Murray, 1868), 23, 27. Indeed, long traditions in both Judaism and Islam hold that certain patriarchs—including Adam, Abraham, Moses, and Mohammed—were born circumcised. See Shaye J. D. Cohen, *Why Aren't Jewish Women Circumcised?: Gender and Covenant in Judaism* (Berkeley: University of California Press, 2005), 23–24; and Isaac Kalimi, "'He Was Born Circumcised': Some Midrashic Sources, Their Concept, Roots and Presumably Historical Context," *Zeitschrift für die Neutestamentliche Wissenschaft und Kunde der Alteren Kirche* 93.1–2 (2002).

5. To set up his argument Weismann presents a number of anecdotes supposedly demonstrating Lamarckian inheritance of acquired characters; many of these anecdotes involve animals that had lost their tails and subsequently produced tailless babies. Along these lines, Jay Geller (knowingly?) writes, "The identity of Jewish males was composed of, if not puppy dog tails, then circumcised penises." See "Identifying 'Someone Who Is Himself One of Them,'" 327.

6. August Weismann, *Essays upon Heredity and Kindred Biological Problems* (Oxford: Clarendon, 1889), 432ff. Though Weismann's experiments with mice may sound ridiculous, they are often credited as having initially demonstrated the untenability of the Lamarckian idea of the inheritance of acquired characters. See, for example, Bowler, *The Non-Darwinian Revolution*, 117.

7. Weismann, *Essays upon Heredity*, 447n441.

8. See Daniel Boyarin, "What Does a Jew Want? or, The Political Meaning of the Phallus," *The Psychoanalysis of Race*, ed. Christopher Lane (New York: Columbia University Press, 1998); Geller, *On Freud's Jewish Body*; and Gilman, *Freud, Race, and Gender*.

9. Freud, "Analysis of a Phobia in a Five-Year-Old Boy ('Little Hans')," 36n.

10. Freud, "Instincts and their Vicissitudes," 121. I would not go quite as far as Franz Maciejewski, who argues that Freud's own circumcision may have been the original trauma of psychoanalysis. See Maciejewski, *Psychoanalytisches Archiv*. I discuss this work in more detail later in this chapter.

11. Sept. 30, 1934, Freud and Zweig, *The Letters of Sigmund Freud and Arnold Zweig*, 91.

12. Freud, "Sexuality in the Aetiology of the Neuroses," 280.

13. August Weismann, *The Germ-Plasm: A Theory of Heredity*, trans. W. N. Parker and Harriet Rönnfeldt (London: W. Scott, 1893). By the early twentieth century Weismann's germ-plasm theory was often cited by scientists and politicians who asserted that Jews could never become fully German, since the properties of the "immortal" (Jewish) germ-plasm were permanent even if the bodily material (such as the individual's penis) could be altered. See Fritz Brenneck, *The Nazi Primer: Official Handbook for Schooling the Hitler Youth*, ed. William E. Dodd, trans. Harwood L. Childs (New York: Harper & Brothers, 1938); and Proctor, *Racial Hygiene*, 54ff.

14. Freud's later diagrams of the psyche, particularly in *The Ego and the Id* (1923), reflect the language and imagery of Weismann's germ-plasm theory and cellular biology: Perceptions must "penetrate" a membrane before reaching the permanent "nucleus" of the psychical system. Mark Solms suggests that Freud's later diagrams of the psyche are derived from his early neurological drawings. However, Freud's drawing in *The Ego and the Id* is markedly different from his earlier diagrams and seems to mirror cellular imagery more than the diagrams, for example, in his letters to Fliess or in *Interpretation of Dreams*. See Freud, *The Ego and the Id*, 24; Freud, *Interpretation of Dreams*, 537; and Lynn Gamwell and Mark Solms, eds., *From Neurology to Psychoanalysis: Sigmund Freud's Neurological Drawings and Diagrams of the Mind* (Binghamton: Binghamton University Art Museum, State University of New York at Binghamton, 2006).

15. While today the term *eugenics* is often "erroneously equated with National Socialist doctrines, . . . in Weimar Germany 'eugenics' was thought of by proto-National Socialist publications and organizations as a kind of leftist deviation. . . . Whether one used the term '*Rassenhygiene*' or '*Eugenik*' became in the late 1920s a kind of political flag, often with the more right-wing members of the movement favoring the first term, the more left-wing members the latter." See Graham, "Science and Values," 1139.

16. Nunberg and Federn, *Minutes of the Vienna Psycho-Analytical Society*, II: 95, 100. While Ehrenfels' emphasis was on the male's sexual needs, Freud evinces some concern for the sexual needs of both males and females. See Freud, "'Civilized' Sexual Morality and Modern Nervous Illness." Ehrenfels published widely on eugenics in the *Archiv für Rassen und Gesellschaftsbiologie* and generally advocated polygamy as a panacea for the degeneration caused by modern industrial society. See Geoffrey G. Field, "Nordic Racism," *Journal of the History of Ideas* 38.3 (1977), 527; and Sander L. Gilman, "Freud and the Sexologists: A Second Reading," *Reading Freud's Reading*, ed. Jay Geller, Sander L. Gilman, and Jutta Birmele (New York: New York University Press, 1994).

17. Nunberg and Federn, *Minutes of the Vienna Psycho-Analytical Society*, II: 93, my emphasis.

18. Of course, what was defined as "unfit" was up for debate. For example, Ehrenfels seems to have lumped Jews and Germans into one "Caucasian race" that was threatened by "Yellow Peril" (the "hordes of Mongols"). As such, he saw the rise of anti-semitism as an anathema: "Among 100 whites there stand two Jews. The German peasant has been awakened and armed with the holy weapons of his ancestors—not to struggle against 80 million Mongols but to confront two Jews! Is this not the height of folly!" Quoted in Gilman, "Freud and the Sexologists," 64.

19. *Sexual Problems* was a continuation of *Mother Protection*, a journal that explicitly focused on questions of eugenics and breeding.

20. Christian Freiherr von Ehrenfels, *Sexualethik (Grenzfragen des Nerven- und Seelenlebens, Heft 56)*, ed. Leopold Löwenfeld (Wiesbaden: J. F. Bergmann,

1907). See also Gilman, "Freud and the Sexologists," 60–65; and Wilhelm Hemcker, "'Ihr Brief war mir so wertvoll' Christian von Ehrenfels und Sigmund Freud—eine verschollene Korrespondenz," *Wunderblock—eine Geschichte der modernen Seele*, ed. Jean Clair, Cathrin Pichler, and Wolfgang Pircher (Vienna: Löcker, 1989).

21. Freud, "'Civilized' Sexual Morality and Modern Nervous Illness," 181.

22. Ibid.

23. Ibid., 202.

24. Ibid., 196.

25. Ibid., 181.

26. G. Stanley Hall, quoted in Stocking, *Race, Culture, and Evolution*, 254–55. Even as the years went on, Hall maintained that while Weismann's theories might apply to bodily structure, they did not detract from the idea that "ancestral experience" could be indefinitely stored in the individual's central nervous system which he saw as the organ of "physiological memory."

27. Hall had invited Weismann to the 1909 events at Clark, but he declined because of old age and bad health. See Rosenzweig, *Freud, Jung, and Hall the King-maker: The Historic Expedition to America (1909), with G. Stanley Hall as Host and William James as Guest* (Seattle: Hogreffe & Huber, 1992), 46.

28. Franz Boas, "Psychological Problems in Anthropology (Lecture delivered at the celebration of the twentieth anniversary of the opening of Clark University, September, 1909)," *American Journal of Psychology* 21 (1910), 371.

29. Boas, "Psychological Problems in Anthropology," 371.

30. Boas and Freud had some interesting similarities that most probably shaped their approaches to the definitions of peoples: Boas was a German-born immigrant to the United States, the grandson of observant Jews, and decidedly private about his Jewish background. As Leonard Glick notes, like many people of his German-Jewish generation, Boas did not convert to Christianity; "he turned instead to a personal philosophy compounded of rationalism, cultural relativism, and ethical humanism, and identified himself as an enlightened universalist who had transcended both ethnic provincialism and supernatural religion." Leonard B. Glick, "Types Distinct from Our Own: Franz Boas on Jewish Identity and Assimilation," *American Anthropologist* 84 (1982), 546. See also Mitchell Bryan Hart, "Franz Boas as German, American Jew," *German-Jewish Identities in America*, eds. Christof Mauch and Joe Salomon (Madison: University of Wisconsin Press, 2003). While a comparison of Boas's and Freud's theorizations of "races" and "types" could be productive, it would need to take into account the very different meanings of "race" in America and in Europe, even as they influenced one another. Boas could become the *white* American "type" whereas darker-skinned Americans continued to struggle for the right to join in the American polis. See Goldstein, *The Price of Whiteness*.

31. On the details of Boas' study, see Stocking's accounts in Franz Boas, *A Franz Boas Reader: The Shaping of American Anthropology, 1883–1911*, ed. George

Stocking (Chicago: University of Chicago Press, 1982), 190; and Stocking, *Race, Culture, and Evolution*.

32. Franz Boas, *The Mind of Primitive Man* (New York: Macmillan, 1911), 196.

33. Boas was famous for proclaiming that while there may be racial differences, there was not necessarily a fixed hierarchy of racial types. In other words, Jews and dark-skinned peoples might be permanently Jewish and dark-skinned, but this did not mean that the Jewishness or dark skin of any individual person permanently doomed him to a particular place in the hierarchy of talents, abilities, and possibilities. However, the reality is that Jewishness or dark skin *could* doom a person to a particular place in the social spectrum—not because these characteristics imply particular abilities or talents (or the lack thereof), but because Jewishness and darker skin can *structurally* limit a person' opportunities in particular historical and social contexts.

34. Freud is reported to have skipped many of the lectures because he found them boring; instead, he went on long walks in the woods with Jung and Ferenczi. See Rosenzweig, *Freud, Jung, and Hall the King-maker*.

35. It is impossible to know how carefully Freud read this book. Aside from Zollschan's hand-written dedication of the book to Freud, there is no evidence of marginalia in his own copy (presently stored at the Freud Museum in London, UK). Nonetheless, aside from a few pages in the index, all the pages have been cut in the style that Freud usually cut his books. Whether Freud read the volume carefully or not, Zollschan's book demonstrates the ubiquity of both Lamarckian racial theories of the Jewish people and a general consciousness of the fact that circumcision would seem to disprove the inheritance of acquired characteristics. I thank Michael Molnar and Keith Davies for assistance with the question of whether Freud actually read this volume.

36. Ignaz Zollschan, *Das Rassenproblem unter besonderer Berücksichtigung der theoretischen Grundlagen der jüdischen Rassenfrage* (Vienna: Braumüller, 1911), 1. All translations of Zollschan are my own.

37. The chapter is entitled *"Die für das Rassenproblem wichtigen Gebiete der Vererbungslehre."* Zollschan, *Das Rassenproblem*, 222.

38. Eduard von Hartmann, approvingly quoted by Zollschan, ibid., 238. Von Hartmann was famous for his work *Philosophy of the Unconscious* (1868), which is sometimes seen as a forerunner of Freud's work on the unconscious.

39. Ibid., 252–53. Interestingly, Zollschan befriended Boas, and together they attempted to organize various international coalitions, including a petition—signed by Freud, among other intellectuals—to oppose Nazi racial science. While I have not yet been able to view this petition, Freud's signature seems to demonstrate that he was well aware of the politics of scientific theories of race in the 1920s and '30s. The 1936 petition, entitled "Initiativcomité zur Veranstaltung einer Welt-Enquete über die Rasssenfrage, An die Vertreter der Wissenschaft!," has never been published. It is mentioned in Paul Weindling,

"Central Europe Confronts German Racial Hygiene: Friedrich Hertz, Hugo Iltis, and Ignaz Zollschan as Critics of German Racial Hygiene," *Blood and Homeland: Eugenics in Central Europe, 1900–1940*, eds. Marius Turda and Paul Weindling (Budapest: Central University Press, 2006); and Paul Weindling, "The Evolution of Jewish Identity: Ignaz Zollschan between Jewish and Aryan Race Theories, 1910–1945," *Jewish Tradition and the Challenge of Darwinism*, eds. Geoffrey Cantor and Marc Swetlitz (Chicago: University of Chicago Press, 2006).

40. As I discuss in Chapter 2, when Freud sent a description of the fourth essay of *Totem* to Ernest Jones in 1912, Jones noticed that there was something new in the "important and far-reaching idea" that repression [*Verdrängung*] was an inheritance, a "result of earlier racial experiences." Jones hoped that this new idea could "stand in harmony" with "the Weismann principle of the non-transmissibility of acquired characters." Though Freud had not referred to either Weismann or Lamarck or used the phrase "racial experiences," Jones' comment may have led him farther down the path of exploring the relationships between "acquired characters" and "racial experiences." Aug. 7, 1912, Freud and Jones, *The Complete Correspondence*, 150.

41. Freud, "The Dynamics of Transference," 99.

42. Ibid., 99n92, my emphasis.

43. Written simultaneously with his essay "On the History of the Psychoanalytic Movement" and his case history of the "Wolf-Man," Freud's essay "On Narcissism" was an explicit defense of the libido theory from the criticisms of Jung. Not insignificantly, Freud wrote these essays immediately after completing his essay on "The Moses of Michelangelo," which has been interpreted as a veiled self-portrait and as a direct anticipation of *Moses and Monotheism*. On the circumstances leading to the composition of this essay and its surprising effects, see Jones, *The Life and Work of Sigmund Freud*, II: 302–6. See also Ilse Grubrich-Simitis, *Michelangelos Moses und Freuds Wagstück: Eine Collage* (Frankfurt am Main: S. Fischer Verlag, 2004).

44. Freud, "On Narcissism," 78, my emphasis. Between writing *Totem* and "On Narcissism," Freud also discussed Weismann's germ-plasm theory in "The Claims of Psycho-Analysis for Scientific Interest," 182.

45. These are the opening lines of the Mishnaic tractate *Avot* as quoted in Yerushalmi, *Freud's Moses*, 29. Yerushalmi explains that the Chain of Tradition is the name that was used to describe a body of literature of the Middle Ages that "surveyed chronologically the transmission of rabbinic law and doctrine by recording the sequence of luminaries who were its bearers through the ages. The purpose was to establish and demonstrate an unbroken succession of teaching and authority from the Bible, through the Talmud, and often up to the time of the author himself." Yerushalmi, *Zakhor*, 33.

46. Freud, "On Narcissism," 78.

47. There is very little commentary on Freud's references to Weismann. One exception is that of Marcia Ian, who compares Freud's and Lacan's uses of

Weismann's germ-plasm theory and argues that "where Freud sees the species [or race] as parasitic upon the individual, Lacan sees the individual as dead vermin hiding in the entrails of species, the undead." Ian, "Freud, Lacan, and Imaginary Secularity," *American Imago* 54.2 (1997), 136. Ian argues that Freud's use of Weismann's germ-plasm theory is particularly (non-)Jewish while Lacan's references to Weismann are particularly (non-)Catholic. While her analysis is provocative, she employs Jewishness and Catholicness as *a priori* explanatory structures, as if they did not have their own complications and contradictions, and as if they do not change over time. We may *begin* with the assumption that our analyses are always shaped by our engagement with (or rejection of) our various religious, ethnic, and racial traditions, but we must also recognize that we change these traditions the moment that we engage with them. Thus, as Freud and Lacan each creatively re-read the Jewish and Catholic traditions, they also contributed to the very definitions of these entities.

48. Freud, "From a History of and Infantile Neurosis (Wolf-Man)," 86. Though this case was not published until 1918, it was written in 1914–15. "At that time," writes Freud, "I was still freshly under the impression of the twisted re-interpretations which C. G. Jung and Alfred Adler were endeavouring to give to the findings of psychoanalysis" (7n1).

49. Ibid., 86. Diane Jonte-Pace suggests that the association of immortality with the figure of the uncanny mother is a counter-thesis running throughout Freud's oeuvre. See Jonte-Pace, *Speaking the Unspeakable: Religion, Misogyny, and the Uncanny Mother in Freud's Cultural Texts* (University of California Press, 2001), 45ff.

50. Eric Kline Silverman, "The Cut of Wholeness: Psychoanalytic Interpretations of Biblical Circumcision," *The Covenant of Circumcision: New Perspectives on an Ancient Jewish Rite*, ed. Elizabeth Wyner Mark (Hanover: Brandeis University Press, University Press of New England, 2003), 53–54.

51. Freud, "On Narcissism," 78.

52. Freud, "Overview of the Transference Neuroses," 19.

53. July 24, 1915, Freud and Ferenczi, *The Correspondence of Sigmund Freud and Sandor Ferenczi*, II: 70.

54. Freud, "Overview of the Transference Neuroses," 20.

55. Ibid., 19.

56. Ibid., 20. This raises the question as to whether the father is propagating only the castration anxiety or also the drive to perpetrate such traumas and anxieties.

57. Ibid. Freud's conundrum is related to the questions that often emerge when circumcision is made the quintessential marker of Jewishness. That is, if circumcision marks a boy as a Jew, is there anything that marks the girl as a Jew?

58. Ibid.

59. See, for example, Brickman, *Aboriginal Populations in the Mind*, 77; and Yerushalmi, *Freud's Moses*, 30.

60. Freud, "Overview of the Transference Neuroses," 20.

61. Jan. 6, 1916, Freud and Ferenczi, *The Correspondence of Sigmund Freud and Sandor Ferenczi*, II: 101.

62. Yosef Hayim Yerushalmi, "Series Z: An Archival Fantasy," *Journal of European Psychoanalysis*. No. 3–4 (1996–1997).

63. Grubrich-Simitis, "Metapsychology and Metabiology," 93ff.

64. Jan. 1, 1917, Freud and Ferenczi, *The Correspondence of Sigmund Freud and Sandor Ferenczi*, II: 169.

65. Nov. 11, 1917, Freud and Abraham, *A Psychoanalytic Dialogue*, 261–62, my emphasis.

66. Freud, *Beyond the Pleasure Principle*, 36.

67. Thomas Laqueur, *Making Sex: Body and Gender from the Greeks to Freud* (Cambridge: Harvard University Press, 1990), 241.

68. Ibid.

69. Freud, *Beyond the Pleasure Principle*, 37.

70. Ibid., 38.

71. Ibid., 24. Whereas most evolutionary theorists assumed that the instincts pushed "forward towards progress and the production of new forms," Freud insisted that the instincts are essentially "conservative" (37).

72. Ibid., 37.

73. Ibid., 37, 38.

74. Ibid., 45–46.

75. If we read psychoanalysis as a sort of continuation or completion of (Freud's version of) Mosaic monotheism, immortality and other such magic would need to be rejected. In *Moses* Freud repeatedly notes that Moses "rejected the illusion, so dear to Egyptians in particular, of a life after death" (20). Indeed, he presents the rejection of immortality as evidence of the Egyptian origins of Mosaic monotheism. See *Moses and Monotheism*, 26, 59. On the idea that psychoanalysis was a sort of godless Judaism, see Yerushalmi, *Freud's Moses*, 99–100. On the comparison between Egyptian and Mosaic monotheism, see Assmann, *Moses the Egyptian*, 153.

76. Freud's dematerialization (or abstraction) of Weismann's materialistic germ-plasm theory is of a piece with his dematerialization of Jewish genealogy, which I discuss in more detail in Chapter 5. It also resonates with the emphasis on Kantian abstraction in the works of modern Jewish intellectuals such as Hermann Cohen, Franz Rosenzweig, and Arnold Schoenberg. See Leora Batnitsky, "The Image of Judaism: German-Jewish Intellectuals and the Ban on Images," in "Icon, Image, and Text in Modern Jewish Culture," Special Issue, *Jewish Studies Quarterly*, 11.3 (2004). Yet simply to interpret Freud's use of Weismann's theory as particularly Jewish (or non-Jewish) is to reduce Jewishness and Judaism to abstraction. While numerous German-Jewish philosophers of the late nineteenth and early twentieth centuries emphasized the supreme abstraction

of Jewish monotheism, there is clearly much in Jewish tradition that resists abstraction: not only circumcision, but also countless proscriptions and prescriptions about Jewish bodies. Moreover, in various canonical Jewish texts not even God is described as entirely abstract or bodiless: In the Bible and Talmud, the Jewish god is described as having a body, a face, and even a phallus. See Daniel Boyarin, "The Eye in the Torah: Ocular Desire in Midrashic Hermeneutic," *Critical Inquiry* 16.3 (1990); Daniel Boyarin, *Carnal Israel*; Eilberg-Schwartz, *God's Phallus and Other Problems for Moses, Masculinity and Monotheism* (Boston: Beacon Press, 1994).

77. Freud developed his theory of the instincts around 1915—that is, in the same time period as his composition of the essay "On Narcissism," "A Phylogenetic Fantasy," and his case of the "Wolf-Man." See Freud, "Instincts and their Vicissitudes," 121.

78. Freud, *Beyond the Pleasure Principle*, 46, my emphasis.

79. Susan Shapiro explores the image of the "Uncanny Jew" (related and sometimes equivalent to the Eternal or Wandering Jew) and its illumination of the deep relationship between the longevity of anti-semitism and of the Jewish people. See Shapiro, "The Uncanny Jew: A Brief History of an Image," *Judaism* 46.1 (1997).

80. Freud, *Moses and Monotheism*, 101.

81. Ibid.

82. The notion that one's own circumcision is not fully remembered (as a narrative of events) is not contradicted by the idea that neonatal traumas—or even the trauma of birth—can have lasting effects on the adult. Even as anti-circumcision activists make this argument, they usually do not claim that a boy can actually recall the sequence of events of the cutting itself. It is significant, however, that the "birth-trauma" was an idea developed by Freud's disciple Otto Rank. Freud saw Rank's book *The Trauma of Birth* (1923) as a rejection of the central psychoanalytic "truth" because it seemed to propose that there was a complex *prior* to the Oedipal complex. And in *Moses and Monotheism*, Freud did not cite Rank's work even as he drew extensively from his book *The Birth of a Hero* (1909) to support his argument that the Bible had distorted the true (Egyptian) origins of Moses. See Rank, "The Essence of Judaism" (1905), *Jewish Origins of the Psycho-analytic Movement*, ed. Dennis B. Klein (Chicago: University of Chicago Press, 1985); Rank, *The Trauma of Birth* (New York: Dover, 1993); Rank, *The Myth of the Birth of the Hero: A Psychological Exploration of Myth*, trans. Gregory Richter and E. James Liberman (Baltimore: Johns Hopkins University Press, 2004); and Rudnytsky, *Reading Psycho-Analysis*.

83. "When our [Jewish] children come to hear of ritual circumcision, they equate it with castration." See Freud, *Totem and Taboo*, 153. The German (as printed in the *Gesammelte Werke*) does not contain the word *Jewish*, which appears in brackets in Strachey's translation.

84. For example, Gilman and Geller read Freud's non-mention of Little Hans' and Otto Weininger's Jewishness as an obvious case of disavowal. Moreover, since Freud's note about circumcision and castration appears in the midst of his discussion of "Little Hans'" realization of gender difference, it clearly aligns male circumcised Jews with penis-less women (or castrated men), and anti-semitism with misogyny. On the idea that Freud displaced his feelings about Jewish difference (self-hatred) onto his feelings about gender difference (misogyny), see Boyarin, "What Does a Jew Want?"; Geller, "A Paleontological View of Freud's Study of Religion: Unearthing the *Leitfossil* Circumcision," *Modern Judaism* 13 (1993); Geller, "The Godfather of Psychoanalysis: Circumcision, Antisemitism, Homosexuality, and Freud's 'Fighting Jew,'" *Journal of the American Academy of Religion* 67.2 (1999); Gilman, *The Jew's Body*; and Gilman, *Freud, Race, and Gender*.

85. My analysis of the famous footnote diverges from the analyses by Boyarin, Geller, and Gilman, who interpret the little boys in Freud's nursery as gentile (uncircumcised) boys rather than as Jewish (circumcised) boys.

86. Freud, "Analysis of a Phobia in a Five-Year-Old Boy ('Little Hans')," 36n31.

87. See Gilman, *Jewish Self-Hatred*.

88. Frantz Fanon, *Black Skin, White Masks*, trans. Charles Lam Markmann (New York: Grove Press, 1967), 111.

89. Ibid., 112.

90. Ibid. Homi Bhabha refers to this description as one of Fanon's "primal scenes." See Bhabha, *The Location of Culture* (New York: Routledge, 1994), 108.

91. Fanon, *Black Skin, White Masks*, 122.

92. Ibid., 115.

93. On the Muslim practice of circumcision (which usually occurs anytime between when the boy is seven days old and when he is thirteen years old), see Anand, "Anxious Sexualities"; Leonard B. Glick, *Marked in Your Flesh: Circumcision from Ancient Judea to Modern America* (New York: Oxford University Press, 2005), 283–84; Rizvi et al., "Religious Circumcision: A Muslim View," *BJU International* 83. Supplement 1 (1999); and F. Sahin, U. Beyazova, and A. Aktürk, "Attitudes and Practices Regarding Circumcision in Turkey," *Child: Care, Health and Development* 29.4 (2003).

94. There is debate about whether Freud's own sons were circumcised: While the Viennese Jewish Community [*Israelitische Kultusgemeinde*] contains no record of their circumcision, it is nearly impossible to know whether they might have been circumcised by a doctor or *mohel* outside the official Viennese Jewish community. For a discussion of the evidence and the debates, see Geller, *On Freud's Jewish Body*, 127, 260n165.

95. Thus it may be possible to put to rest the speculations about whether "Little Hans" (Herbert Graf) was actually circumcised.

96. See Eric Kline Silverman, *From Abraham to America: A History of Jewish Circumcision* (Lanham, MD: Roman and Littlefield, 2006), final two chapters;

Silverman, "Psychoanalyzing Phallacies: Freud and Current Circumcision Controversies," Paper presented at *Freud's Foreskin: A Sesquicentennial Celebration of the Most Suggestive Circumcision in History*, New York Public Library, May 10, 2006.

97. Freud, *New Introductory Lectures on Psycho-Analysis*, 87.

98. Freud, "Analysis of a Phobia in a Five-Year-Old Boy ('Little Hans')," 36n1.

99. Freud, *Moses and Monotheism*, 39.

100. Ibid., 122.

101. Ibid., 91.

102. Ibid., 39, 62, my emphasis. Strachey translates the word "*Zeichen* [sign, symbol]" as "mark."

103. Ibid., 27, 30. "Generally popular custom in Egypt" is my own translation of "*allgemeine Volkssitte in Ägypten geübt wurde.*" Strachey translates this as "universal popular custom," but "general folk-custom" would be a more accurate translation. Katherine Jones translates it as "general custom."

104. Ibid.

105. Ibid. Though Freud acknowledged that circumcision was becoming a general neonatal practice in the United States (among both Jews and non-Jews), he makes only scant reference to the fact that in many parts of the world (but perhaps most significantly among Muslims in Africa and the Middle East), Jews are not the only ones who practice circumcision and that anti-Judaism also exists among people who practice circumcision. Nonetheless, Freud does note that "even to this day a Turk [i.e., a circumcised Muslim] will abuse a Christian as an 'uncircumcised dog.'" Ibid.

106. Ibid., 116.

107. Ibid., 113.

108. Ibid., 121.

109. Ibid., 122.

110. Ibid., 29.

111. Gilman, *Freud, Race, and Gender*, 81.

112. Along these lines, see Connor, "Some of My Best Friends Are Philosemites."

113. While Freud did not explore the significance of the neonatality of the Jewish rite, he alludes to the early age of Jewish circumcision in a footnote in *Totem and Taboo*: "In primaeval times and in primitive races, where circumcision is so frequent, it is performed at the age of initiation into manhood and it is at that age that its significance is to be found; it was only as a secondary development that it was shifted back to the early years of life" (153).

114. Eilberg-Schwartz, *The Savage in Judaism*, 144ff.

115. See Gilman, "Decircumcision: The First Aesthetic Surgery," *Modern Judaism* 17.3 (1997).

116. Eilberg-Schwartz, *The Savage in Judaism*, 176. While Israelite neonatal circumcision might seem to avoid the themes of "virility and social maturity,"

Eilberg-Schwartz writes that "a male's ability to reproduce was not simply the outcome of his maturation but also a privilege of having a certain genealogy. Circumcision was thus a rite which simultaneously conferred and confirmed one's pedigree" (176).

117. Julia Reinhard Lupton, "*Ethnos* and Circumcision in the Pauline Tradition: A Psychoanalytic Exegesis," *The Psychoanalysis of Race*, ed. Christopher Lane (New York: Columbia University Press, 1998), 194.

118. See Cohen, *The Beginnings of Jewishness*, 348.

119. Lennard Davis quoted in Steven Marcus, *Representations: Essays on Literature and Society* (New York: Random House, 1990), 212n.

120. The question of whether Daniel Deronda was "in fact" circumcised remains unknowable, even if it is the subject of seemingly endless discussions. Along these lines, see K. M. Newton, "Daniel Deronda and Circumcision," *Essays in Criticism* 31 (1981); and Louise Penner, "'Unmapped Country': Uncovering Hidden Wounds in *Daniel Deronda*," *Victorian Literature and Culture* 30.1 (2002).

121. "The isolated childhood memories that people have possessed consciously from time immemorial and before there was any such thing as analysis may equally be falsified or at least may combine truth and falsehood in plenty." Freud, *Introductory Lectures on Psycho-Analysis*, 367–68.

122. Etienne Balibar, "Is There a 'Neo-Racism'?" *Race, Nation, Class: Ambiguous Identities*, eds. Etienne Balibar and Immanuel Wallerstein (New York: Verso, 1991), 24. Balibar notes that "anthropological culturalism, which is entirely orientated towards the recognition of the diversity and equality of cultures . . . and also their transhistorical *permanence*, had provided the humanist and cosmopolitan anti-racism of the post-war period with most of its arguments" (21).

123. Ibid., 24.

124. Balibar goes on to argue that "*culture can also function like a nature*, and it can in particular function as a way of locking individuals and groups a priori into a genealogy, into a determination that is immutable and intangible in origin." Ibid., 22. What Balibar does not mention is that this "locking" is itself historically and religiously grounded.

125. Where historians of the ancient world generally refer to the first five centuries of the Common Era as "late antiquity," historians of Judaism refer to this period (specifically 70 C.E. until the sixth century) as the Rabbinic period. Thus the Rabbis (with a capital "R") designates the particular group of Jewish leaders who lived during this period and wrote the body of texts that came to be known as Rabbinic literature (the Mishnah and the Talmudim, among others). Daniel Boyarin argues that Rabbinic Judaism was defined by the fact that it "invested significance in the body which in the other formations [Greek-speaking Jewish formations and much of Christianity] was invested in the soul. That is, for Rabbinic Jews, the human being was defined as a body—animated,

to be sure, by a soul—while for Hellenistic Jews (such as Philo) and (at least many Greek-speaking) Christians (such as Paul), the essence of a human being is a soul housed in a body." Boyarin, *Carnal Israel*, xi, 5. See also Shaye J. D. Cohen, *From the Maccabees to the Mishnah* (Louisville: Westminster John Knox Press, 1987). While the Rabbis were by no means hegemonic during their own time, their writings became the basis for later canonical Jewish texts and practices; on the emergence of Rabbinic authority, particularly regarding the question of whether ancestry or merit defines the people and the priesthood, see Martha Himmelfarb, *A Kingdom of Priests: Ancestry and Merit in Ancient Judaism* (Philadelphia: University of Pennsylvania Press, 2006).

126. Maciejewski, *Psychoanalytisches Archiv und jüdisches Gedächtnis*, 309.

127. Assmann, "Der jüdische Ödipus. Franz Maciejewskis Studie zum Beschneidungsritus," *Neue Zürcher Zeitung* (Dec. 11, 2002).

128. There is an immense body of literature on Paul's letters. Stanley Stowers and John Gager, for example, argue that Paul's Letter to the Romans should be read as an "attempt to clarify for gentile followers of Christ their relation to the law, Jews, and Judaism" rather than as a universal address, or as an address to fellow Jews, whether followers of Christ or otherwise. Stowers, *A Rereading of Romans*, quoted in Gager, *Reinventing Paul* (New York: Oxford University Press, 2002), 107.

129. Assmann, "Das Unbewusste in der Kultur: eine Antwort auf Franz Maciejewski," *Psyche* 62.3 (2008), 253.

130. Assmann is clearly aware of Pauline hermeneutics, so it is all the more noteworthy that he does not acknowledge that he is re-framing what is usually regarded as a split between Judaic and Christian definitions of community rather than between Abrahamic and Mosaic definitions. My point is not that he consciously takes a Christian (or Pauline) perspective, but that, in the context of an argument that downplays the importance of the body and genealogy, it is difficult to see his reference to "circumcision of the heart" as anything other than Pauline. See Cohen, *Beginnings of Jewishness*, 26.

131. Assmann's "inversion" is particularly ironic: In another essay, he argues that *Freud* "knowingly and ironically" inverts the Pauline binary by privileging the Jews' "Advance in Intellectuality [*Geistigkeit*]." See "Der Fortschritt in der Geistigkeit," 166–67. I discuss this inversion in more detail in Chapter 5.

132. While the Torah repeatedly invokes genealogy, it does not clearly state that genealogy is the primary definition of who is a Jew. Such definitions emerge in later texts, most particularly in the fourth to fifth centuries C.E.

133. Silverman, *From Abraham to America*.

134. Silverman demonstrates that circumcision recalls Abraham's narrowly averted sacrifice of Isaac in Genesis 22, as well as the practice of animal sacrifice mentioned in Exodus 22: 28–29: "seven days it shall stay by its mother, on the eighth day it shall be slaughtered." Ibid., chapter 5.

135. Frances Yates, *The Art of Memory* (Chicago: University of Chicago Press, 1966).

136. Maciejewski follows Freud's lead and argues that the Biblical text (imperfectly) documents the already-present practice of circumcision: "Later Scripture is a surface-phenomenon [*Oberflächenphänomen*] superimposed on the complex of dynamic drives operating in the cultural unconscious." Jan Assmann and Franz Maciejewski, "Ein Briefwechsel zwischen Jan Assmann and Franz Maciejewski," *Psyche* 62.3 (2008), 257. I do not agree with Maciejewski's claim that circumcision is the origin and precondition for the development of monotheism, Judaism, or psychoanalysis. However, even as the ritual is extensively discussed and consciously maintained, its power does seem to reside at least partially in the fact that it invokes the very notion of archaic memory or what might be termed the "Jewish cultural unconscious." In other words, because the individual boy's circumcision occurs at a time that will not be remembered in a historical narrative sense, the experience of "recalling" the act seems to fit far more within the realm of unconscious memory than within the realm of history.

137. The emphasis in this sentence is on "unquestioningly": Clearly, there are many individuals who were not born of Jewish women born of other Jewish women but who are nonetheless counted as members of the Jewish community. In such cases, it is rabbis who have generally held the power to do the "counting."

138. Cohen, *Beginnings of Jewishness*, 263.

139. Boyarin, "The Christian Invention of Judaism," 22. Square brackets in original.

140. Freud, *Moses and Monotheism*, 135.

141. Yerushalmi suggests that "on this question of hope or hopelessness, even more than on God or godlessness, [Freud's] teaching may be at its most un-Jewish." *Freud's Moses*, 95. In response to Yerushalmi, Derrida writes, "Jewishness here, if not Judaism, comes down, in its minimal essence, . . . to the openness of the future." *Archive Fever*, 48.

142. Freud, "The Uncanny," 225.

4. SECRET INCLINATIONS BEYOND DIRECT COMMUNICATION

1. "The Dynamics of Transference," 99. While he had privately considered phylogenetic memory in his letter to Jung on Oct. 13, 1911, his first published acknowledgment of the idea appears in this text, published in January 1912.

2. The Freud family installed a telephone sometime before 1895. See Freud, "Project for a Scientific Psychology," 357.

3. July 10, 1915, Freud and Ferenczi, *The Correspondence of Sigmund Freud and Sandor Ferenczi*, II: 64.

4. July 12, 1915, ibid., II: 65.

5. July 18, 1915, ibid., II: 66–67.

6. July 20, 1915, ibid., II: 68.

7. July 20, 1915, ibid., II: 69.

8. July 21, 1915, ibid.

9. Freud, *The Psychopathology of Everyday Life*, 257.

10. Freud, "The Uncanny," 237–38.

11. "It is not a fact that transference emerges with greater intensity and lack of restraint during psychoanalysis than outside it." Freud, "The Dynamics of Transference," 101.

12. Freud, "Five Lectures on Psycho-analysis," 51.

13. Ibid.

14. Lyotard's attempt to distinguish his "jewish" question from the question of "real" Jews seems to (inversely) demonstrate that such distinctions are impossible. As he writes in *Heidegger and the "jews,"* "I use lower case to indicate that I am not thinking of a nation. I make it plural to signify that it is neither a figure nor a political (Zionism), religious (Judaism), or philosophical (Jewish philosophy) subject that I put forward under this name. I use quotation marks to avoid confusing these 'jews' with real Jews. What is most real about real Jews is that Europe, in any case, does not know what to do with them: Christians demand their conversion; monarchs expel them; republics assimilate them; Nazis exterminate them. 'The jews' are the object of a dismissal [*non-lieu*] with which Jews, in particular, are afflicted in reality." Jean-François Lyotard, *Heidegger and "the jews,"* trans. Andreas Michel and Mark S. Roberts (Minneapolis: University of Minnesota Press, 1990), 3.

15. Freud, "Five Lectures on Psycho-analysis," 51.

16. Ibid.

17. Freud, "Address to the Society of B'nai B'rith," 273–74, my emphasis.

18. Freud, *Moses and Monotheism*, 99–100, my emphasis.

19. Jacques Derrida, "Freud and the Scene of Writing," trans. Alan Bass, *Writing and Difference* (New York: Routledge, 1978), 199.

20. There is an immense quantity of scholarship on this topic. Some of the key works that discuss the ways in which Modernist authors and artists incorporated (rather than simply rejected or embraced) the images, anxieties, and aesthetics of new technologies and forms of capitalist production are the following: Tim Armstrong, *Modernism, Technology and the Body* (Cambridge: Cambridge University Press, 1998); Friedrich Kittler, *Discourse Networks 1800/1900*, trans. Michael Metteer and Chris Cullens (Stanford: Stanford University Press, 1990); Kittler, *Gramophone, Film, Typewriter*, trans. Geoffrey Winthrop-Young and Michael Wutz (Stanford: Stanford University Press, 1999); and Avital Ronell, *The Telephone Book: Technology, Schizophrenia, Electric Speech* (Lincoln: University of Nebraska Press, 1989).

21. Pamela Thurschwell, *Literature, Technology and Magical Thinking, 1880–1920* (New York: Cambridge University Press, 2001), 2. See also Kittler, "Romanticism—Psychoanalysis—Film: A History of the Double," trans. Stefanie

Harris, *Literature, Media, Information Systems: Essays* (Amsterdam: Overseas Publishers Association, 1997); Luckhurst, *The Invention of Telepathy*; and Ronell, *The Telephone Book*.

22. I borrow this formulation from Thurschwell, *Literature, Technology and Magical Thinking*, 129. Throughout this chapter, I have found that many of my arguments uncannily correspond with many of Thurschwell's arguments, including the notion that "dangerous proximity" very nearly verges on an invasion of one's psyche, a loss of a sense of originality, and a fear of plagiarism. She follows this anxiety through Ferenczi's work, reiterates Helene Deutsch's remark on this matter ("I became interested at one time in the problems of plagiarism, only to learn much later that these had once weighed very heavily on Freud"), and makes this same point in relation to her own proximity with Eric Santner's work on Schreber's psychosis. Thurschwell, *Literature, Technology and Magical Thinking*, 132, 177n162. See also Eric L. Santner, *My Own Private Germany: Daniel Paul Schreber's Secret History of Modernity* (Princeton: Princeton University Press, 1996); and Thurschwell, "Ferenczi's Dangerous Proximities: Telepathy, Psychosis, and the Real Event," *differences: A Journal of Feminist Cultural Studies* 11.1 (1999).

23. Hart, *Social Science and the Politics of Modern Jewish Identity*, 1–2.

24. One of the most well-known versions of this image is found in Eugene Sue's multi-volume novel *The Wandering Jew*, published in 1844–45. Wherever the Wandering Jew went, he spread cholera in his wake. Sue's work has had an illustrious after-life that is relevant to my discussion: Soon after it was published, it was apparently plagiarized by French satirist Maurice Joly, whose work was in turn plagiarized by Prussian bureaucrat Hermann Goedsche. In his book *Biarritz* (1868) (published using the penname Sir John Retcliffe), Goedsche borrowed from Joly's *The Dialogue in Hell Between Machiavelli and Montesquieu* (1864), but added a crucial scene depicting a cabal of rabbis meeting in a cemetery to discuss their ongoing attempts to establish world domination. Portions of Goedsche's chapter "At the Jewish Cemetery in Prague" were then plagiarized by the Russian Matvei Golovinski. The text was printed as pamphlets widely circulated throughout the world as "The Protocols of the Elders of Zion" and used as evidence of the Jews' conspiracy to take over the world. In this narrative, then, the images of germinological transmission and textual-cultural transmission mirror and reflect one another in fascinating ways. See Norman Cohn, *Warrant for Genocide: The Myth of the Jewish World Conspiracy and the Protocols of the Elders of Zion* (London: Serif, 1996); Ginzburg, "Learning from the Enemy: The French Prehistory of 'The Protocols,'" *Evidence*, eds. John Swenson-Wright, Andrew Bell, and Karin Tybjerg (Cambridge University Press, 2008); and Eugene Sue, *The Wandering Jew* (1844–45), ed. Brian Stableford (New York: Hippocrene, 1990).

25. Shapiro, "The Uncanny Jew," 65.

26. The exploration of these images requires that we be attentive not only to anti-semitic overtones but also to Freud's ultimate concern with why and

how Jews and Jewishness have so persistently survived. In my analysis of these images, I try to withhold judgment about whether they are negative or positive representations of the Jewish people, their circumstances, and their future. Ultimately, it is unclear if anti-semitism and Judaism can ever be separated or if they are part of one "immortal" phenomenon of the drive to understand one's self in relation to an Other. Indeed, these distinctions—between self and other, Jew and non-Jew, and even Judaism and anti-semitism—may be far more unstable than is often presumed.

27. See, for example, James P. Keeley, "'The Coping Stone on Psycho-Analysis': Freud, Psychoanalysis, and The Society for Psychical Research," PhD dissertation, Columbia University, 2002; Roger Luckhurst, "'Something Tremendous, Something Elemental': On the Ghostly Origins of Psychoanalysis," *Ghosts: Deconstruction, Psychoanalysis, History*, eds. Peter Buse and Andrew Stott (New York: Macmillan, 1999); and Thurschwell, "Ferenczi's Dangerous Proximities."

28. Alan Bass, "Translator's Introduction: L Before K," *The Post Card: From Socrates to Freud and Beyond* (Chicago: University of Chicago Press, 1978), ix.

29. Sigmund Freud, "The Unconscious," 187.

30. Harold Bloom, *The Anxiety of Influence: A Theory of Poetry*, 2nd ed. (New York: Oxford University Press, 1997), 6. A (perhaps spurious) anecdote illuminates Bloom's idea of the "anxiety of influence": Isaac Newton is reported to have said, "I could only see so far because I was standing on the shoulders of giants." Yet as the years passed, other scientists began to stand on Newton's shoulders. Rising from the dead, the ghost of Newton remarked, "I could have seen further if I didn't have all these giants standing on my shoulders." I thank Geoffrey Bowker for sharing this anecdote in private correspondence.

31. Ibid.

32. Oscar Wilde, quoted in ibid.

33. In his essay on "the original and belated testaments," Bloom acknowledges that when authors see themselves and their own texts as fulfillments of earlier texts, there is the danger that the later text (in this case, the Gospel according to St. John) will supplant and destroy the earlier text (the Hebrew Bible). See Bloom, "'Before Moses Was, I Am': The Original and the Belated Testaments," *Notebooks in Cultural Analysis: An Annual Review*, eds. Norman F. Cantor and Nathalia King (Durham: Duke University Press, 1984).

34. In Santner's version of this joke, there is also an American who presents a paper on "How to Breed Bigger and Better Elephants." Santner, "Freud, Žižek, and the Joys of Monotheism," 197. The inclusion of the American as a national type is itself a funny (though uncommented) addition to the joke, because the premise of the joke is the Europeans' confidence in typologies. Like the Jewish type, the American type has also been defined by a sort of postmodern instability that can incorporate just about anything into its (bigger and better) "melting pot." However, it is this very instability that also allows national

leaders to proclaim a confidence in such universal ideals as American freedom and democracy. Indeed, the definition of who is an American and who is a Jew are similarly all-incorporative as opposed to who is counted as a German or a Frenchman. Whoever is born a Jew is Jewish (regardless of language, feelings, practices, or passports), and whoever is born in America can claim American citizenship (regardless of language, feelings, or practices). The same is not true of Germany or France, where, until recently, children and grandchildren of immigrants have not necessarily been incorporated into the national body legally or conceptually.

35. Santner, "Freud, Žižek, and the Joys of Monotheism."

36. Slavoj Žižek, quoted in ibid., 198–99.

37. Ibid., 199.

38. Freud, *The Future of an Illusion*, 19.

39. Santner, "Freud, Žižek, and the Joys of Monotheism," 201. Santner develops his interpretation of *jouissance* in *On the Psychotheology of Everyday Life*, 31–33.

40. Santner, "Freud, Žižek, and the Joys of Monotheism," 202.

41. Santner, *On the Psychotheology of Everyday Life*, 8.

42. Santner, "Freud, Žižek, and the Joys of Monotheism," 201.

43. Santner, "Freud's *Moses* and the Ethics of Nomotropic Desire," 34.

44. I realize that in reading Freud's theory of transference as a theory of Jewishness, I seem to be suggesting that one of the most fundamental psychoanalytic concepts is implicitly Jewish. While this may be true, it is not my point. My point is only that Freud's construction of transference is particularly relevant to understanding the persistent transmission and survival of Jewishness. The psychoanalytic concept of transference illuminates a range of relationships and interactions between individuals and generations, not all of whom are Jewish.

45. As Gilman and Efron have each noted, Jewish physicians and racial scientists were stuck in a similar double bind, since they were both the investigators and the objects of such investigation. See Efron, *Defenders of the Race*, 2–3; and Gilman, *Freud, Race, and Gender*, 3. The problem of objectivity is not limited to the natural sciences. As Yerushalmi notes, "The problem of objectivity is common to all historians, not just to historians of the Jews who are themselves Jews. Why should my anxiety be greater than that of a French and a Russian historian, each writing about the Napoleonic wars? My own conception of historical research and writing is that of a constant oscillation between empathy and distance." See "Yerushalmi, Yosef Hayim (1932–)."

46. Indeed, in *The Psychopathology of Everyday Life*, Freud remarks that psychoanalysis transformed the "construction of a supernatural reality" into a scientific "psychology of the unconscious," or "metaphysics into metapsychology" (259).

47. Keeley, "'The Coping Stone on Psycho-Analysis,'" 38, my emphasis. In 1882, Henry Sidgwick (along with Frederic Myers and Edmund Gurney)

founded the Society for Psychical Research in part as an attempt to distinguish their own "real" (objective) scientific research on these matters from the religious explorations and charlatan demonstrations of such phenomena. The Society still exists and maintains a website with copious information about their history: www.spr.ac.uk.

48. See Freud, "A Comment on Anti-Semitism."

49. Freud, "Observations on Transference-Love," 164.

50. Bernadette Bensaude-Vincent, "Lessons in the History of Science," *Configurations* 8 (2000), 204.

51. See Jones, *The Life and Work of Sigmund Freud*, III: 313, 394.

52. Freud, *Totem and Taboo*, 158, my emphasis. The German reads: "welcher Mittel und Wegen sich die eine Generation bedient, um ihre psychischen Zustände auf die nächste zu *übertragen*."

53. Freud, "Analysis Terminable and Interminable," 240–41.

54. Freud, *Moses and Monotheism*, 69, my emphasis.

55. Ibid., 93, my emphasis.

56. Freud, *Totem and Taboo*, 158.

57. Ibid.

58. Ibid., 159. "Even the most ruthless suppression must leave room for distorted surrogate impulses and for reactions resulting from them."

59. I discuss this in more detail in Chapter 1.

60. June 23, 1913, Freud and Ferenczi, *The Correspondence of Sigmund Freud and Sandor Ferenczi*, I: 494, my emphasis.

61. Freud, *New Introductory Lectures on Psycho-Analysis*, 55.

62. Freud, *Moses and Monotheism*, 124, my emphasis.

63. In fact, Freud uses many images that allude to conspiracy theories and, in particular, theories that allude to the idea of Jewish world conspiracy. See L. J. Rather, "Disraeli, Freud, and Jewish Conspiracy Theories," *Journal of the History of Ideas* 47.1 (1986).

64. There are numerous letters in which Freud tells Jung and Ferenczi to "keep quiet about" their explorations of the occult, and often these admonitions appear in the very same letters in which he expresses concern about their explorations of their feelings for their patients. See, for example, Freud's letter to Ferenczi, Oct. 6, 1909, *The Correspondence of Sigmund Freud and Sandor Ferenczi*, I: 79.

65. See Luckhurst, " 'Something Tremendous, Something Elemental,' " 55.

66. June 7, 1909, Freud and Jung, *The Freud/Jung Letters*, 230–31.

67. Freud, "Five Lectures on Psycho-analysis," 51.

68. In a more speculative mode, I would suggest that Freud's meditations on transference inside and outside psychoanalysis are homologous with certain aspects of Jewish transference inside and outside Jewish communities and even in communities with no Jews. That is, there is no need to know "real Jews" for there to be a Jewish Question, a suspicion of Jews (as Others) within the midst,

or even within oneself. The question is what serves as the catalyst in these situations. What is it that causes a person to fall into these patterns of love, of repetition, of transference, of anti-semitism, of Jewishness, and of Judaism?

69. Dec. 31, 1911, Freud and Jung, *The Freud/Jung Letters*, 475–76.

70. See the editor's note in Freud, "Psycho-Analysis and Telepathy," 175–76. On the "secret" committee, see Grosskurth, *The Secret Ring*.

71. June 18, 1909, Freud and Jung, *The Freud/Jung Letters*, 235. Freud cites this same sentence in *Jokes and Their Relation to the Unconscious*, 82. More could probably be said about Freud's reference to Ferdinand Lassalle, who was well known not as a chemist, but as a Jewish German socialist. Indeed, Freud quotes the penultimate sentence of Lassalle's *Science and the Workingmen: An argument in his own defense before the Criminal court of Berlin on the charge of having publicly incited the unpropertied classes to hatred and contempt of the propertied classes* (1900). In the following and final sentence, Lassalle appeals to the court to acquit him. One could speculate that Freud's citation of Lassalle's text suggests that he felt as if he needed to defend psychoanalysis against the accusation that it shifted the structure of power and "incited" rebellion.

72. Freud, "The Future Prospects of Psycho-Analytic Therapy," 145.

73. Ibid., 144–45.

74. Freud, "Recommendations to Physicians Practising Psycho-Analysis," 115.

75. See Thurschwell, "Ferenczi's Dangerous Proximities."

76. Freud, "Recommendations to Physicians Practising Psycho-Analysis," 115–16.

77. Ibid.

78. See Ronell, *The Telephone Book*; and Thurschwell, "Ferenczi's Dangerous Proximities."

79. Freud, *Civilization and Its Discontents*, 88.

80. Ibid., 90.

81. Ibid., 91.

82. Most famously, in the nineteenth century Jules Verne wrote science-fiction novels about air, underwater, and space travels long before airplanes, submarines, and space shuttles had been invented (or were even feasible, given the knowledge of the time period).

83. Thurschwell, *Literature, Technology and Magical Thinking*, 121.

84. Freud, *New Introductory Lectures on Psycho-Analysis*, 36.

85. Ibid., 39.

86. Ibid.

87. Ibid., 55.

88. In his four-volume *Outline of Science*, Lodge devotes an entire chapter to "Psychic Science" (in which he discusses telepathy and the survival of the mind after bodily death), and another chapter to "The Body Machine and Its Work" (in which he extensively discusses Freud and psychoanalysis). See Oliver Lodge,

Outline of Science, ed. J. Arthur Thompson, 4 vols. (New York: G. P. Putnam's Sons, 1922).

89. A sampling of *New York Times* articles from 1927—the year the first images were seen televisually—shows that scientists, journalists, and politicians widely and openly discussed such possibilities. See, for example, "British to Try to Broadcast Telepathic Messages Feb. 16," *New York Times*, Jan. 24, 1927; "Says Telepathy is Next: Professor Low Predicts Transmission of Thoughts Without Speech," *New York Times*, Jan. 16, 1927; and "'Thinkers-In' Guess In Telepathy Test, Thousands of 'Ideas' Sent to British Psychical Society in Thousands of Letters, Two Seem to Have Hit It, One Correctly Describes the 'Thought Broadcaster's' Attire, the Other a Box in the Room," *New York Times*, Feb. 18, 1927. Moreover, somewhat serious discussions of telepathy continue today: See, for example, Rupert Sheldrake, *Dogs That Know When Their Owners Are Coming Home and Other Unexplained Powers of Animals* (New York: Three Rivers Press, 1999).

90. Freud, *New Introductory Lectures on Psycho-Analysis*, 55.

91. Ibid., my emphasis.

92. Marc Redfield, "The Fictions of Telepathy," *Surfaces* 2.27 (1992), 6.

93. Indeed, when *Der Sturmer* ran contests encouraging German children to send their thoughts on Jews, one little girl wrote, "People are so bothered by the way we're treating the Jews. They can't understand it, because they are God's creatures. But cockroaches are also God's creatures, and we destroy them." Quoted in Eliahu Ellis and Shmuel Silinsky, *The War Against the Jews* (2005).

94. Luckhurst, "'Something Tremendous, Something Elemental,'" 59–60.

95. Freud explicitly addresses the question of how psychoanalysis incorporates telepathy and the occult in the following works: Freud, "Dreams and Telepathy"; Freud, "Some Additional Notes upon Dream-Interpretation as a Whole"; Freud, *New Introductory Lectures on Psycho-Analysis*; and Freud, "Psycho-Analysis and Telepathy." A couple of notes about these texts: "Psychoanalysis and Telepathy" was prepared as a lecture for the "secret" committee in 1921, but it was not published until after Freud's death. In "Some Additional Notes upon Dream Interpretation," Freud includes a section on "The Occult Significance of Dreams." In his *New Introductory Lectures* (1933), he returned to many of the themes he had first explored in his earlier *Introductory Lectures* (1915–16), but now he included a lecture on "Dreams and Occultism."

96. Oppenheim, *The Other World*, 62ff.

97. Keeley, "'The Coping Stone on Psycho-Analysis,'" 39.

98. Luckhurst, "'Something Tremendous, Something Elemental,'" 57–58.

99. Keeley, "'The Coping Stone on Psycho-Analysis,'" 44ff.

100. Frederic Myers, et al., "First Report of the Literary Committee (December 9, 1882)," *Proceedings of the Society for Psychical Research* (London: Trübener, 1883), 81, my emphasis.

101. Freud, *Civilization and Its Discontents*, 91–92.
102. Freud, *The Interpretation of Dreams*, 613.
103. Freud, *Introductory Lectures on Psycho-Analysis*, 278.
104. Freud, *Moses and Monotheism*, 111.
105. Ibid., 113, my emphasis.
106. Freud, *Introductory Lectures on Psycho-Analysis*, 278.
107. Freud, *Group Psychology and the Analysis of the Ego*, 75n71.
108. Freud, *Moses and Monotheism*, 21, 63–64.
109. Ibid., 85.
110. Shapiro, "The Uncanny Jew," 65.
111. Santner, *On the Psychotheology of Everyday Life*, 9.
112. Freud, "The Unconscious," 191.
113. Thus, for example, Freud (in)famously refers to the adult woman's sexuality as the "dark continent." See "The Question of Lay Analysis," 212.
114. Boyarin, "What Does a Jew Want?," 219.
115. This is Homi Bhabha's formulation of the colonial subject's doubled consciousness in *The Location of Culture*. Quoted in Boyarin, "What Does a Jew Want?," 219.
116. See, for example, Keeley, " 'The Coping Stone on Psycho-Analysis' "; Luckhurst, " 'Something Tremendous, Something Elemental' "; and Thurschwell, *Literature, Technology and Magical Thinking*.
117. On Jones' attempt to understand Freud's Lamarckism as an effect of his Jewishness, see page 89.
118. Jones, *The Life and Work of Sigmund Freud*, III: 381. Jones does not say what year this conversation took place.
119. Quoted in ibid., III: 395.
120. Ibid., III: 395–96.
121. Jacques Derrida, "Telepathy," *Oxford Literary Review* 10 (1988), 35.
122. Nicholas Royle, *After Derrida* (Manchester: Manchester University Press, 1995), 64. While Derrida focuses on Freud's use of the term *foreign body*, it is actually his translators and interpreters who have taken this term and used it to more generally describe telepathy's position within psychoanalysis. For example, Maria Torok argues that "*telepathy* was probably the name Freud unwittingly gave to a *foreign body* within the corpus of psychoanalysis, a foreign body that retains its own individuality, walls, and partitions." Like the unconscious, telepathy and the occult are the names given to "that which cannot be fully assimilated, interpreted or incorporated within the rational structure of psychoanalysis." Torok, "Afterword: What is occult in Occultism? Between Sigmund Freud and Sergei Pankeiev Wolf Man," *The Wolf Man's Magic Word: A Cryptonomy*, trans. Nicholas Rand (Minneapolis: University of Minnesota Press, 1986), 86.
123. Similarly, in her essay "Ferenczi's Dangerous Proximities," Thurschwell responds to Freud's 1926 letter to Jones in which he explicitly links telepathy, smoking, and Jewishness. She writes, "I will leave aside the intriguing

question of just how private Jewishness and smoking are in relation to psycho-analysis" (120).

124. Feb. 25, 1926, Freud and Jones, *The Complete Correspondence of Sigmund Freud and Ernest Jones*, 33–34.

125. Freud, *Civilization and Its Discontents*, 114.

126. See, for example, Geoffrey Bennington and Jacques Derrida, *Jacques Derrida* (Chicago: University of Chicago Press, 1999); Ronell, *The Telephone Book*; Nicholas Royle, "Phantom Review," *Textual Practice* 11.2 (1997); and Royle, *Telepathy and Literature: Essays on the Reading Mind* (Cambridge: Blackwell, 1991).

127. Derrida, "Telepathy," 36.

128. "Parousia" refers to the Second Coming of Jesus Christ at the end of time, or a messianic or apocalyptic event comparable to the Second Coming. The word derives from the Greek for "parallel to but beyond presence; or analogous but separate from essence." *Oxford English Dictionary Online*, s.v. "parousia." Derrida's reference to parousia evokes and anticipates Bloom's discussions of prophetic texts, family romances, and the "anxiety of influence" discussed earlier in this chapter. See Bloom, "'Before Moses Was, I Am'"; and Bloom, *The Anxiety of Influence*.

129. Derrida, "Telepathy," 33–34; Freud, *New Introductory Lectures on Psycho-Analysis*, 56.

130. Ibid.

131. Aug. 20, 1910, Freud and Ferenczi, *The Correspondence of Sigmund Freud and Sandor Ferenczi*, I: 211, my emphasis.

132. Thomas Ollive Mabbott, "Text of 'The Purloined Letter' by Edgar Allan Poe, with Notes," *The Purloined Poe: Lacan, Derrida and Psychoanalytic Theory*, eds. John P. Muller and William J. Richardson (Baltimore: Johns Hopkins University Press, 1988).

133. Barbara Johnson, "The Frame of Reference: Poe, Lacan, Derrida" (1977), *The Purloined Poe*, 242.

134. Jacques Lacan, "Seminar on 'The Purloined Letter,'" *The Purloined Poe*, 53.

135. Johnson, "The Frame of Reference," 249.

136. Derrida, loosely quoted in Johnson, "The Frame of Reference," 226.

137. Derrida, *Archive Fever*.

138. Derrida, "Telepathy," 16.

139. Just as Derrida and Lacan facilitate the transmission of Freud's letters, Žižek (with the help of Louis Althusser) carries Derrida's and Lacan's letters one step further.

140. Žižek, *Enjoy Your Symptom! Jacques Lacan in Hollywood and Out* (New York: Routledge, 1992), 12. Althusser's "call of ideology" will return in my "Belated Speculations."

141. Ibid.

142. *Deuteronomy* 29: 14–15.

143. Nicholas Rand, "Introduction: Renewals of Psychoanalysis," in Nicolas Abraham and Maria Torok, *The Shell and the Kernel: Renewals of Psychoanalysis*, ed., trans. Nicholas Rand (Chicago: University of Chicago Press, 1994), 22.

144. Nicolas Abraham, "Notes on the Phantom: A Complement to Freud's Metapsychology," *The Shell and the Kernel*, 176.

145. Ibid.

146. Ibid., 172.

147. Ibid., 172–73.

148. Ibid., 171.

149. Ibid., 175.

150. Though I presume that I am not the first to notice this lacuna, I have not come across any mention of Abraham's and Torok's non-mention of their own relationships to the Jewish Question, even when their work is cited in the context of discussions of Jewishness and memory. See, for example, Caruth, *Unclaimed Experience*, 136n122; Maria Damon, "Hannah Weiner Beside Herself: Clairvoyance After Shock or The Nice Jewish Girl Who Knew Too Much" *The East Village* (1999); and Martin Kavka, *Jewish Messianism and the History of Philosophy* (New York: Cambridge University Press, 2004). Elizabeth Bellamy notes that Abraham and Torok were Jewish, but not how she knew this information: *Affective Genealogies: Psychoanalysis, Postmodernism, and the Jewish Question After Auschwitz* (Lincoln: University of Nebraska Press, 1997), 21–22. Note: After completing the manuscript, I learned from various secondary sources (people who know people who knew Abraham and Torok) that Abraham and Torok *were* "in fact" both Jewish.

151. Rand, "Introduction: Renewals of Psychoanalysis," 1–2.

152. Before Freud became friends with Karl Abraham, he slyly asked Jung in a postcard whether Abraham was "a descendant of his eponym." Aug. 27, 1907, Freud and Jung, *The Freud/Jung Letters*, 80.

153. Particularly in his discussions of Holocaust historiography, Dominick LaCapra notes that the historian (or "interviewer-cum-therapist") is always in danger of also becoming a "secondary witness," infected by the traumas he describes and documents. See LaCapra, *Writing History, Writing Trauma* (Baltimore: Johns Hopkins University Press, 2000), 97ff; LaCapra, *Representing the Holocaust*; and LaCapra, *History in Transit*.

154. Laurie Johnson reports that "both [Abraham and Torok] lost their [families] to the genocide." Johnson, "'I Wish to Dream' and Other Impossible Effects of the Crypt," *Psychoanalytic Review* 92.5 (2005), 735. Elisabeth Roudinesco also discusses Abraham's and Torok's lives and bases her account on an interview with Maria Torok and Nicholas Rand. See Roudinesco, *Jacques Lacan and Co. A History of Psychoanalysis in France, 1925–1985*, trans. J. Mehlman (Chicago: University of Chicago Press, 1990), 598–603.

155. James Herzog, "World Beyond Metaphor: Thoughts on the Transmission of Trauma," *Generations of the Holocaust*, eds. Martin S. Bergmann and Milton E. Jucovy (New York: Basic Books, 1982), 104–5. See also Dorothy Burlingame, "Child Analysis and the Mother (An Excerpt)," *Psychoanalysis and the Occult*, ed. George Devereux (New York: International Universities Press, 1953).

156. Grubrich-Simitis, "Trauma or Drive—Drive and Trauma," 25n29, my emphasis.

157. Grubrich-Simitis, *Early Freud and Late Freud*, 69.

158. This same language—of bodily haunting and transgenerational telepathy—has been incorporated in a number of films and novels about the Holocaust and its descendants as well as in films and novels about African American slavery and its descendants. See, for example, Octavia Butler, *Kindred* (Garden City: Doubleday, 1979); David Grossman, *See Under: LOVE* (New York: Farrar, Straus & Giroux, 1989); Toni Morrison, *Beloved: A Novel* (New York: Knopf, 1987); and D. M. Thomas, *The White Hotel* (New York: Viking, 1981).

159. See Davidman and Tenenbaum, "It's in My Genes."

160. Michaels, "Race into Culture," 682.

5. IMMATERIAL MATERIALITY: THE "SPECIAL CASE" OF JEWISH TRADITION

1. A very small sampling of the enormous recent trans-disciplinary literature on this subject includes the following: Jan Assmann, *Das kulturelle Gedächtnis* (Munich: C. H. Beck, 1992); Mieke Bal, Jonathan Crewe, and Leo Spitzer, eds., *Acts of Memory: Cultural Recall in the Present* (Hanover: University Press of New England, 1999); Cathy Caruth, *Trauma: Explorations in Memory*; James Fentress and Chris Wickham, *Social Memory* (Cambridge: Blackwell, 1992); Kerman Lee Klein, "On the Emergence of Memory in Historical Discourse," *Representations* 69 (2000); David Farrell Krell, *Of Memory, Reminiscence, and Writing: On the Verge* (Bloomington: Indiana University Press, 1990); Matt Matsuda, *The Memory of the Modern* (New York: Oxford University Press, 1996); Jeffrey K. Olick and Joyce Robbins, "Social Memory Studies: From 'Collective Memory' to the Historical Sociology of Mnemonic Practices," *American Review of Sociology* 24 (1998); Paul Ricoeur, *Memory, History, Forgetting*, trans. Kathleen Blamey and David Pellauer (Chicago: University of Chicago Press, 2005); David G. Roskies, *The Jewish Search for a Usable Past* (Bloomington: Indiana University Press, 1999); Michael Roth, *The Ironist's Cage: Memory, Trauma, and the Construction of History* (New York: Columbia University Press, 1995); Edward Said, "Invention, Memory, Place," *Critical Inquiry* 26 (2000); and Daniel L. Schacter, ed., *Memory Distortion: How Minds, Brains, and Societies Reconstruct the Past* (Cambridge: Harvard University Press, 1995).

2. Said, *Freud and the Non-European*, 35.

3. Ibid., 50.

4. As I discuss in Chapters 2 and 3, it is at the end of the section entitled "Difficulties" that Freud admits that he had "behaved for a long time as though the inheritance of memory-traces of the experience of our ancestors, *independently of direct communication* and of the influence of education by the setting of an example, were established beyond question. When I spoke of the *survival of a tradition* among a people or of the formation of a people's character, I had mostly in mind *an inherited tradition* of this kind and *not one transmitted by communication.*" *Moses and Monotheism*, 99–100, my emphasis.

5. To maintain consistency, I include the German wherever Freud uses the word *Geistigkeit* or *geistig(e)*.

6. Freud, *Moses and Monotheism*, 99. Michael Mack explores the relationship between Freud's thought and the German Idealist tradition in much more detail. Specifically, he suggests that Freud ironically inverted Kant's proposal that Christ was a revolutionary who inaugurated "an overthrow" of Jewish moral philosophy and thereby "turned the tables on Kant by shedding light on reason's irrationality." See Mack, *German Idealism and the Jew: The Inner Anti-Semitism of Philosophy and German Jewish Responses* (Chicago: University of Chicago Press, 2003), 152, 154.

7. Freud, *Moses and Monotheism*, 111–15. That Freud saw "The Advance in *Geistigkeit*" as the quintessence of his work is evidenced by the fact that he had his daughter Anna read this section as a ventriloquized lecture at the 1938 Psychoanalytic Congress in Paris. Indeed, even as he thought he might not publish the work in its entirety, he published this section separately in the winter of 1939. See Assmann, "Der Fortschritt in der Geistigkeit," 157; and Bernstein, *Freud and the Legacy of Moses*, 82–89.

8. Freud, *Moses and Monotheism*, 99.

9. For a more detailed discussion of the Mosaic opposition to Egyptian and "primitive" religions, see Assmann, *Moses the Egyptian*, 151.

10. Freud, *Moses and Monotheism*, 47.

11. The apparent contradiction between the claim to biological purity and the insistence on spiritual superiority was common in Nazi racial theories. As David Biale notes, the Nazis' "hyper-literal or physical understanding of blood contradicted [their] insistence that they represented the 'spiritual' (*Geist*), contrasting with Jewish materialism." *Blood and Belief: The Circulation of a Symbol between Jews and Christians* (Berkeley: University of California Press, 2007), 139.

12. For Freud and his contemporaries, genealogy was defined materially both in terms of archival practices documenting descent from a particular ancestor and of the idea that certain biological materials are transmitted from one generation's bodies to the next. Indeed, the idea of biology as a separate field of study emerged only in the early nineteenth century, when the term was coined by German naturalist Gottfried Reinhold in his 1802 work *Biologie* and, most significantly for this story, adopted in French in the same year by Lamarck in his *Hydrologie*. *Oxford English Dictionary Online*, s.v. "biology."

13. This was true for a number of Freud's contemporaries such as Benjamin Disraeli, who is generally regarded as the first Jewish prime minister of England, though he was baptized as an Anglican at the age of 13. Freud uses Disraeli's Jewishness as indirect evidence of Moses' Egyptianness: Like Disraeli (whose name indicates that he "was indeed an Italian Jew"), Moses' name suggests that he was indeed Egyptian. See *Moses and Monotheism*, 9.

14. When Max Graf (the father of "Little Hans") asked Freud whether he should raise his son as a Jew or have him baptized, Freud responded, "If you do not let your son grow up as a Jew, you will deprive him of those sources of energy which cannot be replaced by anything else. He will have to struggle as a Jew, and you ought to develop in him all the energy he will need for that struggle. Do not deprive him of that advantage." In other words, even if Graf did not raise his son as a Jew, he would be regarded as such, and Graf should let him know what it means to be a Jew from an insider's perspective so that he would have the energy to struggle with other (external and/or anti-semitic) perspectives. Max Graf, "Reminiscences of Professor Sigmund Freud," *The Psychoanalytic Quarterly* 11 (1942), 473.

15. "The story is told in New York of the banker Otto Kahn and the humorist Marshall P. Wilder, who was a hunchback. Strolling along Fifth Avenue, the banker pointed to a church and said: 'Marshall, that's the church I belong to. Did you know that I once was a Jew?' The hunchback answered: 'Yes, Otto, and once I was a hunchback.'" Theodor Reik, *Jewish Wit* (New York: Gamut Press, 1962), 90. Reik was a Viennese (Jewish) psychoanalyst who trained with Freud and immigrated to New York City in 1938.

16. See Assmann, *Moses the Egyptian*; Assmann, "Der Fortschritt in der Geistigkeit"; and Boyarin, *Unheroic Conduct*.

17. See Gilman, *Freud, Race, and Gender*; Stewart, "Freud Before Oedipus"; and Yerushalmi, *Freud's Moses*.

18. Yerushalmi, *Freud's Moses*, 90.

19. Bernstein, *Freud and the Legacy of Moses*, 113.

20. Jacques Le Rider, "Jewish Identity in *Moses and Monotheism*," *The Psychohistory Review* 25 (1997), 247.

21. As Jonathan Boyarin argues, "Many critical analyses of psychoanalysis and authority share in Freud's view of ancestral authority as a problem to be overcome through the achievement of autonomy, rather than as a facultative condition of human existence." It seems, however, that Freud did not necessarily believe that overcoming ancestral authority (through achieving autonomy) was desirable or possible. See Boyarin, "Another Abraham: Jewishness and the Law of the Father," *Yale Journal of Law and the Humanities* 9.2 (1997), 347.

22. Freud and Andreas-Salomé, *Letters*, 206.

23. See Bernstein, *Freud and the Legacy of Moses*, 119; and Yerushalmi, *Freud's Moses*, 78.

24. Freud, *Moses and Monotheism*, 53.

25. Freud, *Totem and Taboo*, 1, my emphasis.

26. Ibid., 132–36, 152–55. Freud mentions Robertson Smith's study of the *Religion of the Semites*, but he focuses on his treatment of the sacrificial meal rather than the intellectual [*geistig*] "prohibitions" and "renunciations" (which are a central focus of *Moses and Monotheism*).

27. I discuss Freud's initial resistance to (and eventual acceptance of) the notion of inherited memory in Chapters 2 and 3.

28. As he explains in the March 1938 prefatory note to the third essay of *Moses*, "Not that I should have anything to say that would be new or that I did not say clearly a quarter of a century ago" (55).

29. Ibid., 52–53, my emphasis.

30. Of course, by being identified as Jewish, people have been regularly subjected to political powers with real material ramifications, both negative (as in most of Europe for most of recorded history) and positive (as in present-day Germany and Israel). In Freud's Vienna, however, a Jewish person was less likely to receive material benefits from being identified as Jewish. The question that Freud seems to be posing, then, was why have individuals persistently submitted to the "yoke" of being Jewish? What convinces individuals that they are Jewish and that they should practice Jewish traditions even as the Jewish tradition (itself) does not satisfy any material needs?

31. Freud, *Moses and Monotheism*, 19. Freud explains that Christianity "did not maintain the high level in things of the mind [*hielt die Höhe der Vergeistigung nicht ein*] to which Judaism had soared. It was no longer strictly monotheist, it took over numerous symbolic rituals from surrounding peoples. . . . Above all, it did not, like the Mosaic [religion] . . . exclude the entry of superstitious, magical and mystical elements, which were to prove a severe inhibition upon the intellectual [*geistige*] development of the next two thousand years" (88).

32. Ibid., 9, 28–29n2.

33. Ibid., 32.

34. On the concept of tradition as a religious category, see Gershom Scholem, "Revelation and Tradition as Religious Categories in Judaism," trans. Michael Meyer, *The Messianic Idea in Judaism and Other Essays* (New York: Schocken Books, 1995).

35. See Jean LaPlanche and Jean-Bertrand Pontalis, *The Language of Psycho-Analysis*, trans. Donald Nicholson-Smith (London: Hogarth Press and the Institute of Psycho-analysis, 1973), xi–xiii.

36. Freud, *Moses and Monotheism*, 68–69.

37. Ibid., 93.

38. Ibid.

39. Ibid., my emphasis.

40. Freud, *Moses and Monotheism*, 93–94.

41. Ibid.

42. Freud, *Totem and Taboo*, 159.

43. Freud, *Moses and Monotheism*, 113.

44. Ibid., 101, my emphasis.

45. Ibid., 100.

46. It is impossible to determine (once and for all) how Freud felt about his Jewishness since, not surprisingly, his feelings changed over time and in different contexts. The strength and importance of Freud's theory of Jewishness—and Rosenzweig's for that matter—is that it does not shy away from some of the most problematic and paradoxical aspects of Jewish definition. See Shapiro, "The Uncanny Jew," 72.

47. On the similarities between racial anti-semitism in twentieth-century Germany and fifteenth-century Spain, see Yerushalmi, *Assimilation and Racial Anti-Semitism*.

48. See Jan Assmann, *Die Mosaische Unterscheidung: oder der Preis des Monotheismus* (Wien: Carl Hanser Verlag, 2003), 166–67.

49. Assmann, "Der Fortschritt in der Geistigkeit," 166–67; and Assmann, "The Advance in Intellectuality: Freud's Construction of Judaism," *New Perspectives on Freud's Moses and Monotheism*, eds. Ruth Ginsburg and Ilana Pardes (Tübingen: Max Niemeyer Verlag, 2006), 16.

50. As I discuss in Chapter 3, Assmann himself ironically employs Pauline hermeneutics in privileging the "continuation and completion" of circumcision through a life of Jewish study and practice. Like Paul, Assmann privileges "circumcision of the heart" over and against circumcision of the body. See Assmann, "Das Unbewusste in der Kultur"; and Assmann and Maciejewski, "Ein Briefwechsel Zwischen Jan Assmann und Franz Maciejewski."

51. Grubrich-Simitis, *Early Freud and Late Freud*, 77–78.

52. Freud, *Moses and Monotheism*, 113.

53. Gilman has thoroughly explored the ways in which Jewish bodies and bodily parts have been portrayed, specifically in terms of penises, feet, noses, smells, and hair. See Gilman, *The Jew's Body*; and Gilman, *Creating Beauty to Cure the Soul: Race and Psychology in the Shaping of Aesthetic Surgery* (Durham: Duke University Press, 1998). See also Boyarin, *Unheroic Conduct*, 244–48.

54. Eilberg-Schwartz, *People of the Body*, 5. Other revivals of the "Tough Jew" can be found in the revival of the Maccabees' "heroic" story, the delight in Alan Dershowitz's *Chutzpah*, and the romanticization of Jewish gangsters in two books titled *Tough Jews*. See Paul Breines, *Tough Jews: Political Fantasies and the Moral Dilemma of American Jewry* (New York: Basic Books, 1990); and Rich Cohen, *Tough Jews: Fathers, Sons and Gangster Dreams* (New York: Simon and Schuster, 1998).

55. See, for example, Batnitsky, "The Image of Judaism"; Boyarin, *Unheroic Conduct*, 246ff; and Hermann Cohen, *Religion of Reason: Out of the Sources of Judaism*, trans. Simon Kaplan (New York: Frederick Ungar, 1972).

56. Eilberg-Schwartz, *People of the Body*, 1. On the recent return to matters of the Jewish body, see Kirshenblatt-Gimblett's recent essay documenting the split in Jewish Studies between the new "Berkeley (or California) school" of studies of the "People of the Body" and the older (East Coast–based) school of studies of the "People of the Book." Barbara Kirshenblatt-Gimblett, "The Corporeal Turn," *Jewish Quarterly Review* 95.3 (2005).

57. Or, as one Holocaust museum website put it, "Among all the things that Judaism is, the one thing it is not is a race." See Florida Holocaust Museum, *What Is Judaism?* (2003).

58. For example, to counter William Z. Ripley's claims that the Jews were not a race, Joseph Jacobs argued that they were the most pure race. See Joseph Jacobs, "Are Jews Jews?" *Popular Science Monthly* 55 (1899); Jacobs, *The Jewish Race: A Study in National Character* (London: Privately printed, 1899); and William Z. Ripley, "The Racial Geography of Europe: A Sociological Study. Supplement: The Jews," *Popular Science Monthly* 54 (1899). By contrast, Maurice Fishberg went to anthropological lengths to demonstrate that the Jews were *not* a distinct racial group. See Fishberg, *The Jews: A Study of Race and Environment* (New York: The Walter Scott Publishing Company, 1911). See also Abu El-Haj, "The Genetic Reinscription of Race," *Annual Review of Anthropology* 36 (2007); Efron, *Defenders of the Race*; Raphael Falk, "Zionism and the Biology of the Jews," *Science in Context* 11.3–4 (1998); and Eric L. Goldstein, "'Different Blood Flows in Our Veins': Race and Jewish Self-Definition in Late Nineteenth Century America," *American Jewish History* 85.1 (1997).

59. Ibid., 123, my emphasis.

60. In *Civilization and Its Discontents*, Freud reiterates that he had come to this conclusion by analyzing Christianity specifically. "From the manner in which, in Christianity, this redemption is achieved—by the sacrificial death of a single person, who in this manner takes upon himself a guilt that is common to everyone—we have been able to infer what the first occasion may have been on which this primal guilt, which was also the beginning of civilization, was acquired" (136). See also Freud, *Totem and Taboo*, 153–55.

61. Jacqueline Rose, "Response to Edward Said," *Freud and the Non-European* (New York: Verso, 2003), 75.

62. Freud, *Moses and Monotheism*, 69–70, my emphasis.

63. Ibid., 115.

64. Ibid.

65. Ibid., 51, my emphasis.

66. I thank Ruth Liberman for her insightful illumination of this passage.

67. Freud, *Moses and Monotheism*, 111.

68. Ibid., 7.

69. Eliot Oring seems to present one of the more extreme versions of this argument: "If Moses was not a Jew then neither was Freud." Oring, *The Jokes*

of Sigmund Freud: A Study in Humor and Jewish Identity (Philadelphia: University of Pennsylvania Press, 1984), 101. Le Rider argues that it is precisely by making Moses an Egyptian that Freud demonstrated his ultimate rejection of Jewish racial definitions: "In denying the Jewish birth of Moses, Freud denied his own descendance." Le Rider, "Jewish Identity in *Moses and Monotheism*," 247. See also Robert, *From Oedipus to Moses*, 278.

70. In *Freud and the Legacy of Moses*, Bernstein repeatedly interprets various passages as evidence that Freud took pride in his Jewishness. For example, he writes, "Freud . . . is . . . taking pride in the spiritual and intellectual power of his *own* tradition" (35); "in a passage where Freud's pride in his Jewish heritage shines through" (51); "a legacy with which Freud proudly identifies" (84); and "Freud's pride in identifying himself with this tradition" (85). I am not suggesting that Freud had *no* pride in his Jewish heritage, or that his presentation was completely disinterested. Rather, I am interested in the ways in which his book compels us to examine the complexities of Jewishness that often give rise to *both* pride and embarrassment, and often simultaneously.

71. Freud and Andreas-Salomé, *Letters*, 206–7. See Yerushalmi, *Freud's Moses*, 78; and Bernstein, *Freud and the Legacy of Moses*, 32.

72. Yerushalmi, *Freud's Moses*, 7.

73. Jan. 6, 1935, Freud and Andreas-Salomé, *Letters*, 204.

74. Freud, *Moses and Monotheism*, 100.

75. Yerushalmi, *Freud's Moses*, 85.

76. Ibid., 90.

77. While Yerushalmi implicitly seems to worry that Jewishness (ethnicity "freed" of its religious content) will not be able to survive on its own, Moshe Gresser expresses this concern more explicitly: "In that sense, Freud's view simply reflects the prejudice of his age and its anti-Jewish culture (one that dispensed with 'the Law' in order to free 'the Spirit'), and is therefore thoroughly inadequate to sustain Jewish life. Though Freud's own children married Jews (at least in their first marriages), the next generation married out and effectively left the Jewish community. Freud's family is in fact another casualty of assimilation, and his psychological Judaism bears some responsibility. The loss bears witness to the risk of dual allegiance in the absence of Jewish content." Gresser, *Dual Allegiance*, 249.

78. Yerushalmi, *Freud's Moses*, 53, my emphasis.

79. Though recent work has tried to prove the unity of Jews' genetics, I use this term in a more etymological sense to refer to common genealogical origins, whether real or imagined (and I suspect that this is what Yerushalmi also intended by using this word). An individual's inheritance of Jewishness does not necessarily suggest that he would share genetic commonalities with all (or any) other Jews other than known immediate family members. Nonetheless, a number of twentieth-century scientific studies (and studies of these studies) tried to

prove either common genetic origins or the fallacy of such unity. On the former, see Abu El-Haj, "The Genetic Reinscription of Race"; and Abu El-Haj, "A Tool to Recover Past Histories," *Occasional Papers of the School of Social Science* 19 (2004). On the latter, see Raphael Patai and Jennifer P. Wing, *The Myth of the Jewish Race* (New York: Scribner's, 1975).

80. Freud, *Moses and Monotheism*, 123, my emphasis.

81. Bernstein, *Freud and the Legacy of Moses*, 113, my emphasis.

82. Efron, *Defenders of the Race*, 8.

83. Freud, *Moses and Monotheism*, 52. In itself, this is not so unusual, since many accounts of ancient Jewish history refer to the twelve tribes of Israel.

84. Ibid., 42.

85. Ibid., 113.

86. Ibid., 114. Freud does not just mention this transition in passing; he reiterates it: "An advance in intellectuality [*Geistigkeit*] consists in deciding against direct sense-perception [*direkte Sinneswahrnehmung*] in favour of what are known as the higher intellectual processes—that is, memories, reflections and inferences. It consists, for instance, in deciding that paternity is more important than maternity, although it cannot, like the latter, be established by the evidence of the senses [*Zeugnis der Sinne erweisbar*], and that for that reason the child should bear his father's name and be his heir [*nach ihm erben*]" (117–18).

87. See Assmann, *Die Mosaische Unterscheidung*, 166–67.

88. Boyarin, *Unheroic Conduct*, 260.

89. It is possible, though unlikely, that Freud did not know (or care) that, according to rabbinic definitions, Jewishness is transmitted through the mother's genealogy. Some evidence suggests that even if he knew about the matrilineal definition, such factors were not important in determining one's Jewishness in the everyday life of Freud's Vienna. In *The Psychopathology of Everyday Life*, he tells an anecdote about a Jewish-born colleague who had converted in order to marry a Christian woman. The colleague had two sons who were also baptized but who apparently knew about their Jewish background. When they were staying at an inn, the host made some anti-semitic comments. The father worried that his sons "would betray the momentous truth" of the "fact that we were Jews," so he told the sons to "go into the garden, *Juden* [Jews]," after which he quickly corrected himself and said, "*Jungen* [boys]." Thus, concludes Freud, the man learned the lesson "that the 'faith of our fathers' cannot be disavowed with impunity if one is a son and has sons of one's own" (93). Nonetheless, it seems that Freud would not bother making such a big point of the "preference for paternity" if he did not know that he was inverting the matrilineal principle.

90. Cohen, *The Beginnings of Jewishness*, 263–307.

91. Freud, *Moses and Monotheism*, 114.

92. Whereas Boyarin argues that Freud masculinizes and Aryanizes Jewish tradition in a number of ways, he overlooks Freud's particular inversion of the

matrilineal principle. Indeed, he specifically argues that Freud masculinizes the Jews by rejecting their carnality: "Where the Jews have been accused of carnality and, therefore, of being like women, Freud . . . would demonstrate that they are more spiritual, and more rational, than the Others, and therefore more masculine than the accusers themselves. . . . Freud set out to counter antisemitic charges that Jews are not spiritual but carnal, female and not male." Boyarin, *Unheroic Conduct*, 253.

93. Freud's move is further demonstrated by his allusion to Aschylus' play *Oresteia* to suggest that the only true parent is the one whose contribution is the invisible *eidos* (i.e., the father). The discovery (or invention) of the invisible Mosaic god runs parallel to a Greek prioritization of the invisible realm of intellectuality [*Geistigkeit*] over the visible and material realm of sensuality [*Sinnlichkeit*]. I thank an anonymous reviewer of an earlier draft of this chapter for alerting me to this connection.

94. Sander Gliboff suggests that the plight of Kammerer was similarly determined by shifting scientific standards of documentation. While nineteenth-century scientists regularly doctored their evidence or provided drawings of their observations, by the 1920s the scientific establishment began to expect untouched photographs documenting all scientific experiments and observations. See Gliboff, "The Case of Paul Kammerer." See also Chandler, Davidson, and Harootunian, eds., *Questions of Evidence*; and Léon Chertok and Isabelle Stengers, *A Critique of Psychoanalytic Reason: Hypnosis as a Scientific Problem from Lavoisier to Lacan*, trans. Martha Noel Evans (Stanford: Stanford University Press, 1992).

95. See Freud, "Recommendations to Physicians Practising Psycho-Analysis"; Freud, "Lines of Advance in Psycho-Analytic Therapy"; and Freud, *The Future of an Illusion*.

96. Freud, *Moses and Monotheism*, 113.

97. See Abu El-Haj, "The Genetic Reinscription of Race"; Efron, *Defenders of the Race*; and Falk, "Zionism and the Biology of the Jews."

98. In comparing Freud and Rosenzweig, I draw from the comparative analyses by Santner and Shapiro. See Santner, "Freud's *Moses* and the Ethics of Nomotropic Desire"; Santner, *On the Psychotheology of Everyday Life*; and Shapiro, "The Uncanny Jew."

99. Franz Rosenzweig, *The Star of Redemption*, trans. William W. Hallo (Notre Dame: University of Notre Dame Press, 1985), 300.

100. Ibid., 302.

101. Freud, *Moses and Monotheism*, 115.

102. Drawing from Freud's *Moses*, Žižek sees this radical deterritorialization as a fundamental characteristic of the modern subject, always unsure of his proper place in the social fabric. See Santner, "Freud, Žižek, and the Joys of Monotheism"; and Žižek, *The Sublime Object of Ideology*.

103. Nora, "Between Memory and History: Les Lieux de Memoire" in "Special Issue: Memory and Counter-Memory," *Representations* 26 (1989), 7. In

this essay (a re-publication of Nora's introduction to a massive collaborative history of France), Nora uses the term *lieux de mémoire* to refer to "sites of memory" whose significance has intensified "because there are no longer *milieux de mémoire*, real environments of memory." He correlates this renewed interest in such sites as part of a "particular historical moment, a turning point where consciousness of a break with the past is bound up with the sense that memory has been torn—but torn in such a way as to pose the problem of the *embodiment* of memory in certain sites where a sense of historical continuity persists" (7, my emphasis). While this "particular historical moment" may have been felt as various post-colonial nation states began to recognize their fractiousness and multiple identities, it is, I think, emblematic of both Freud's and Rosenzweig's definitions of Jewish tradition. On European Jewishness in the early twentieth century as a colonial encounter, see Boyarin, *Unheroic Conduct*, 271ff.

104. Freud, *Moses and Monotheism*, 105, my emphasis.

105. Derrida, *Archive Fever*, 76–77.

106. Rosenzweig, *The Star of Redemption*, 300. Oddly, the standard English translation of Rosenzweig's text does not include this concluding line of this paragraph: "The people is a people only through the people." See Franz Rosenzweig, *Der Stern der Erlosung* (Freiburg im Breisgau: Universitätsbibliothek, 2002), 345.

107. I thank Geoffrey Bowker for suggesting this comparison.

108. Slavoj Žižek, *Enjoy Your Symptom! Jacques Lacan in Hollywood and Out* (New York: Routledge, 1992), 14.

109. Here I draw from Boyarin, *A Radical Jew*, 240–41.

110. See Walter Benn Michaels, "The No-Drop Rule," *Critical Inquiry* 20 (1994).

111. Assmann, *Moses the Egyptian*, 7.

112. Similarly, a number of scholars have expressed discomfort with Rosenzweig's concept of the "community of blood" and suggest that it should be understood symbolically rather than as an expression of racial or ethnic identification. See, for example, Peter Eli Gordon, "Rosenzweig Redux: The Reception of German-Jewish Thought," *Jewish Social Studies* 8.1 (2002), 94–95; and Gordon, *Rosenzweig and Heidegger: Between Judaism and German Philosophy* (Berkeley: University of California Press, 2003), 212–14. Certainly Freud engaged with scientific questions of race far more than Rosenzweig, but my point is that the very *use* of such terminology itself amounts to an engagement with the questions and images of race.

113. Race is not exactly a taboo topic within Jewish studies: See, for example, the brief essays in Alan Arkush, ed., "The Jewish Race?" Special Issue, *AJS Perspectives: The Magazine of the Association of Jewish Studies* (Fall 2007).

114. See Goldschmidt, *Race and Religion Among the Chosen Peoples of Crown Heights*.

115. Cohen, *The Beginnings of Jewishness*, 348.

116. Freud, *Moses and Monotheism*, 85.

BELATED SPECULATIONS: EXCUSE ME, ARE YOU JEWISH?

1. Althusser, "Ideology and Ideological State Apparatuses," 174.

2. Freud, "Five Lectures on Psycho-analysis," 51.

3. Ibid.

Abraham, Karl. "Amenhotep IV (Ichnaton): Psychoanalytische Beiträge zum Verständnis seiner Persönlichkeit und des monotheistischen Atonkultes." *Imago: Zeitschrift für Anwendung der Psychoanalyse auf die Geisteswissenschaften* 1 (1912): 334–60.

Abraham, Nicolas. "Notes on the Phantom: A Complement to Freud's Metapsychology" 1975. Trans. Nicholas Rand. *The Shell and the Kernel: Renewals of Psychoanalysis*. Chicago: University of Chicago Press, 1987.

Abraham, Nicolas, and Maria Torok. *The Shell and the Kernel: Renewals of Psychoanalysis*. 1978. Ed., trans. Nicholas Rand. Chicago: University of Chicago Press, 1987.

———. *The Wolf Man's Magic Word: A Cryptonomy*. 1976. Trans. Nicholas Rand. Minneapolis: University of Minnesota Press, 1986.

Abu El-Haj, Nadia. "'Bearing the Mark of Israel?' Genetics and the Quest for Jewish Origins." Unpublished draft [personal communication] (2004).

———. "The Genetic Reinscription of Race." *Annual Review of Anthropology* 36 (2007): 283–300.

———. "A Tool to Recover Past Histories." *Occasional Papers of the School of Social Science* 19 (2004). www.sss.ias.edu/publications/papers/paper19.pdf. Accessed December 29, 2008.

Adams, Michael Vannoy. "'It Was All a Mistake': Jung's Postcards to Ernest Jones and Kipling's Short Story 'The Phantom Rickshaw.'" (2006). www .jungnewyork.com/jung_postcards.shtml. Accessed August 1, 2006.

Adler, Jerry, with Anne Underwood. "Freud Is (Not) Dead." *Newsweek*, March 27, 2006.

Althusser, Louis. "Ideology and Ideological State Apparatuses (Notes Towards an Investigation)." Trans. Ben Brewster. *Lenin and Philosophy and Other Essays*. New York: Monthly Review Press, 1971.

Anand, Dibyesh. "Anxious Sexualities: Masculinity, Nationalism and Violence." *British Journal of Politics and International Relations* 9.2 (2007): 257–69.

Arkush, Allan, ed. "The Jewish Race?" Special issue, *AJS Perspectives: The Magazine of the Association of Jewish Studies* (Fall 2007). www.ajsnet.org/ajsp07fa .pdf. Accessed December 1, 2007.

Armstrong, Tim. *Modernism, Technology and the Body*. New York: Cambridge University Press, 1998.

Assmann, Jan. "The Advance in Intellectuality: Freud's Construction of Judaism." *New Perspectives on Freud's Moses and Monotheism*. Eds. Ruth Ginsburg and Ilana Pardes. Tübingen: Max Niemeyer Verlag, 2006.

———. "Der Fortschritt in der Geistigkeit. Sigmund Freuds Konstruktion des Judentums." *Psyche* 2.56 (2002): 154–71.

———. "Der jüdische Ödipus. Franz Maciejewskis Studie zum Beschneidungsritus." *Neue Zürcher Zeitung*, December 11, 2002.

———. *Das kulturelle Gedächtnis*. Munich: C. H. Beck, 1992.

———. *Die Mosaische Unterscheidung: oder der Preis des Monotheismus*. Vienna: Carl Hanser Verlag, 2003.

———. *Moses the Egyptian: The Memory of Egypt in Western Monotheism*. Cambridge: Harvard University Press, 1997.

———. *Of God and Gods: Egypt, Israel and the Rise of Monotheism*. Madison: University of Wisconsin Press, 2008.

———. "Sigmund Freud und das Kulturelle Gedächtnis." *Psyche* 58.1 (2004): 1–25.

———. "Das Unbewusste in der Kultur: eine Antwort auf Franz Maciejewski." *Psyche* 62.3 (2008): 253–56.

Assmann, Jan, and Franz Maciejewski. "Ein Briefwechsel zwischen Jan Assmann und Franz Maciejewski." *Psyche* 62.3 (2008): 257–65.

Aubry Kaplan, Erin. "Black Like I Thought I Was." *L.A. Weekly*, October 7, 2003.

Bakan, David. *Sigmund Freud and the Jewish Mystical Tradition*. Princeton: Van Nostrand, 1958.

Bal, Mieke, Jonathan Crewe, and Leo Spitzer, eds. *Acts of Memory: Cultural Recall in the Present*. Hanover: University Press of New England, 1999.

Balibar, Etienne. "Is There a 'Neo-Racism'?" *Race, Nation, Class: Ambiguous Identities*. Eds. Etienne Balibar and Immanuel Wallerstein. New York: Verso, 1991: 17–28.

Balter, Michael. "Genetics: Was Lamarck Just a Little Bit Right?" *Science*, April 7, 2000: 38.

Bass, Alan. "Translator's Introduction: L Before K." In Jacques Derrida, *The Post Card: From Socrates to Freud and Beyond*. Chicago: University of Chicago Press, 1978.

Batnitsky, Leora. *Idolatry and Representation: The Philosophy of Franz Rosenzweig Reconsidered*. Princeton: Princeton University Press, 2000.

———. "The Image of Judaism: German-Jewish Intellectuals and the Ban on Images." In "Icon, Image, and Text in Modern Jewish Culture," Special issue, *Jewish Studies Quarterly*. 11.3 (2004): 259–81.

Bellamy, Elizabeth. *Affective Genealogies: Psychoanalysis, Postmodernism, and the "Jewish Question" after Auschwitz*. Lincoln: University of Nebraska Press, 1997.

Bennington, Geoffrey, and Jacques Derrida. *Jacques Derrida*. Chicago: University of Chicago Press, 1999.

Bensaude-Vincent, Bernadette. "Lessons in the History of Science." Trans. Matthew Tiews and Trina Marmarelli. *Configurations* 8 (2000): 201–14.

Bernstein, Richard J. *Freud and the Legacy of Moses*. New York: Cambridge University Press, 1998.

Bhabha, Homi K. *The Location of Culture*. New York: Routledge, 1994.

Biale, David. *Blood and Belief: The Circulation of a Symbol between Jews and Christians*. Berkeley: University of California Press, 2007.

Bloom, Harold. *The Anxiety of Influence: A Theory of Poetry*. 2nd ed. New York: Oxford University Press, 1997.

———. "'Before Moses Was, I Am': The Original and the Belated Testaments." *Notebooks in Cultural Analysis: An Annual Review*. Eds. Norman F. Cantor and Nathalia King. Durham: Duke University Press, 1984.

Boas, Franz. *A Franz Boas Reader: The Shaping of American Anthropology, 1883–1911*. Ed. George Stocking. Chicago: University of Chicago Press, 1982.

———. *The Mind of Primitive Man*. New York: Macmillan, 1911.

———. "Psychological Problems in Anthropology (Lecture delivered at the celebration of the twentieth anniversary of the opening of Clark University, September, 1909)." *American Journal of Psychology* 21 (1910): 371–84.

Bori, Pier Cesare. "Una pagina inedita di Freud: la premessa al romanzo storico su Mosè." *Rivista di storia contemporanea* 7 (1979): 1–16.

Bowler, Peter J. *The Non-Darwinian Revolution: Reinterpreting a Historical Myth*. Baltimore: Johns Hopkins University Press, 1988.

Boyarin, Daniel. *Carnal Israel: Reading Sex in Talmudic Culture*. Berkeley: University of California Press, 1993.

———. "The Christian Invention of Judaism: The Theodosian Empire and the Rabbinic Refusal of Religion." *Representations* 85 (2004): 21–57.

———. *A Radical Jew: Paul and the Politics of Identity*. Berkeley: University of California Press, 1994.

———. *Unheroic Conduct: The Rise of Heterosexuality and the Invention of the Jewish Man*. Berkeley: University of California Press, 1997.

———. "What Does a Jew Want? or, The Political Meaning of the Phallus." *The Psychoanalysis of Race*. Ed. Christopher Lane. New York: Columbia University Press, 1998.

Boyarin, Jonathan. "Another Abraham: Jewishness and the Law of the Father." *Yale Journal of Law and the Humanities* 9.2 (Spring 1997): 345–94.

Breines, Paul. *Tough Jews: Political Fantasies and the Moral Dilemma of American Jewry*. New York: Basic Books, 1990.

Brenneck, Fritz. *The Nazi Primer: Official Handbook for Schooling the Hitler Youth*. Ed. William E. Dodd. Trans. Harwood L. Childs. New York: Harper & Brothers, 1938.

Brickman, Celia. *Aboriginal Populations in the Mind: Race and Primitivity in Psychoanalysis*. New York: Columbia University Press, 2003.

"British to Try to Broadcast Telepathic Messages Feb. 16." *New York Times*, Amusements, January 24, 1927: 19.

Britt, Brian. *Rewriting Moses: The Narrative Eclipse of the Text*. New York: T&T Clark, 2004.

Bruder, Edith. *The Black Jews of Africa: History, Religion, Identity*. New York: Oxford University Press, 2008.

Brunner, José. *Freud and the Politics of Psychoanalysis*. 1995. New Brunswick: Transaction Publishers, 2001.

Buell, Denise. *Why This New Race? Ethnic Reasoning in Early Christianity*. New York: Columbia University Press, 2005.

Burlingame, Dorothy. "Child Analysis and the Mother (An Excerpt)." 1935. *Psychoanalysis and the Occult*. Ed. George Devereux. New York: International Universities Press, 1953: 188–91.

Butler, Octavia. *Kindred*. Garden City: Doubleday, 1979.

Carotenuto, Aldo. *A Secret Symmetry: Sabina Spielrein Between Freud and Jung*. Trans. Aldo Pomerans, John Shepley, and Krishna Winston. New York: Pantheon, 1982.

Caruth, Cathy. *Trauma: Explorations in Memory*. Baltimore: Johns Hopkins University Press, 1995.

———. *Unclaimed Experience: Trauma, Narrative, and History*. Baltimore: Johns Hopkins University Press, 1996.

Center for Holocaust and Genocide Studies. "Histories and Narratives: Documentary Evidence." Regents of the University of Minnesota (2008). www.chgs.umn.edu/histories/documentary/hadamar/racism.html. Accessed July 4, 2008.

Certeau, Michel de. *The Writing of History*. Trans. Tom Conley. New York: Columbia University Press, 1988.

Chandler, James, Arnold I. Davidson, and Harry Harootunian, ed. *Questions of Evidence: Proof, Practice, and Persuasion across the Disciplines*. Chicago: University of Chicago Press, 1994.

Chertok, Léon, and Isabelle Stengers. *A Critique of Psychoanalytic Reason: Hypnosis as a Scientific Problem from Lavoisier to Lacan*. Trans. Martha Noel Evans. Stanford: Stanford University Press, 1992.

Clifford, James. *The Predicament of Culture: Twentieth-Century Ethnography, Literature, and Art*. Cambridge: Harvard University Press, 1994.

Coen, Deborah. "Living Precisely in Fin-de-Siècle Vienna." *Journal of the History of Biology* 39.3 (2006): 493–523.

Cohen, Hermann. *Religion of Reason: Out of the Sources of Judaism*. 1919. Trans. Simon Kaplan. New York: Frederick Ungar, 1972.

Cohen, Shaye J. D. *The Beginnings of Jewishness: Boundaries, Varieties, Uncertainties*. Berkeley: University of California Press, 1999.

———. *From the Maccabees to the Mishnah*. Louisville, KY: Westminster John Knox Press, 1987.

———. "Why Aren't Jewish Women Circumcised?" *Gender & History* 9.3 (1997): 560–78.

———. *Why Aren't Jewish Women Circumcised?: Gender and Covenant in Judaism*. Berkeley: University of California Press, 2005.

Cohn, Norman. *Warrant for Genocide: The Myth of the Jewish World Conspiracy and the Protocols of the Elders of Zion*. London: Serif, 1996.

Collingwood, R. G. *The Idea of History*. 1946. New York: Oxford University Press, 1994.

Connor, Steven. "Some of My Best Friends Are Philosemites." Paper presented at a panel marking the publication of *The Jew in the Text: Modernity and the Construction of Identity*, ed. Tamar Garb and Linda Nochlin, Institute of Contemporary Arts, London, (1995). www.bbk.ac.uk/english/skc/skcphil.htm. Accessed July 1, 2008.

Damon, Maria. "Hannah Weiner Beside Herself: Clairvoyance After Shock or The Nice Jewish Girl Who Knew Too Much." *The East Village* (1999). www.fauxpress.com/t8/damon/p1.htm. Accessed October 5, 2006.

Danto, Elizabeth Ann. *Freud's Free Clinics: Psychoanalysis and Social Justice, 1918–1938*. New York: Columbia University Press, 2005.

Darwin, Charles. *The Variation of Animals and Plants under Domestication*. Vol. 2. London: Murray, 1868. www.gutenberg.org/dirs/etext01/2vapd10.txt. Accessed August 31, 2007.

Davidman, Lynn, and Shelly Tenenbaum. "It's in My Genes: Biological Discourse and Essentialist Views of Identity among Contemporary American Jews." *The Sociological Quarterly* 48.3 (2007): 435–50.

Decker, Hannah S. "The Medical Reception of Psychoanalysis in Germany, 1894–1907: Three Brief Studies." *Bulletin of the History of Medicine* 45 (1971).

Derrida, Jacques. *Archive Fever: A Freudian Impression*. Trans. Eric Prenowitz. Chicago: University of Chicago Press, 1996.

———. "Freud and the Scene of Writing." *Writing and Difference*. Trans. Alan Bass. New York: Routledge, 1978: 196–231.

———. *The Post Card: From Socrates to Freud and Beyond*. Trans. Alan Bass. Chicago: University of Chicago Press, 1987.

———. "Telepathy." Trans. Nicholas Royle. *Oxford Literary Review* 10 (1988): 3–41.

Dobbelaere, Karel. "Some Trends in European Sociology of Religion: The Secularization Debate." *Sociological Analysis* 48.2 (1987): 107–37.

Efron, John M. *Defenders of the Race: Jewish Doctors and Race Science in Fin-de-Siècle Europe*. New Haven: Yale University Press, 1994.

Ehrenfels, Christian Freiherr von. *Sexualethik (Grenzfragen des Nerven- und Seelenlebens, Heft 56)*. Ed. Leopold Löwenfeld. Wiesbaden, Germany: J. F. Bergmann, 1907.

Eilberg-Schwartz, Howard. *God's Phallus and Other Problems for Moses, Masculinity and Monotheism*. Boston: Beacon Press, 1994.

———. *The Savage in Judaism: An Anthropology of Israelite Religion and Ancient Judaism*. Bloomington: Indiana University Press, 1990.

Eilberg-Schwartz, Howard, ed. *People of the Body: Jews and Judaism from an Embodied Perspective*. Albany: State University of New York Press, 1992.

Eliot, George. *Daniel Deronda*. 1889. New York: Penguin, 1995.

Ellis, Eliahu, and Shmuel Silinsky. "The War Against the Jews" (2005). www.aish.com/holocaust/overview/The_War_Against_the_Jews.asp. Accessed October 2, 2007.

Falk, Raphael. "Zionism and the Biology of the Jews." *Science in Context* 11.3–4 (1998): 587–607.

Fanon, Frantz. *Black Skin, White Masks*. Trans. Charles Lam Markmann. New York: Grove Press, 1967.

Felman, Shoshana, and Dori Laub. *Testimony: Crises of Witnessing in Literature, Psychoanalysis, and History*. New York: Routledge, 1992.

Fentress, James, and Chris Wickham. *Social Memory*. Cambridge: Blackwell, 1992.

Ferenczi, Sandor. *Thalassa: A Theory of Genitality*. 1924. Trans. Henry Alden Bunker. London: Karnac, 1989.

Field, Geoffrey G. "Nordic Racism." *Journal of the History of Ideas* 38.3 (1977): 523–40.

Fishberg, Maurice. *The Jews: A Study of Race and Environment.* New York: Walter Scott Publishing Company, 1911.

Florida Holocaust Museum. *What Is Judaism?* (2003). www.flholocaustmuseum
.org/history_wing/antisemitism/related_topics/judaism.cfm. Accessed September 26, 2005.

Freedman, H., and Maurice Simon, eds. *The Midrash Rabbah.* Trans. H. Freedman and Maurice Simon. Vol. 2, *Exodus* and *Leviticus.* New York: Soncino Press, 1977.

Freud, Sigmund. "Address to the Society of B'nai B'rith." 1926 [1925]. *S.E.*
Vol. 20: 271–74.

———. "Analysis of a Phobia in a Five-Year-Old Boy ('Little Hans')." 1909.
S.E. Vol. 10: 1–149.

———. "Analysis Terminable and Interminable." 1937. *S.E.* Vol. 23: 209–53.

———. "Autobiographical Study." 1925. *S.E.* Vol. 20: 1–74.

———. *Beyond the Pleasure Principle.* 1920. *S.E.* Vol. 18: 1–64.

———. "Charcot." 1893. *S.E.* Vol. 3: 7–23.

———. *Civilization and Its Discontents.* 1930. *S.E.* Vol. 21: 57–145.

———. "'Civilized' Sexual Morality and Modern Nervous Illness." 1908. *S.E.*
Vol. 9: 177–204.

———. "A Comment on Anti-Semitism." 1938. *S.E.* Vol. 23: 287–93.

———. "Dreams and Telepathy." 1922. *S.E.* Vol. 18: 195–220.

———. "The Dynamics of Transference." 1912. *S.E.* Vol. 12: 97–108.

———. *The Ego and the Id.* 1923. *S.E.* Vol. 19: 1–66.

———. "Five Lectures on Psycho-analysis." 1910 [1909]. *S.E.* Vol. 11: 1–55.

———. "From a History of an Infantile Neurosis (Wolf-Man)." 1918 [1914].
S.E. Vol. 17: 1–122.

———. *The Future of an Illusion.* 1927. *S.E.* Vol. 21: 1–56.

———. "The Future Prospects of Psycho-Analytic Therapy." 1910. *S.E.* Vol.
11: 139–51.

———. "Heredity and the Aetiology of the Neuroses." 1896. *S.E.* Vol. 3:
141–56.

———. *Group Psychology and the Analysis of the Ego.* 1921. *S.E.* Vol. 18: 65–143.

———. "Instincts and their Vicissitudes." 1915. *S.E.* Vol. 14: 109–40.

———. *The Interpretation of Dreams.* 1900. *S.E.* Vol. 4–5.

———. "Introduction to the Manuscript Draft (1934) of *Der Mann Moses.*"
Trans. Yosef Hayim Yerushalmi. In Yosef Hayim Yerushalmi, *Freud's Moses:
Judaism Terminable and Interminable.* New Haven: Yale University Press,
1991: 17, 101–3.

———. *Introductory Lectures on Psycho-Analysis.* 1916–17 [1915–17]. *S.E.* Vol.
15–16.

———. *Jokes and Their Relation to the Unconscious*. 1905. *S.E.* Vol. 8.

———. *The Letters of Sigmund Freud*. Ed. Ernst L. Freud. Trans. Tania and James Stern. New York: Basic Books, 1960.

———. "Letter to the Editor of the *Jewish Press Centre in Zurich*." 1925. *S.E.* Vol. 19: 291.

———. "Lines of Advance in Psycho-Analytic Therapy." 1919 [1918]. *S.E.* Vol. 17: 157–68.

———. *Moses and Monotheism*. 1939 [1934–38]. *S.E.* Vol. 23: 1–137.

———. *Moses and Monotheism*. 1939 [1934–38]. Trans. Katherine Jones. New York: Vintage, 1967.

———. "The Moses of Michelangelo." 1914. *S.E.* Vol. 13: 211–38.

———. *New Introductory Lectures on Psycho-Analysis*. 1933 [1932]. *S.E.* Vol. 22: 1–182.

———. "Observations on Transference-Love (Further Recommendations on the Technique of Psycho-Analysis III)." 1915 [1914]. *S.E.* Vol. 12: 157–71.

———. "Obsessive Actions and Religious Practices." 1907. *S.E.* Vol. 9: 115–27.

———. "On Narcissism: An Introduction." 1914. *S.E.* Vol. 14: 67–102.

———. "On the History of the Psycho-Analytic Movement." 1914. *S.E.* Vol. 14: 1–66.

———. "Overview of the Transference Neuroses." [1915]. *A Phylogenetic Fantasy: Overview of the Transference Neuroses*. Ed. Ilse Grubrich-Simitis. Trans. Axel and Peter T. Hoffer. Cambridge: Harvard University Press, 1987.

———. "Psycho-Analysis and Telepathy." 1941 [1921]. *S.E.* Vol. 23: 173–93.

———. "The Psychogenesis of a Case of Homosexuality in a Woman." 1920. *S.E.* Vol. 18: 145–72.

———. *The Psychopathology of Everyday Life*. 1901. *S.E.* Vol. 6.

———. "The Question of Lay Analysis: Conversations with an Impartial Person." 1926. *S.E.* Vol. 20: 179–258.

———. "Recommendations to Physicians Practising Psycho-Analysis." 1912. *S.E.* Vol. 12: 109–20.

———. "Sexuality in the Aetiology of the Neuroses." 1898. *S.E.* Vol. 3: 259–85.

———. "Some Additional Notes upon Dream-Interpretation as a Whole." 1925. *S.E.* Vol. 19: 123–38.

———. *Three Essays on the Theory of Sexuality*. 1905. *S.E.* Vol. 7: 123–245.

———. *Totem and Taboo*. 1913 [1912–13]. *S.E.* Vol. 13: 1–161.

———. "The Uncanny." 1919. *S.E.* Vol. 17: 217–56.

———. "The Unconscious." 1915. *S.E.* Vol. 14: 159–216.

Freud, Sigmund, and Karl Abraham. *A Psychoanalytic Dialogue: Letters of Sigmund Freud and Karl Abraham, 1907–1926*. Eds. Hilda C. Abraham and Ernst

L. Freud. Trans. Bernard Marsh and Hilda C. Abraham. New York: Basic Books/Hogarth Press, 1965.

Freud, Sigmund, and Lou Andreas-Salomé. *Letters.* 1966. Ed. Ernst Pfeiffer. Trans. William Robson-Scott and Elaine Robson-Scott. New York: Harcourt, Brace, Jovanovich, 1972.

Freud, Sigmund, and Josef Breuer. *Studies on Hysteria.* 1893–95. *S.E.* Vol. 2.

Freud, Sigmund, and Sandor Ferenczi. *The Correspondence of Sigmund Freud and Sandor Ferenczi.* Vol. I–III. Eds. Eva Brabant, Ernst Falzeder, Patrizia Giampieri-Deutsch, and André Haynal. Trans. Peter T. Hoffer. Cambridge: Harvard University Press, 1993–2000.

Freud, Sigmund, and Wilhelm Fliess. *The Complete Letters of Sigmund Freud to Wilhelm Fliess, 1877–1904.* Ed. Jeffrey M. Masson. Cambridge: Harvard University Press, 1985.

———. *The Origins of Psycho-Analysis.* Eds. Marie Bonaparte, Anna Freud, and Ernst Kris. New York: Basic Books, 1954.

Freud, Sigmund, and Ernest Jones. *The Complete Correspondence of Sigmund Freud and Ernest Jones.* Ed. Andrew Paskauskas. Cambridge: Harvard University Press, 1993.

Freud, Sigmund, and Carl Gustav Jung. *The Freud/Jung Letters: The Correspondence between Sigmund Freud and C. G. Jung.* Ed. William McGuire. Trans. R. F. C. Hull and Ralph Manheim. Princeton: Princeton University Press, 1974.

Freud, Sigmund, and Arnold Zweig. *The Letters of Sigmund Freud and Arnold Zweig.* Trans. Elaine Robson-Scott and William Robson-Scott. New York: Harcourt, 1970.

Frey-Rohn. *From Freud to Jung: A Comparative Study of the Psychology of the Unconscious.* Trans. Fred E. Engreen and Evelyn K. Engreen. New York: Putnam, 1974.

Fromm, Erich. *Sigmund Freud's Mission.* New York: Harper, 1959.

Gager, John. *Reinventing Paul.* New York: Oxford University Press, 2002.

Galton, Francis. *Inquiries into Human Faculty and Its Development.* 1893. New York: Dutton, 1907.

Gamwell, Lynn, and Mark Solms, eds. *From Neurology to Psychoanalysis: Sigmund Freud's Neurological Drawings and Diagrams of the Mind.* Binghamton: Binghamton University Art Museum, State University of New York, 2006.

Gay, Peter. *Freud: A Life for Our Time.* New York: Norton, 1988.

———. *A Godless Jew: Freud, Atheism, and the Making of Psychoanalysis.* New Haven: Yale University Press, 1987.

Geller, Jay. "*Atheist* Jew or Atheist *Jew*: Freud's Jewish Question and Ours." *Modern Judaism* 26.1 (2006): 1–14.

———. "The Godfather of Psychoanalysis: Circumcision, Antisemitism, Homosexuality, and Freud's 'Fighting Jew.'" *Journal of the American Academy of Religion* 67.2 (1999): 355–85.

———. "Identifying 'Someone Who Is Himself One of Them': Recent Studies of Freud's Jewish Identity." *Religious Studies Review* 23.4 (1997): 323–31.

———. "Little Hans: A Footnote in the History of Circumcision." Paper presented at *Freud's Foreskin: A Sesquicentennial Celebration of the Most Suggestive Circumcision in History*, New York Public Library, May 10, 2006.

———. *On Freud's Jewish Body: Mitigating Circumcisions*. New York: Fordham University Press, 2007.

———. "A Paleontological View of Freud's Study of Religion: Unearthing the *Leitfossil* Circumcision." *Modern Judaism* 13 (1993): 49–70.

Gilman, Sander L. *Creating Beauty to Cure the Soul: Race and Psychology in the Shaping of Aesthetic Surgery*. Durham: Duke University Press, 1998.

———. "Decircumcision: The First Aesthetic Surgery." *Modern Judaism* 17.3 (1997): 201–10.

———. *Difference and Pathology: Stereotypes of Sexuality, Race, and Madness*. Ithaca: Cornell University Press, 1985.

———. "Freud and the Sexologists: A Second Reading." *Reading Freud's Reading*. Eds. Sander L. Gilman, Jay Geller, and Jutta Birmele. New York: New York University Press, 1994: 47–76.

———. *Freud, Race, and Gender*. Princeton: Princeton University Press, 1993.

———. *Jewish Self-Hatred: Anti-Semitism and the Hidden Language of the Jews*. Baltimore: Johns Hopkins University Press, 1990.

———. *The Jew's Body*. New York: Routledge, 1991.

Gilroy, Paul. *Against Race: Imagining Political Culture Beyond the Color Line*. Cambridge: Harvard University Press, 2000.

Ginzburg, Carlo. "Checking the Evidence: The Judge and the Historian." *Questions of Evidence: Proof, Practice, and Persuasion across the Disciplines*. Eds. James Chandler, Arnold I. Davidson, and Harry Harootunian. Chicago: University of Chicago Press, 1991: 290–303.

———. *Clues, Myths, and the Historical Method*. Baltimore: Johns Hopkins University Press, 1992.

———. "Learning from the Enemy: The French Prehistory of 'The Protocols.'" *Evidence*. Eds. John Swenson-Wright, Andrew Bell, and Karin Tybjerg. New York: Cambridge University Press, 2008.

Gitelman, Zvi, Barry Kosmin, and András Kovács, eds. *New Jewish Identities: Contemporary Europe and Beyond*. New York: Central European University Press, 2003.

Gliboff, Sander. "The Case of Paul Kammerer: Evolution and Experimentation in the Early 20th Century." *Journal of the History of Biology* 39.3 (2006): 525–63.

———. "The Pebble and the Planet: Paul Kammerer, Ernst Haeckel, and the Meaning of Darwinism." PhD dissertation, Johns Hopkins University, Baltimore, 2001.

Glick, Leonard B. *Marked in Your Flesh: Circumcision from Ancient Judea to Modern America*. New York: Oxford University Press, 2005.

———. "Types Distinct from Our Own: Franz Boas on Jewish Identity and Assimilation." *American Anthropologist* 84 (1982): 545–65.

Goldschmidt, Henry. *Race and Religion Among the Chosen Peoples of Crown Heights*. New Brunswick: Rutgers University Press, 2006.

Goldstein, Eric L. "'Different Blood Flows in Our Veins': Race and Jewish Self-Definition in Late Nineteenth Century America." *American Jewish History* 85.1 (1997): 29–55.

———. *The Price of Whiteness: Jews, Race, and American Identities*. Princeton: Princeton University Press, 2006.

Gordon, Lewis. "Foreword." *In Every Tongue: The Racial and Ethnic Diversity of the Jewish People*. Eds. Diane Tobin, Gary Tobin, and Scott Rubin. San Francisco: Institute for Jewish & Community Research, 2005.

Gordon, Peter Eli. *Rosenzweig and Heidegger: Between Judaism and German Philosophy*. Berkeley: University of California Press, 2003.

———. "Rosenzweig Redux: The Reception of German-Jewish Thought." *Jewish Social Studies* 8.1 (2002).

Gorenberg, Gershom. "How Do You Prove You're a Jew?" *New York Times Magazine*, March 2, 2008.

Gould, Stephen Jay. *Ontogeny and Phylogeny*. Cambridge: Harvard University Press, 1977.

Goux, Jean-Joseph. *Symbolic Economies: After Marx and Freud*. 1973. Trans. Jennifer Curtiss Gage. Ithaca: Cornell University Press, 1990.

Graf, Max. "Reminiscences of Professor Sigmund Freud." *The Psychoanalytic Quarterly* 11 (1942).

Graham, Loren R. "Science and Values: The Eugenics Movement in Germany and Russia in the 1920s." *The American Historical Review* 82. 5 (1977): 1133–64.

Gresser, Moshe. *Dual Allegiance: Freud as a Modern Jew*. Albany: State University of New York Press, 1994.

Grosskurth, Phyllis. *The Secret Ring: Freud's Inner Circle and the Politics of Psychoanalysis*. Reading: Addison-Wesley, 1991.

Grossman, David. *See Under: LOVE*. New York: Farrar, Straus & Giroux, 1989.

Grubrich-Simitis, Ilse. *Back to Freud's Texts: Making Silent Documents Speak.* Trans. Phillip Slotkin. New Haven: Yale University Press, 1996.

———. *Early Freud and Late Freud: Reading Anew Studies on Hysteria and Moses and Monotheism*. Trans. Philip Slotkin. New York: Routledge, 1997.

———. "Extreme Traumatization as Cumulative Trauma: Psychoanalytic Investigations of the Effects of Concentration Camp Experiences on Survivors and Their Children." *Psychoanalytic Study of the Child* 36 (1981): 415–50.

———. "From Concretism to Metaphor: Thoughts on Some Theoretical and Technical Aspects of the Psychoanalytic Work with Children of Holocaust Survivors." *Psychoanalytic Study of the Child* 39 (1984).

———. "Metapsychology and Metabiology." Trans. Axel and Peter T. Hoffer. *A Phylogenetic Fantasy: Overview of the Transference Neuroses, by Sigmund Freud*. Cambridge: Harvard University Press, 1987: 73–107.

———. *Michelangelos Moses und Freuds "Wagstück": Eine Collage*. Frankfurt: S. Fischer Verlag, 2004.

———. "Trauma or Drive—Drive and Trauma: A Reading of Sigmund Freud's Phylogenetic Fantasy of 1915." *The Psychoanalytic Study of the Child* 43 (1988): 3–32.

Guttman, Samuel A., et al. *The Concordance to the Standard Edition of the Complete Psychological Works of Sigmund Freud*. 2nd ed. New York: International Universities Press, 1984.

Hacking, Ian. *The Taming of Chance*. New York: Cambridge University Press, 1990.

Haeberle, Erwin J. "The Transatlantic Commuter: An Interview with Harry Benjamin on the Occasion of His 100th Birthday." *Sexualmedizin* 14.1 (1985). www2.hu-berlin.de/sexology/gesund/archiv/trans_B5.htm. Accessed April 5, 2006.

Halberstam, Yitta. "Choosing Judaism." *Jewish Action* 5766 (Summer 2006): 11–16. ou.org/pdf/ja/5766/summer66/11_17.pdf. Accessed August 31, 2007.

Handelman, Susan. *The Slayers of Moses*. Albany: State University of New York Press, 1982.

Harmon, Amy. "Seeking Ancestry in DNA Ties Uncovered by Tests." *New York Times*, National, April 12, 2006.

Harrington, Ralph. "The Railway Accident: Trains, Trauma and Technological Crisis in Nineteenth-Century Britain" (2004). www.york.ac.uk/inst/irs/irshome/papers/rlyacc.htm. Accessed June 27, 2007.

Hart, Mitchell Bryan. "Franz Boas as German, American, Jew." *German-Jewish Identities in America*. Eds. Christof Mauch and Joe Salomon. Madison: University of Wisconsin Press, 2003.

———. *Social Science and the Politics of Modern Jewish Identity*. Stanford: Stanford University Press, 2000.

Hartmann, Eduard von. *Philosophy of the Unconscious*. 1868. London: Routledge & Kegan Paul, 1950.

Harwood, Jonathan. *Styles of Scientific Thought: The German Genetics Community, 1900–1933*. Chicago: University of Chicago Press, 1993.

Hauschild, Thomas. "Christians, Jews, and the Other in Germany Anthropology." *American Anthropologist* 99.4 (1997): 746–53.

Haynal, André E. "Freud and His Intellectual Environment: The Case of Sándor Ferenczi." *Ferenczi's Turn in Psychoanalysis*. Ed. Peter L. Rudnytsky. New York: New York University Press, 1996: 25–40.

———. "Introduction." *The Correspondence of Sigmund Freud and Sandor Ferenczi*. Vol. I–III. Eds. Eva Brabant, Ernst Falzeder, Patrizia Giampieri-Deutsch, and André Haynal. Trans. Peter T. Hoffer. Cambridge: Harvard University Press, 1993–2000.

———. *Psychoanalysis and the Sciences: Epistemology—History*. Berkeley: University of California Press, 1991.

Hemcker, Wilhelm. "'Ihr Brief war mir so wertvoll.' Christian von Ehrenfels und Sigmund Freud—eine verschollene Korrespondenz." *Wunderblock—eine Geschichte der modernen Seele*. Eds. Jean Clair, Cathrin Pichler, and Wolfgang Pircher. Vienna: Löcker, 1989: 561–70.

Henninger, Joseph. *P. Wilhelm Schmidt S. V. D., 1868–1954: Eine biographische Skizze*. Freiburg, Germany: Paulusdruckerei, 1956.

Herzog, James. "World Beyond Metaphor: Thoughts on the Transmission of Trauma." *Generations of the Holocaust*. Eds. Martin S. Bergmann and Milton E. Jucovy. New York: Basic Books, 1982.

Himmelfarb, Martha. *A Kingdom of Priests: Ancestry and Merit in Ancient Judaism*. Philadelphia: University of Pennsylvania Press, 2006.

Hobsbawm, Eric. "Inventing Tradition." *The Invention of Tradition*. Eds. Eric Hobsbawm and Terence Ranger. New York: Cambridge University Press, 1983.

Hoffer, Peter T. "The Concept of Phylogenetic Inheritance in Freud and Jung." *Journal of the American Psychoanalytic Institution* 40.2 (1992): 517–30.

Hopwood, Nick. "Book Review: August Weismann's *Ausgewählte Briefe und Dokumente*, ed. Frederick B. Churchill and Helmut Risler." *Bulletin of the History of Medicine* 76.2 (2002): 382–84.

Hurston, Zora Neale. *Moses, Man of the Mountain*. 1939. New York: Harper Perennial, 1991.

Ian, Marcia. "Freud, Lacan, and Imaginary Secularity." *American Imago* 54.2 (1997): 123–47.

———. "'Invisible Religion': The Extimate Secular in American Society." *Jouvert: A Journal of Postcolonial Studies* 3.1–2 (1999). social.chass.ncsu.edu/ Jouvert/v3i12/ian.htm. Accessed August 28, 2007.

Iltis, Hugo. *Der Mythus von Blut und Rasse*. Vienna: R. Harand, 1936.

———. *Gregor Johann Mendel: Leben, Werk und Wirkung*. Berlin: J. Springer, 1924.

———. "Rassenwissenschaft und Rassenwahn." *Die Gesellschaft: Internationale Revue für Sozialismus und Politik* 4 (1927).

———. *Volkstümliche Rassenkunde*. Jena, Germany: Urania-Verlagsgesellschaft, 1930.

Jablonka, Eva, and Marion Lamb. *Epigenetic Inheritance and Evolution: The Lamarckian Dimension*. New York: Oxford University Press, 1995.

Jacobs, Janet Liebman. *Hidden Heritage: The Legacy of the Crypto-Jews*. Berkeley: University of California Press, 2002.

Jacobs, Joseph. "Are Jews Jews?" *Popular Science Monthly* 55 (1899): 502–11.

———. *The Jewish Race: A Study in National Character*. London: privately printed, 1899.

Jewish Museum Vienna. *Vienna, City of the Jews* (2004). www.jmw.at/en/ vienna_city_of_the_jews_-_walk.html. Accessed July 25, 2006.

Johnson, Barbara. "The Frame of Reference: Poe, Lacan, Derrida." 1977. *The Purloined Poe: Lacan, Derrida & Psychoanalytic Reading*. Eds. John P. Muller and William J. Richardson. Baltimore: Johns Hopkins University Press, 1988: 213–51.

Johnson, Laurie. "'I Wish to Dream' and Other Impossible Effects of the Crypt." *Psychoanalytic Review* 92.5 (2005): 735–45.

Jones, Ernest. *The Life and Work of Sigmund Freud*. Vol. I–III. New York: Basic Books, 1953–57.

———. "The Psychology of the Jewish Question." *Essays in Applied Psycho-Analysis*. Vol. 1. London: Hogarth Press and the Institute of Psycho-Analysis, 1951: 284–300.

Jonte-Pace, Diane. *Speaking the Unspeakable: Religion, Misogyny, and the Uncanny Mother in Freud's Cultural Texts*. Berkeley: University of California Press, 2001.

Joravsky, David. "Soviet Marxism and Biology before Lysenko." *Journal of the History of Ideas* 20.1 (1959): 85–104.

Judd, Robin. *Contested Rituals: Circumcision, Kosher Butchering, and Jewish Political Life in Germany, 1843–1933*. Ithaca: Cornell University Press, 2007.

———. "Cutting Identities: German Jewish Bodies, Rituals and Citizenship." PhD dissertation, University of Michigan, Ann Arbor, 2000.

Jung, Carl Gustav. *Memories, Dreams, Reflections.* Ed. Aniela Jaffé. Trans. Richard and Clara Winston. New York: Vintage Books, 1965.

———. "The Psychology of *Dementia Praecox*." 1906. *Collected Works.* Vol. 3. Princeton: Princeton University Press, 1953–77.

———. *Psychology of the Unconscious: A Study of the Transformations and Symbolisms of the Libido.* 1911–12. *Collected Works.* Vol. Supplementary B. Ed. William McGuire. Trans. Beatrice M. Hinkle. Princeton: Princeton University Press, 1953–77.

Kalimi, Isaac. "'He Was Born Circumcised': Some Midrashic Sources, Their Concept, Roots and Presumably Historical Context." *Zeitschrift für die Neutestamentliche Wissenschaft und Kunde der Älteren Kirche* 93.1–2 (2002): 1–12.

Kammerer, Paul. *Rejuvenation and the Prolongation of Human Efficiency: Experiences with the Steinach-Operation on Man and Animals.* New York: Boni and Liverlight, 1923.

Kavka, Martin. *Jewish Messianism and the History of Philosophy.* New York: Cambridge University Press, 2004.

Kaye, Howard L. "Was Freud a Medical Scientist or a Social Theorist? The Mysterious 'Development of the Hero.'" *Sociological Theory* 21.4 (2003): 375–97.

Keeley, James P. "'The Coping Stone on Psycho-Analysis': Freud, Psychoanalysis, and The Society for Psychical Research." PhD dissertation, Columbia University, New York, 2002.

Kerr, John. *A Most Dangerous Method: The Story of Jung, Freud, and Sabina Spielrein.* New York: Knopf, 1993.

Kessel, Barbara. *Suddenly Jewish: Jews Raised as Gentiles Discover Their Jewish Roots.* Hanover: University Press of New England, 2000.

Kirshenblatt-Gimblett, Barbara. "The Corporeal Turn." *Jewish Quarterly Review* 95.3 (2005): 447–61.

Kitcher, Patricia. *Freud's Dream: A Complete Interdisciplinary Science of Mind.* Cambridge: MIT Press, 1992.

Kittler, Friedrich. *Discourse Networks 1800/1900.* Trans. Michael Metteer and Chris Cullens. Stanford: Stanford University Press, 1990.

———. *Gramophone, Film, Typewriter.* Trans. Geoffrey Winthrop-Young and Michael Wutz. Stanford: Stanford University Press, 1999.

———. "Romanticism—Psychoanalysis—Film: A History of the Double." Trans. Stefanie Harris. *Literature, Media, Information Systems: Essays.* Amsterdam: Overseas Publishers Association, 1997.

Klein, Emma. *Lost Jews: The Struggle for Identity Today.* New York: St. Martin's Press, 1995.

Klein, Kerman Lee. "On the Emergence of Memory in Historical Discourse." *Representations* 69 (2000): 127–50.

Koppers, Wilhelm, ed. *Festschrift P. W. Schmidt: 76 sprachwissenschaftliche, ethnologische, religionswissenschaftliche, prähistorische und andere Studien.* Vienna: Mechitharisten-Congregations-Buchdruckerei, 1928.

———. "Obituary of Pater Wilhelm Schmidt." *Mitteilungen der Anthropologischen Gesellschaft in Wien* 83 (1954): 87–96.

Kramer, Michael P. "Race, Literary History, and the 'Jewish Question.'" *Prooftexts* 21.3 (2001): 287–321.

Kris, Ernst. "Freud in the History of Science." *The Listener*. Vol. 55. London: BBC, 1956: 631–33.

Krüll, Marianne. *Freud and His Father*. Trans. Arnold Pomerans. New York: Norton, 1986.

Lacan, Jacques. *The Four Fundamental Concepts of Psychoanalysis*. Ed. Jacques-Alain Miller. Trans. Alan Sheridan. New York: Norton, 1998.

———. "Seminar on 'The Purloined Letter.'" 1956. *The Purloined Poe: Lacan, Derrida and Psychoanalytic Reading*. Eds. John P. Muller and William J. Richardson. Baltimore: Johns Hopkins University Press, 1988.

LaCapra, Dominick. *History in Transit: Experience, Identity, Critical Theory*. Ithaca: Cornell University Press, 2004.

———. *Representing the Holocaust: History, Theory, Trauma*. Ithaca: Cornell University Press, 1994.

———. *Writing History, Writing Trauma*. Baltimore: Johns Hopkins University Press, 2000.

Lampert-Weissig, Lisa. "Race, Periodicity, and the (Neo-) Middle Ages." *MLQ: Modern Language Quarterly* 65.3 (2004): 391–421.

Langston, Scott. *Exodus Through the Centuries*. Malden: Blackwell, 2006.

LaPlanche, Jean, and Jean-Bertrand Pontalis. *The Language of Psycho-Analysis*. Trans. Donald Nicholson-Smith. London: Hogarth Press and the Institute of Psycho-analysis, 1973.

Laqueur, Thomas. *Making Sex: Body and Gender from the Greeks to Freud*. Cambridge: Harvard University Press, 1990.

Lassalle, Ferdinand. *Science and the Workingmen: An argument in his own defense before the Criminal court of Berlin on the charge of having publicly incited the unpropertied classes to hatred and contempt of the propertied classes*. 1863. Trans. Thorstein Veblen. New York: International Library, 1900. de.geocities.com/veblenite/txt/workmen.txt. Accessed October 29, 2006.

Lenz, Fritz. "Der Fall Kammerer und seine Umfilmung durch Lunatscharsky." *Archiv für Rassen- und Gesellschaftsbiologie* 21 (1929).

————. "Die Stellung des Nationalsozialismus zur Rassenhygiene." *Archiv für Rassen- und Gesellschaftsbiologie* 25 (1931): 300–8.

Lenz, Fritz, Erwin Baur, and Eugen Fischer. *Human Heredity [Menschliche erblichkeit].* 1921. New York: Macmillan, 1931.

Lepicard, Etienne. "Eugenics and Roman Catholicism, An Encyclical Letter in Context: *Casti connubii*, December 31, 1930." *Science in Context* 11.3–4 (1998): 527–44.

Le Rider, Jacques. "Jewish Identity in *Moses and Monotheism.*" *The Psychohistory Review* 25 (1997): 245–54.

Lewontin, Richard. "Facts and the Factitious in Natural Sciences." *Questions of Evidence: Proof, Practice, and Persuasion across the Disciplines.* Eds. James Chandler, Arnold I. Davidson, and Harry Harootunian. Chicago: University of Chicago Press, 1991.

————. "A Rejoinder to William Wimsatt." *Questions of Evidence: Proof, Practice, and Persuasion across the Disciplines.* Eds. James Chandler, Arnold I. Davidson, and Harry Harootunian. Chicago: University of Chicago Press, 1991.

Lewontin, Richard, and Richard Levins. "The Problem of Lysenkoism." *The Dialectical Biologist.* Cambridge: Harvard University Press, 1985: 163–96.

Lipphardt, Veronika. "Biowissenschaftler mit jüdischem Hintergrund und die Biologie der Juden: Debatten, Identitäten, Institutionen (1900–1935)." PhD dissertation, Humboldt Universität, Berlin, 2006.

Lodge, Oliver. *Outline of Science.* Ed. J. Arthur Thompson. 4 vols. New York: Putnam, 1922.

Logan, Cheryl. "Overheated Rats, Race, and the Double Gland: Paul Kammerer, Endocrinology and the Problem of Somatic Induction." *Journal of the History of Biology* 40.4 (2007): 683–725.

Luckhurst, Roger. *The Invention of Telepathy, 1870–1901.* New York: Oxford University Press, 2002.

————. " 'Something Tremendous, Something Elemental': On the Ghostly Origins of Psychoanalysis." *Ghosts: Deconstruction, Psychoanalysis, History.* Eds. Peter Buse and Andrew Stott. New York: Macmillan, 1999: 50–71.

Lupton, Julia Reinhard. "*Ethnos* and Circumcision in the Pauline Tradition: A Psychoanalytic Exegesis." *The Psychoanalysis of Race.* Ed. Christopher Lane. New York: Columbia University Press, 1998.

Lyotard, Jean-François. *Heidegger and "the jews."* Trans. Andreas Michel and Mark S. Roberts. Minneapolis: University of Minnesota Press, 1990.

Mabbott, Thomas Ollive. "Text of 'The Purloined Letter' by Edgar Allan Poe, with Notes." *The Purloined Poe: Lacan, Derrida and Psychoanalytic Theory.* Eds. John P. Muller and William J. Richardson. Baltimore: Johns Hopkins University Press, 1988.

Maciejewski, Franz. "Freud, Beschneidung und Monotheismus." *Psyche* 58.5 (2004): 458–63.

———. *Psychoanalytisches Archiv und jüdisches Gedächtnis: Freud, Beschneidung und Monotheismus*. Vienna: Passagen Verlag, 2002.

———. "Das Unbewusste in der Kulture: Von der Schwierigkeit, die psychoanalytische Kulturtheorie (Freud) in eine kulturwissenschaftliche Gedächtnistheorie (Assmann) zu überführen." *Psyche* 62.3 (2008): 235–52.

Mack, Michael. *German Idealism and the Jew: The Inner Anti-Semitism of Philosophy and German Jewish Responses*. Chicago: University of Chicago Press, 2003.

Mahfouz, Naguib. *Akhenaten, Dweller in Truth*. Trans. Tagreid Abu-Hassabo. New York: Random House, 1998.

Maidenbaum, Aryeh, and Stephen A. Martin. *Lingering Shadows: Jungians, Freudians, and Anti-Semitism*. Boston: Shambhala, 1991.

Marcus, Steven. *Representations: Essays on Literature and Society*. 1976. New York: Random House, 1990.

Masson, Jeffrey M. *The Assault on Truth: Freud's Suppression of the Seduction Theory*. 1984. New York: Harper Perennial, 1992.

Matsuda, Matt. *The Memory of the Modern*. New York: Oxford University Press, 1996.

Mayr, Ernst. *The Growth of Biological Thought: Diversity, Evolution and Inheritance*. Cambridge: Harvard University Press, 1982.

———. "Weismann and Evolution." *Journal of the History of Biology* 18.3 (1985): 295–329.

Merton, Robert K. *On Social Structure and Science*. Chicago: University of Chicago Press, 1996.

Michaels, Walter Benn. "The No-Drop Rule." *Critical Inquiry* 20 (1994): 758–69.

———. "Race into Culture: A Critical Geneaology of Identity." *Critical Inquiry* 18 (1992): 655–85.

Montserrat, Dominic. *Akhenaten: History, Fantasy, and Ancient Egypt*. New York: Routledge, 2000.

Moreau-Ricaud, Michelle. "The Founding of the Budapest School." *Ferenczi's Turn in Psychoanalysis*. Eds. Peter L. Rudnytsky, Antal Bókay, and Patrizia Giampieri-Deutsch. New York: New York University Press, 1996.

Morrison, Toni. *Beloved: A Novel*. New York: Knopf, 1987.

Myers, Frederic W. H., W. F. Barrett, C. C. Massey, Rev. W. Stainton Moses, Frank Podmore, and Edmund Gurney. "First Report of the Literary Committee (December 9, 1882)." *Proceedings of the Society for Psychical Research* (London: Trübner, 1883).

Newton, K. M. "Daniel Deronda and Circumcision." *Essays in Criticism* 31 (1981): 313–27.

Nora, Pierre. "Between Memory and History: Les Lieux de Memoire." In "Memory and Counter-Memory," Special issue, *Representations* 26 (1989): 7–24.

Nunberg, Herman, and Ernst Federn. *Minutes of the Vienna Psycho-Analytical Society, 1906–1915.* Trans. M. Nunberg. New York: International Universities Press, 1962–75.

Olick, Jeffrey K., and Joyce Robbins. "Social Memory Studies: From 'Collective Memory' to the Historical Sociology of Mnemonic Practices." *American Review of Sociology* 24 (1998): 105–40.

Oring, Eliot. *The Jokes of Sigmund Freud: A Study in Humor and Jewish Identity.* Philadelphia: University of Pennsylvania Press, 1984.

Otis, Laura. *Organic Memory: History and the Body in the Late Nineteenth and Early Twentieth Centuries.* Lincoln: University of Nebraska Press, 1994.

Oxford English Dictionary Online. Oxford University Press (2002), dictionary.oed.com.

Patai, Raphael, and Jennifer P. Wing. *The Myth of the Jewish Race.* New York: Scribner's, 1975.

Paul, Robert. "Freud's Anthropology: A Reading of the Cultural Books." *The Cambridge Companion to Freud.* Ed. Jerome Neu. New York: Cambridge University Press, 1991: 267–86.

Pellegrini, Ann. *Performance Anxieties: Staging Psychoanalysis, Staging Race.* New York: Routledge, 1997.

Penner, Louise. "'Unmapped Country': Uncovering Hidden Wounds in *Daniel Deronda.*" *Victorian Literature and Culture* 30.1 (2002): 77–97.

Piper, Adrian. "Passing for White, Passing for Black." Adrian Piper Research Archive (2004). www.adrianpiper.com/docs/passing.pdf. Accessed August 10, 2007.

Popper, Karl R. *Conjectures and Refutations: The Growth of Scientific Knowledge.* 1963. New York: Routledge, 2002.

Proctor, Robert. "Nazi Medicine and the Politics of Knowledge." *The "Racial" Economy of Science.* Ed. Sandra Harding. Bloomington: Indiana University Press, 1993.

———. *Racial Hygiene: Medicine Under the Nazis.* Cambridge: Harvard University Press, 1988.

———. *Value-Free Science? Purity and Power in Modern Knowledge.* Cambridge: Harvard University Press, 1991.

Rand, Nicholas. "Introduction: Renewals of Psychoanalysis." In Nicolas Abraham and Maria Torok, *The Shell and the Kernel: Renewals of Psychoanalysis.* Ed., trans. Nicholas Rand. Chicago: University of Chicago Press, 1975.

Rand, Nicholas, and Maria Torok. *Questions for Freud: The Secret History of Psychoanalysis*. Cambridge: Harvard University Press, 1997.

Rank, Otto. "The Essence of Judaism." 1905. *Jewish Origins of the Psychoanalytic Movement*. Ed. Dennis B. Klein. Chicago: University of Chicago Press, 1985.

———. *The Myth of the Birth of the Hero: A Psychological Exploration of Myth*. Trans. Gregory Richter and E. James Liberman. Baltimore: Johns Hopkins University Press, 2004.

———. *The Trauma of Birth*. 1909. New York: Dover, 1993.

Rather, L. J. "Disraeli, Freud, and Jewish Conspiracy Theories." *Journal of the History of Ideas* 47.1 (1986): 111–31.

Redfield, Marc. "The Fictions of Telepathy." *Surfaces* 2.27 (1992): 4–20. tinyurl.com/RedfieldTelepathy. Accessed July 24, 2006.

Reik, Theodor. *Jewish Wit*. New York: Gamut Press, 1962.

Remennick, Larissa. "'Idealists Headed to Israel, Pragmatics Chose Europe': Identity Dilemmas and Social Incorporation among Former Soviet Jews Who Migrated to Germany." *Immigrants & Minorities* 23.1 (2005): 30–58.

Rice, Emanuel. *Freud and Moses: The Long Journey Home*. Albany: State University of New York Press, 1990.

Ricoeur, Paul. *Memory, History, Forgetting*. Trans. Kathleen Blamey and David Pellauer. Chicago: University of Chicago Press, 2005.

Rieff, Philip. *Freud: The Mind of the Moralist*. New York: Viking, 1959.

Ripley, William Z. "The Racial Geography of Europe: A Sociological Study. Supplement: The Jews." *Popular Science Monthly* 54 (1899): 163–75, 338–51.

Ritvo, Lucille B. *Darwin's Influence on Freud: A Tale of Two Sciences*. New Haven: Yale University Press, 1990.

Rizvi, S. A. H., et al. "Religious Circumcision: A Muslim View." *BJU International* 83, Supplement 1 (1999): 13–16.

Robert, Marthe. *From Oedipus to Moses: Freud's Jewish Identity*. Trans. Ralph Manheim. London: Routledge & Kegan, 1977.

Robertson, Ritchie. "'My True Enemy': Freud and the Catholic Church, 1927–39." *Austria in the Thirties: Culture and History*. Eds. Kenneth Segar and John Warren. Riverside: Ariadne Press, 1990.

Ronell, Avital. *The Telephone Book: Technology, Schizophrenia, Electric Speech*. Lincoln: University of Nebraska Press, 1989.

Rose, Jacqueline. *The Last Resistance*. New York City: Verso, 2007.

———. "Response to Edward Said." *Freud and the Non-European*. New York: Verso, 2003.

Rosenzweig, Franz. *Der Stern der Erlosung*. 1921. Freiburg im Breisgau, Germany: Universitätsbibliothek (2002). www.freidok.uni-freiburg.de/volltexte/310/pdf/derstern.pdf. Accessed October 13, 2006.

———. *The Star of Redemption*. 1921. Trans. William W. Hallo. Notre Dame: University of Notre Dame Press, 1985.

Rosenzweig, Saul. *Freud, Jung, and Hall the King-Maker: The Historic Expedition to America (1909), with G. Stanley Hall as Host and William James as Guest.* Seattle: Hogreffe & Huber, 1992.

Roskies, David G. *The Jewish Search for a Usable Past*. Bloomington: Indiana University Press, 1999.

Roth, Michael. *The Ironist's Cage: Memory, Trauma, and the Construction of History*. New York: Columbia University Press, 1995.

Roudinesco, Elisabeth. *Jacques Lacan and Co.: A History of Psychoanalysis in France, 1925–1985*. Trans. J. Mehlman. Chicago: University of Chicago Press, 1990.

Royle, Nicholas. *After Derrida*. Manchester: Manchester University Press, 1995.

———. "Phantom Review." *Textual Practice* 11.2 (1997): 386–98.

———. *Telepathy and Literature: Essays on the Reading Mind*. Cambridge: Blackwell, 1991.

———. *The Uncanny*. New York: Routledge, 2003.

Rudnytsky, Peter L. *Reading Psycho-Analysis: Freud, Rank, Ferenczi, Groddeck.* Ithaca: Cornell University Press, 2002.

Sahin, F., U. Beyazova, and A. Aktürk. "Attitudes and Practices Regarding Circumcision in Turkey." *Child: Care, Health and Development* 29.4 (2003).

Said, Edward. *Freud and the Non-European*. New York: Verso, 2003.

———. "Invention, Memory, Place." *Critical Inquiry* 26 (2000): 175–92.

Santner, Eric L. "Freud, Žižek, and the Joys of Monotheism." *American Imago* 54.2 (1997): 197–207.

———. "Freud's *Moses* and the Ethics of Nomotropic Desire." *October* 88 (1999): 3–41.

———. *My Own Private Germany: Daniel Paul Schreber's Secret History of Modernity*. Princeton: Princeton University Press, 1996.

———. *On the Psychotheology of Everyday Life: Reflections on Freud and Rosenzweig.* Chicago: University of Chicago Press, 2001.

"Says Telepathy Is Next: Professor Low Predicts Transmission of Thoughts Without Speech." *New York Times*, Editorial General News. January 16, 1927: E2.

Schacter, Daniel L., ed. *Forgotten Ideas, Neglected Pioneers: Richard Semon and the Story of Memory*. Philadelphia: Psychology Press, 2001.

———. *Memory Distortion: How Minds, Brains, and Societies Reconstruct the Past.* Cambridge: Harvard University Press, 1995.

Schäfer, Peter. "Geschichte und Gedächtnisgeschichte: Jan Assmanns *Mosaische Unterscheidung.*" *Memoria—Wege jüdischen Erinnerns, Festschrift für Michael Brocke zum 65. Geburtstag.* Eds. Birgit Klein and Christiane E. Müller. Berlin: Metropol Verlag, 2005: 19–39.

———. "The Triumph of Pure Spirituality: Sigmund Freud's *Moses and Monotheism.*" Trans. Johanna Hoornweg and Annette Reed. *Jewish Studies Quarterly* 9 (2002): 381–406.

Schmidt, Wilhelm. "Befreiung Wiens vom jüdischen Bolshewismus! Eine Katholikentagsrede von Professor Dr Wilhelm Schmidt S.V.D." *Das Neue Reich* 3 (1920): 42–43.

———. "Blut-Rasse-Volk." *Kirche im Kampf.* Ed. Clemens Holzmeister. Vienna: Seelsorger Verlag, 1936: 43–81.

———. *The Culture Historical Method of Ethnology: The Scientific Approach to the Racial Question.* Trans. S. A. Sieber. New York: Fortuny's, 1939.

———. "Der Ödipus-Komplex der Freudschen Psychoanalyse und die Ehegestaltung des Bolshewismus. Eine kritische Prüfung ihre ethnologischen Grundlagen." *Nationalwirtschaft* 2 (1928): 401–36.

———. *The Origin and Growth of Religion: Facts and Theories.* 1931. Trans. H. J. Rose. London: Methnon, 1935.

———. *Rasse und Volk: eine Untersuchung zur Bestimmung ihrer Grenzen und zur Erfassung ihrer Bezeihungen.* Munich: J. Kösel & F. Pustet, 1927.

———. "Das Rassenprinzip des Nationalsozialismus." *Schönere Zukunft* 7 (1931–32): 999–1000.

———. "Eine wissenschaftliche Abrechnung mit der Psychoanalyse." *Das Neue Reich* 11 (1928–29): 266–77.

Scholem, Gershom. "Revelation and Tradition as Religious Categories in Judaism." 1962. Trans. Michael Meyer. *The Messianic Idea in Judaism and Other Essays.* New York: Schocken, 1995: 282–303.

Schwartz, Regina. *The Curse of Cain: The Violent Legacy of Monotheism.* Chicago: University of Chicago Press, 1997.

Seidman, Naomi. *Jewish-Christian Difference and the Politics of Translation.* Chicago: University of Chicago Press, 2006.

Sengoopta, Chandak. "Glandular Politics: Experimental Biology, Clinical Medicine, and Homosexual Emancipation in Fin-de-Siècle Europe." *Isis* 89.3 (1998): 445–73

———. *The Most Secret Quintessence of Life: Sex, Glands, and Hormones, 1850–1950.* Chicago: University of Chicago Press, 2006.

Shapiro, Susan. "The Uncanny Jew: A Brief History of an Image." *Judaism* 46.1 (1997): 63–78.

Sheldrake, Rupert. *Dogs That Know When Their Owners Are Coming Home and Other Unexplained Powers of Animals*. New York: Three Rivers Press, 1999.

Shell, Marc. *Children of the Earth: Literature, Politics and Nationhood*. New York: Oxford University Press, 1993.

Shengold, Leonard. "A Parapraxis of Freud in Relation to Karl Abraham." *American Imago* 29 (1972): 123–59.

Silverman, Eric Kline. "The Cut of Wholeness: Psychoanalytic Interpretations of Biblical Circumcision." *The Covenant of Circumcision: New Perspectives on an Ancient Jewish Rite*. Ed. Elizabeth Wyner Mark. Hanover: Brandeis University Press, University Press of New England, 2003: 43–57.

———. *From Abraham to America: A History of Jewish Circumcision*. Lanham, MD: Roman and Littlefield, 2006.

———. "Psychoanalyzing Phallacies: Freud and Current Circumcision Controversies." Paper presented at *Freud's Foreskin: A Sesquicentennial Celebration of the Most Suggestive Circumcision in History*, New York Public Library, May 10, 2006.

Slezkine, Yuri. *The Jewish Century*. Princeton: Princeton University Press, 2004.

Society for Psychical Research. Website. www.spr.ac.uk. Accessed July 10, 2008.

Spencer, Herbert. "The Inadequacy of 'Natural Selection.'" *Contemporary Review* 63 (1893): 153–66, 439–56.

———. "Professor Weismann's Theories." *Contemporary Review* 63 (1893): 743–60.

———. "A Rejoinder to Professor Weismann." *Contemporary Review* 66 (1893): 592–608.

Steele, Edward, Robyn Lindley, and Robert Blanden. *Lamarck's Signature: How Retrogenes Are Changing Darwin's Natural Selection Paradigm*. Reading: Perseus, 1998.

Stewart, Larry. "Freud Before Oedipus: Race and Heredity in the Origins of Psychoanalysis." *Journal of the History of Biology* 9.2 (1976): 215–28.

Stocking, George W., Jr. *Race, Culture, and Evolution: Essays in the History of Anthropology*. New York: Free Press, 1968.

Strachey, James, ed. *The Standard Edition of the Complete Psychological Works of Sigmund Freud*. Trans. James Strachey and Anna Freud. 24 vols. London: Hogarth Press and the Institute of Psycho-Analysis, 1953.

Stratton, John. *Coming Out Jewish: Constructing Ambivalent Identities*. New York: Routledge, 2000.

Sue, Eugene. *The Wandering Jew*. 1844–45. Ed. Brian Stableford. New York: Hippocrene, 1990.

Sulloway, Frank J. *Freud, Biologist of the Mind: Beyond the Psychoanalytic Legend.* New York: Basic Books, 1979.

"'Thinkers-In' Guess In Telepathy Test, Thousands of 'Ideas' Sent to British Psychical Society in Thousands of Letters, Two Seem to Have Hit It, One Correctly Describes the 'Thought Broadcaster's' Attire, the Other a Box in the Room." *New York Times*, February 18, 1927: 1.

Thomas, D. M. *The White Hotel.* New York: Viking, 1981.

Thurschwell, Pamela. "Ferenczi's Dangerous Proximities: Telepathy, Psychosis, and the Real Event." *differences: A Journal of Feminist Cultural Studies* 11.1 (1999): 150–78.

———. *Literature, Technology and Magical Thinking, 1880–1920.* New York: Cambridge University Press, 2001.

Timpanaro, Sebastiano. "Freud's Roman Phobia." *New Left Review* 1.147 (1984).

Torok, Maria. "Afterword: What Is Occult in Occultism? Between Sigmund Freud and Sergei Pankeiev Wolf Man." In Torok and Abraham, *The Wolf Man's Magic Word: A Cryptonomy.* Trans. Nicholas Rand. Minneapolis: University of Minnesota Press, 1986.

Warner, Silas L. "Freud the Mighty Warrior." *Journal of the American Academy of Psychoanalysis* 19.2 (1991): 282–93.

Wasserstein, Bernard. *Vanishing Diaspora: The Jews in Europe Since 1945.* Cambridge: Harvard University Press, 1996.

Webber, Jonathan. *Jewish Identities in the New Europe.* London: Littman Library of Jewish Civilization, 1994.

Weber, Max. *Ancient Judaism.* Trans. Hans Gerth and Don Martindale. New York: Free Press, 1952.

Webster, Richard. "The Bewildered Visionary." *Times Literary Supplement*, May 16, 1997.

———. *Why Freud Was Wrong: Sin, Science and Psychoanalysis.* New York: Basic Books, 1995.

Weigel, Sigrid. *Genea-Logik: Generation, Tradition und Evolution zwischen Kultur- und Naturwissenschaften.* Munich: Fink, 2006.

Weikart, Richard. *From Darwin to Hitler: Evolutionary Ethics, Eugenics, and Racism in Germany.* New York: Macmillan, 2004.

Weindling, Paul. "Central Europe Confronts German Racial Hygiene: Friedrich Hertz, Hugo Iltis, and Ignaz Zollschan as Critics of German Racial Hygiene." *Blood and Homeland: Eugenics in Central Europe, 1900–1940.* Eds. Marius Turda and Paul Weindling. Budapest: Central University Press, 2006.

———. "The Evolution of Jewish Identity: Ignaz Zollschan between Jewish and Aryan Race Theories, 1910–1945." *Jewish Tradition and the Challenge of Darwinism*. Eds. Geoffrey Cantor and Marc Swetlitz. Chicago: Chicago University Press, 2006.

———. *Health, Race, and German Politics Between National Unification and Nazism, 1870–1945*. New York: Cambridge University Press, 1989.

Weismann, August. "The All-Sufficiency of Natural Selection: 1) A reply to Herbert Spencer, and 2) Conclusion." *Contemporary Review* 64 (1893): 309–38, 596–610.

———. *Essays upon Heredity and Kindred Biological Problems*. Oxford: Clarendon, 1889.

———. *The Germ-Plasm: A Theory of Heredity [Das Keimplasma]*. 1892. Trans. W. N. Parker and Harriet Rönnfeldt. London: W. Scott, 1893.

Weissberg, Liliane. "Introduction: Freudian Genealogies." In "Three Essays on Freud," Special Issue, *The Germanic Review* 83.1 (2008): 5–10.

Winther, Rasmus G. "August Weismann on Germ-Plasm Variation." *Journal of the History of Biology* 34.3 (2001): 517–55.

Wrong, D. H. *The Problem of Order: What Unites and Divides Society*. New York: Free Press, 1994.

Yates, Frances A. *The Art of Memory*. Chicago: University of Chicago Press, 1966.

Yerushalmi, Yosef Hayim. *Assimilation and Racial Anti-Semitism: The Iberian and the German Models*. New York: Leo Baeck Institute, 1982.

———. *Freud's Moses: Judaism Terminable and Interminable*. New Haven: Yale University Press, 1991.

———. "The Moses of Freud and the Moses of Schoenberg: On Words, Idolatry, and Psychoanalysis." *The Psychoanalytic Study of the Child* 47 (1992): 1–20.

———. "Reflections on Forgetting." *Zakhor: Jewish History and Jewish Memory*. Address delivered at the Colloque de Royaumont. Seattle: University of Washington Press, 1996.

———. "Series Z: An Archival Fantasy." *Journal of European Psychoanalysis* 3–4 (1996–97). www.psychomedia.it/jep/number3–4/yerushalmi.htm. Accessed October 22, 2001.

"Yerushalmi, Yosef Hayim (1932–)." *Contemporary Authors Online*. The Gale Group (2002). Accessed October 2, 2003.

Yerushalmi, Yosef Hayim, and Frédéric Brenner. *Marranes*. Paris: Editions de la Différence, 1992.

Žižek, Slavoj. *Enjoy Your Symptom! Jacques Lacan in Hollywood and Out*. New York: Routledge, 1992.

————. *Metastases of Enjoyment: Six Essays on Woman and Causality*. London: Verso, 1994.

————. *The Parallax View*. Cambridge: MIT Press, 2005.

————. *The Sublime Object of Ideology*. London: Verso, 1989.

Zollschan, Ignaz. *Das Rassenproblem unter besonderer Berücksichtigung der theoretischen Grundlagen der jüdischen Rassenfrage*. Vienna: Braumüller, 1911.

Zweig, Arnold. *Bilanz der Deutschen Judenheit 1933. Ein Versuch*. Leipzig: Reclam-Bibliothek, 1991.